Seeing and Being Seen

Seeing and Being Seen
Tourism in the American West

Edited by David M. Wrobel
and Patrick T. Long

Foreword by Earl Pomeroy

Published for
The Center of the American West
University of Colorado at Boulder by the

University Press of Kansas

Chapter 2, "Seeing and Being Seen: Tourism in the American West," by Patricia Nelson Limerick published with permission from Valerie Matsumoto, Blake Allmendinger, *Over the Edge: Remapping the American West.* Copyright © 1998, The Regents of the University of California

Chapter 3, "Why I Love Tourists: Confessions of a Dharma Bum," © 2001 by Rudolfo Anaya

Published by the University Press of Kansas (Lawrence, Kansas 66049), which was organized by the Kansas Board of Regents and is operated and funded by Emporia State University, Fort Hays State University, Kansas State University, Pittsburg State University, the University of Kansas, and Wichita State University.

Library of Congress Cataloging-in-Publication Data
Seeing and being seen : tourism in the American West /edited by David
  M. Wrobel and Patrick T. Long, foreword by Earl Pomeroy.
     p. cm.
    Includes index.
    ISBN 0-7006-1082-0 (cloth : alk. paper) — ISBN 0-7006-1083-9 (pbk. :
alk. paper)
    1. Tourism—West (U.S.) I. Wrobel, David M. II. Long, Patrick T.
G155.U6 S42 2001
338.4'791780434—dc21   00-012389

British Library Cataloguing in Publication Data is available.

Printed in the United States of America
10 9 8 7 6 5 4 3 2 1

The paper used in this publication meets the minimum requirements of the American National Standard for Permanence of Paper for Printed Library Materials Z39.48-1984.

For Earl Pomeroy

Contents

Foreword: Still Searching for the Golden West

Earl Pomeroy

Americans often have been greatly interested in what tourists, among other visitors, say about their country—in the nineteenth century, especially about the western part of it; yet tourists in the American West were late in interesting historians as subjects. The great themes of American history from the Revolution through the Civil War, as historians ordinarily conceived them, were political and national. Economic and social change interested them chiefly insofar as politicians responded to it in national settings. Historians were far more interested in the personnel of national political action and controversy than in casual visitors, especially to a region that was at most secondary in political influence. Yet by the late nineteenth century, history, like the West itself, was changing, even within the academy.

In 1889, Henry Adams drew at length on accounts of foreign visitors for his history of the United States in the administrations of Presidents Jefferson and Madison.[1] By the 1900s, Frederick Jackson Turner diverged from the historical establishment of his time in incorporating units on diverse ethnic cultural heritages in his course on the American West. Championing environmental alternatives to the then-dominant interpretations that ascribed social origins to inheritance, he used and recommended previously overlooked sources, prompting others to use them also as they tried to flesh out accounts of institutional change in their teaching and writing.

In 1953–1954, when I began my first year outside the classroom after graduate school, I had announced a course on the West in which the second half would concern only developments in the twentieth century, before I found that library catalogues and published bibliographies did not suggest much parallel reading. Compelled to strike out on my own, I unsystematically followed Turner's lead, plowing through what I could find on the West in magazines, both popular and promotional, journals of history and the social sciences, corporate reports, government documents, biographies, and memoirs, including memoirs of tourists and other travelers. I did not intend to write at length about tourists until friends encouraged me to develop a draft of a possible article into a book.[2]

Now, nearly a half-century after I published that book, the western tourist industry has grown so much that it warrants extended analysis simply as a major sector of regional and national economies. It often enlists larger workforces and capital investments and yields larger returns than the extractive industries that dominated the West over centuries of European penetration and occupation. Moreover, tourism often has developed most rapidly at what had been the centers of those industries. Developers have, for example, converted depleted gold and silver mining towns to ski lodges and golf courses, marginal grazing land to suburban ranchettes.

Las Vegas, Nevada, well illustrates the scale and significance of tourism in the West. It has more in the way of hotel accommodations than any other city on the continent, and passenger traffic in proportion. The city commits much more water and energy to the casinos and theaters that entertain its visitors than its natural environment alone could support. It shows in characteristically gargantuan and flamboyant style how some of the most advanced technology and largest investments of capital have been employed in parts of the West farthest from main concentrations of population, in some of the most unpromising locations; becoming a major metropolitan center, the Las Vegas suburb of Henderson is currently the fastest growing city in the nation.

As the authors of the essays in this volume remind us, what tourists do and require and how others respond to their demands represent some of the most dynamic and revealing factors in regional and national development, and some of the most promising opportunities for scholars.

Notes

1. Henry Adams, *History of the United States during the Administrations of Jefferson and Madison*, 9 vols. (New York: Scribner's, 1889–1891).

2. Earl Pomeroy, *In Search of the Golden West: The Tourist in Western America* (New York: Alfred A. Knopf, 1957).

Acknowledgments

In the late spring of 1997 the Center of the American West at the University of Colorado at Boulder hosted a conference titled "Seeing and Being Seen: Tourism and the American West." The event brought together a wide range of people: scholars from the humanities and social sciences, business faculty, National Park Service employees, representatives from boards of tourism and chambers of commerce, and a sizable number of Boulderites and residents of the surrounding Front Range area who are interested in the forces shaping the region in which they live. The event, typical of the interdisciplinary outreach activities of the center, was a successful effort to bring a wide range of expert perspectives to bear on issues of interest to those inside and outside the academy. Very much in the tradition of all the center's work, the conference was an example of how institutions of higher learning can and must reach out to their surrounding communities and of how scholars and other experts can and must be public intellectuals. The "Seeing and Being Seen" conference successfully put the issues before the public, placed them into historical context, and explored them from a range of disciplinary angles.

Two years later the content of the conference became the primary foundation of the present project. We utilized a selected number of papers from the conference in revised form and solicited new essays from other scholars on topics that we felt were vital to the volume. In addition, we decided, in several cases, to include revised versions of previously published essays or book chapters that fit well with the volume's overall structure. We are grateful to all the contributors for the patient, timely, and good-humored manner in which they responded to our requests for revisions.

We are indebted to previous and present staff, faculty, and affiliates of the Center of the American West: Leslie Durgin, Julia Hobson, David Hoffman, Roni Iris, Patricia Nelson Limerick, Tom Precourt, and Bill Riebsame, who all contributed in important ways to the construction and conceptualization of the volume. Bradley Johnson, former staff member at the Center of the American West, deserves special mention here for his role in organizing the original conference; he provided close readings of all the essays in their various stages, made extensive and insightful suggestions for revisions, and helped gather illustrations for the volume. Richard Wobbekind, director of the business research division at the University of Colorado, Boulder, kindly provided office space for us to work on the volume in spring 1999. We are also grateful to Nancy Scott Jackson of the University Press of Kansas, who saw the promise in the project and helped guide it through the various stages of development. Virginia Scharff of the University of New Mexico offered important advice in the early stages of the project.

The end product will, we hope, serve as a useful introduction to a subfield of American western studies that blossomed in the last decade of the twentieth century. The first major treatment of American western tourism in historical context was Earl Pomeroy's *In Search of the Golden West: The Tourist in Western America*, published in 1957. It is especially fitting, in light of Pomeroy's pioneering work, that his reflections on tourism, four and a half decades later, should serve as the foreword for the present volume. We are grateful to Earl Pomeroy for effectively launching an entire subfield and for offering his reflections as a beginning for this book, and we dedicate *Seeing and Being Seen* to him.

This book seeks to answer some of the difficult questions that surround western tourism and to raise some important questions for other scholars to explore. If it can do this much it will be a worthy part of the Pomeroy legacy of complex explorations of western American issues. And in the spirit of the Center of the American

West's commitment to scholarly endeavors that heighten public interest and understanding, we hope that *Seeing and Being Seen* proves of use to those outside the academy as well as those within it. It seems especially crucial in a collection of scholarly treatments of tourism—a topic so vitally important to the public—that scholars do much more than talk to just each other. The cultural and economic exchanges that comprise tourism shape western lives and places in vital ways. This volume should hence prove of interest to some of the tourists who do the seeing, and to the residents of those communities who see the tourists and are seen by them.

A final word of thanks is reserved for our families for their constant support and encouragement. Patrick wishes to thank especially his wife, Marlene Long, and his mother, Anna Rose Long. David wishes to thank especially his wife, Janet Ward, and his mother, Evelyn Hawro. Reflecting back on our childhood and youth, we see clearly that Anna Rose and Evelyn were the ones who first made tourists of us and demonstrated enduring patience as they taught us to be responsible visitors. Marlene and Janet have provided sound advice that has sharpened our thinking about tourism. It is their love and good company that have made our respective travels so enjoyable.

Chapter One

Introduction: Tourists, Tourism, and the Toured Upon

David M. Wrobel

Travelers and Tourists

Growing up in London, England, in the 1970s I developed an unusual empathy for tourists, particularly American tourists. On my regular trips into central London from the city outskirts, one of the most frequent phrases I would hear was the impassioned Cockney lament: "bloody tourists." Those words seemed as common as rain in the misty city, and Londoners uttered them often and loudly, generally in reference to visitors from the United States; there were many more choice labels for visitors from other countries, but Americans were the "bloody tourists." The sentiment was quite pervasive in British popular culture and reflected currents of both anti-Americanism and island provincialism.[1] One indicator of the extent of its cultural pervasiveness was the 1978 release of the album "Bloody Tourists" by the rock/pop group 10CC.[2]

Now, there was some irony in Londoners' cynical reactions to tourists a generation ago, since the English were, and still are, among the most feared tourists on the European continent, seemingly more prone to acts of drunken destructiveness than their European Community counterparts. Still, the irony did not seem to bother the city's permanent residents. I can vividly recall London bus conductors, newspaper vendors, and other assorted characters bragging about

1

having shortchanged American tourists. There seemed to be a deep Cockney pride in fleecing the proverbial "other." London locals vilified the tourists, and in doing so those locals perhaps developed the necessary self-justification to victimize the tourists, and then brag about it, without the accompanying moral qualms that their actions might be expected to stir up. My Cockney counterparts also liked to have a little fun at American tourists' expense, purposefully providing bad directions and then joking with their pals in the pubs about the dumb rich Americans looking for the Houses of Parliament in London's East End, or searching for Buckingham Palace in Brixton.[3] I eventually chose the tourists' side, viewing them as unfortunate victims of London's unscrupulous streetwise locals, and developed a sense of empathy for them.

When, a couple of decades later, I began to read academic literature about tourism in general, and more specifically about tourism in the western United States, I was struck by the lack of empathy for tourists among professional writers and scholars, and was reminded of my youth. Academics have exhibited a proclivity for fleecing tourists a little more indirectly, but no less subtly than Londoners. It is common practice among cultural critics and journalists to set the tourist up as a pitiful straw man or woman for the purpose of expressing their intellectual laments over the artificiality and soullessness of modern corporate, capitalist culture.[4] Frequently, tourists are seen as shallow, gullible, and ignorant, a general "bane to civilization,"[5] and tourism is viewed as the new imperialism of the postmodern, postcolonial world.[6] In scholarly discourse, residents of tourist communities generally become the long-suffering hosts and victims of a reprehensible force and of its tiresome representatives.[7] Perhaps academics even exhibit a sort of "ascetic priest" mentality in their emphasis on the inherent wastefulness and pleasure-based purposelessness of touristic consumption.[8]

This intellectual fleecing of tourists is not quite as old as the human tendency for "locals" to fleece "outsiders"; still, one can find critical commentaries on tourists in the American West in literature more than a century old as well as in current academic writing. In the early 1870s, a century before Edward Abbey's impassioned tirade against "industrial tourists," naturalist John Muir was expressing his disdain for visitors who crowded into Yosemite and quickly perused its "points of interest" before hurrying off to superficially experience other natural wonders.[9] Yet Muir would also comment in 1898 that "the tendency nowadays to wander in the wilderness is delightful to see," and lauded the healing power of wilderness for "thousands of tired, nerve-shaken, over-civilized people."[10] Given the power of Muir's descriptions of Yosemite and other western wonderlands (combined with improvements in rail transportation), it is hardly surprising that visitors began to come in droves.[11] Muir reflected the divided mind and the great dilemma that surrounds tourism. "He was torn," historian Earl Pomeroy notes, "between his conviction that conservation could come only through popular support and his contempt for 'the rough vertical animals called men, who occur in and on these mountains like sticks of condensed filth.'"[12] Muir lamented that most tourists in the national parks "are content with what they can see from [railway] car windows or the verandas of hotels, and in going from place to place cling to their precious trains and stages like wrecked sailors to rafts."[13] Still, Muir was hopeful that tourists might become enlightened appreciators of wilderness.

Muir, like later advocates of wilderness, including photographer Ansel Adams and Edward Abbey, faced what historian Roderick Nash calls "the chronic preservation *vs* enjoyment dilemma"—how to simultaneously preserve wild nature and promote it, in order to gain the necessary support for its preservation.[14] Muir walked a fine line between biocentric and anthropocentric attitudes toward nature—between the preservation of environments and the provision of pleasure for an increasingly large and urbanized public (the dual goals of the National Park Service's 1916 "Organic Act").[15] Tourists were the very heart of the dilemma, and Muir and Adams (and Abbey perhaps less so) clearly understood the impossibility of maintaining theoretical consistency while walking the line between preservation and pleasure. But not all late-nineteenth- and early-twentieth-century critics of tourism were as understanding. One travel writer, in 1905, assured more refined "travelers" that the remoteness of the West's natural wonders from its centers of population provided some protection from the "hordes of hoodlums who desecrate nearby beauty spots."[16]

These early criticisms of tourism were largely class-based, reflecting the disdainful response of the wealthy "traveler" to the democratization of the travel experience. As middle-class Americans, imbued with some financial means and leisure time (but standing outside the American and European aristocracies), began to travel to nearby and faraway American attractions around the turn of the century, the term "tourist" came to be used to describe them and distinguish them from the "higher breed" of "travelers." Ironically, then, the practice of these elites in defining their socioeconomic "other" was a precursor of sorts to more recent academic criticism of tourists, which often focuses on the tourists' racially motivated "imperial gaze" upon a group of "others" composed of peoples of color.[17]

Tourists, while commonly painted as phonies, shallow incompetents—pitiful beings who are naive enough to get caught in "tourist traps"—are, at the same time, often characterized as dangerous consumers, commodifiers, exoticizers, and objectifiers of other cultures. The tourist is left in the unenviable position of being considered both incompetent and malign at the same time. The tourist becomes both the villain who destroys cultural purity and the victim of his/her own shallowness, which prevents him/her from really seeing anything of value while touring. Yet contemporary criticism of the "hordes" or "waves" of mass tourism sparks a sense of déjà vu in those familiar with the criticisms leveled by a "traveling" cultural elite against the "touring" masses a century ago.[18] Interestingly, the same terms—"hordes," "waves," "tides," and the like—were very much a part of the anti-immigrant sentiment of the late nineteenth and early twentieth centuries (and have been a constant undercurrent in American thought since then). The use of similar terminology is hardly surprising, since the fear of so many residents of tourist communities is that tourists will not be mere "birds of passage," but will end up staying.

An influential example of the common academic denigration of tourists deserves extended commentary. Back in 1962, best-selling historian and former librarian of Congress Daniel Boorstin, in his book *The Image; or, What Happened to the American Dream,* lamented the transition, as he saw it, "from traveler to tourist." Boorstin noted that while "[m]any Americans now 'travel,' few are travelers in the old sense of the word." Travel had become cheaper, easier, more readily available to more people, he explained. Yet Boorstin was not lauding the democratization of travel. While travel had become more affordable, "the experience of travel," he contended, had been cheapened, "diluted, contrived, prefabricated." The "experience of going there, the experience of being there, and what is brought back from there are all very different" from what they used to be, he suggested. Indeed, the change was so significant that Boorstin contended that "[t]he modern American tourist now fills his experience with *pseudo-events*" (italics mine). The tourist, he continued, "has come to believe that he can have a lifetime of adventure in two weeks and all the thrills of risking his life without any real risk at all." "Expecting all this," Boorstin further added, the tourist "demands that it be supplied to him. Having paid for it he likes to think he got his money's worth. He has demanded that the whole world be made a stage for pseudo-events. And there has been no lack of honest and enterprising suppliers who try to give him what he wants, to help him inflate his expectations, and to gratify his insatiable appetite for the impossible."[19]

For Boorstin, the democratization of travel and the accompanying growth of tourism were marked by a decline in cultural and regional distinctiveness and a concordant rise in standardization and homogenization.[20] Furthermore, a decrease in cultural and experiential authenticity and a rise in artificiality, or pseudoreality, characterized this transition. The modern tourist was, Boorstin insisted, merely searching after that which he/she was expected to experience. The tourist even visited sites depicted in movies and matched the actual reality of the site against the hyperreality of its celluloid presentation, and often ended up disappointed by the actual site.[21]

It is worth adding that this phenomenon of visiting places that have been seen on the big screen is sometimes so pronounced that a historic site becomes significant as a tourist attraction largely because it has been depicted in a movie. Signs alongside Interstate 70 in western Kansas, in addition to promoting the world's largest prairie dog (unfortunately a large concrete sculpture and not the really huge, live prairie dog I had hoped to see), used to also promote a significant historic site, Fort Hays, in a particularly memorable manner. One of the signs read: "VISIT HISTORIC FORT HAYS, AS FEATURED IN THE MOVIE *DANCES WITH WOLVES*." The 1990 movie, directed by and starring Kevin Costner, was a blockbuster and multi-Oscar winner that helped to reignite the Western as a popular movie genre, and that genre would remain popular for the first half of the 1990s. The movie was memorable, and so, the sign suggested, the site was worth seeing. Indeed, the sign somehow added a new layer of authenticity to the site, while at the same time suggesting a somewhat convoluted representational process of life imitating art imitating life.[22]

Now historical purists might be alarmed at this process by which a historic site seeks tourist traffic based on the cachet of its celluloid history and not on the richness of its actual history. But this process should not be instantly dismissed as impure and artificial. These purists may be expecting too much and not fully accepting that places, cultures, even historic sites are always in a state of flux.[23] The idea of a static, immutable past that can be discovered and preserved is perhaps the greatest of all historical myths.[24] People with no illusions concerning the presumed purity of the preserved past simply view Fort Hays's depiction in a hugely successful movie as a fortuitous event that put it, quite literally, back on the map.[25]

These concepts of flux and impurity are worth keeping in mind as we consider the complexities surrounding tourism, particularly the thorny issue of authenticity. Identifying a lamentable transition away from cultural authenticity and toward a staged reality of pseudo-events, toward cultural decline and impurification, is unlikely to illuminate all of those complexities (though it is likely to play to certain academic prejudices). That model is a little too dramatic and dualistic; we should instead consider some finer gradations in the theoretical landscape that surrounds tourism. We need to remember that all places change and that tourism, though it may speed up the rate of change, does not create the process of change. We need to consider, too, that authenticity and artificiality are not absolute values; still, the tendency among academic and literary commentators on tourism has often been to take the easy way out and treat them as such.[26]

Take, for example, writer Ian Frazier, who takes a casual stab or two at tourists in his popular work *Great Plains* (1989). He recounts a scene at Fort Union, Montana: "One woman tourist to another: 'I had so many clothes in my closet I broke the closet rods!'"[27] I do not doubt that the conversation or the event took place; the point is that such incidents—stupid tourist stories, as they are often referred to— are rather readily recounted in western travel literature. Both the event and the verbal exchange it inspired—a few broken closet rods in a motel room, one marginally interesting anecdote—are not terribly significant in and of themselves; but if we place them within the dualistic framework adopted in commentaries on tourism, then we find that the events resonate; they speak volumes. The closet rods were broken by the weight of one woman's cultural baggage, her inability to travel without the array of sartorial possibilities she would enjoy closer to home. The implication is clear: the woman never left home. She will not experience anything of cultural significance because she is wearing cultural blinders. What is more, she does not even get the joke that she has become and proceeds to recount the event to a tourist friend, who probably does not get it either. The closet rod–breaking tourist can safely recount her experience to a tourist companion without the irony becoming apparent to either of them, for they are both mere tourists.

Thus, Frazier, as a "traveler," the paragon of authenticity, illuminates for his readers the artificiality of the tourist experience.[28] And, whether consciously or not, he places himself in a long line of travel writers in America. The line stretches back to Lewis and Clark at the beginning of the nineteenth century, through Horace Greeley and Sir Richard Burton around the middle of the century, to Mark Twain, Robert Louis Stevenson, Oscar Wilde, Rudyard Kipling, and Charles F. Lummis, later that century, and onward in time to Agnes Laut, Emily Post, Sinclair Lewis, John Steinbeck, Jack Kerouac, Charles Kuralt, William Least Heat-Moon, Dayton Duncan, Robert Kaplan, Timothy Egan, and countless others in the twentieth century.[29] All of them, Frazier included, would probably define, or would have defined, themselves as travelers, not tourists. Lummis had walked, or as he put it, "tramped" 3,500 miles across the continent, from Chillicothe, Ohio, to Los Angeles, California, in 1884, prior to beginning work at the *L.A. Times*. The physical demands and dangers of his experience, its authenticity (as Boorstin would have it), is hard to question. Lummis truly "traveled." Still, it is worth noting that undertaking this marathon pedestrian continent-crossing was, at least in part, an act of self-promotion (as well as place-promotion) on Lummis's part. His "travels" both to California and throughout the Southwest in later years, the voluminous publications that resulted from them, and his energetic editorship of the promotional journal *Land of Sunshine/Out West* certainly encouraged multitudinous others to "travel," or "tour" (depending upon one's definition).[30]

Still, in the modern age, one did not need to walk across the continent in pioneer fashion or cross it in a covered wagon to be deemed a "traveler"; one merely needed to record the experience in publishable format and thereby gain an audience. With publication came authenticity. Transcontinental railroad trips were turned into travel accounts, Richard Harding Davis's *The West from a Car Window* (1892) being one of the most notable examples. The issue of "authenticity" certainly did arise with respect to rail travel. By the late nineteenth century, western pioneer societies were taking chartered group rail excursions in luxurious Pullman Palace cars across the continent. On the trips members of the societies juxtaposed the dangerous and physically demanding transcontinental treks of their earlier years, on foot and by covered wagon, with the opulent travel accommodations available to later post-pioneer generations. The old pioneers, in their accounts of these modern trips, often waxed eloquently on the subject of their earlier trailblazing. They recounted how their journeys had paved the way for the taming of the wilderness and made the rail lines possible; or, to put it another way, how their travels had made the West safe to tour and settle. They insisted upon the authenticity of their experience as real travelers, real pioneers, and sometimes referred derisively to the "Pullman Pioneers" who came later.[31] Most old pioneers would have agreed wholeheartedly with historian Hal Rothman's suggestion that "the railroad made tourists out of travelers."[32] The old pioneer society members were not embarrassed about being tourists in their twilight years; indeed, from all accounts, they reveled in their Pullman journeys. Those journeys provided them the perfect stage for contrasting their elevated moral characters and physical constitutions—as shaped by the age of rough travel—with those of later generations raised in the age of easy touring.

By the first decade of the twentieth century, the first transcontinental auto travelers were publishing book-length accounts of their experiences. In these works they portrayed themselves as authentic pioneers, and given the near total lack of paved roads between cities in this period and the comparative fragility of their vehicles, there was some truth to their claims.[33] Scores of these accounts were published in the first three decades of the century.[34] As the roads improved in the teens and twenties and as the automobile became more widely available, the transcontinental auto trip lost much of its pioneer status. And as the Depression of the thirties began, such accounts became increasingly uncommon. By the post–World War II years, the transcontinental auto narrative had largely become the purview of professional writers. By the time Steinbeck left on his *Travels with Charley in Search of America* (1962), roads were further improved, and the interstate highway system was under construction. Traversing the national and western landscapes was quicker, easier, and infinitely more comfortable, even if Steinbeck and his chronicling successors often (and William Least Heat-Moon, exclusively), stuck to the blue highways (secondary roads marked in blue on the maps of the day). Still, despite the comparative comfort of their travels, the resulting chronicles claimed considerable authenticity. The journeys of these professional writers were deemed reflective by the reading public, and their vision was considered to be unblinkered. They were supposedly less encumbered by their own cultural baggage. They were travelers, not tourists. Their experience was real, not artificial.[35]

But the equation is not so simple, and the traveler-tourist dichotomy warrants further exploration. In his seminal work on the topic, *The Tourist: A New Theory of the Leisure Class* (1976, 1989, 1999), Dean MacCannell builds on the premise that "we are all tourists" to construct a more complex model. MacCannell explores the fuzziness of authenticity and inauthenticity. He is critical of Boorstin's traveler-tourist dichotomy and points to a "rhetoric of moral superiority" on Boorstin's part, "a pronounced dislike, bordering on hatred, for other tourists, an attitude that turns man against man in a *they are tourists, I am not* equation" (italics MacCannell's).[36] MacCannell overstates his case, to be sure: Boorstin was primarily interested in tourism within the context of his broader and quite innovative examination of American pseudo-events; and while Boorstin clearly exhibits disdain for tourists, it hardly borders on hatred. Still, for all MacCannell's impressive model building (in contrast to Boorstin's more dualistic framework), all of which has spawned myriad studies of tourism in the social sciences and in cultural studies, one suspects that Boorstin's "tourist as easy target" approach is still the more common one.[37] French postmodern theorist Jean Baudrillard, in his oft-cited book of reflections on the United States, *America* (1988), rejects tourism and the very notion that he might be considered a tourist. He echoes Boorstin, and generations of other travel writers, in commenting that "nothing is further from pure traveling than tourism or holiday travel."[38] Furthermore, Baudrillard, in positing tourists and tourism as the "other," in stark opposition to himself and the art of traveling, engages in the "rhetoric of moral superiority" that MacCannell points to.

Boorstin's, Baudrillard's, and Frazier's critical take on tourists seems to be the more common one; it is likely that most scholars (at least in the liberal arts) share their assumptions. One can imagine academics strolling around mystical New Mexican towns such as Santa Fe and Taos, looking at the tourists around them and thinking up clever ways to conceptualize the objectification of the "other" by visitors, and unaware that other academics may be looking at them and thinking precisely the same thing. It would rarely dawn on an academic that he/she might be a tourist. Perish the very suggestion, the academic might think, since self-identification as a tourist would set him/her up as an example of the very shallowness, hollowness, and artificiality that so often mark the tourist. But we academics can only take the "fieldwork" argument so far, and in the end we need to accept our positions as tourist affines, as we interpret other times and places and peoples, in the hope that our peers will find our work "authentic." We are ourselves part of the genealogy of tourism, notwithstanding any elevated claims to the contrary. Just as anthropologists constantly question whether even a long-term stint living in another culture can make them full enough participants in that culture to be accurate recorders of it, so we scholars of tourism should consider ourselves tourists in the places we study.[39]

We would do well in our academic inquiries to move beyond the by now well "traveled" distinction between traveler and tourist and the authenticity-artificiality dichotomy that accompanies it. Still, one suspects that the dichotomy is too pervasive in print culture and too firmly engrained in the popular consciousness to fade away quickly. Examples of it abound. If parents are considering trips with the children to America's national parks, one of the preparatory readings they will find is Paris Permenter's and John Bigley's *National Parks with Kids: Be a Traveler—Not a Tourist* (1999), part of a series of guidebooks, all with the same catchy subtitle. The net surfer would also come across David Blomstrom's *(Ir)rational Parks: An Offbeat Look at Wilderness, Tourism, and America* (1996), proudly billed as "[t]he first and foremost collection of stupid tourist questions from America's national parks."[40]

Contemporary films (in addition to occasionally reigniting public interest in historic sites) provide further evidence of the cultural pervasiveness of pejorative usage of the word "tourist" and of easy assumptions about the inauthenticity of the tourist experience. In fact, in popular culture, "tourist" has become virtually synonymous with inauthenticity and artificiality. A memorable recent example of this is the movie *Fight Club* (dir. David Fincher, 1999), starring Brad Pitt and Ed Norton. In the film Norton plays a young man so thoroughly alienated from the excesses of his impersonal, postmodern, consumer-driven existence that he seeks solace in support groups for victims of terminal diseases (none of which he suffers from). He remarks that people who are dying are more likely to listen to him. His presence at these meetings is, of course, a sham. However, he refers to Marla, the movie's female lead, another "healthy" group-goer (played by Helena Bonham-Carter), as a "tourist," someone who is not there for the authentic experience. Marla is a mere gate-crasher. These two pathetic seekers of authentically tragic emotional experiences are unable to achieve the necessary levels of catharsis when they are in attendance together at the same support group meetings; each is irritated by the other's inauthenticity. So, they decide to coordinate their presence at separate meetings—they split up the groups between them. They each consider their own individual presence at the meetings to be a genuine journey in search of emotional catharsis. They each make their separate claims to being travelers, yet each considers the other to be a tourist. Boorstin would perhaps view their actions as the ultimate expression of "diluted, contrived, prefabricated" "pseudo-event" seeking.[41] MacCannell might view their experience as the ultimate expression of "the alienation of the sightseer."[42] Whatever the case, these characters reflect the ubiquitousness of the denigration of tourists in popular culture.

Certainly, the tourist is an easy target for writers and for the broader public because the tourist's actions in and reactions to places so often seem to reflect a lack of understanding, or a "stereotyped understanding," or a kind of "simulacrum" of experience.[43] Boorstin noted that "American tourists" have a tendency to become "naïve, to the point of gullibility."[44] (Many Americans would probably agree, and yet would almost certainly insist, in Baudrillardian fashion, that they themselves were not tourists). But one wonders how it could be otherwise? To accuse tourists of not being travelers, of being gullible and of not developing a full and authentic understanding of the peoples and places they visit, would be akin to the full professor chiding the first-year college student for having a meager publication record. The tourist, by virtue of wanting to see and experience different cultures and environments, opens him/herself up to the ridicule of locals and the ire of academics. And the critics emphasize that very lack of familiarity (on the tourists' part), which, in turn, is perhaps the factor that at least motivates the more adventurous and inquiring tourist to want to know more. The easy verbal and written assault on the modern tourist, especially when leveled by academics, is uncomfortably reminiscent of late-nineteenth- and early-twentieth-century ridiculing of southern and eastern European immigrant children by culturally insensitive teachers. At least tourists are trying, with varying degrees of commitment to be sure, to find out about other people and places, trying to operate, if only for a week or two at a time, in another world apart from their own.

Now, as noted, tourists go about this business of broadening their cultural horizons in a variety of ways. It seems plausible enough that some tourists are shameless seekers of the exotic, "psychic trophy hunters" (as Rothman calls those on this extreme end of the spectrum) out to bag some experience just so they can share it with their well-heeled, well-traveled friends and acquaintances.[45] One assumes there is a "been there, done that" kind of motivation (or lack thereof) behind this kind of tourism. Nonetheless, it seems to be the case that some other tourists are literally carried away, mentally, by the stimulation of their experiences, a phenomenon that British journalist Jeremy Laurance refers to, somewhat caustically, as "sudden unhinged tourist syndrome." Those afflicted with SUTS (not an officially classified condition, it should be noted) often suffer complete mental breakdowns when they visit places of great spiritual or cultural significance. In Jerusalem it is not unheard of for visitors to don sheets from their hotel rooms and wander the streets in a spiritual trance chanting psalms.[46] In Florence, Italy, an average of ten or so tourists a year were hospitalized between 1977 and 1986 after exhibiting "outburst[s] of anxiety reaching psychotic dimensions," generally after viewing firsthand a small detail in a work of art with which they had had some prior familiarity.[47] Laurance continues the long tradition of poking fun at tourists, but follows a less common substrain of that tradition by chiding them for achieving too elevated an experience, for straying too far from the "been there, done that," run-of-the-mill brand of tourism, for being *too* "authentic," getting *too* caught up in the moment, for not bagging their "psychic trophies" but being psychically bagged by them.

Now, we need not take this spirited defense of tourists, this chronicling of their easy targeting by academics and others, too far. Even with the increasing democratization of travel since the late nineteenth century, tourists are people who have the disposable time and income to travel away from home, and that very fact alone places them in the minority among a world population to whom such luxuries are largely unknown. (Tourists are, to draw a parallel, akin to people in the developed world who have the time to worry about pollution and overpopulation in third-world countries, but drive large, fuel-inefficient sports utility vehicles and do not themselves suffer the consequences of overpopulation). Still, as academics we can have too jaundiced a view of tourists as conquering hordes of thrill-seeking, authenticity-craving slaves to modern consumer culture. One suspects that tourists actually comprise a representative cross-sampling of the socioeconomic and cultural groups from which they hail.[48] Their experiences probably fall most often into the larger, murkier, and generally less dramatic space that lies between the extremes of "psychic trophy hunters" and "SUTS-sufferers."[49] Furthermore, so-called "mass" tourism, it is worth remembering, probably has as much to do with the economic means of the participants as with their respective levels of craving for authenticity (itself a profound intangible for which there is no reliable yardstick for measurement). To criticize charter tourists on package tours for allowing themselves to be sold a thoroughly inauthentic bill of experiential goods places academics in a situation uncomfortably similar to that of the late-nineteenth-century critics of the democratization of travel, critics who bemoaned the presence of barbaric crowds at the gates of their private paradises. Academics' anti-tourist proclamations can sound like, and often are, thinly veiled expressions of classism.

British novelist David Lodge provides a hilarious example of this academic targeting of tourists and tourism in his novel *Paradise News* (1991), set in Hawaii. In the novel, Bernard Walsh, an agnostic theologian, is subjected to the self-promotional and theoretical excesses of one Roger Sheldrake, an anthropologist writing on tourism and the author of a book entitled *Sightseeing*. Sheldrake explains to the affable Bernard that his book treats "sightseeing as a substitute for religious ritual. The sightseeing tour as a secular pilgrimage. Accumulation of grace by visiting the shrines of high culture. Souvenirs as relics. Guidebooks as devotional aids. You get the picture."[50] "Tourism," Sheldrake then proclaims to his captive audience of one, "is the new world religion," and he is "doing to tourism what Marx did to capitalism, what Freud did to family life. Deconstructing it." Sheldrake explains that people do not really like holidays, but have been brainwashed into thinking they do, and even if they seem cheerful it is only "[a]n artificial cheerfulness." Since the anthropologist and the agnostic are both on their way to Hawaii, the tourism as "passport to paradise" theme (the ultimate sacred metaphor) naturally emerges, and Sheldrake explains that the mission of his research endeavors is "[t]o save the world." "Tourism," he informs his attentive yet mildly skeptical listener, "is wearing out the planet." To back up his claim he notes (exaggerating his case rather brazenly) that "in 1963 forty-four people went down the Colorado river on a raft, now there are a thousand trips a day." (Just over twenty thousand people made the trip in 1991, and the figure has been quite stable in the last decade.)[51] Sheldrake concludes his gratuitous lecture in fine rhetorical style:

> The only way to put a stop to it, short of legislation, is to demonstrate to people that they really aren't enjoying themselves when they go on holiday, but engaging in a superstitious ritual. It's no coincidence that tourism arose just as religion went into decline. It's the new opium of the people, and must be exposed as such.

Bernard's innocent, but revealing, reply to this impassioned academic outburst is: "Won't you do yourself out of a job if you're successful?" But Sheldrake rightly replies in his only, though albeit unconscious, moment of insightfulness: "I don't think there's any immediate risk of that."[52]

Since an end to tourism will not be legislated, and since it is more than a popular new opiate, and since its scholarly critics really do not want to put themselves out of work and are in no real danger of doing so, but, since some of them are in danger of becoming objects of novelistic humor, it is well worth moving beyond simple dualisms and easy presumptions to establish a closer empathy with tourists, the objects of the academic gaze.

Tourism: Definitions and Destinations

Having reflected a little on tourists, we might find it worth considering what we actually mean by tourism. Definitions abound, and only a few of them are shared here, but the variety that exists among them is noteworthy. According to the World Tourism Organization (WTO): "Tourism is the activity of persons traveling to and staying in places outside their usual environment for not more than one consecutive year for leisure, business or any other purposes." This is one of my favorite definitions since it includes "business" trips as tourism and thereby renders the conference-going academician a tourist.[53] (Incidentally, the definition, by virtue of the phrase "or any other purposes," seems to also render as tourists those from Eugene, Oregon, and other places who protested violently against another WTO, the World Trade Organization, in Seattle in late 1999). The definition is also notable for its use of the phrase "outside their usual environment," a rather loose, yet (as we will see) potentially useful, way of referencing the destination. Finally, it should be emphasized that the World Tourism Organization's definition of tourism places a limit of one year (of residence) on the tourist experience. So, duration of stay is also a factor in defining tourism. At some point the tourist becomes, as Rothman puts it, a "neo-native."[54]

The Travel Industry Association of America's (TIA) definition is a little more precise in some areas than the WTO's and more problematic as a result. According to the TIA, tourism encompasses: "All round-trips with a one-way route mileage of 100 miles or more and all trips involving one or more nights away from home, regardless of distance." So Los Angeles residents going to Las Vegas for the weekend (a four-hour drive or forty-minute commuter flight across the desert), and doing so twice a month, are tourists, even though Las Vegas may be no further "outside their usual environment," than Atlantic City is for Philadelphians (a ninety-minute road trip). But by this definition, residents of rural far-western Nebraska traveling to Cheyenne, Wyoming (an hour's drive) for the Frontier Days festival are not tourists. Boulder, Colorado, to the southern end of Fort Collins, Colorado (just under a hundred miles), for a one-week visit, does not make the grade, but Boulder to Colorado Springs (a little over a hundred miles) for a single night is a tourist outing. Or consider, for example, that a five-hundred-mile trip to one's old hometown to visit relatives (a trip that might not involve hotel stays or dining out), hardly places one outside of one's usual environment, but does count as tourism, according to the TIA. But a day trip to a neighboring town to go to the beach (presumably involving parking, cabana fee, and meals out) does not count as tourism. Definitional precision has its problems.[55]

Perhaps we need a definition of tourism that is less vague and yet less tied to the variable of the distance one travels from home or the length of time one stays away. Surely a resident of the Bronx visiting Ellis Island on a day trip for the first time is a tourist in much the same way that a resident of Flagstaff, Arizona, on a first visit to the Grand Canyon is. In both cases the distance is too short to meet the TIA's definition of tourism. Yet in both cases the experience, one hopes, is significant. Meanwhile, some residents of suburban Philadelphia, after an initial trip to Lancaster County, Pennsylvania, to experience Amish culture, discover the outlet malls and make subsequent trips back to the region to purchase consumer goods at reduced rates. (Or perhaps their first visit there is primarily motivated by a desire to experience the outlets and not the Amish.) Now, the point here is not to argue that shopping is not and never can be a significant experience (it could be noted, too, that the tourist is a shopper seeking packaged experiences), but rather to note that the primary purpose of such Amish-country shoppers is not to see and experience anything out of the ordinary, but to purchase familiar items more cheaply. Are they really tourists (even if they have driven the requisite distance and stayed the requisite length of time to meet the definitional standards), or shoppers?[56]

Perhaps the tourist is simply "someone who travels to experience unfamiliar surroundings." Now this definition certainly reflects my empathy for tourists and faith in their efforts to at least try and experience that which is out of the ordinary; my definition does imbue tourists with a degree of authenticity. Critics might charge that the primary motivation of many tourists is not to actually experience those surroundings, but to bag another set of experiences that can be talked about with friends and associates. Steinbeck suggested as much in *Travels with Charley*, when he wrote that "one goes, not so much to see but to tell afterward."[57] But how can we effectively measure the nature of tourists' motivations and the quality of tourist experiences? Those motivations are as varied and as difficult to measure as people's sense of place. It does seem that a Los Angelean's bimonthly overnight trips to Las Vegas may become, after a time, decidedly nontouristic, though the explosive rate at which new hotels are constructed and old ones are imploded on the Strip places Las Vegas in a constantly heightened state of flux.[58] Still, the frequent visitor to a place probably does stop experiencing anything terribly "out of the ordinary," and the place that is revisited becomes a part of the familiar environment. "Someone who travels to experience unfamiliar surroundings" may be a consciously open-ended definition of the tourist, but it does seem to get at the issue of the cultural significance of the experience.[59]

Sticking with this theme of multiple and ambivalent contexts, I am reminded of the opening line of John Jakle's rich and important study *The Tourist* (1985): "Tourism is a state of mind."[60] Likewise, I am reminded of western historians' and writers' debates in the early 1990s over "where the West is" and the not uncommon response from some of them that "the West is a state of mind." However, I would venture that the word *tourism* prompts rather different mental images in the minds of those in different fields of inquiry and endeavor. For those in the fields of business and hospitality management, tourism constitutes a massive sector of the economy, and the primary concern is with how to conduct the business of tourism more effectively. This is not to say that business scholars are uninterested in the cultural or environmental impacts of tourism; rather, such interests are less likely to be their primary concern. But for scholars in anthropology, cultural studies, geography, history, literature, and sociology, analyzing the growth of sectors of the tourist economy is of less concern than assessing the environmental, social, and cultural impact, and representations of, tourists on the people and places they visit, and the impact of those people and places on the tourists. In short, the business scholar focuses more squarely on tourism (as the tourist industry), while those in the humanities and social sciences focus more on tourists and on the people and places that are toured upon. This is a generalization, to be sure, yet it does help to illuminate the broad division in the field of tourism studies between those in business and hospitality on the one hand and those in the liberal arts on the other.[61] One suspects that both broad camps of scholars can learn from each other's work and that interdisciplinary approaches to tourism afford great possibilities.[62] Still, in light of the tremendous variety of disciplinary and cross-disciplinary approaches to tourism, constructing a definition that works for everyone is an impossibly tall order.

The Toured Upon: Peoples and Places

In the field of western American history, the most studied of the three broad elements under discussion here—tourists, tourism, and the toured upon—is probably the last. Scholars of the West have become increasingly interested in the impact of tourists and the tourism industry on the environments and communities that are visited. This awakening of heightened interest, reflected in the appearance of numerous books, articles, and doctoral dissertations, should hardly come as a surprise.[63] The field has often taken its theoretical cues from developments in disciplines other than history (which itself is a sign of healthy cross-disciplinarity rather than theoretical dependency), and scholars in those fields—cultural studies, environmental studies, sociology, and anthropology in particular—have been interested in tourism for some time.[64] What is more, the increasing centrality of tourism to American western economies has rendered "the toured upon" (peoples and places) natural subjects for study.

The grand landscapes and diverse inhabitants of the American West today draw visitors in huge numbers. The national parks (most of which are located in the West), for example, annually attract a total visitor population roughly equal in size to the population of the nation itself. John Muir's vision of "thousands of tired, nerve-shaken, over-civilized people" experiencing mental and spiritual rejuvenation through contact with wilderness has become for the National Park Service a vision (a nightmare vision, some scholars and environmentalists might say) of hundreds of millions. The West's distinctive societies—Indian, Hispanic, or Mormon villages, mining, ranching, or logging towns—also form a set of experiential alternatives in an

increasingly urbanized, suburbanized, and, perhaps, homogenized
nation.

Residents and visitors have viewed the West as a place of adventure and excitement, refuge and restoration, for more than two
centuries now. The West's "frontier heritage"—that is, the multitudinous mythologized versions of its past—constitutes, like the heritage of any region, a sanitized, simplified version of a messier, more
ambiguous history. It is that sanitized mode of representation that
provides the stock symbols of western tourism—the quaint false-
front buildings of old western towns, or the ubiquitous cowboy and
Indian and pioneer iconography. It is not essential that the symbols
bear any definite connection to the historical realities of an actual
western locale for the promotion of place to be successful.[65] Touristic representations need only invoke a semblance, or a "simulation,"
of an imaginary past to be effective.[66] Authenticity is hence not always the key issue.

The West has been viewed by European-Americans through
mythic lenses for centuries; the presumed inauthenticity of tourist
communities is actually part of this much longer tradition. The
"West of the Imagination" has departed cavalierly from the complexities and ambiguities of the region's past to present its presumed
"essence," and western tourism has followed suit.[67] That mythic
heritage has generated a great deal of income for some western residents and, in most cases, more for outside corporations. Whatever
the historical inaccuracies in the presentation of places to tourists,
whatever the nature of the motivations that inspire the touristic journeys, visiting the West has meant spending money there, and that
fact has gained significance with every passing year, any qualms
concerning inauthenticity notwithstanding. As historian Bonnie
Christensen notes in her study of Red Lodge, Montana, residents
"played with the past" in response to touristic opportunities in the
present. In the space of a few decades the town had "miners dressed
up like cowboys, miners dressed up like Italian immigrants, cowboys wrestling steers from speeding cars, cowboys who were really
Indians (and vice versa) and trout dumped from airplanes to make
nature more 'natural.'"[68] One suspects that Red Lodge is typical of
many western towns in its evolving processes of heritage creation.
As with Fort Hays, Kansas, and its fortuitous representation in
Dances with Wolves, the recreation of a semblance of the past in west-

ern towns reminds us of the dictum "you take what you can get." And in representing a past wrapped in multiple layers of mythology, you can get away with a great deal in the West, and qualms over inauthenticity are unlikely to act as much of a brake on the process. Still, it is important to note that many other western towns have not "played with the past" so frivolously; indeed, many have developed very thoughtful and historically accurate community heritage tourism plans, driven by a desire for authentic representation of the past.

As the region's traditional extractive economies, such as mining and logging, have gone into decline in recent decades, tourism has often seemed like the wave of the economic future, a "clean" and controllable alternative.[69] But the equation (like the authenticity-artificiality equation discussed earlier) is not so simple. This tourism boom offers categorically good and bad news, and plenty of mixed news, too. Some communities have been able, to some degree, to set the terms of tourism and reap significant benefits. Others have seen their homes turned into theme parks, where big-spending outsiders inflate local prices and locals in some measure sacrifice their cultural integrity to meet outsiders' high standards for proper quaintness.[70] Many westerners have themselves been instrumental in transforming their landscapes and sometimes their customs, in a form of "playing to the camera," to meet the expectations of tourists.[71]

Still, much like the processes of defining tourism and interpreting tourist motivations and experiences, assessing tourism's impact on communities and environments can lead easily to supposition, but not so easily to answers. For example, we can view tourism as another wave of extractive industry in the West and lament that the entertainment infrastructure—hotels, restaurants, theme parks, golf courses, ski slopes, and so on—is often owned by corporate interests centered far outside the community.[72] More than a half century ago Carey McWilliams issued a warning to the West that those states in which the tourist trade was the most important income producer "are economically vulnerable, puppets of forces which they find it difficult to influence or control."[73] We can point to the growth of low-wage service economies in tourist towns such as Aspen, Colorado, and view the workers as a later generation of colonial servants to imperial guests, servants who often cannot afford to live in the communities where they work.[74] We can envision a process in which

cultural integrity dissolves as western communities prepare themselves for the process of being seen by their "other," the tourists. Or
we can emphasize a range of positive outcomes from well-managed,
locally directed, and locally owned tourist operations. We can highlight cases in which western communities have engaged in cultural
heritage tourism and become more cognizant of their own community heritages and perhaps developed deeper, more cohesive community consciousnesses as a result. As was the case with descriptions
of tourist motivations—from the "psychic trophy hunters" to the
SUTS-sufferers—we are likely to find here a rather murky middle
ground between the most extreme examples of tourism's cultural
and environmental impacts.

Tourism, when placed within a broad framework, one comprising the full range of advantages and disadvantages experienced by
the "toured upon," becomes a sweeping category for analysis, much
like "work," or "leisure," or "commerce." Tourism, like "work," is
a part of everyday life in much of the modern West, and we need to
move beyond the "visited as victims" model in studying the "toured
upon," just as we need to move beyond the authenticity-artificiality paradigm in studying tourists.

We need to ask difficult questions about the "toured upon": Can
we determine a point at which tourist communities lose control of
the processes by which their attractions are presented to tourists?
Does our common emphasis on the "impurification" of resident
cultures through contact with visitors leave us in the position of
suggesting that cultures are static, rather than in a constant state of
flux? Do we end up, through the use of concepts such as the "toured
upon," viewing the resident communities as groups of people who
are merely "acted upon"?[75] (And, similarly, do we have a tendency
to view tourists as "acted upon," as passive consumers of the images, merchandise, and constructed landscapes engineered in almost
militaristic fashion by the tourist industry?)[76] Should communities
that consciously promote tourism be so adamant in expressing the
sentiment that visiting is okay, but staying (establishing residency)
is unwelcome? Do the oft-recounted stupid-tourist stories tell as
much about the locals as the visitors—or more? Are tourists' perceptions of residents as "other" matched sometimes in their cultural
arrogance by resident perceptions of tourists as "other"? Should our
emphasis on the exploitation of workers in tourism service econo-

mies focus less on the perceived malign nature of service sector labor and more on specific forms of exploitation that are particular to, or particularly acute in, the tourism service sector (e.g., the seasonal nature of employment and the unaffordability of housing close to places of work)? Still, it is doubtful that white middle-class "ski bums" working in the service sectors of upscale resorts such as Aspen see their plight as particularly dire. What is more, Hispanic maids working in the same kinds of resorts have chosen to be there because their level of compensation exceeds that in their former places of work and residence. Of course such workers are exploited by the corporations that employ them, but to view them as helpless victims hardly does justice to their significant efforts to gain a foothold on a somewhat higher rung of an exploitative service economy. Service economies, like tourism (contrary to the hopes of the fictional Roger Sheldrake and many real academics), are unlikely to crumble in the face of academic disdain, but scholars can certainly offer constructive, insightful analyses of labor in tourism service sectors that might help illuminate specific areas for improvement.[77]

Hopefully, the essays in *Seeing and Being Seen*, comprising, as they do, a range of perspectives and disciplinary approaches, can help us frame the important questions more clearly and even move us toward some of the answers. Given the extent of scholarship on western tourism, a single collection of essays can hardly provide a comprehensive overview. A cursory glance at the volume's contents will suggest that much has been left out. The book might have included a section on different kinds of western tourism, with essays on skiing, gambling, fishing, cultural heritage tourism, and ecotourism. A section might have focused on tourism in western cities, since that is where a good portion of the tourism business is centered, and where the vast bulk of the West's population resides. Chapter-length case studies of the growth and impact of tourism on particular western communities could have been included. But the intent here is to be provocative rather than comprehensive, to raise a range of interesting and important issues for other scholars to consider.

Instead of aiming for complete coverage of the topic, the volume emphasizes three main areas. Part I, "Perspectives: Scholars and Tourists," like this introductory essay, addresses some of the complex issues surrounding perceptions of tourism, of tourists, and of those who are "toured upon." Part II, "Processes: Tourism and Cultural Change," examines tourism in historical context and seeks to address its cultural impact on communities and, to some degree, on the tourists. Part III, "Parks: Tourism in Western Wonderlands," explores the history and impact of tourism in the West's national parks from the late nineteenth century to the present, with particular emphasis on efforts to maintain the delicate balance between natural preservation and public enjoyment. Together the essays perhaps move us a little further toward the loftier motivations behind tourism and tourism studies—to better understand others, and ourselves, in unfamiliar surroundings.

Notes

1. It is important to note that Londoners' designation of Americans as "bloody tourists" has a good deal to do with a broader anti-American sentiment among the generation of English people who came after the World War II generation.

2. 10CC, "Bloody Tourists." The album included the U.K. no. 1 hit single "Dreadlock Holiday."

3. Dona Brown provides a brief and useful discussion of anti-tourist attitudes in *Inventing New England: Regional Tourism in the Nineteenth Century* (Washington and London: Smithsonian Institution Press, 1995), 2–3. She mentions Cape Codders' T-shirts bearing the proud proclamation "I cheat drunks and tourists," 2. See also Jean Kristian Steen Jacobsen, "Anti-Tourist Attitudes: Mediterranean Charter Tourism," *Annals of Tourism Research* 27, no. 2 (2000): 284–300.

4. This essay takes a non-gender-specific approach to the topic. For a gender-based analysis see Caren Kaplan's chapter "Postmodern Geographies: Feminist Politics of Location," in her book *Questions of Travel: Postmodern Discourses of Displacement* (Durham: Duke University Press, 1996), 143–87; see also Inderpal Grewal and Caren Kaplan, "Transnational Feminist Practices and Questions of Postmodernity," in Grewal and Kaplan, eds., *Scattered Hegemonies: Postmodernity and Transnational Feminist Practices* (Minneapolis: University of Minnesota Press, 1994), 1–33.

5. John Jakle provides good coverage of the tendency to ridicule tourists in his "Introduction" to *The Tourist: Travel in Twentieth-Century North America* (Lincoln and London: University of Nebraska Press, 1985), 1–22, especially 3–4. One suspects that the general tone of derision in journalistic writing on tourism is at least partly subconscious. For example, Nancy Lofholm, *Denver Post* staff writer, in discussing the changing face of tourism in Grand Junction and Mesa County, Colorado, notes: "you won't find hordes of the luggage-toting, picture-snapping variety of travelers here"; see Lofholm, "New Breed of Tourism Is Tops in Mesa County," *Denver Post*, February 7, 1999, L1. Lofholm's choice of vocabulary is not especially harsh—"hordes" being the only unqualified term of derision—but the general effect is far from neutral.

6. For more on this topic see Dennison Nash, "Tourism as a Form of Imperialism," in Valene L. Smith, ed., *Hosts and Guests: The Anthropology of Tourism*, 2nd ed. (Philadelphia: University of Pennsylvania Press, 1989; first published 1977), 37–52. Deborah McLaren in *Rethinking Tourism and Ecotravel: The Paving of Paradise and What You Can Do to Stop It* (Washington, D.C.: Kumarian Press, 1998), actually uses the phrase "invasion by tourists" in the index. While clearly a concerted effort to promote more ecofriendly and culturally sensitive tourism, McLaren's book does serve as a good example of the easy and very critical stereotyping of tourists in much contemporary literature.

7. A typical example of this common attitude toward tourists, tourism, and the "toured upon" is Norbert Blei's *Chronicles of a Rural Journalist in America* (Sister Bay, Wisc.: Chronicles of a Rural Journalist, 1991). An excerpt from the book is published in the *Utne Reader* 46 (July/August 1991), as an inset in Jim Robbins's essay "Tourism Trap: The Californication of the American West," 89–93, 90–91.

8. For more on the "ascetic priest" mentality in western European culture see Friedrick Nietzsche, *The Genealogy of Morals: A Polemic*, trans. Douglas Smith (New York: Oxford University Press, 1996; originally published 1887).

9. The Muir quotation is from John F. Sears's excellent study *Sacred Places: American Tourist Attractions in the Nineteenth Century* (New York: Oxford University Press, 1989), 149; see also p. 155. Edward Abbey, *Desert Solitaire: A Season in the Wilderness* (Tucson: University of Arizona Press, 1989; first published 1968).

10. John Muir, "The Wild Parks and Forest Reservations of the West," *Atlantic Monthly* 81 (January 1898): 15–28; republished in Muir's *Our National Parks* (Boston: Houghton Mifflin, 1901), 1–36.

11. See, for example, Muir's 1871 description of the Yosemite Valley region in his chapter "The Glacier Lakes," in his *The Mountains of California* (New York: Century Co., 1894), 98–124.

12. Earl Pomeroy, *The Pacific Slope: A History of California, Oregon, Washington, Idaho, Utah, and Nevada* (Lincoln: University of Nebraska Press, 1991; previously published, New York: Knopf, 1965), 345. Pomeroy is quoting Muir's letter to Emily Pelton (April 2, 1872), in William F. Bade, *The Life and Letters of John Muir*, vol. 1 (Boston: Houghton Mifflin Co., 1924), 325.

13. Muir, "Wild Parks and Forest Reservations," 25, quoted in Pomeroy, *Pacific Slope*, 345.

14. For an excellent discussion of Ansel Adams's attitudes toward tourism promotion and wilderness preservation, see Jonathan Spaulding, "Yosemite and Ansel Adams: Art, Commerce, and Western Tourism," in Susan Rhoades Neel, ed., "Tourism and the American West," Special Issue, *Pacific Historical Review* 65 (November 1996): 615–39; and Spaulding, *Ansel Adams and the American Landscape: A Biography* (Berkeley: University of California Press, 1996). The phrase "chronic preservation *vs* enjoyment dilemma" is from Nash, *Wilderness and the American Mind*, 328.

15. For more on anthropocentric and biocentric attitudes toward wilderness see Roderick Nash, *Wilderness and the American Mind*, 3rd ed. (New Haven: Yale University Press, 1982; previously published, Yale, 1973, and Yale, 1967), 325–29. For more on the 1916 "Organic Act," see the essays in Part III of this volume, "Tourists in Western Wonderlands." William Cronon in his "Introduction: In Search of Nature," and "The Trouble with Wilderness; or, Getting Back to the Wrong Nature," and Richard White, in "Are You an Environmentalist or Do You Work for a Living," in Cronon, ed., *Uncommon Ground: Towards*

Reinventing Nature (New York: W. W. Norton, 1995), 23–25, 69–90, and 171–85, respectively, take us beyond the biocentric-anthropocentric dichotomy.

16. Henry F. Cope, "A Nation's Playground," *World Today* 8 (June 1905): 634 and 639, quoted in Robert Athearn, *The Mythic West in Twentieth Century America* (Lawrence: University Press of Kansas, 1986), 137.

17. For more on the concept of the "other," see Edward W. Said, *Orientalism* (New York: Random House, 1979). For a fuller discussion of the application of the concept of the "other" in travel writing see Sara Mills, *Discourses of Difference: An Analysis of Women's Travel Writing and Colonialism* (New York: Routledge, 1992). For more on tourist perceptions of the "other," see Andrew McGregor, "Dynamic Texts and Tourist Gaze: Death, Bones, and Buffalo," *Annals of Tourism Research* 27, no. 1 (2000): 27–50.

18. Lofholm, "New Breed of Tourism," L1.

19. Daniel Boorstin, "From Traveler to Tourist: The Lost Art of Travel," in *The Image: A Guide to Pseudo-Events in America*, 25th anniversary ed. (New York: Vintage Books, 1987), 77–117, 79–80. The book was first published under the title *The Image; or, What Happened to the American Dream* (New York: Atheneum, 1962).

20. For more on the theme of standardization and homogenization and the decline of regional cultures in the United States, see Lucy Lippard, *Lure of the Local: Senses of Place in a Multicentered Society* (New York: New Press, 1998); and David M. Wrobel and Michael C. Steiner, "Many Wests: Notes toward a Dynamic Western Regionalism," in Wrobel and Steiner, eds., *Many Wests: Place, Culture, and Regional Identity* (Lawrence: University Press of Kansas, 1997), 1–30.

21. Boorstin, while regarded as an important and intuitive interpreter of American events, is not thought of as a jaded chronicler of the American experience. His three-volume work *The Americans*, vol. 1: *The Colonial Experience*, vol. 2: *The National Experience*, vol. 3: *The Democratic Experience* (New York: Random House, 1958, 1965, 1973), is generally regarded as a staple of "consensus history," which de-emphasized conflict as a factor in the nation's past and emphasized American exceptionalism. But his book *The Image* suggests a deep cynicism, on the author's part, with the standardization, homogenization, and Disneyfication of American life. That cynicism, on occasion, actually seems more similar to that of the New Left historians and cultural critics of the early 1960s than to the tone of the writings of Boorstin's consensus history counterparts.

22. By the late 1990s, with the film no longer a significant element in the public's popular culture consciousness, the sign was gone. The Fort Hays–*Dances With Wolves* connection is reminiscent of that between the Grand Hotel on Mackinac Island, Michigan, and the movie *Somewhere in Time*.

23. For a good discussion of this theme of cultural flux in relation to tourism and how that cultural flux makes the authenticity or inauthenticity of an experience virtually impossible to gauge, see M. Crick, "Sun, Sex, Sights, Savings and Servility: Representations of International Tourism in the Social Sciences," *Criticism, Heresy, and Interpretation* 1 (1988): 37–76. See anthropologists Simone Abram's and Jacqueline Waldren's "Introduction," in their edited collection, *Tourists and Tourism—Identifying with People and Places* (New York: Berg, 1997), 1–11; Dean MacCannell, "Staged Authenticity," *American Journal of Sociology* 79 (November 1973), 589–603; and "Cannibalism Today," in *Empty Meeting Grounds: The Tourist Papers* (New York: Routledge, 1992), 17–73; Bonnie Christenson, "Playing with the Past: Heritage and Public Identity Formation in the American West (Ph.D. dissertation, University of Washington, 1999); and

Susan G. Davis, "Landscapes of Imagination: Tourism in Southern California," in William Deverell, Greg Hise, and David C. Sloane, guest eds., "Orange Empires," special issue of *Pacific Historical Review* 68 (May 1999): 145–316, 173–91; and John Findlay, *Magic Lands: Western Cityscapes and American Culture after 1940* (Berkeley: University of California Press, 1992). Hal Rothman provides important coverage of the touristic search for authenticity in his chapter "Tourism on the Actual Periphery: Archeology and Dude Ranching," in *Devil's Bargains: Tourism in the Twentieth Century American West* (Lawrence: University Press of Kansas, 1998).

24. Ironically enough, Daniel Boorstin provides an excellent examination of the unrepresentativeness of the preserved past (and how this factor complicates the authenticity-artificiality issue) in his essay "The Historian: A Wrestler with the Angel," in *Hidden History: Exploring Our Secret Past* (New York: Harper and Row, 1987), 3–23.

25. The process is reminiscent of that which E. H. Carr explained in his insightful work *What Is History?* (1966)—a highly subjective one by which things that happened in the past become "historical facts" by virtue of being footnoted and re-footnoted by historians—Fort Hays was effectively re-footnoted by Kevin Costner, and its significance as a historic site was enlarged, reborn, even. See E. H. Carr, *What Is History?* (New York: Penguin Books, 1978), 7–30; originally published by Macmillan, 1961. For more on historic sites as tourist attractions, see Barbara Kirshenblatt-Gimblett, *Destination Culture: Tourism, Museums, and Heritage* (Berkeley: University of California Press, 1998); Michael Kammen, *Mystic Chords of Memory: The Transformation of Tradition in American Culture* (New York: Alfred A. Knopf, 1991); John F. Sears, *Sacred Places: American Tourist Attractions in the Nineteenth Century* (New York: Oxford University Press, 1989); Hal K. Rothman, *Preserving Different Pasts* (Urbana: University of Illinois Press, 1989); Daniel Boorstin, "An American Style in Historical Monuments," in *America and the Image of Europe* (New York: Meridian Books, 1960), 82–91; and John D. Dorst, *Looking West* (Philadelphia: University of Pennsylvania Press, 1999).

26. Nigel Morgan and Annette Pritchard, in *Tourism, Promotion and Power: Creating Images, Creating Identities* (Chichester, England: John Wiley and Sons, 1998; reprinted 1999), note the need to "mov[e] the debate on from the increasingly stale polarization of tourism as an authentic or inauthentic experience, a debate which is increasingly irrelevant as the experience itself becomes the reality," 12. Patricia Nelson Limerick discusses the issue of authenticity, or "purity," in her essay in Part I of this volume. Mike Davis, in his book *Ecology of Fear: Los Angeles and the Imagination of Disaster* (New York: Henry Holt, 1998), provides a classic case of commentary on the dichotomy between the authentic and the artificial when he contrasts the "tourist bubbles" (theme parks, malls, etc.) that are "partitioned off from the rest of the city," and emphasizes Los Angeles as "the world capital of such 'hyperreality.'" He further notes that "tourists are increasingly reluctant to venture into the imagined dangers of Los Angeles's 'urban jungle,'" and instead engage in a "junk-food version of urbanity," consequently experiencing "little of the real promiscuity" that animated cities such as Chicago and New York in the 1920s; see 392–93. Still, one wonders if Davis is not drawing the dichotomy between the "real promiscuity" of 1920s urban life and the "hyperreality" of "tourist bubbles" a little too dramatically. And Chicago, of course, had its own massive tourist bubble from 1893–1894, i.e., the World's Fair, for which a virtual sister city was constructed

and then later torn down; and the same process occurred in cities all over the country when they hosted World's Fairs. Furthermore, one suspects that even the "imagined dangers of Los Angeles's 'urban jungle'" are real enough to suggest that the average tourist family is not making a thoroughly unreasonable decision in visiting Disneyland or Knott's Berry Farm rather than parts of downtown L.A. For more on tourist bubbles, see Dennis R. Judd, "Constructing the Tourist Bubble," in Dennis R. Judd and Susan S. Fainstein, eds., *The Tourist City* (New Haven: Yale University Press, 1999), 35–53; and S. Davis, "Landscapes of Imagination."

27. Ian Frazier, *Great Plains* (New York: Farrar, Straus and Giroux, 1989), 121.

28. It is worth noting that Frazier's most recent book, *On the Rez* (New York: Farrar, Straus and Giroux, 2000), sees him grappling more consciously with this issue of authenticity. In the book he considers his strong identification with the Oglala Sioux and the reality that for all his time spent on the Pine Ridge Reservation, he is not one of them. Gwen Fiorio emphasizes the authenticity theme in a review of Frazier's book, entitled "Outsider Brings Sympathy to Reservation," *Philadelphia Inquirer*, January 9, 2000, K1 and K4.

29. For more on travel writers and tourists, see Patrick Holland and Graham Huggan, *Tourists with Typewriters: Critical Reflections on Contemporary Travel Writing* (Ann Arbor: University of Michigan Press, 1998); and Michael Kowalewski, ed., *Temperamental Journeys: Essays on the Modern Literature of Travel* (Athens: University of Georgia Press, 1992). For an interesting American-European comparative context, see James Buzard, *The Beaten Track: European Tourism, Literature, and the Ways to Culture, 1800–1918* (New York: Oxford University Press, 1993). See also Mills, *Discourses of Difference*; and Mary Louise Pratt, *Imperial Eyes: Travel Writing and Transculturation* (New York: Routledge, 1992). Edward Said deals with "traveling theories" in *The World, the Text, and the Critic* (Cambridge: Harvard University Press, 1983).

30. Lummis sent back accounts of his journey to the *Chillicothe Leader;* see Lummis, *A Tramp across the Continent* (New York: Charles Scribner's Sons, 1892; republished, Lincoln: University of Nebraska Press, 1982), and as *Letters from the Southwest: September 20, 1884, to March 14, 1885,* ed. James W. Byrkit (Tucson: University of Arizona Press, 1989).

31. George E. Place, untitled speech in *Annual Report of the L.A. County Pioneers of Southern California, 1909–1910* (no publisher listed; probably L.A.: print of Gazette Publishing Co.), 5; available in *L.A. County, Pioneer Society Annual Reports, 1908–1915,* Henry E. Huntington Library, Rare Book #106161, hereafter referred to as HEH, RB. The juxtaposition of the Palace car and the prairie schooner is ubiquitous in pioneer society proceedings and in published pioneer reminiscences from the late nineteenth and early twentieth centuries. Among the more notable examples are: Emiline L. Fuller, *Left by the Indians: Story of My Life* (Mount Vernon, Iowa: Hawkeye Steam Print, 1892), 7; Robert Vaughn, *Then and Now; or, Thirty-Six Years in the Rockies* (Minneapolis: Tribune Printing Co., 1900), 63; Mrs. William Markland Molson, "Glimpses of Life in Early Oregon," *Quarterly of the Oregon Historical Society* 1 (June 1900): 158–64, 158; Sarah Fells, *Threads of Alaskan Gold* (no publisher listed, probably Omaha, Neb., 1904), 35; Arthur L. Stone, *Following Old Trails* (Missoula, Mont.: Morton John Elrod, 1913), 195 and 302; Minnie Moeller to John Burt Colton, January 16, 1914, Jayhawker Collection, HEH, Box #6; Mrs. Helen B. Ladd, president of the Pioneer Women, address delivered on "Pioneer and Old Settlers' Day," October 16, 1915, at the Panama-Pacific Exposition, in *California Pioneers of Santa*

Clara County: Pioneer and Old Settlers' Day (no place, publisher, or date), HEH, RB #260530, 53–54; George W. Riddle, *History of Early Days in Ore.*: (Riddle, Ore.: Riddle Enterprise, 1920), 30. A final example worth mentioning appears in the poem "The Disappointed Tenderfoot," reprinted in Luke Voorhees, *Personal Recollections of Pioneer Life on the Mountains and Plains of the Great West* (Cheyenne, Wyo.: privately published, 1920), in the Ayer Collection, Newberry Library, #128.5 V8. The poem begins, "He reached the West in a palace car, Where the writers tell us the cowboys are." For the railroad's advertising of tourism in the late nineteenth and early twentieth centuries, see Alfred Runte, "Promoting the Golden West: Advertising and the Railroad," *California History* 70 (Spring 1991): 63–75.

32. Rothman, *Devil's Bargains*, 39. Rothman, though he does distinguish between tourists and travelers, does not engage in the easy dichotomization of the two groups. In fact, his observation that "people became tourists because they could" (p. 31) effectively parallels the motivation behind aristocratic "travel" and mass "tourism," and categorizes them jointly.

33. For further discussion of the early automobilers see Pomeroy, *The Pacific Slope*, 359–61, and the essays by Marguerite Shaffer in Part II and David Louter and Peter Blodgett in Part III of this volume.

34. For a quite extensive listing of transcontinental auto-travel narratives see Carey S. Bliss, *Autos across America* (Los Angeles: Dawson's Bookshop, 1972; reprint Austin, Tex.: Jenkins and Reese, 1982). Archibald Hanna Jr., curator, *From Train to Plane: Travelers in the American West, 1866–1936: An Exhibition in the Beinecke Rare Book and Manuscript Library, Yale University* (New Haven, Conn.: Yale University Library, 1979). See also Warren James Belasco, *Americans on the Road: From Autocamp to Motel, 1910–1945* (Cambridge, Mass.: MIT Press, 1979); Rothman, "Intraregional Tourism: Automobiles, Roads, and the National Parks," in *Devil's Bargains*, 143–67; and Walter Nugent, "The 'Finding' of the West," in Robert C. Ritchie and Paul Andrew Hutton, eds., *Frontier and Region: Essays in Honor of Martin Ridge* (San Marino, Calif.: Huntington Library Press, and Albuquerque: University of New Mexico Press, 1997), 3–26, especially the section on pp. 10–20, on "Cross-Country Motoring, 1903–1930s."

35. Interestingly, the same claim to authenticity has been made by advocates of certain kinds of tourism. For example, advocates of ecotourism, such as John Gilbert, argue that ordinary touristic experiences "are not linked to a sense of place," while the ecotourist "is experiencing nature and reality first hand, not viewing it from a bus window or a video screen." See Gilbert, *Eco-Tourism Means Business* (Wellington, New Zealand: GP Publications, 1997). Deborah McLaren in *Rethinking Tourism and Ecotravel*, provides a far more critical picture of ecotourism, noting that "[a]t its worst ecotravel is environmentally destructive, economically exploitative, culturally insensitive, 'greenwashed' travel," 98. McLaren comments critically on young "budget . . . backpackers" who "like to distinguish themselves as 'travelers' not 'tourists,'" 83. For more on the experience of the ecotourist, see Chris Ryan and Karen Hughes Sharon Chirgwin, "The Gaze, Spectacle and Ecotourism," *Annals of Tourism Research* 27, no. 1 (2000): 148–63. For more on the topic of tourism and the environment, see Tensie Whelan, *Nature Tourism: Managing for the Environment* (Washington, D.C.: Island Press, 1991), and U.S. Travel Data Center, *Discover America: Tourism and the Environment: A Guide to Challenges and Opportunities for Travel Industry Businesses*, commissioned by the Discover America Implementation Task Force (Washington, D.C.: Travel Industry Association of America, 1992).

36. Dean MacCannell, *The Tourist: A New Theory of the Leisure Class* (Berkeley and Los Angeles: University of California Press, 1999; first published in 1976, republished in 1989), 9, 107. MacCannell's seminal work prompted numerous sociological studies of tourism. The following year, 1977, saw the publication of Valene L. Smith's important edited collection *Hosts and Guests: The Anthropology of Tourism*, 2nd ed. (Philadelphia: University of Pennsylvania Press, 1989), which provided the intellectual impetus for the growth of tourism studies in anthropology. Boorstin's analysis of tourism in *The Image* comprises just a segment of the narrative (one of six chapters), yet it has proven highly influential. MacCannell's criticism of Boorstin is overly harsh. It is worth noting that in his essay "An American Style in Historical Monuments," Boorstin emphasized, in quite positive terms, the essentially democratic nature of the nation's cultural heritage sites. Still, Boorstin's tourist-traveler dichotomy, with its strong emphasis on the inauthenticity of the former and the authenticity of the latter, has been criticized by a number of scholars. For a summary of these criticisms see Morgan and Pritchard, *Tourism, Promotion and Power*, 8–9. For an interesting and sophisticated critique of MacCannell, see Kaplan's chapter "The Question of Moving: Modernist Exile/Postmodernist Tourism," in *Questions of Travel*, 27–64.

37. J. Thurot and G. Thurot, "The Ideology of Class and Tourism: Confronting the Discourse of Advertizing," *Annals of Tourism Research* 10, Special Issue (1983), 173–89, note that "The leisure of the masses, which is very recent, has received from the intellectuals more criticism in 10 years than aristocratic leisure received in 2,000 years," 184; Thurot and Thurot are quoted in Morgan and Pritchard, *Tourism, Promotion and Power*, 8.

38. Jean Baudrillard, *America*, trans. Chris Turner (New York: Verso, 1988; originally published as *Amérique* [Paris: Bernard Grasset, 1986]). For an interesting reading of the tourist-traveler dichotomy in Boudrilliard's *America* see Kaplan, *Questions of Travel*, 78–79.

39. See Vasiliki Galani-Moutafi, "The Self and the Other: Traveler, Ethnographer, Tourist," *Annals of Tourism Research* 27, no. 1 (2000): 203–224.

40. Paris Permenter and John Bigley offer the following confident advice to the imminent "traveler": "Talk it over with the whole family so everyone will be excited about the trip, then head off down the road. Like America's earliest explorers, you've got an incredible journey ahead of you," *National Parks with Kids: Be a Traveler—Not a Tourist* (Cold Spring Harbor, N.Y.: Open Road Publishers, 1999), 13; Stephanie Gold, *San Francisco Guide: Be a Traveler—Not a Tourist* (Cold Spring Harbor, N.Y.: Open Road Publishers, 1999); Larry Ludmer, *Utah Guide: Be a Traveler—Not a Tourist* (Cold Spring Harbor, N.Y.: Open Road Publishers, 1999); David Blomstrom, *(Ir)rational Parks: An Offbeat Look at Wilderness, Tourism, and America* (Seattle, Wash.: Geobopological Survey, 1996). The quotation is from Amazon.com's "Book Description" section. Paul Schullery, in his essay "Privations and Inconveniences: Early Tourism in Yellowstone National Park," in this volume (a revised version of his previously published chapter "Privations and Inconveniences," in *Searching for Yellowstone: Ecology and Wonder in the Last Wilderness* [Boston: Houghton Mifflin Company, 1997], 89–107), provides an excellent discussion of responses to tourist behavior, but takes us way beyond the "stupid tourist stories" approach to the subject.

41. Boorstin, *The Image*, 79.

42. MacCannell, *The Tourist*, 6.

43. The phrase "stereotyped understanding" is from Jakle, *The Tourist,* 3. Jean Baudrillard, in *America,* uses the concept of "simulacrum" (his definition of postmodern consumer society) to describe a virtual, mediated version of reality that becomes more real than "actual" experience; see also his *Simulacra and Simulation (The Body, in Theory: Histories of Cultural Materialism)* (Ann Arbor: University of Michigan Press, 1994). MacCannell, in "Cannibalism Today," uses the term "pseudo-authenticity" in a similar vein, see p. 31; Rothman uses the term "manufactured authenticity," *Devil's Bargains,* 118.

44. Boorstin, *The Image,* 107.

45. Rothman, *Devil's Bargains,* 14–15.

46. The issue of whether religious pilgrimages can be considered touristic is an interesting one. Many would argue that they should not be, because the pilgrimage is a thoroughly authentic spiritual experience, but this supposition reopens the tourist-traveler, artificiality-authenticity dichotomy. Tourism could perhaps be viewed as a substitute for its religious origin, the pilgrimage.

47. Jeremy Laurance, "Oh no, it's sudden unhinged tourist syndrome," *Independent* (UK), December 27, 1999, 1.

48. For more on the theme of tourism and socioeconomic status, see Limerick's essay in Part I of this volume.

49. Pierrer L. Ven Den Berghe provides sense of the range of tourist motivations and expectations in his book *The Quest for the Other: Tourism in San Cristobal, Mexico* (Seattle: University of Washington Press, 1994); see especially his chapter "The Tourists: Twenty-Five Vignettes," 100–121.

50. David Lodge, *Paradise News* (New York: Penguin Books, 1992), 75. The fictional Roger Sheldrake's intellectual debt to MacCannell, who argued that "tourist attractions are precisely analogous to the religious symbolism of primitive peoples," is obvious; see *The Tourist,* 2. Bruce K. Martin provides good critical analysis of *Paradise News* in his book *David Lodge* (New York: Twayne, 1999), 131–41.

51. For figures on rafting and on general visitation in the Grand Canyon, see Stephen J. Pyne, *How the Grand Canyon Became Grand: A Short History* (New York: Penguin Books, 1998), figures A-4 and A-5 in unnumbered appendix pages.

52. Lodge, *Paradise News,* quotations from pages 76–79; the novel was first published in 1991 by Secker and Warburg. For a very early account of travel/ tourism in Hawaii, see Isabella Bird, *The Hawaiian Archipelago: Six Months among the Palm Groves, Reefs, and Volcanoes of the Sandwich Islands* (London: John Murray, 1881). For a fascinating account of efforts on the part of the U.S. government and armed forces to sell the experience in Hawaii as tourism to the servicemen, servicewomen, and support workers stationed there during World War II, see David Farber and Beth Bailey, "The Fighting Man as Tourist: The Politics of Tourist Culture in Hawaii during World War II," in Susan Rhoades Neel, ed., special issue, *Pacific Historical Review* 65 (November 1996): 641–60.

53. For a contrasting definition, see Charles R. Goeldner, J. R. Ritchie, and Robert W. Intosh, who define tourists as people who "travel from place to place for nonwork reasons," in their widely used text *Tourism: Principles, Practices, Philosophies,* 8th ed. (New York: John Wiley and Sons, 2000), 14. *Tourism* also offers quite precise definitions of the various elements—the tourist, businesses, governments of host communities, and host communities themselves—that make up tourism; see p. 724.

54. Rothman, *Devil's Bargains.*

55. The World Tourism Organization and Travel Industry Association of America definitions of tourism are reproduced in Goeldner, Ritchie, and McIntosh), *Tourism*, 16 and 17, respectively.

56. Useful sources for making determinations concerning who meets the definition of "tourist" are John D. Hunt and Donlynne Layne, "Evolution of Travel and Tourism: Terminology and Definitions," *Journal of Travel Research* 29 (Spring 1991): 7–11; Clive L. Morley, "What Is Tourism: Definitions, Concepts and Characteristics," *Journal of Tourism Research* 1 (May 1990): 3–8; E. Cohen, "Who Is a Tourist: A Conceptual Clarification," *Sociological Review* 22 (November 1974): 527–55; and Peter Burns and Andrew Holden, *Tourism: A New Perspective* (New York: Prentice Hall, 1995), 4–6. *The Compact Edition of the Oxford English Dictionary (OED)* defines the tourist as "one who makes a tour or tours; esp. one who does this for recreation; one who travels for pleasure or culture, visiting a number of places for their objects of interest, scenery, or the like." Interestingly, in defining "tourism," the *OED* notes that the context in which the word is used is "[u]sually depreciatory"; see *OED*, vol. 2: P–Z (Oxford, England: Oxford University Press, 1986), 3363.

57. It is interesting that Steinbeck's wonderfully entertaining book *Travels With Charley in Search of America* (New York: Bantam Books, 1963; originally published by Viking, 1962), was published the same year as Boorstin's *The Image*. The phrase "one goes, not so much to see but to tell afterward," Steinbeck said marked "the American tendency in travel," 161.

58. It is interesting to note that the imploding of old casinos has itself become a tourist attraction on The Strip, and major implosions draw major crowds in cities across the country. For more on Las Vegas, see Rothman, *Devil's Bargains*, particularly the chapters "Entertainment Tourism: Making Experience Malleable," and "Purifying the Wages of Sin: Corporate Las Vegas," 287–312 and 313–37, respectively; Eugene P. Moehring, *Resort City in the Sunbelt: Las Vegas, 1930–1970* (Reno and Las Vegas: University of Nevada Press, 1989); Mike Davis and Hal K. Rothman, *The Grit beneath the Glitter: Tales from the Real Las Vegas* (Berkeley: University of California Press, 1998); John Findlay, *People of Chance: Gambling in American Society from Jamestown to Las Vegas* (New York: Oxford University Press, 1986); and Robert E. Parker, "Las Vegas: Casino Gambling and Local Culture," in Judd and Fainstein, eds., *The Tourist City*, 107–23.

59. This definition of the tourist as "someone who travels to experience unfamiliar surroundings" is similar to the perspective of Eric Cohen, who emphasized the desire to visit unfamiliar peoples and places, to see and experience that which is different. Eric Cohen, "Towards a Sociology of International Tourism," *Social Research* 39 (1972): 164–82. A similar definition is provided by Smith in her "Introduction" to *Hosts and Guests*, 2nd ed.: "in general, a tourist is a temporarily leisured person who voluntarily visits a place away from home for the purpose of experiencing a change," 1–17. Of course, the danger of definitions of tourism that emphasize the centrality of the unfamiliar to the tourist experience is that they can lead us back into the murky arena of authenticity/inauthenticity. Smith actually provides a table of "tourist types," which is reminiscent of Boorstin's tourist-traveler dichotomy, but with more gradations. At the top of the table is the "explorer," who "accepts fully" the local norms of the location being visited. At the bottom of the table are the "mass tourist" and the "charter tourist," who "expect," and "demand," respectively, "Western amenities" wherever they happen to be; see Smith, "Introduction," 12. Implicit

in the model is the authenticity of the explorer's experience and the superficiality of the mass and charter tourist experiences.

60. Jakle, *The Tourist*, 1.

61. Morgan and Pritchard, in *Tourism, Promotion and Power*, write that "thirty years after the emergence of tourism as a field of study there remains little crossover between those taking a business perspective and those pursuing a more sociological or historical perspective," 4.

62. Earl Pomeroy's foreword to the present volume also points to the rich intellectual rewards to be reaped when disciplinary lines are crossed in tourism studies.

63. Examples of the heightened scholarly interest in tourism in the United States and the West in the 1980s include: Jakle, *The Tourist*; J. Valerie Fifer, *American Progress: The Growth of Transport, Tourist, and Information Industries in the Nineteenth-Century West* (Chester, Conn.: Globe Pequot Press, 1988); Sears, *Sacred Places*; Athearn's chapter "The Dude's West," in *The Mythic West*. Another interesting overview from the 1980s is Maxine Feifer's *Tourism in History: From Imperial Rome to the Present* (New York: Stein and Day, 1985). American western tourism has received increasing attention from historians in the 1990s; see, for example, Stanford E. Demars, *The Tourist in Yosemite, 1855–1985* (Salt Lake City: University of Utah Press, 1991); Neel, ed., *Pacific Historical Review*, special issue, "Tourism and the American West"; Leah Dilworth, *Imagining Indian in the Southwest: Persistent Visions of a Primitive Past* (Washington, D.C.: Smithsonian Institution Press, 1996); Marg Weigle and Barbara Babcok, eds., *The Great Southwest of the Fred Harvey Company and the Santa Fe Railway* (Phoenix, Ariz.: Heard Museum, 1996); Chris Wilson, *The Myth of Santa Fe: Creating a Modern Regional Tradition* (Albuquerque: University of New Mexico Press, 1997); Walter Nugent's chapter "Tourists, Honyockers, Mexicans and More, 1914–1929," in *Into the West: The Story of Its People* (New York: Alfred A. Knopf, 1999), 174–226; and, most importantly, Rothman's *Devil's Bargains*. The large number of doctoral dissertations on western American tourism, either in progress or undergoing revision for publication, is further testimony to the growth of this subfield; for a listing of these dissertations and for a fuller bibliographic essay on tourism, see *Devil's Bargains*, 423–25.

64. Earl Pomeroy's *In Search of the Golden West: The Tourist in Western America* (New York: Alfred A. Knopf, 1957), Daniel Boorstin's chapter "From Traveler to Tourist: The Lost Art of Travel," in *The Image* (1962); Pomeroy's informative chapter on "The Changing Outdoors," in *The Pacific Slope*; and Roderick Nash's "The Irony of Victory," in *Wilderness and the American Mind*, 3rd ed., 316–41 (the "Irony of Victory" section first appeared in the 1973 ed.), all predated the innovative work in the fields of anthropology and sociology. Sociologist MacCannell's *The Tourist* (1976, 1989, 1999); and Smith's edited collection *Hosts and Guests: The Anthropology of Tourism* (1977, 1989), are among the more influential theoretical works on the topic in their respective fields. Influential recent works include John Urry, *The Tourist Gaze: Leisure and Travel in Contemporary Societies* (New York: Routledge, 1990); Dean MacCannell, *Empty Meeting Grounds: The Tourist Papers* (New York: Routledge, 1992). The *Annals of Tourism Research*, begun in 1973, is also a crucial source for theoretical writings on tourism. The journal has always treated tourism as a multidisciplinary field and publishes the work of scholars in a wide range of fields. For a good introduction to the work in the field as represented in the journal, see Margaret Byrne Swain, Maryann Brent, and Veronica H. Long, "Annals and Tour-

ism Evolving: Indexing 25 Years of Publication," 25th Anniversary Edition, *Annals of Tourism Research* 25, Supplement (1998): 991–1014.

65. Bonnie Christensen's doctoral dissertation, "Playing with the Past: Heritage and Public Identity in the American West" (University of Washington, 1999) provides excellent examples of the incongruity between touristic representations of the past and the actual past in Red Lodge, Montana.

66. Mitchell Schwarzer, in his fascinating recent article, "Off-World in the Far West: On Yosemite Valley and the Las Vegas Strip," *Harvard Design Magazine* (Winter/Spring 1998): 60–65, notes: "Whereas the crossing of the Great Basin deserts once inspired fear, it now elicits fear's simulations," 60. In comparing two ostensibly very different landscapes—the Las Vegas Strip and the Yosemite Valley—Schwarzer provides a model for the examination of constructed environments. He suggests that "Yosemite, typically seen as Snow White to Las Vegas's Evil Queen, is as much a site for experiencing 'postmodern aura' as its gaming counterpart to the southeast," 60. Yosemite and the Strip, Schwarzer further notes, "construct extreme environments that appeal to the mass public's restlessness with everyday life," and offer something that is larger than everyday life. So, the "amazing popularity" of these two places may be testimony "to the fact that people are running toward something as much as away from something," 64–65.

67. For a thorough overview of mythic representations of the West by painters, see William M. Goetzmann and William N. Goetzmann, *The West of the Imagination* (New York: W. W. Norton, 1986).

68. Christensen, "Playing with the Past."

69. For more on the transformation of western places in the wake of tourism development, see Raye Ringholz, *Little Town Blues: Voices from a Changing West* (Salt Lake City: Peregrine Smith Books, 1992); Ringholz, *Paradise Paved: The Challenge to Growth in the New West* (Salt Lake City: University of Utah Press, 1996); and Duane A. Smith, *Rocky Mountain Boom Town: A History of Durango, Colorado* (Niwot: University Press of Colorado, 1992; first published, 1980), especially 176–79 and 200–201.

70. For more on the physical transformation of tourist areas, see Clare A. Gunn, *Vacationscape: Designing Tourist Regions*, 2nd ed. (New York: Van Nostrand Reinhold, 1988). Rothman's *Devil's Bargains* provides the fullest examination of the impact of tourism on the western communities that are toured upon.

71. See Richard Butler and Douglas Pearce, eds., *Change in Tourism: People, Places, Processes* (New York: Routledge, 1995); Simon Abram, Jacqueline Waldren, and Donald V. L. Macleod, eds., *Tourists and Tourism: Identifying with People and Places* (New York: Berg, 1997); and John E. Rosenow and Gerald L. Pulsipher, eds., *Tourism: The Good, the Bad, and the Ugly* (Lincon, Neb.: Century Three Press, 1979).

72. See Annie Gilbert Coleman, "The Unbearable Whiteness of Skiing," in Neel, ed., "Tourism and the American West," special issue, *Pacific Historical Review*: 583–614; Anne F. Hyde, "Round Pegs in Square Holes: The Rocky Mountains and Extractive Industry," in David M. Wrobel and Michael C. Steiner, eds., *Many Wests: Place, Culture, and Regional Identity* (Lawrence: University Press of Kansas, 1997), 93–113; and William G. Robbins, "Historical Commentary: Creating a 'New' West: Big Money Returns to the Hinterland," *Montana: The Magazine of Western History* 46 (Summer 1996): 66–72.

73. Carey McWilliams, "Introduction," in Ray B. West Jr., ed., *Rocky Mountain Cities* (New York: W. W. Norton, 1949), 1–25, 22.

74. See Rothman, *Devil's Bargains*, passim, but especially chapter 13, "The Mélange of Postmodern Tourism," 338–70.

75. For more on the possible pitfalls of viewing resident communities as the "others" that are "acted upon," see Neel, "Tourism and the American West: New Departures," in Neel, ed., "Tourism and the American West," special issue, *Pacific Historical Review:* 517–23, 521. So-Min Cheong and Marc L. Miller provide an interesting discussion of the tourist as "acted upon" by tourism brokers and host communities in "Power and Tourism: A Foucauldian Observation," *Annals of Tourism Research* 27, no. 2 (2000): 371–90.

76. Davis, in her discussion of Southern California tourism, comments that "the fiscal need to pull tourists into controlled landscapes and to keep them circulating on fairly tight paths is giving rise to more concentrated tourist districts." She cites Las Vegas's MGM Grand entertainment complex as an example; see "Landscapes of Imagination," 182. However, this leaves the impression of tourists as mere regimented minions of the tourist industry, or hamsters in a cage, who will trundle around on the little metal wheel if you place it there for them. But tourists do make decisions; they are not merely the "acted upon," the choiceless and unknowingly coerced victims of corporate tourism. Perhaps tourists even play a role in determining what the tourist industry provides for them.

77. It is hardly the case that these questions about tourism are being raised here for the first time. Indeed, scholars outside of the humanities (those in business and the social sciences in particular) are addressing them—a review of articles in the *Annals of Tourism Research* over the last decade attests to this. But in American western history scholars still have some theoretical catching up to do. In *Devil's Bargains*, the first wide-ranging examination of western American tourism in nearly half a century, Hal Rothman raises some of these questions, and his study should serve as an important catalyst to further exploration.

Part I

Perspectives:
Scholars and Tourists

Western tourism and tourists have been the subjects of both rash judgments and reasoned reflection for well over a century. Historians, literary and cultural theorists, sociologists, anthropologists, and others have been reflecting, at least sporadically, on the meaning and the impact of tourism in the region since the arrival of the first large groups of tourists there. The scholarly outpouring of interest in western American tourism in the last decade is a testimony to the fuller recognition of its powerful economic, environmental, and cultural impacts on peoples and places. While tourism has been a vital part of the formation of western economies and of perceptions of the West since the late nineteenth century, it is only more recently that scholars have fully grasped the centrality of the tourism industry for understanding the contemporary West. With that recognition a veritable cottage industry of western tourism studies has followed.

Part I presents four perspectives on tourism in the West as well as tourism more broadly conceived. None of the perspectives is categorically favorable or unfavorable toward tourism. Historian Patricia Nelson Limerick and writer Rudolfo Anaya are both cautiously positive concerning the motivations of tourists and the potential benefits of tourism's outcomes. Both write about how their personal experiences have shaped their perspectives on western tourism. Limerick recounts her experience as a worker in the tourism service industry, and Anaya reflects on his seemingly impossible boyhood dreams of growing up to be a tourist. Each of them empathizes with tourists and emphasizes that touristic motivations, in the best of all possible case scenarios, can be honorable and inspired. Yet both scholars are certainly far from uncritical of the range of downsides that can accompany tourism and the shallower motivations that can "inspire" tourists.

Limerick surveys the advent of travel in America from the pre-cash trading economies of Indian people, through the journeys of early European-American explorers, the democratization and expansion of travel since the late nineteenth century, and the great dilemmas facing the national parks (as they seek to accommodate ever larger numbers of visitors) in the present. She wonders if we might not be inspired to expand our horizons concerning the nature of western tourism, to the point where a Nevada bombing range might warrant national park status, since it is a vital historic site, a central element of a complicated western heritage.

Anaya explores a southwestern regional heritage that is sensitive when it comes to tourists, especially those who might stay, since natives are so closely attached to the region and have developed such a deep sense of place. Similar claims to an elevated sense of place could surely be made by residents of all the West's regions. Yet Anaya hits on one of the key western sensitivities concerning tourism: the fear that visitors will become residents and change western places forever and not for the better. And he hits on one of the key oversights: the fact that Mexican migrant workers, and other peoples of color, who are shaping the West through their labor and their geographic mobility, are not considered tourists. Anaya, like Limerick, calls for an expansion of our conceptions of tourism and for increased sensitivity and mutual respect.

Sociologist and business scholar Patrick Long, who has conducted numerous studies of tourism in smaller western communities, emphasizes specific strategies for reducing the negatives that can accompany tourist development and highlights the benefits that the industry can have for both residents and visitors alike. Fully aware of the many downsides of tourism development for smaller communities, Long emphasizes that community involvement in the decision-making processes can enable small western towns to take advantage of the economic benefits that accompany expanded interest in rural recreational opportunities. Those towns need to be wary, and they need to plan meticulously, but if they do so, they can use tourism to their advantage.

Historian Hal Rothman, author of the first full-scale study of tourism in the twentieth-century West (the first major overview of western tourism since Earl Pomeroy's seminal 1957 volume), is more critical in his assessment of the impact of tourism on western communities and his analysis of the factors that motivate the tourist. Rothman argues that tourism is essentially a devil's bargain, one that promises much and almost invariably fails to deliver on its promises. While it is often the only viable economic recourse open to many western places, it nonetheless "typically fails to meet the expectations of communities and regions that embrace it as an economic strategy." Furthermore, Rothman emphasizes the strains that tourism development can place on already fragile community bonds and the cultural compromises that residents have to make to meet the expectations of visitors.

Whether these four scholars are offering fundamentally divergent perspectives on tourist motivations and the impact of tourism or just differences in emphasis is left to the reader's judgment. What is clear from all of the perspectives offered is that tourism provides a valuable window through which to view relations between socioeconomic classes and between races, between "natives," "neo-natives," and "visitors," between people and nature, between advertisers and their audiences, and between scholars and the people, places, and processes they write about. Tourism is the engine driving so many contemporary western debates over land use and culture—over where we live and who we are. Its importance to the West is so great, and the issues surrounding it so complex, that we would do well to look through that window of tourism carefully and reflectively.

Perhaps the scholar should view the neo-native's expression of disdain over the arrival of the new season's latest batch of tourists as something not unique to the contemporary West, but very much in keeping with the western tradition of critical and defensive responses to new arrivals. Perhaps the natives' responses are fully in keeping with a tradition of understandable concern over the failure of visitors to appreciate the complexities and the ecological fragility of so many of the West's places and the cultural integrity of its peoples. Whatever the case, when we study tourism in the West and the cultural, economic, political, environmental, and even scholarly conflicts it engenders, we do well to remember that the sources of the debates are deeply rooted in American western history, as well as in all human history. We can regard tourism as the archetypal postmodern service economy of the West—an economic activity that departs from extractive industries such as mining and logging in important ways—yet, we need to remember that the debates over land, power, and cultural identity that accompany tourism are age-old debates. Tourism, when analyzed as a mirror through which we can reflect on both the contemporary West and the nature of human thought and action, might even throw new light on old issues. Certainly, the perspectives of Limerick, Anaya, Long, and Rothman can facilitate our reflections on these matters.

Chapter Two

Seeing and Being Seen: Tourism in the American West

Patricia Nelson Limerick

In the summer of 1970, I undertook unintended fieldwork in the subject of western tourism. I was attending the University of California at Santa Cruz, and that fact set certain limits on summer employment. Before Santa Cruz was a university town, it was a tourist town. Bordering on the beach and boardwalk was a jumble of motels. In the summer of 1970, I worked as a maid at the St. Charles Motel. This was pretty hard work, really an indoor version of stoop labor: stooping to strip beds, stooping to make beds, stooping to vacuum, stooping to clean toilets and scrub tubs. I was only nineteen, but every evening, my back hurt and I felt like a zombie. At the end of the day, the one point of clarity in my head was my feeling toward tourists. When the motel guests had eaten potato chips in their rooms, and ground some of those potato chips into the rug, I had particularly clear—really quite radiantly clear—feelings about tourists. When it comes to understanding the feelings of local residents about tourists, and when it comes to understanding the frustrations of the service jobs attached to tourist economies, the summer of 1970 gave me a certain intellectual and psychological advantage.

My employer at the St. Charles Motel made me wear a white uniform, with white stockings, and white shoes, and a white kerchief. With that costume, in a blizzard in Colorado, I would have

39

been invisible. In the summer in Santa Cruz, far from blizzard conditions, I was very visible indeed; I was virtually central casting's archetype of The Maid. This visibility gave me one of my few occupational satisfactions. Every day at noon, I would take my sack lunch down to the boardwalk along the beach. Then I would sit on a bench and eat my lunch, among the swirl of tourists lining up for the roller coaster and the carousel. As I sat there, I would say, nonverbally but (thanks to my uniform) still very clearly, "You are having fun, but I am the Maid. In other words, the fact that *you* are having fun correlates directly to the fact that I am leading such a dreary life."

Even as I did my best to advertise my resentment of the people who made my employment possible, I believe I knew that the situation was more complicated than my emotions. I knew that when I sat, in a manner a little reminiscent of Edgar Allan Poe's reproachful raven (though opposite in color), on the Santa Cruz boardwalk, I was not really confronting a privileged class. Santa Cruz was not Newport or Aspen; Santa Cruz was a working-class tourist town. Most of the people who were at the Santa Cruz beach would return to put on their own working-class uniforms at the end of that vacation.

I open with this story because I believe that scholars writing about western tourism can be tempted to adopt the point of view of the locals, to see the tourist from the outside, to cast the tourist as an alien, even contemptible, other. In thinking about tourism one runs a constant risk of casting the tourists themselves as boorish, invasive, repellent, and insensitive. This casting of the tourist as unappealing other is, of course, exactly the skill I mastered in 1970, when I ate my lunch at the Santa Cruz boardwalk and, as we would say now, "performed" my victimization.

My lunches on the Santa Cruz boardwalk call our attention to another risk in the scholarship on tourism: the risk of missing the class differences within the unit we call tourists. There have been very rich people with second homes in Aspen, Colorado, and Jackson, Wyoming. There have been much-less-rich people who have pulled their resources together for a week of vacationing in budget motels near beaches and boardwalks. Unless we watch ourselves, we fall into the habit of clumping all these people together, simply, as tourists. That clumping permits a not very accurate drawing of class lines: the outsider-tourists become the privileged middle or upper class; the insider-providers of tourist services become the working class. With that formulation, we miss the many and consequential occasions in which working-class people have been themselves tourists, a situation that fit, I think, most of the people I glowered at along the Santa Cruz boardwalk.

In fact, if one thought of the categories, tourist versus tourist-industry worker, as separate and exclusive, my own background would be an anomalous one. My heritage is very much mixed, with a line of descent on both sides. Tourism was a big element in my hometown, Banning, California. The resort town of Palm Springs was just down the road, and many people who worked there—as maids, gardeners, bellmen, waitresses—lived in Banning because they could not afford to live in Palm Springs. Travelers driving through Banning on their way to Palm Springs were also a source of income, and no one knows this better than I. My father owned and operated a date shop—a roadside store selling chocolate-covered dates and walnut-stuffed dates, date malts, and date shakes. My mother worked full-time as a legal secretary, and so my family's California Date Shop proved to be my day-care center.

When I was still a toddler, my parents bought me some cowgirl clothes—a fringed vest and skirt, and the proper boots. With this purchase, we might now say, my parents took the first step in my commodification. Before I was three years old, I had been added to the resources, amenities, and attractions of the California Date Shop. Quite a number of my father's customers made regular stops at the store, and they soon took up a custom of inquiring after the "cowgirl." "How's the cowgirl?" they would say. If I now have considerable empathy for the residents of tourist towns who live in a constant muddle of authenticity and constructed identity, then early days at the California Date Shop provided my first round of experiential learning and fieldwork in the subject of western tourism.

But my parents were also tireless tourists themselves, packing us off for an extended car trip at least once a year, with the forests of the Sierras, the beach, and the Grand Canyon as our most frequent destinations. Thus I was in childhood both the touring and the toured upon, both the subject doing the seeing and the object being seen. If we take tourism to be an example of the sin of snoopishness, as it appears in some of the critical literature, then I was indeed both sinned against and sinning. And I suspect that that mixed experience is the bedrock reason why I cannot muster the purity of outlook that other writers can bring to the subject of tourism. I do not know if I was, in the usual equation, subject or other, other or subject, or some unholy combination of the two. My vivid memories of how a motel maid's back feels at the end of the day prevent me from celebrating the fine economic opportunities of a regional shift to tourism. On the other side, I remember too clearly my pleasure in watching Indian dances in northern Arizona, or in watching waves crash on Southern California beaches, to damn tourists as a kind of invasive infection, spreading the viruses and microbes of inauthenticity and commodification. Forty years ago, when I put on the uniform of the cowgirl, I gave up my claim to purity and authenticity. After spending one's formative years in the California Date Shop, one can never claim to be untainted by contact with the coins, dollars, traveler's checks, and credit cards of the tourist.

We form a larger subculture than we realize, those of us who were raised, supported, formed, and informed by western tourism. If there is accuracy in the predictions that tourism will prove to be the principal industry in many areas of the West, this is a subculture that is going to grow and grow. But where did we come from, or, more precisely, where did western tourism come from? When did western tourism begin?

North America was full of paths and trails that served the purposes of hunting, gathering, seasonal migration, and trade. One stimulant for Indian mobility was, however, curiosity: too many Indian stories tell of travels undertaken for the purposes of inquiry and adventure to suggest that Indian people traveled only for economic purposes. Every seashell, from the Atlantic or the Pacific, that ended up in the interior is its own testimony that travel has a long history on this continent. But should we call this tourism? The very question raises the matter of how much purity we are inclined to hold out for in defining what tourism is. To be a true tourist, must an individual be embedded in the emotions and economies of modern industrial, capitalistic society? Or did true tourism come to this planet before the cash economy? Here we confront an oddly inverted and yet very high standard of purity. To be a *true* tourist, one must meet high standards for impurity, for holding motives considerably more tangled and corrupted than pure curiosity, and for engaging in transactions mediated much more by paper and plastic currency than by direct human contact. In truth, the standards for impurity are set too high here. There are good reasons to look for behavior that bears some resemblance to tourism before the arrival of the cash economy, and there are also good reasons to look for motives that are not always tainted and exploitative in postlapsarian, conventional, modern tourism. So however one thinks of early Indian travel, one has to recognize it as curious, active travel, and recognize in it at least a small degree of kinship with the tourism of the last century and a half. Part of that more recent travel is, after all, Indian travel to Europe and to the eastern United States, a revealing counterpoint to the travel, in the opposite direction, of Europeans and Euro-Americans visiting Indian territory.

In the first half of the nineteenth century, Anglo-American explorers-writers introduced a practice more directly connected, and, indeed, precedent-setting for what we now think of as tourism. To William Clark and Meriwether Lewis, to Zebulon Pike, to Stephen Long, to John C. Fremont, the West was the exotic place of their adventuring and self-testing. They treated their western experiences in a manner very similar to the way later Anglo-Americans would treat beaver pelts, buffalo hides, minerals, trees, grasses, and soil. The explorers extracted western experience and packed it out of the West. They then processed and refined it into the form of reports. When explorers wrote their reports, their literary activity was directly parallel to the activities of the felters and hatters who made western beaver pelts into hats, parallel to the activities of the men who refined western minerals in mills and smelters.

The explorers supplied these refined and processed parcels of experience to readers eager to learn about the Far West. These were writers of remarkable intellectual confidence. In their travels, they traced only a narrow line across the West, and yet they wrote confidently of the character of the whole region. If, over the centuries, we have taken a long time to reckon with the reality of the American West, this surely is one of the reasons: many of our ideas about the West originated in the minds of people who were just passing through, people who saw only a little and who still wrote as if they knew the whole. For these travelers, their relationship to their audience made it necessary to cast the West as that exotic place "out there." To dramatize their own daring and mark their own achievement, these explorers had to dramatize the West's strangeness, novelty, unpredictability, and general wildness. The explorers of the first half of the nineteenth century thus built the foundation for later tourism. Offering an image of the West defined by its separateness from the familiar, the explorers' reports provided a portrait of a place that was, if dangerous and threatening, also very interesting. It is important to note that none of these explorers traveled through empty or "virgin" space. All of them made frequent references to inhabitants, particularly Indians, Mexicans, and the mixed-blood families of fur traders.

Explorers may have been laying the foundation for tourism, but they were government men, federal agents, people on official business, and not exactly tourists. Sometimes accompanying them were people closer to the model of tourism: gentlemen, sometimes European aristocrats, sometimes artists or naturalists, out to see the sights in the West. Some of these fellows do give the impression of taking part in a mid-nineteenth-century anticipation of Outward Bound. My own favorite for this category has been Sir William Drummond Stewart, a Scottish nobleman who took the artist Alfred Jacob Miller along on his outing to the Rockies in the 1830s. In an archetypal moment of early tourism, Miller told the story of the party's approach to a fiercely overflowing river, with tree trunks and branches bobbing wildly in the flood. They reached the river, and Stewart plunged in. Miller plunged in after him, and, miraculously, made it to the far shore. As he fought his way up on the bank, Miller said to Stewart, "You know, sir, I do not know how to swim." "Neither do I," replied Stewart. "You know not what you can do until you have tried."[1]

I am surprised that Outward Bound has not taken this as its founding moment, surprised that Stewart's words are not the celebrated slogan for adventure tourism all around the planet. But as advertising slogans go, "You know not what you can do until you have tried," has its weaknesses. One does not have to contemplate Miller's story very long (or especially to contemplate his drawing of the fiercely flooding river) to realize that this story could easily have delivered up the opposite ending, with Miller and Stewart both drifting downstream and off the pages of history. "You know not what you *cannot* do until you have tried" is as good a moral to this story, but not a particularly affirmative way to advertise adventure tourism.

An enthusiasm for tourism on Stewart's scale of strenuosity was slow to develop. Indeed, to see the emergence of tourism on a sizable scale, one has to look to a more "facilitated" form of travel. The completion of the transcontinental railroad in 1869 and the expansion of luxury travel by Pullman Palace cars unleashed a tourism boom on the West. This was, of course, insulated travel, insulated both from nature and from natives. These tourists were people of means, people who wanted comfort and service, people for whom the era of conquest was a little too recent and raw. Predictably, much of the effort of recruiting these tourists rested on reassurance, repeating the promise that the West was safe now, with tame hotels, parlors, and verandas from which the wild scenery could be calmly viewed. This enterprise in promotion also played on the nineteenth-century American inferiority complex. By one common perception among intellectuals and the upper and middle classes, the United States, in comparison to Europe, was simply too new, too young, too short on history; by the same pattern of thinking, western scenery was too different, too big, too stark, too dry. Thus tourist promotion in the late nineteenth century sought legitimacy through European analogies: California was the Mediterranean, a transplanted Italy; Colorado was Switzerland, with replicas of the Alps. Western resort hotels had, by the same token, to match European luxury; for this elite and well-financed type of tourist, European-like scenery had to be accompanied by European-like buildings and services.

These mid- and late-nineteenth-century tourists had an influence and impact far beyond their numbers. Quite a number of these people had contacts and ties with publishers and editors, and thus they found a direct channel to influencing public opinion. These were journal-keepers, diary-writers, impression-recorders, and word-mongers, and many of them could not look out a train window at a wide open western horizon without reaching for their pens. The result of their compulsive literacy was, by 1900, a western landscape blanketed by words, covered two or three inches deep with the littered vocabulary of romantic scenery appreciation. By 1900, a place like Yellowstone had already been the scene of so much published scribbling and emotion that it was extremely difficult for anyone to have an immediate, direct response to the landscape, without a chorus of quotations going off in the head. Before the eye could take in the walls of Yosemite, the mind had already provided the caption: soaring, sublime, uplifting; grandeur, glory, and spirit. With the script of response already written, one's only remaining task was to try to feel what one already knew one was *supposed* to feel.

My own favorite example of this pattern has long been the Southern Californian George Wharton James, former minister, reborn promotional writer who, at the turn of the century, unleashed a flood of words promoting everything possible in the Southwest. As a literary hired hand of the railroads and resorts, George Wharton James said, in pages of text one could measure by the pound, that everything—deserts, mountains, oases, Indians, Mexican American villagers, irrigated farms, growing towns and cities—was colorful and fun . . . and totally risk-free. No threats here, every page of James's slick and slippery prose said; the threats are all gone; it's your playground now.[2]

This enterprise was, of course, a little more complicated than it seemed at first. It was not easy to hit the balance in this constant effort of packaging and manipulating the image of the West. The West had to be cast as tame and safe, with no features that would seriously scare tourists. At the same time, it could not be so tame and safe that it went over the edge and became dull and familiar. This pressure, by the turn of the century, brought a withdrawal of many of the European analogies and a move toward a greater accent on more interesting and distinctive elements of westernness. This shift in accent appeared in the proliferation of dude ranches and the recognition that one could sometimes make more money by herding tourists down a trail than by herding cattle. One could see the shift, as well, in the rise of rodeos as tourist entertainment, where skills once used for work now became skills used for show.

As both these examples indicate, the accenting of western distinctiveness was a very selective matter. The process worked by freezing a moment in an imagined past, disconnecting cattle-working techniques from their real-life context, and locating them instead in a timeless moment when real westerners were cowboys, when the mark of real westernness hinged, by everyone's understanding, on a certain close, cooperative, and even affectionate relationship with a horse. In much more recent times, the movie *City Slickers* reinvigorated the appeal of dude ranches. Dude ranching bookings accelerated; and the old formula—by which one is repaired from the injuries of urban, industrial civilization with an interlude of simple, rural western life—gained new force. As historian Earl Pomeroy has observed, this had long been a very illuminating choice: developers marketing western rural authenticity to urbanites chose to sell them the experience of simulated work on a cattle ranch, and not simulated work in a copper mine or on a sugar beet farm.[3]

The rise of this kind of western tourism, at the turn of the century, might well strike some historians as a watershed moment in western history, perhaps the best indicator of the end of the frontier. When places and people that were once frightening and threatening turned quaint and fun, when Indians did war dances for tourists at train stations (and skipped the attack on the invaders that might logically follow a war dance), when visitors flocked to the stores and restaurants of San Francisco's Chinatown, when painters set themselves to extracting the charm from the Indian and Hispano people of Taos, when deserts, which had terrified overland travelers, turned pretty and appealing in their colors and clear lines, then it might well seem that the frontier was over and the distribution of power clearly settled in the American West. Here, one could think, the violent history of conquest ended, and a new, tame history of buying souvenirs and taking photographs began.

To my mind, the unsettled issues of conquest did not disappear, even if tourists could not see them. But I can get a glimpse of why other historians might think that the flood of tourists into the West provided the clearest and most dramatic statement: the war was over; white people had won; the West was subdued; the West was an occupied terrain, and the tourists were the army of occupation.

With the gradual shift away from the railroad and toward the automobile as the vehicle of tourism, the flood of tourists only broadened and deepened. For the first two decades of the twentieth century, the automobile remained primarily an additional toy for the vacationing rich. But by the 1920s, the automobile was serving as the agent for the democratization of tourism, for the redefinition of western tourism as a mass experience. There were still a lot of poor people left out of this mobile festival, since one still needed the resources to afford a car, leisure, gasoline, shelter, and food. But the group on the road, from the 1920s on, was *much* broader in its origins and occupations than the nineteenth-century tourists had been. With auto camps, motels, gas stations, roadside restaurants, and commercial strips, as J. B. Jackson has argued, a new kind of land-scape came to exist in support of automotive tourism.[4] Following the well-set patterns of western economic development, the federal government's role was crucial, with federal money and direction playing an important part in the construction of highways. West-ern tourism has been in a long phase of expansion, pressed by the power of the word "more"—more motels, more gas stations, more attractions, more communities trying to figure out how to get in on this action.

More confusion and more discontent have also been a part of this expansion. A coherent history of the resistance to and rejection of the tourist industry is a hard thing to come by, but it is an enor-mously rich topic. The signs of rejection are fairly widespread today. In November of 1993, the voters of the state of Colorado rejected a tax, in existence for ten years, that supported a state tourism board and a range of promotional activities. In the Northwest, the perma-nent residents of La Conner, Washington, recently began a campaign to institute a "tourist-free zone" in the center of their town, with a La Conner resident, the novelist Tom Robbins, also proposing that developers wear identifying tags so that they might be properly shunned. One suspects that quite a number of residents of western tourist towns understand the appeal of this idea. As a number of them have said, living in these towns is like always having houseguests, guests who may rotate but who never go away.[5]

Certainly, Edward Abbey was industrial tourism's most persis-tent and audible critic. Tourism, Abbey wrote in one essay, "is al-ways and everywhere a dubious, fraudulent, distasteful, and in the long run, degrading business, enriching a few, doing the rest more harm than good," and this is one of his more moderate statements. And yet Abbey, in his vigorous and appealing writing about the southwestern deserts and especially about the Colorado Plateau's canyonlands, had a significant impact in increasing tourism in the area, putting a little-known area squarely at the center of the read-ing public's attention. Abbey was equally important for denounc-ing tourism and for recruiting more tourists, and that is only one of the many paradoxes that run through western tourism.[6]

The national parks have long represented the best documented case of the puzzles and paradoxes of tourism. From the beginnings of the National Park Service in 1916, its officials knew that they had to sell the parks. Unless they could get significant numbers of Americans to visit the parks, the parks would be without a political constituency. And so the Park Service was placed, from the beginning, at the sharp edge of the divide between the goals of "providing for the enjoyment" of the parks and preserving the parks, in some more or less intact form, for "future generations."[7]

The sharpness of that edge has not been blunted over time, as the Park Service hops between increasing tourist access with more roads and more facilities and regulating and restraining crowds and traffic. A 1990 survey asked national park visitors what factors governed their choice of which parks to visit. First on the list of the public's criteria was natural beauty. Second was the factor "how crowded the park is," and there is some kind of deep and puzzling irony in the workings of this factor that I cannot begin to untangle. Spend a few hours behind a parade of Winnebagoes heading into Yellowstone, and you might begin to think that this criterion of "crowdedness" functions in the opposite way one might expect: the more crowded the park, the more people want to go there. But third on the list of decision-making factors was the availability of restrooms, and fourth was the availability of parking.[8]

When one first contemplates it, this survey provides one of the occasions for a "Hmph!" response to western tourism. Is this the best that members of the American public can do? They are presented with the opportunity for moving and instructive encounters with nature, and their attention stays fixed on the prospect of restrooms and convenient parking spaces? But this survey also presents an opportunity to go beyond the "Hmph!" response—to recognize that a preference for comfort and convenience is, in truth, a hallmark of current times, and, further, it is an enthusiasm often shared by scholars and historians. Who among us has not felt some desperation in midtown Manhattan, confronting an urban wilderness with neither restrooms nor parking spaces? Just how high is the ground we can occupy in judging the crassness and baseness of the tourist mind? Should there not be a little more in the way of solidarity among philistines?

There may be nothing inherently disillusioning or disheartening about people's concern for porta-potties, but one might be more actively disheartened by the ranking, in that survey, awarded to the very last item on the list of criteria. In last place, as a reason to visit a park, came "educational program." But does it have to be this way? Could not education, reconceived and redirected, make for more vigorous tourism, with more productive social consequences? Could we not widen the concept of sites worth seeing? I think here, especially, of the photographer Richard Misrach's work on a northern Nevada naval bombing range. This piece of the Great Basin absorbed bomb after bomb, with quite a number of them still lying unexploded on the site, and with shells and devastated bombing targets all over the place. Misrach has photographed the bombing range extensively, but his book *Bravo 20* goes beyond collecting images to suggest the creation of a Bravo 20 National Park. This would be a "unique and powerful addition to our current park system," Misrach says. "In these times of extraordinary environmental concern, it would serve as a permanent reminder of how military, government, corporate, and individual practices can harm the earth. In the spirit of Bull Run and the Vietnam Memorial, it would be a national acknowledgment of a complex and disturbing period in our history."[9]

Working with landscape architects, Misrach has drawn up the plans for this park. Like most parks, this one would have a loop road, this time called Devastation Drive; to view the somewhat risky terrain of unexploded bombs, the tourists would walk along a boardwalk, very much like the boardwalk leading through the geysers of Yellowstone, but called the Boardwalk of the Bombs. Misrach has even made plans for the gift shop, with books and videos on military and environmental issues, as well as "imprinted clothing such as camouflage-style caps, t-shirts, pants; 'Nevada Is Not a Wasteland' and 'Bombs Away' mugs, tote bags, and bumper stickers; and for the kids, Mattel models based on the most advanced, top-secret military designs—up-to-date delivery systems and Stealth bombers."[10]

It is impossible to look at Misrach's proposal without thinking that we have, as a society, been *very* limited and unimaginative in our thinking about the possibilities of tourism. I myself never took a more interesting tour than the one we had a few years ago, of the Hanford Nuclear Reservation in eastern Washington. Begun in 1943 to produce the plutonium for the Manhattan Project's bombs, Hanford now has eight retired nuclear reactors, a number of retired production facilities, and *a lot* of radioactive and chemical waste. The day at Hanford was the most memorable and unsettling day of my life as a tourist. The impact of that visit tells me that western tourism will have arrived, become mature, gained its full meaning, realized its deeper possibilities, when Hanford, the Nevada Test Site, and the northern Nevada Bravo 20 pull in as many visitors as Disneyland or Las Vegas. But, for now, we remain stuck in a mode in which a visit to an important site in western history is still supposed to mean *escape* from the world's problems, and not a way of reckoning with them.

The history of western tourism does provide the material for explaining one of the most complicated issues of historical thought today. For one example, consider the experience of the wildlife at the base of Pike's Peak. In the 1880s, in Colorado Springs, the local coyotes got the jump on postmodernist theory. General W. A. J. Palmer of the Denver and Rio Grande Railroad had planned the town of Colorado Springs as an upper-class resort, and participants at an upper-class resort had to have proper entertainment. So they had dinners and dances, and they played polo, and they rode to hounds. But if the tourists at Colorado Springs were going to play the part of British aristocrats, who would play the part of the fox? This is where the Colorado coyotes stole the march on postmodernism; in the absence of proper foxes, coyotes had to fill in.[11] And so the Colorado Springs coyotes had their chance to learn, early on, what it meant to be a part of a constructed experience, to be conscripted into someone else's act of representation, to carry the burdens of an imagined and inauthentic identity, and to suffer all the real-life, down-to-earth consequences and injuries of that burdensome construction.

This is one element that all theoretically inclined historians can celebrate in the topic of western tourism: this is the subject that makes all the abstractions of cultural theory—construction, authenticity, appropriation, identity, representation, performance—concrete and clear. Nearly everyone associated with the subject of western tourism has had moments when they looked like, acted like, talked like case studies designed for the express purpose of illustrating postmodernist theory.

As one of the best possible examples of what I mean here, consider the interesting recent mobility of the Grand Tetons. The Tetons are, usually, located right next to the site of Jackson, Wyoming. They have been in that neighborhood for some millennia. But, in the late

1980s, they hit a phase of remarkable mobility. A handsome photograph of the Tetons appeared in a brochure advertising Amtrak, which does not run through Wyoming. The Tetons appeared, as well, in an ad for a resort in Montana. And, in what seems to have irritated Wyomingites the most, the Tetons then moved south, to lend their authority and appeal to a condominium project in the Colorado Rockies. "We are more than a little miffed that our competitors continue to use our assets to promote their areas," said a spokesman for the Jackson Hole Chamber of Commerce, who went on to remark that Jackson Hole was "seriously considering trademarking the Tetons." The ad agency that put together the brochure for the Colorado condominiums denied culpability: "It was just a case of mistaken identity," this group said. The manager of the Montana resort was more willing to admit errors of judgment: "I was totally against using the Tetons, but we had to get something out on the market immediately."[12]

"Wyoming Insists That Tetons Must Stay," said one headline in the *New York Times*.[13] In this whole episode, as in many others, western tourism delivers on its full, instructional promise. If you have a student or colleague who does not understand the meaning of appropriation of identity or the politics of representation, then let that individual contemplate the restlessness of the Tetons, and contemplate the jealous possessiveness of the Jackson Chamber of Commerce, tugging away for commercial *and* emotional control of an image.

Or consider my neighboring city of Denver. Every year or so, Denver collapses into a fit of anxious self-consciousness and worries about its image. Should it surrender the fight for sophistication and package itself as a cow town? While the smell of a feedlot is *not* a much sought after *experience*, tourists love many of the associations of cow towns: handsome men on horseback, rugged outdoor life, the heritage of the Wild West, the contact with lives more grounded, authentic, and real than lives in cities, offices, and industries. But just as a wave of enthusiasm for embracing the role of the cow town begins to build, then the anxieties break right behind. If Denver capitalizes on its frontier history and advertises itself as a cow town, will it not, by that act, move toward the past and away from the future, rendering itself into a backwater town, a town of the nineteenth century where no twenty-first-century high-tech company would want to locate? Every year or so, a group of consultants pitch into this problem. Poor Denver sits like a hopeful star, forgotten in the green room, overlooked and immobilized while the makeup and costume experts debate what look would best distract attention from the subject's many flaws.[14]

Or consider the example of Cheyenne, Wyoming. In 1989, the mayor of Cheyenne tried to address the problem of tourist disappointment in the city. Cheyenne is a town heavily dependent on the federal government and defense spending, and it is a town that suffered from the slump in oil and energy production. Despite its modern complexities, Cheyenne has still chosen to dramatize its Wild West identity, adopting the slogan, "Live the Legend." Once a year, during Frontier Days, Cheyenne goes all-out for Wild West imagery, with plenty of cowboys, horses, bulls, and dust. But the rest of the year, tourists pulling off the interstate experience considerable disappointment. Live the Legend? What Legend? As one young visitor said, "There's got to be some cowboys around here somewhere"; instead, there were businesspeople and secretaries, service station attendants and waitresses.[15]

To ease this disappointment, the mayor in 1989 recommended that all residents offer their visitors various signifiers of westernness. They should wear western dress and say "howdy" instead of "hello." Moreover, a troop of real estate agents, carpenters, and servicemen responded to the mayor's initiative, and pitched in to stage periodic gunfights in the street. Once again, it would take only three or four "howdies" from real estate agents dressed, perhaps more authentically than the mayor intended, as bandits and outlaws for even a very prosaic student to begin to get a firm grasp on the notion of constructed and appropriated identity, and on the contested meanings of authenticity.[16]

In Kellogg, Idaho, the rush of towns capitalizing on westernness brought forth an even more remarkable demonstration in cultural theory. Kellogg had gone into a terrible, possibly terminal, slump from the recession in mining and logging. The landscape in large areas around Kellogg spoke of those earlier industries, with large sections "deforested from acid rain and pollution from a smelter that is no longer in use." In 1989, with the inspiration provided by a $6.5 million federal grant to engineer a ski slope, Kellogg considered its image. Would the town adopt a western theme to accompany its ski resort? Too many towns in the area had already made that choice. So Kellogg settled on "old Bavarian" as its image of choice. Not everyone was enthusiastic. "I have," said one resident in a wonderful and memorable line, "some real reservations about going Bavarian."[17]

"I have some real reservations about going Bavarian" is a sentiment to savor, but it is also a sentiment to challenge. "So you have some reservations about going Bavarian," one wants to say to the speaker from Kellogg. "Would you have any reservations about going back to mining? Isn't a bit of Alpine bric-a-brac a small price to pay compared to those earlier prices of acid rain, pollution, deforestation, and cyclical economic collapse?"

Here is the central question of western tourism, past and present. Given the instability and even decline of the conventional, rural western enterprises, given the economic troubles afflicting mining, logging, ranching, and farming, does not the lesson of history point in the direction of tourism? The lesson of western history is that extractive industries have provided a treacherous foundation for permanent and stable communities. If one looks for a different, and more reliable, kind of foundation, all roads seem to lead to tourism, to the preservation and publicizing of local natural and cultural resources, as a permanent attraction for visitors with deep pockets. Here, the theory goes, is the clean industry, the sustainable industry. By this thinking, the residents of Kellogg, Idaho, may feel a little goofy in their pinafores and lederhosen, but wearing silly clothes is a small price to pay for escape from the environmental injury and economic instability represented in the town's old smelter.

Whether one calls it the end of the frontier or not, some sort of major shift is indeed under way in the American West today. The rural extractive industries are undeniably on the ropes. The only question is whether they have one or two more rides left on the boom/bust roller coaster, or whether the whole ride is over. Under those circumstances, it is hard to find economic options other than tourism. In tourism's third-world labor arrangements, in its often terrible disparity between rich and poor in places like Aspen, in its various environmental impacts from sewage to air pollution, and in its ongoing vulnerability to the swings of the American economy, tourism may be an unappealing alternative to mining, logging, ranching, and farming. But what else is there?

At this point in my reflections, I come face to face with a pow-erful, if unexamined, urge among historians of my generation to steer their narratives toward some sort of happy, or at the least promis-ing, ending. The lessons of western history, one feels certain in say-ing, tell us that the extractive uses of western resources come with a very definite limit in time and extent. On that count, one cannot fudge. But my own inclination to fudge evidently becomes more powerful when it comes to the appraisal of tourism as an alterna-tive to these dead-end enterprises. I would like to believe that there are better ways to *do* tourism, ways that give greater respect to the dignity of the toured upon—or, probably more important, that give greater *wages* to the toured upon. I would like to believe that at the heart of tourism is a very understandable human curiosity, a sym-pathetic impulse to go beyond the limits of one's own familiar world, and to see and to learn about new places and new people. I would like to believe that this curiosity is not intrinsically damaging and degrading.

Consider, for instance, the pattern adopted by visitors to Utah and Salt Lake City before 1890. The one feature of local society on every non-Mormon visitor's mind was polygamy. Visitors to Salt Lake were thus the living, walking embodiments of the component of snoopishness in tourism. If visitors walked past a Mormon house and the door happened to be open, they would peer in, hoping for a glimpse of polygamy in private life.

This was tourism at its peak of snoopishness, tourism as intru-sion, tourism as psychological and domestic invasion. But this is also where a suspension of the casting of the tourist as contemptible, intrusive other seems in order. Is there anyone among us who does *not* find polygamy very interesting? Jessie Embry's fine book on Mormon polygamous families is a case in point.[18] It is a well-done book in scholarly terms, but one reads it eagerly, energetically, not simply out of admiration for its scholarship, but also for reasons not all that removed from the snoopishness of the gentile tourists of the late nineteenth century. One turns the pages of Embry's book in a spirit not entirely separate from the eagerness with which tourists hoped that a door would open and they could get a glimpse of a polygamous family at home. The curiosity that drives the historian and the curiosity that drives the tourist have a certain amount in common. The spirit of inquiry with which the historian pokes into the lives of people of the past bears a certain resemblance to the spirit of inquiry with which tourists have poked into the lives of their contemporaries. Historians had better put some effort into a sympathetic understanding of the interior world of tourists, because tourists are, in some not necessarily very agreeable way, our kinfolk.

But the relation of historians to tourists is even more tangled than this, because contemporary tourism relies heavily on the *marketing* of history. When you track the history of western American tourism, you arrive, ironically, at a branch of tourism that rests on the marketing of the romance, color, and interest of western American history. To use the term employed by professionals in this field, you confront heritage tourism, tourism that capitalizes on the attractions and interest of the past. This kind of tourism has a way of rendering western history in pastel colors, sketching a cheery and inconsequentially quaint past. And yet the messages of heritage tourism reach a much larger audience than writings of academic historians will ever reach; it does not seem entirely justifiable for historians to turn on our heels and retreat in contempt from the impurity of heritage tourism.

I am willing to go pretty far in asking for a reconsideration of tourism, and for a reconsideration of our usual portrait of the tourist as a bumbling, contemptible, invasive other. But I recognize that, even with this reconsideration, what tourists want from western history and what historians are willing to give them may be fundamentally at odds. This is a struggle not likely to dissolve in friendly, reciprocal empathy and understanding.

When art tourism hit Taos, New Mexico, early in the twentieth century, Anglo-American artists rushed in to paint Indians and Mexican Americans, producing appealing images that in turn inspired further waves of tourism. When I am starting to get too cheery and soft-headed in my appraisal of tourism, it helps to remember a story that anthropologist Sylvia Rodriguez tells in an article on the Taos Art Colony. Joseph Sandoval was a child in Taos Pueblo when art tourism hit the area. Sandoval's father served as a model for the artists, and then, at age six, Joe himself began to pose. Years later, Joseph Sandoval described his start in modeling. "When sitting as a young child for [the painter Irving] Couse, Joe remembers that he became frightened at the idea of the artist's 'catching' his image in paint and ran out of the studio down the street. However, he was soon overtaken by Mrs. Couse who brought him back, chained him around the waist to a chair within easy reach of a great bowl of luscious fruit and a tempting mound of cookies. A blanket was draped over the chain, says Joe, and Couse, without further complications, completed the painting."[19]

I end with this story to counteract any tendency toward the suspension of critical judgment that I may have shown in this essay. This image of a chained child, with a blanket placed over the chain to make the picture pretty, is part of the heritage of western tourism. As we examine the rising influence of tourism in the western economy, we return to pay attention to that chain.

Notes

1. Marvin C. Ross, ed., *The West of Alfred Jacob Miller* (Norman: University of Oklahoma Press, 1951), 119.

2. Patricia Nelson Limerick, *Desert Passages: Encounters with the American Deserts* (Albuquerque: University of New Mexico Press, 1985), 113–126.

3. Earl Pomeroy, *In Search of the Golden West: The Tourist in Western America* (New York: Alfred A. Knopf, 1957), 172.

4. J. B. Jackson, "The Stranger's Path," *Landscape* 7 (Autumn 1957): 11–15.

5. Michelle Mahoney and Steve Lipsher, "Tourist Bureau Closing," *Denver Post*, November 4, 1993; Timothy Egan, "What Attracts Tourists Repels Some Residents," *New York Times*, June 1989.

6. Edward Abbey, *Abbey's Road* (New York: E. P. Dutton, 1979), 86.

7. Alfred Runte, *National Parks: The American Experience* (Lincoln: University of Nebraska Press, 1979), 104.

8. Michael deCourcy Hinds, "Anxious Armies of Vacationers Are Demanding More from Nature," *New York Times*, July 8, 1990.

9. Richard Misrach, with Myriam Weisang Misrach, *Bravo 20: The Bombing of the American West* (Baltimore: Johns Hopkins University Press, 1990), 95.

10. Ibid., 96.

11. Pomeroy, *In Search of the Golden West*, 21.

12. "Photogenic Tetons Get Around a Lot More Than Wyoming Likes," *Denver Post*, December 26, 1989.

13. "Wyoming Insists That Tetons Must Stay," *New York Times*, December 27, 1989.

14. "Denver Told Image Will Lasso Tourists," *Denver Post*, March 15, 1991; "Visitors Cool on Denver," *Denver Post*, June 24, 1993.

15. "'Not-So-Wild West Disappointing," *Denver Post*, July 2, 1989.

16. Ibid.

17. Timothy Egan, "Kellogg Journal: Mining Town Given Lift in Effort to Be a Resort," *New York Times,* July 13, 1989.

18. Jessie L. Embry, *Mormon Polygamous Families: Life in the Principle* (Salt Lake City: University of Utah Press, 1987).

19. Quoted in Sylvia Rodriguez, "Art, Tourism, and Race Relations in Taos: Toward a Sociology of the Art Colony," *Journal of Anthropological Research* 45, no. 1 (1989): 83.

Chapter Three

Why I Love Tourists: Confessions of a Dharma Bum

Rudolfo Anaya

I was born on the eastern llano of New Mexico—at just the right moment, so my mother said—a tourist from the great beyond. Just another guest on Earth looking for his dharma nature. I discovered the core of my nature in the people of my region. But we also discover elements of our essential nature by traveling to other places, by meeting other people. To tour is to move beyond one's circle. So we're all tourists on Earth, we go from here to there if only to just have a look.

But tourists and natives often clash, perhaps because the tourist cannot love the place as much as the native. We learn to love the land that nurtures us. We, the natives, become possessive about "our place." Westerners especially feel a great love toward this land that stretches north and south along the spine of the Rocky Mountains. I believe this sense of possessiveness about "our land" means we, the denizens of the West, are turning inward. We now truly understand that "there's no where else to go," so we had better take care of what's left.

The open spaces of the West once allowed for great mobility, and so the nature of those who came here was more ample, more extroverted. Today the real and the mythic frontier has disappeared, so we seem to be growing more introverted. Maybe we just want to be left alone.

Change and the progress of technology are bothering us. Next to Alburquerque where I live, a city has been built around the Intel Corporation; the subdivisions spread across sand hills where once only coyotes and jackrabbits roamed. Along the Rio Grande valley subdivisions cover farming land. We know what overdevelopment of the land can do. We know we're running out of water, out of space, out of clean air to breathe.

Westerners seem bound by one desire: to keep the land the way it was. Now the megacities are crowding us in. More and more people seem to be touring our turf. Are all those tourists looking for a place to settle? That's what bothers us. There are just too many tourists discovering and rediscovering the West. The tourist has become the "other" to the westerner. I hear my New Mexican paisanos say: "Take their money but let them go back where they came from. Please don't let them settle here."

Tourism is a very important segment of the western economy. Tourists bring bucks to grease Las Vegas, Disneyland, L.A., Seattle, and San Francisco, bucks to oceanside resorts and Rocky Mountain ski slopes, bucks for boating and hunting and fishing. Tourism has become the west's clean industry. But deep inside we, the natives, know it's got its inherent problems.

Tourism affects our lives, we believe, because it affects not only the topography; it also affects the sacred. We believe there is a spirit in the land; we know we cannot trample the flesh of the Earth and not affect its soul. Earth and spirit of the place go hand in hand. The transcendent has blessed this land and we don't want it ruined, we don't want it destroyed. We have a covenant with the land, we have become the keepers of the land. No wonder so many dharma bums— those looking for their essential relationship to the Earth—have crossed the West's rugged terrain, looking for a home, not just a home with a majestic view, but a home rooted to a landscape that allows the true nature of the person to develop.

We have all been tourists at one time or another. We have traveled to distant places to entertain and rest the body, and also to enlighten the spirit. The two are intertwined. We go looking for that revelation on the face of the Earth that speaks to the soul.

There are sensitive tourists, dharma bums who care about illuminating their nature and who appreciate the region and people they experience on their journey. There are some who respect the place and allow themselves to be changed by the people and region they visit. They return from the journey fulfilled, more aware of other cultures.

Then there are those who breeze through the place, accepting nothing of the local culture, learning little, complaining constantly, and leaving in their wake a kind of displacement. The natives take their money and are thankful when they're gone. Those travelers return home to complain about the food, the natives, and about the different lifestyles they encountered. They should never have left home. They did not travel to illuminate the spirit.

The land draws tourists to the West. They come to see the majestic mountains, arid deserts, the Pacific Ocean. Some come to experience our diverse cultural groups. Others come only to visit the cultural artifacts of the west: Las Vegas, Disneyland, L.A., Silicon Valley, Hoover Dam. Those who experience only the artifacts miss the spirit we natives find imbued in the landscape. Those who deal *only* in artifacts miss the history and culture of the West's traditional communities. And so tourists also symbolize that tension between tradition and change, a change that in some places carries the weight of impending doom.

Have the traditionalists grown tired of sharing the spirit of the West? Are we tired of those who come and trample our sacred land? And is the West really one unified region? When we speak of tourism are we only talking about people visiting here from outside the West, or do we also speak of internal tourism? From Montana to New Mexico, we hear complaints about tourists from outside the region. But in New Mexico, for example, we also complain about the Texans as tourists. Today I hear complaints about the nouveau riche Californians. Even Oregonians shrink from California tourists. "Please don't let them settle here," they whisper to each other.

The West was never one homogenous region; it is not only the land of the pioneers and the cowboy of the western movies. The West is a grouping of micro-regions and cultural groups. Even the grandeur of the Rocky Mountains can't unify us, because there are too many different landscapes in the West, too many different indigenous histories. My home, the northern Rio Grande, is such a micro-region, with its unique history and people. It is—and here I show my indigenous bias—one of the most interesting multicultural areas of the West.

The Spanish/Mexicano side of my ancestors were tourists who journeyed to this region in the late sixteenth century. Imagine the Pueblo Indians seeing the Spanish colonists coming up the Rio Grande in 1598. I'm sure they shook their heads and said, "There goes the neighborhood." In many ways *it did go*. If anyone has suffered from tourists, it is the Native American communities.

But the tourists kept coming into the land of the pueblos. The first entradas were from south to north as Spanish-speakers expanded north. In the nineteenth century the east to west migrations began. In a scene from my novel *Shaman Winter*, I describe Kearny marching into New Mexico with the Army of the West in 1846. The Mexicanos in the crowd yell: "Why don't you go back where you came from!" "Go home gringos!" "Hope they keep going right on to California." "We ought to pass a Spanish Only law if they stay."

Of course those "tourists" didn't go home. And they changed the West forever. Each group introduced a new overlay of culture. Each brought a new set of stories, their own history and mythology to the West. Now the balance of what the land can hold has reached a critical point. Maybe we're uncertain about tourists because they represent the unknown. If the tourist decides to return to settle—and history teaches us that's the pattern—each one is a potential threat to the land, each one represents one more house to be built, more desert to be plowed up, more water consumed. They represent development in a fragile land already overdeveloped.

It's not just the growth in numbers we fear. We are convinced that outsiders know nothing of the nature of our relationship to the earth. This relationship defines our nature. I feel connected to la tierra de Nuevo México. This Earth is all I know, it nourishes my soul, my humanity. The gods live in the Earth, the sky, the clouds.

Growing up in eastern New Mexico, I felt the llano speak to me. The llano as brother, father, mother. Constant breezes caressed me, sang to me, whispered legends, stirred my memory. The Pecos River engulfed me with its bosque of alamos, river willows, Russian olives, thick brush. It sang a song of memory as it flowed south to empty into the Rio Grande, from there into the Gulf of Mexico. Truly, time and the river sang in my heart.

This early attachment and sensibility to the land became love, love for the place and the people. The people molded me. The

Hispano/Mexicanos of the llano were cattlemen and sheepmen who taught me a way of relating to the earth. The farmers from the Pecos River Valley initiated me into another relationship with nature; they planted my roots in that earth as they planted seeds. I saw the people struggle to make a living, I heard the stories they told. History and traditions were passed down, and everything related to the place and the people. Some of the teaching was unspoken; it was there in the silence of the llano, the faces of the people.

People told stories, joys and tragedies carried in the breezes, so I, too, became a storyteller. Listening to the people's story and then retelling the story relates one to the place. Will tourists who visit our land pause long enough to listen to our stories? The bones buried in the earth tell the story. Who will listen?

This spiritual connection to the land seems to describe the westerner. Even in the harshest weather and the longest drought, we stand in awe of the earth. Awe describes our relationship to the land. Perhaps tourists are simply people who don't stand still long enough to feel the immediacy of awe. They don't understand the intimacy of relationships woven into the people of the land.

As a child I felt this awe on the llano, along the river, on those hills which shaped my childhood. So the Earth for me has a particular feel, it is the New Mexican landscape, the llano and Pecos River of childhood, the Rio Grande and Sangre de Cristo Mountains of my later life, the desert which is always at the edge.

Still, we must be kind to tourists. It's part of our heritage to be kind to strangers. And we have all been tourists at one time or another. I, too, have been a tourist, a seeker who wanted to explore beyond the limits of my immediate environment.

One description of the Anglo-American culture has been its mobility. Anglo-Americans, we are told, are a restless lot. They couldn't just stay over there in the thirteen colonies, no, they had to go West. They love to quote the oft-repeated "Go west, young man, go west." So much a part of the history and mythology of this country is known from that western movement. Land, they smelled land, and gold and beaver pelts and gas and oil, all of which drew them west. So, Anglos are natural-born tourists. Now they've even been to the moon. Maybe some people just take to touring better than others. Or perhaps there are times when mass migrations take place; need and adventure move entire populations.

The Indohispanos of New Mexico have ancient roots in the land. Our European ancestors settled in the Hispano homeland along the northern Rio Grande in 1598. Remember those Espanioles coming up the Rio Grande? They took to the land, became as indigenous and settled as their vecinos in the pueblos. Wars, adventure, and extreme economic necessity have taken them beyond the homeland's frontier.

In this region Hispanics also claim tourist heroes. Cabeza de Vaca comes to mind. Shipwrecked on the coast of Texas, he set out on an odyssey that lasted seven or eight years. He is the Odysseus of the Southwest. Never mind that he was lost. Perhaps to be "lost" as a tourist is essential. Only thus can you enter fully into the place and the people. He was the first European tourist in Texas. Can you imagine the awe he experienced?

And he turned out to be a typical tourist. He went back to Mexico and spread the word. "Texas was great," Cabeza de Vaca told the viceroy in Mexico City. "The streets are paved with gold. There are pueblos four or five stories high. And a strange animal called a buffalo roams the plains by the millions."

Other Spanish explorers quickly followed Cabeza de Vaca. Coronado came north. A tourist looking for gold and the fabled cities of Cibola. He found only Indian pueblos, the original natives living in houses made of adobes. Accommodations in Native America weren't the best in the sixteenth century, so the Spanish tourists returned home, discouraged they hadn't found cities with streets paved with gold.

But the Spaniards were consumate note-takers. They mapped the land, described it and the natives, and they sent letters to their neighbors back in Mexico. "You've got to see this place. La Nueva México is virgin land. Very little traffic, and the native arts and crafts are out of this world. I brought a clay pot for dos reales. I can sell it in Spain for twice that. In a few years the place will be spoiled. Come see it before it's gone."

Gone? That's what we fear. What if the spirit that attracted us here in the first place leaves?

Tourists do spoil things. The minute tourists discover a new place, they also bring their garbage with them. Some set up businesses to ship the clay pots back home, organizing the natives in ways the natives never wanted to be organized. Tourism leads to strange kinds of enterprises, some good, some not very humanistic.

But I didn't learn about tourism in the West by reading the Spanish explorer's notes. In my childhood we weren't taught the history of our land as it occurred from the colonizations that came to el norte from the south. We were only taught the history of the pioneers, the western movement. How many times did little Chicanitos in school have to sing "Oh My Darling Clementine?".

The first tourists I encountered were in Santa Rosa, New Mexico, my home town. On highway 66, right after World War II. It was the best of times, it was the worst of times. People were moving west, tourists in search of California. I remember one particular afternoon at a gas station where we went to fill our bike tires after goathead punctures. A car stopped. Dad, mom, son, and daughter. Blonde, blue-eyed gringos from the east. They usually didn't pay attention to the brown Mexicanitos gathered at the gas station. But this Ozzie and Harriet Nelson family did. They talked briefly to me.

"Where you from?" Ozzie asked.
"Here," I said.
"Just here?" he said, looking around.
"Yes." I had never considered anyplace other than just here. Here was home.
He wasn't too interested. "Oh," he said and went off to kick his car's tires.
"Where are *you* from?" I asked Harriet.
"Back east."
"Where are you going?" I asked.
"We're tourists," she answered. "We're going to California."

Heading west on highway 66, into the setting sun.

Imagine, I thought to myself. A family can travel to California as tourists. Just to go look. Look at what? The Pacific Ocean. I knew it from the maps at school. I knew then I wanted to be a tourist.

I ran home and told my mother. "Mama, I want to be a tourist."

Her mouth dropped. She stopped rolling tortillas and made the sign of the cross over me. "Where did you get that idea?" I told her about the family I had just met.

"No, mijito," she said. "Only the Americanos can be tourists. Now go help Ultima with her herbs and get those crazy ideas out of your mind."

I went away saddened. Why was it a crazy idea to be a tourist? Was my mother telling me to beware of tourists?

"Why is it only the Americanos get to be tourists?" I asked Ultima. She knew the answer to almost any question that had to do with healing and sickness of the soul, but I could see that tourists puzzled her.

"They have cameras, they take pictures," she finally answered.

"What's wrong with that?"

"The spirit of who we are cannot be captured in the picture," she said. "When you go to a different place you can know it by taking a picture, or you can let the place seep into your blood. A real turista is one who allows the spirit of that place to enter."

She looked across the hills of the llano, then turned her gaze to the river. "The river is like a turista. The water moves, but yet the river remains constant. So to travel also means to go within. This place, or any place, can change you. You discover pieces of yourself when you go beyond your boundaries. Or you can stay in one place and learn the true nature of your soul."

I knew Ultima had never been a tourist. She only knew the few villages around Santa Rosa. But she was far wiser than anyone I knew. She had traveled within, and so she knew herself. She knew the land and its people.

Still I questioned her. "My tio Benito and his family are tourists, aren't they? They're always going to Colorado or Texas."

Again she shook her head. "They go to work in the beet fields of Colorado and to pick cotton in Texas. Poor people who go to work aren't turistas."

So, tourists didn't go to work. They just went to look, and maybe take pictures. What a life. I knew I *really* wanted to be tourist.

"Who knows," Ultima said, "maybe someday you will travel beyond this river valley. You may even go to China."

China, I thought. On the round world globe at school it was directly across from Santa Rosa. One day I dug a hole in the schoolyard. "You better watch out, Rudy," the girls warned me. "You could fall through to China." They ran away laughing.

For a class project I wrote away to cruise lines and did a report on cruise ships. They circled the globe. They went to Greece. Spain. Italy. They went to the Mediterranean world. Maybe someday I will take a ship on the Mediterranean, I thought.

For another project I made a sculpture of clay. The pyramids of Giza and the Sphinx. Set on a plaster board with sand for the desert and twigs for palm trees. It was real to me. I got an A.

"What do you want to be when you grow up?" the teacher asked.

"I want to be a tourist," I said.

"Esta loco," the kids whispered.

Yes, to dream of travel in that time and place was to be a little crazy. I settled for books to bring distant places to me.

But I did go to China. In 1984 my wife and I and a small group of colleagues traveled through China. I saw wonders my ancestors of the Pecos River could only imagine. Bejing, Xian, the Yangtze River, the Great Wall. I got so much into the place and the people at one point I felt transformed into a Chinese man. That's the kind of transformation the sensitive tourist looks for, becoming one with the place and people. If only for a short while. I have never written travel journals, but I did write one about China. *A Chicano in China.*

The memory of who I am stretches beyond the here and now. It resides in the archetypes, a biologic stream that is a strand into the past, to distant places and people. We sense the truth of images in stories and myths. And so we set out to test the memory. Was I related to China and its people? Was the Chinese dragon the Quetzalcoatl of the Aztecs? Was the god of nature, the golden carp which I described in *Bless Me, Ultima,* related to the golden carp that thrive in Chinese lakes? Was the bronze turtle resting at temple entrances related to the boy called Tortuga in my novel by that name?

We travel to seek connections. What are the tourists who come west seeking? Is our job to take their money and be done with them, or should we educate them? Should they read our books and history before applying for visas to our sacred land?

Later in life I did cruise on the Mediterranean, from the Greek Isles through the Bosporus into magical Constantinople. From Spain— where I practiced my New Mexican Spanish in many a tapas bar—to

Italy down to Israel and into Eygpt. Cruising the Nile, like a lowrider on Saturday night, I was transported into a past so deep and meaningful, I became Egyptian. I cut my hair like an Egyptian, wore the long robe, prayed at the temples, and entered into the worship. A tourist must also be a pilgrim.

I didn't participate in any revolutions like Lawrence of Arabia. I was a tourist. I knew my role and my parameters. But even as tourists we can enter the history of the place. I would go back to the Nile at the drop of a tortilla. Now I consider my Rio Grande a sister of the Nile. Long ago Mediterranean people, my ancestors, came to Rio Grande, bringing their dreams. I am part of that dream that infused the land. I am part of all the dreams that have settled here.

How do we teach these connections to tourists that visit our Rio Grande, or the Colorado River, or the Columbia? There are relationships of rivers. Those from the east bring knowledge of their Mississippi, their Ohio, their Hudson. They bring a knowledge of their place and history. How we connect to each other may show us how we can save the West, and save the world.

Still we fear that tourism has become just one more consumer item on the supermarket shelf. Tourists who come only to consume and don't connect their history to ours leave us empty.

Is there an answer to this topic of tourism in the West? The issue is complex. My tio Benito and his family, who as I mentioned earlier went as workers to Texas and Colorado, weren't considered tourists, and yet they gave their work and sweat to the land. But they remained invisible. They worked the earth of the West, like prior groups have worked the western land, but they remained invisible.

The Mexicano workers who right now are constructing the history of the West through their work in the fields are not considered tourists. And yet they are lending their language, their music, and their food to enrich our region. The Pacific Rim has been connected to Asia for a long time, and that relationship continues to thrive in our time. The West now speaks Japanese, Chinese, and Korean.

Maybe the West is going through a new era. We are a vast and exciting region where new migrations of people are creating an exciting multicultural world, one that has very little in common with the older, conservative myth of the West. Perhaps the idea of the West as the promised land isn't dead; a new infusion of cultures continues even as postmodern technology changes our landscape once again.

I am fascinated with the migrations of people. I have tried to emphasize this by saying some of those past migrations to the West were tourists. I don't mean to be flippant. We know most often it is necessity that moves groups of people. But migrations are a normal course of human events. Today, as in the past, it isn't only curiosity and available leisure time that creates the tourist. When people have to feed their families they will migrate.

Our challenge is to be sensitive to those who migrate across the land. A lot of mistakes were made in the past by those too arrogant to appreciate the native ways. Clashes between the cultural groups of the West exploded into atrocities. That, too, is part of our history. To not repeat that waste is the challenge. The answer lies in how we educate ourselves and those tourists exploring our region. In this effort major attention has to be paid to the migrant workers, those who put sweat and labor into the land but may not have the leisure time we normally associate with tourists. In many ways they know our region better than most of us, and many are settling into the land.

In Spanish we have a saying: Respeto al ajeno. Respect the other person's property, respect the foreigner. As we respect places and people in our travels, we expect to be respected by those who travel through our land. Respect can be taught. After all, we are on Earth "only for a while" as the Aztec poet said. We are all dharma bums learning our true nature from the many communities of the West. Let us respect each other in the process.

Chapter Four

For Residents and Visitors Alike: Seeking Tourism's Benefits, Minimizing Tourism's Costs

Patrick T. Long

Recently I was introduced to a "hockey mom"—a person who spends endless hours in cold places or driving to and from such places as well as an inordinate amount of money to ensure her child fulfills his/her ice hockey dreams. When she learned that I was a hockey dad, she proceeded to tell me about her family's weekend travels to Fargo, North Dakota, where her son's hockey team participated in a tournament. Upon finishing her story she asked me what I did for work. I told her I was on the business faculty at the local university, where I taught tourism. She couldn't help herself and spontaneously burst out laughing, a response I have become somewhat accustomed to when people hear about my academic discipline.

Still giggling, she asked me, "What's tourism?" I pointed out that for her family to travel to Fargo, they probably purchased airline tickets, stayed in a motel, rented a car and purchased gasoline, ate meals at local restaurants, paid tournament registration fees and bought souvenirs—all typical travel expenditures. I suggested that her family probably interacted with local business personnel and residents, as well as with other travelers participating in the tournament. Her travel experience, I pointed out, was a rather typical tourism experience that as a member of the academic community, I was interested in better understanding. My response seemed to satisfy her curiosity about my work.

This hockey mom, despite her unintended (I certainly hope) ridicule of my discipline, helped me tremendously in thinking about the issues that are fundamental to this chapter. She reminded me that many western communities benefit from the development and presentation of a local tourism industry frequently anchored by cultural, historic, and nature-based tourism initiatives.

Tourism throughout the western United States is intrinsically a public and private partnership. For instance, in Colorado, the Division of State Parks annually hosts more than 12 million visitors to its forty sites. Located throughout the state, these sites provide employment to 190 full-time and 500 seasonal workers. The Colorado Division of Wildlife reported in 1996 that hunting and fishing contributed $1.7 billion to the state's economy, while the Colorado River Outfitters Association estimated that in 1997 there were 489,000 commercial rafting user days, resulting in an economic impact exceeding $106 million. Colorado offers its visitors twenty-two designated scenic byways, forty dude and guest ranches, eleven National Park Service units, and twelve national forests and grasslands, most of which are located in rural areas throughout the state.[1] These destinations provide the catalyst for substantial private sector development.

The woman's story about her travels to Fargo for a youth hockey tournament made an important point for me: it served as a reminder of just how appropriate thoughtful and intelligent tourism can be for a community, particularly when such tourism is well planned and integrated into a community's overall economic and social fabric—where, in fact, residents and visitors alike can benefit. In the case of Fargo, one anchor for the local tourism economy is the fast-emerging area of sports tourism. Sports tourism involves hosting sporting events that result in substantial expenditures within the destination by visiting participants and their families and friends. Such sporting events can include both local and regional offerings, such as softball and hockey tournaments, and more substantial events, such as the National Junior College Baseball Tournament held annually in Grand Junction, Colorado, or the Division I NCAA baseball tournament annually held in Omaha, Nebraska.

Over the past decade, due to shifts in the economic base of America's western rural communities, there has been much attention placed on tourism as a revitalization tool for expanding local

economies. This phenomenon reflects what is happening throughout the world as nations, states, regions, and communities seek to
capture a share of the vacation and business travel markets by promoting tourism. Increasingly, tourism, particularly in the U.S. West,
is being looked upon as filling the void left by the decline of traditional resource extraction industries (mining, timber, agriculture,
energy) as well as manufacturing, or as a potential avenue for stimulating new development and economic opportunities. For many
rural communities tourism often emerges as one of the few remaining options to revitalize a local economy, or, in some cases, simply
to survive.

Tourism is important to the economy of most rural communities because tourism businesses provide both jobs and careers for
local residents. Seasonal and part-time tourism jobs are critical in
filling employment needs of high school and college students, retired individuals or couples, and the undereducated or underemployed, of residents needing to supplement household income, and
of those consciously choosing to work in a tourism area to pursue
their chosen lifestyle. Career owners and operators of businesses that
provide consumers with such services as travel arrangements, accommodations, community attractions, technology, real estate, and
hospitality services, have a vocation that can be as significant to the
community as that of the rancher, farmer, miner, manufacturer, or
forester.

Tourism in America's West is not limited to a specific set of
destinations or to visitors only from out of the region. Area residents
traveling within the West to visit family and friends, attend a family or class reunion, participate in a sporting event, look for antiques,
or attend a weekend concert are as much a part of western tourism
as a person traveling from Illinois or Ireland to ski, camp, or attend
a conference. Tourism is essentially felt everywhere throughout the
region, whether it be Moab, Utah; Colorado Springs, Colorado; or
Taos, New Mexico. One might not think of a remote agricultural
community such as Sterling, Colorado, as a community that benefits
from tourism, yet approximately 20 percent of its economy depends
on visitor expenditures.

This money typically is spent in small tourism businesses such
as food stores, eating and drinking establishments, accommodations,
travel arrangements, retail sales, recreation, and ground and air

transport. For the rural economy these are major employers, and they generate taxes that flow from lodging, retail sales, fuel purchases, and personal and corporate assessments. These tourism businesses impact the local and state economies through employment, payroll, expenditures, and local and state tax receipts.

But important questions face communities pursuing tourism. What is the attraction that will draw people to the community? Can the community afford the investment necessary to attract tourists and their money? How much physical, social, and environmental change (and how quickly) must residents endure to be successful in tourism? How much economic dependence should be placed on a tourism economy? Can the delicate balance that ensures that tourism does not overwhelm residents and compromise the community's well-being beyond the point of redemption be achieved?

Now, the world, not just the American West, has its examples of tourism gone bad. Inflated housing costs, low wages, changed culture, diminished or destroyed natural resources, and unappreciative guests are just a few of the reasons often noted for communities to avoid becoming tourist destinations. At best, for some, tourism is viewed as a "doomsday" economic development strategy, one to be pursued when all else has failed—and abandoned as soon as any acceptable alternative is identified.

It is no secret that many destinations have been severely challenged as a result of their efforts to establish or expand their tourism economy. Many negative issues can confront a community if tourism is allowed to reach a scale that exceeds the capacity of the destination or if a community's quality of living is severely altered due to mass—or as some refer to it, industrialized—tourism. Many of the negative outcomes of tourism can be traced to a fixation on increased numbers of tourists rather that the right ones or on attempts to provide every imaginable experience and amenity a tourist might want rather than to tailor the tourism offering to unique cultural, historic, or nature-based resources. In addition, monetary greed can drive a destination's tourism policies, resulting in unconstrained development.

Some of this "dubious" tourism has been documented in my own research. Through the mid 1980s, with two professional colleagues and numerous students, I studied residents' perceptions of various dimensions of community life in locations with varying degrees of dependence on tourism and recreation. In research conducted in twenty-three Colorado communities, we found that residents perceived lower to moderate levels of tourism development as quite beneficial; but as development continued, perceptions of community life declined, particularly as related to public services and opportunities for citizen social and political involvement.[2] Communities tend to support tourism when they view it as "the best imaginable alternative." However, western rural communities are not positively predisposed toward tourism—they don't view it as a recourse to be undertaken regardless of the community's economic need; rather, they view it as an option that sometimes has to be undertaken when a local economy is faltering.

This being the case, further research indicated that support for additional tourism development was positively related to the level of perceived positive impact derived from tourism and negatively related to the level of perceived negative impact. Not surprisingly, we also found that as the perceived future of the community without tourism improved, support for tourism declined. Finally, we documented that support for restrictive tourism development policies was negatively related to support for tourism development.[3]

In a more recent research effort conducted in the early 1990s, we measured resident attitudes regarding the early impacts of limit-stakes casino gambling in the communities of Deadwood, South Dakota, and Central City, Cripple Creek, and Black Hawk, Colorado.[4] This research provided evidence of resident dissatisfaction with several aspects of community life that had dramatically changed due to the new gambling economy. Regarding political empowerment (an understanding of the importance of involvement in the political process), residents from all four gambling towns indicated rather strongly that their ability to influence local political decisions had negatively changed. Even the control-town respondents from Grand Lake, Colorado, a nongambling rapid-growth tourist town experiencing similar changes, expressed doubts about the effectiveness of their vote.

Also, when residents of the gambling towns were asked whether they agreed with the statement "My town is an ideal place to live," 76 percent of the residents from Central City and 56 percent of the residents of Cripple Creek expressed strong disagreement. About 40 percent of respondents from both Deadwood and Black Hawk also disagreed strongly. When asked whether they would consider moving from their community, 44 percent of the Cripple Creek residents, 39 percent of Central City residents, 32 percent of Black Hawk residents, and 29 percent of Deadwood residents said they would consider moving. This is in contrast to the 15 percent response from residents of a nongambling tourist community.

Further evidence of the negative implications of tourism that we have been tracking surfaces in western Colorado in the five counties of Garfield, Eagle, Lake, Pitkin, and Summit. The resort destinations of Vail (Eagle County), Aspen (Pitkin County), and Copper Mountain, Keystone, and Breckinridge (Summit County) create tremendous wealth for their respective counties due to the demand for skiing and other year-round, natural-resource-based recreation activities. But due to the high cost of housing in the resort counties, many workers are imported from the poorer counties of Lake and Garfield, creating transportation, child care, and family domestic problems, among others.

Private and public sector leaders from these five counties, recognizing the challenges the region faces, have been working cooperatively to "Create a working partnership that addresses the economic and human needs of the Rural Resort Region."[5] These leaders are attempting to address the uneven distribution of costs and benefits created by the growth and development of the destination resorts and tourism economy. They realize that the health, human services, and public safety issues related to providing a basic level of service for residents are best analyzed and understood on a regional basis.

In Eagle and Pitkin Counties, approximately 70 percent of workers are employed in the services industry, while in Lake and Summit Counties about 50 percent are considered service-industry employees. In Garfield County, only about 30 percent are counted as such. The annual wage (1992) of those working in the recreation sector in this region was $18,486, with those working in the eating and drinking sector earning $12,319 and in the hotel and lodging sector, $15,605. In Pitkin County, where Aspen Ski Company is located, and Eagle County, where Vail Resort is located, there is a particularly high percentage of service workers.

Because of the abundant numbers of workers imported from Lake and Garfield Counties to Aspen and Vail, the expenditures within these counties for day care is substantial—especially in contrast to the expenditures for day care of the destination counties. In 1992, Lake County exported 21 percent of its workers to Summit County and 31 percent to Eagle County, spending in excess of $100,000 for low-income day care. Garfield County spent more than $150,000. Medicaid births in Lake County exceeded 50 percent of all births that year, this being a substantial increase from each of the two previous years. In Garfield County, over 30 percent of the county's total budget was spent on social services; in Lake County, it was in excess of 24 percent. It is clear that much of the burden for social services of workers in the resort communities is borne by those counties that have the least financial capability.

But my concerns are more about the communities that singer John Prine refers to when he sings about "small towns, bright lights, Saturday night!" These rural western communities will never be mass tourism destinations, but they seek to offer a glimpse of the charm, beauty, and genuineness of rural western life in trade for the traveler's money. Much has been written about the issues facing Vail and Estes Park, Colorado; Moab and St. George, Utah; Santa Fe and Taos, New Mexico; or Jackson and West Yellowstone, Wyoming. That is not to suggest that there is not a great deal to learn from their experience—or that these destinations are not, in fact, aggressively and creatively addressing the challenges they face as a result of tourism.

But for every Vail or Santa Fe, there are scores of communities such as Fargo and Minot (North Dakota), Pierre and Aberdeen (South Dakota), Lewiston and Glasgow (Montana), Thermopolis and Sheridan (Wyoming), Grand Junction and Lamar (Colorado), Carlsbad and Ruidoso (New Mexico), Sandpoint and Ketchum (Idaho), Cedar City and Vernal (Utah), and Globe and Kingman (Arizona)—all western communities reaping some economic benefits from tourism.

Tourism, like other western industries such as mining, forestry, fishing, and ranching, has generated a number of positive outcomes as well as the often cited negative ones. Like the previously dominant western economies of mining, forestry, and agriculture, even well-intentioned tourism development can bring about a certain degree of unwanted change. No other industry requires residents to play "host" to visiting "guests" (tourism consumers). While such intimacy can be most rewarding, it can also, as the cliché goes, "breed contempt," stemming from potential negative impacts on the community's social fabric, natural environment, infrastructure, and superstructure.[6]

But change is typically judged "through the eyes of the beholder" and thus assessed differently by various groups holding differing opinions about tourism's impact. Throughout the remainder of this chapter I would ask you to consider the various perspectives of the major players of the western tourism experience. These perspectives include those of the tourist, tourism business owners/managers, public policy makers, and residents of host communities.

The tourist to the West today is generally seeking a safe and affordable destination that provides family attractions and amenities based on culture, history, or outdoor recreation opportunities. Business owners and managers are seeking an increase in the number of new or repeat visitors, in the average length of stay in the area, and in cash flow and profits; expanded markets for local products; and an improvement of the local lifestyle for both family and employees.

Public policy makers (elected and hired officials) are frequently seeking a reversal to the downturn of the local economy and an increase in tax revenues to support existing and new services. They are also seeking an increase in local job opportunities and in capital investment in the community, and are eager to leave their mark on the community's history.

Residents, in turn, are thinking about whether they can get primary or supplemental income or business ownership and how they and their children can afford to continue living in the area. They also are seeking a general improvement in the economy and their social environment. But residents are also concerned about inflated housing costs and real estate values, the influx of seasonal workers and low-paying jobs, increased congestion and interference with daily living routines, the loss of local culture and the natural environment, and the downturn in the general quality of community life.

Now, in addition to the Fargos and Minots mentioned earlier, there are hundreds of smaller communities across the West, such as Trinidad and Burlington, Colorado, which simply want a small piece of the tourism action to help in their economic revitalization efforts. They are part of the ever-growing group of communities in the West seeking to develop an attraction base from their heritage, culture, and natural resource amenities and striving to effectively plan and manage their tourism industry from its conception. They are not seeking to become full-scale tourism destinations or to shift yet again to a single-industry economy. Rather, they would like to complement and supplement the struggling economy they currently have.

For tourism to be successful as a long-term economic development strategy in rural western communities, it needs the support and input of a significant majority of community residents. Therefore, it is important that tourism be positioned as an industry that can yield a positive return on the local investment without exceeding the social and physical carrying capacity. Sociologist Elizabeth Moen notes that smaller rural towns that experience rapid growth and change are subjected to the realization that "the capacity of a community's facilities, services, and administrative capability can be quickly exceeded, that the power structure and socioeconomic relationships of the community can experience dramatic change in a very short time, and that conflict can arise between long-term residents and newcomers."[7]

Trinidad, Colorado, is located near the New Mexico border on the northern route of the historic Santa Fe Trail. It is located adjacent to U.S. Interstate 25 and is the site of one of Colorado's state welcome centers. Historically, Trinidad served as a rest station for travelers attempting to traverse Raton Pass, and today it possesses a rich mining, railroad, and agricultural history. Trinidad has a population of about nine thousand residents and is particularly challenged with increasing its per capita income, which is about $13,500—almost $7,000 below the state average. The community has been designated to benefit from the state's Enterprise Zone Tax Credit Program, has a junior college, is culturally diverse, has good weather and excellent access to outdoor recreation. It is part of the Highway of Legends Scenic Byway. It also has a number of vacant main-street buildings—many of historic value. The community also faces resident uncertainty and apathy about economic and social change.

At a community forum held a few years ago addressing general issues of community development and specific issues of economic development, delegates "envisioned a way of life that combined traditional values with the benefits that people in larger, more prosperous parts of Colorado enjoy." The delegates also expressed the wish "to preserve the natural beauty of the area, the healthy environment, the pleasant climate, the friendliness and helpfulness of people, the small scale and unhurried pace of day-to-day life, and the history and cultural influences that give the area an identity and sense of uniqueness."[8]

Regarding tourism specifically, the delegates noted that with the "climate, scenery, open landscape, museums, architectural heritage, and advantageous location that many other successful tourist towns lack," tourism has the potential to be a powerful industry in Trinidad. But despite a general sense of optimism regarding tourism, some expressed fear the area might evolve into a tourist town like Santa Fe and Taos (the feared SF & T words!), towns that may be losing their culture to tourism. Those holding this belief expressed the attitude that "no tourism is better than the wrong kind of tourism."[9] It should be noted that a vote to legalize gambling tourism in Trinidad was soundly defeated only a short while ago. Yet, with its wonderful museums and the richness of the area's culture, history, and natural resources, Trinidad's future in tourism appears bright if the community can come to agreement on the role tourism should play in its overall economy.

Burlington, Colorado, with a population of about three thousand, is located in Kit Carson County just off Interstate 70 on Colorado's eastern border. It is located just west of the most traveled entrance point to the state. Historically an agricultural community, Burlington has been seeking to complement a stalled economy by sharing its history and culture, but from the beginning, there was concern that tourism development be controlled.

As part of the "Colorado Outback" regional promotion, Burlington has good highway access, a state welcome center, Bonnie Reservoir, and the attractiveness of a rural, agricultural, farming community. It also has an internationally renowned carousel that was featured on a National Geographic television special. Its most significant attraction, Old Town, is one that came about due to a broad-based community effort and a good deal of local political will.

This attraction is a replication of a late 1800s–early 1900s village and consists today of twenty restored historic buildings. Located on a six and one-half acre site and adjacent to a Colorado state welcome center, this village preserves the history and culture of the plains and creates local income through employment and the sale of home-based products. Visitors to Old Town and the carousel eat at local restaurants, shop at local stores, and enjoy the generally friendly atmosphere of the community. By the way, Burlington folks feel passionate about their beef industry. When the cattle ranchers found out the Chamber of Commerce was serving chicken at an annual meeting, they printed and distributed a bumper sticker that read "Support the Beef Industry—Run Over a Chicken!"

What are the strengths of Burlington's tourism development? It is an initiative that the community rallied behind and worked on together—a true community development effort. It has resulted in new revenue to local businesses, a new tax source for local government, and an increase in personal income. It attracts a type of tourist that "fits" with the expectations of the community, and the scale of tourism is appropriate for the community's size. Burlington has benefited from strong political leadership and the rural work ethic. Does everyone in the community agree on the direction of this initiative? Are there detractors? Of course—this is rural America. But it seems that the positive outcomes of tourist development in Burlington outweigh any negative consequences, and the levels of community disagreement are actually comparatively low.

The emerging interest in developing tourism in Trinidad and Burlington as well as many other rural areas of the United States is easily understood. On the tourism *supply* side it is the need for local economic development and the fact that tourism expansion represents possibly the only alternative economic opportunity for rural America. The country's most precious scenic beauty and a sense of open space are found in the natural amenities of our hinterlands. There also appears to be a general perception that rural America represents certain values and a general aura of friendliness that seems increasingly more attractive to many Americans as the nation becomes more "metropolitan," and consequently more crowded and fast-paced.

A National Policy Study on Rural Tourism and Small Business Development completed in 1989 reported that "the rural areas of the US are badly in need of economic revitalization, yet these same areas have an abundance of cultural, historical and natural resource amenities around which to expand or build a tourism economy."[10] Even former President Bush had some words to say about rural tourism during his administration. Before a meeting of the nation's travel and tourism leaders he noted: "This solid record of the [economic] growth of tourism has not gone unnoticed by small communities and by rural areas facing the challenge to diversify their economies. More and more rural communities are making tourism a part of their economic diversification options for the nineties."[11]

On the *demand* side of tourism, an increasing number of visitors are seeking the rural experience, having already tasted the offerings of urban America. The U.S. Travel Data Center has discovered through its inbound survey of international air passengers that the repeat visitor is frequently returning to see America's "heartland." The domestic traveler, today vacationing more frequently for shorter time periods, is seeking the history, culture, and outdoor experiences offered in a more readily accessible rural environment. The issues of safety and affordability that face our major cities also help to make rural America attractive.

But many traveling Americans are simply seeking the rural nostalgia described by Douglas Duncan, newspaper editor in Shelton, Nebraska. When asked by CBS correspondent Charles Kuralt how one knows if he or she is in a small town, Duncan responded that you know you are in a small town when "Third Street is on the edge of town; when you're born on June 13th and your family receives gifts from the local merchants because you're the first baby of the year; when you dial a wrong number and talk for fifteen minutes anyway; when the biggest business in town sells farm machinery; and when someone asks you how you feel and spends the time to listen to what you have to say."[12]

Despite notable examples of negative outcomes from tourism development, rural communities across the country are seeking economic relief through tourism. Few are pursuing full-scale development—most simply are hoping to beautify their community and attract a few more tourist dollars. On what basis do they presume they can be successful?

First, there are substantial traveler expenditures to be captured. The Travel Industry Association of America recently reported that travel and tourism is the nation's third-largest retail sales industry behind automotive dealers and food stores, and continues to be a growth industry.[13] In 1995 travel and tourism generated $430 billion in expenditures. As the United States's largest services export, travel and tourism generated $79 billion in expenditures from 45 million international visitors who spent, on average, $210 per day. This is in addition to the $350 billion spent by domestic travelers.

For the nine western states of North Dakota, South Dakota, Montana, Wyoming, Colorado, New Mexico, Idaho, Utah, and Arizona, this meant total tourism expenditures by domestic travelers of $24 billion and international expenditures of $2.8 billion. There are local jobs to be created and filled. Travel and tourism over the last decade has created jobs at a faster rate than the rest of the economy. In 1994, travel and tourism supported 6.3 million direct and 8 million indirect jobs, a total of 14.3 million jobs, of which 650,000 were executive-level positions. For the nine western states this has meant approximately 471,000 jobs.

That same year, the travel and tourism industry ranked only second behind health care as the largest source of jobs in the United States and was among the top three employers in thirty-four states. Besides the full-time jobs created through travel and tourism, many rural communities find value in the part-time and seasonal employment opportunities that supplement household income and allow families to remain in the community. In addition to the general expenditures and potential for jobs, travel and tourism also generated $58.4 billion in tax revenues for federal, state, and local governments, $8.8 billion of which went to local units of government.[14]

The West can also benefit from recreation patterns that favor rural economies. In a report titled "Outdoor Recreation in America 1996" prepared for the Recreation Roundtable, an organization of the CEOs of the major recreation companies in the United States, it was noted that the top outdoor recreation activities in 1995 included walking, driving, swimming, picnicking, fishing, camping, off-road bicycling, and horseback riding.[15] The report also noted that seven in ten Americans reported no visits to federal recreation areas in the past year. Thus the two billion visits in 1995 represent a large number of visits by a relatively small group of travelers, mostly highly educated and affluent Americans. Clearly there is an untapped market and a market that, should recreation patterns change even slightly, could easily overwhelm our national outdoor recreation venues.

In addition, this report identified the qualities and experiences of desired vacations as well as the motivations and values of the frequent traveler and what they predict about vacation spending and choices. Virtually all of the vacation preferences expressed by the survey group match up with the offerings of a western tourism experience. And the reported average household income of $58,500, exceeding the national average income by about $18,000, indicates sufficient affluence for travel.[16]

Without going into great detail on what the tourism industry in the western United States needs to strive for to be successful over the next decade, I would like to highlight at least a few of the more important elements. First, our "tourism resources," the natural and man-made features that attract people to an area for recreation, relaxation, and education, must be managed with an increased sense of stewardship. To do so, we must more effectively distribute the visitors we currently are attracting and must market to future visitors who are inclined to appreciate our natural environment and cultural and historic amenities. More initiatives such as the Old Works Golf Course near Deer Lodge, Montana, an environmentally sensitive golf course development built upon land that once was the site of the town's first smelter, are vitally important. States and communities can come to better know their cultural heritage through initiatives such as the Colorado Heritage Area Partnership Project, which promotes wise stewardship of landscapes, rivers, wildlife, trails, parks, and historical sites in order to build healthy communities. An improved and more consistent funding base must be secured to preserve the natural resource "treasures" found in the West. We must find a way to limit actions such as covering previously excavated areas at such sites as Chaco Canyon, New Mexico, due to erosion and the lack of funding for management and security. If we put greater emphasis on preserving and managing our natural treasures, their importance and value will increase, as will their likelihood of preservation.

Our "traveler services," which include accommodations, food establishments, shopping, convention services, and state and local visitor centers, must improve their level of service and hospitality. The competition for new and return visitors is fierce, and deciding factors for future success will be the quality and availability of information, the uniqueness of the tourism product, and the quality of service provided. Bed and breakfasts, guest ranches, and small regional convention centers such as the one in Yuma, Colorado, are the type of venues currently most attractive to both the regional and the statewide traveling public. It is critical that financial lending institutions increase their understanding of the legitimacy of tourism businesses and the effect of such businesses on creating business ownership, jobs, and tax revenues. Neighboring rural communities within any geographic region need to pursue all avenues of cooperation and communication in order to provide a critical mass of the experiences and services tourists are seeking, as well as to promote such opportunities.

Our "tourism infrastructure," including "trains, planes, and automobiles" as well as our communication and Internet technology, must be brought up-to-date. Recently I previewed the rural vacation Web sites of three locations I plan to visit—Italy, Ireland, and Texas—and I am well aware of the quality of the tourist information provided on the Internet and its ease of access. Clearly the Internet creates a more level playing field between richer, more developed tourist destinations and those rural areas with limited budgets attempting to enter the marketplace. Thus, western states need to improve their Web site presence on the Internet.

The continuation and expansion of the Federal Department of Transportation Scenic Byways and All-American Roads program is important to funding corridor planning and roadway development, highway safety improvements, dissemination of tourism information, and improved roadway access for recreation purposes. This program has served as a major catalyst to effective regional planning for corridor development by local communities, state and federal agencies, and environmental advocacy groups. In addition to our scenic roadway designations, we need a more reliable method to sustain regional air and rail transportation. This will ensure that travelers can efficiently be transported to their more distant destinations.

Our "tourism markets" are changing—the international visitors, particularly those from the Far East, offer an opportunity to increase tourist revenues and share our western culture. Whether international or domestic, travelers, particularly families, seeking adventure travel, and what is more commonly known today as the ecotourism experience, are abundant. So are those travelers seeking an authentic cultural and historic experience. Senior adult travelers, grandparents traveling with grandchildren, and minority groups, including blacks and Hispanics, are emerging target markets around which a local tourism economy can expand. In addition, gamblers seeking a gaming experience can mean substantial revenue to a local community (e.g., Black Hawk, Colorado), but unfortunately much of their spending immediately leaves a region.

Finally, residents, policy makers, and business owners of our "host communities" are less inclined today to be "taken in" by tourism. They are more willing to inquire about the costs of tourism to their community, not just about revenue projections, and are willing to take an active role in planning, developing, and managing their community's tourism economy. Residents want to have tourism as a piece of their overall economy, to keep money at home, to restore and preserve precious resources, and to protect and improve their quality of economic and social well-being. They also want tourism to "fit" with their community, not to have their community be forced to adapt to the plans and demands of outside commercial forces.

Now, what must we do in the western region to make tourism work? What will make the embracing of a tourism industry acceptable for western communities? Successful tourism does not happen serendipitously. If we fail to plan? Well, we have learned that without planning, we are destined to take what we get. For rural communities, where human, financial, and physical resources are already at a premium, the gravity of the tourism planning situation is magnified, thus amplifying the need for an applied planning process that is rooted in, but not consumed by, systems theory.

A number of tourism planning models have been developed to help guide communities through the development of a tourism economy—models that balance economic growth with protection of a community's cultural, social, and environmental assets. Such planning models typically stress broad-based community involvement, the establishment of an organization's main purpose or mission, formulation of ways to achieve those purposes, and direction for implementing operational or tactical plans.

One such mode has been tailored to the unique needs and demands of western rural communities.[17] It recognizes the challenges of establishing a "sustainable" tourism industry but also the reality that tourism is an effective way to revitalize or expand the local economy. In the context of rural tourism development, organiza-

tional, physical, and marketing planning should, ideally, incorporate ten planning activities, including: (1) gathering information, (2)
identifying community values, (3) developing a vision, (4) identifying critical concerns and opportunities, (5) formulating a mission,
(6) developing goals, (7) developing objectives corresponding to each
goal, (8) outlining actions and funding strategies, (9) evaluating
progress, and (10) updating and modifying the plan. A brief overview of this model should indicate the importance of a conscious
effort to plan and manage tourism.

The first steps in this model guide the identification of a community's capability of developing tourism, articulate the community's
perspective of positive and negative impacts of tourism on the community, and also provide a clear picture of the "place" that the residents of the community want to live in.

In terms of public involvement, identifying values, creating a
common vision, and identifying critical concerns and opportunities
are perhaps the most important of all the steps, and the outcomes
should be seriously considered only if the views of a representative
sample of community residents are included. This is where the interaction of business, public policy makers, and community representatives is critical. Establishing a clear vision becomes central to
formulating and achieving community tourism goals. Without this
vision, actions may be taken that empty the community of its current
residents by creating a place in which they no longer want to live.

The next three steps, developing goals, objectives, and actions,
are standard in translating values and vision into action. With a clear
vision and mission statement, these three steps become a measur-
able problem of strategy execution. Goals and objectives are developed to guide and direct a group's efforts and its allocation of
typically scarce resources. These goals are broad statements directed toward fulfilling the community's mission and serve to provide guidance for the various committees. In order to be successful,
these tourism development goals must mesh with overall community goals, thus reinforcing the importance of integrating tourism
with community, regional, and economic development.

The final two steps formalize the fact that tourism development
and the associated impacts are complex, iterative, and evolving.
These activities are evaluating progress and updating and modifying the tourism development plan as needed, while ensuring that

the values, mission, and vision of the organization are not lost in the transition.

No one can or should presume to know the exact outcomes of tourism development; however, a community must continually focus on the degree to which it is willing to alter its character—its soul—to attract and satisfy visitor needs. Constant revisions and modifications are essential during these planning phases.

I would like to suggest that tourism and the West will continue to have a tension-filled relationship, but success is achievable. For this success, the federal land-management agencies, having already assumed a far greater role in the provision of recreation than ever before, must expand their efforts to work in partnership with local communities in a region's economic development. State tourism divisions must be charged by their legislatures to focus as much on developing quality products and destinations as they do on promotion and marketing. In addition, local communities, seeing tourism for the economic potential it has, must strive to provide a tourism experience that is better tailored to their resources and their values—one that attracts the type of tourist whose expectations and expenditures are best matched with the experience the community is providing. This will result only from a greater local commitment to effective tourism planning and the establishment of more stringent tourism policies.

Communities seeking economic relief through tourism must strive for what the tourism planning committee from the Northwest Territory of Canada has identified as the characteristics of "Good Tourism." Such tourism

- Is beneficial to local residents;
- Results in local purchases and local profits;
- Results in preservation of the natural environment;
- Preserves traditional values and lifestyles;
- Results in local employment and management;
- Provides secondary infrastructure benefits;
- Informs and educates visitors and promotes understanding;
- Results in local control and ownership;
- Does not overwhelm communities; and,
- Advocates external investments directed to meeting these ends.[18]

Unfortunately, planning for tourism has all too often been "too little too late" or simply nonexistent. Western tourism development, to be successful

- Must be viewed not simply as an economic development strategy, but also as a *modus operandi* related to broader aspects of community development;
- Must mesh with the values, opinions, and ideas of local community residents who ultimately must live with the inevitable positive and negative changes to their environment and quality of life; and
- Must be guided by strong and representative local leadership, be well planned, and include access to outside expertise and resources to achieve success and mitigate the negative effects.

In rural settings, where most decisions pertaining to community development readily affect every member of the local populace, interactive planning and decision making is imperative. Due to the intimate nature of rural tourism, the potential impacts felt directly by the community are heightened. Thus, when tourism is being considered as a part of the community development mix, incorporating a "transactive planning orientation" is recommended in order to accomplish a strategic plan for developing a sustainable tourism industry.[19] Such an orientation emphasizes the use of existing community knowledge and expertise and extensive interaction of locals, lessening the reliance on outside "experts." Comprehensive tourism development requires integrating a variety of development and management strategies relating to organizational development, physical development, resource management, marketing, and business.

Developing a successful tourism industry is not a task to be taken lightly. In fact, in rural settings, it requires striking a delicate balance between often limited or strained human, physical, and financial resources. Successful and sustainable tourism development in rural settings depends on the synergistic relationship of effective local leadership, thoughtful planning, and competent technical assistance. Even the most modest attempts, however, to approach rural tourism development in a holistic manner will increase the likelihood that a community will develop a tourism product that captures and fulfills the needs and interests of both the desired target markets and the local community.

All the thinking about tourism outlined here is probably best summed up by the comment of one visitor to the West, responding to a questionnaire regarding tourism development: "I think tourism is like seasoning on food. Some can make an improvement, a little more can make it perfect. A lot ruins it and makes a good thing disgusting."[20] What is served to the public as tourism needs to be very carefully prepared if it is to be palatable for both residents and visitors alike.

Notes

1. P. Long, "Tourism Makes a Difference in Rural Colorado," Insight: The American West Series, *Boulder Camera*, November 22, 1998.

2. P. Long, R. Perdue, and L. Allen, "Rural Resident Tourism Perceptions and Attitudes by Community Level of Tourism," *Journal of Travel Research* 12, no. 1 (1990): 18–23.

3. R. Perdue, P. Long, and L. Allen, "Resident Support for Tourism Development," *Annals of Tourism Research* 17, no. 4 (1990): 586–99.

4. P. Long, J. Clark, and D. Liston, *Win, Lose or Draw! Gambling with America's Small Towns* (Washington, D.C.: Aspen Institute, 1994).

5. "Opening Presentation" (5 County Rural Resort Region Symposium, December 1994, Beaver Creek, Colorado; prepared by the members of the Rural Resort Region Planning Team, Northwest Colorado Council of Governments, Frisco, Colorado).

6. *Superstructure* is a term used by some authors to describe the "services" side of the tourism industry, including but not limited to accommodations, food and beverage, retail, transportation, and information campaigns developed primarily for the vacationing or business traveler or visitor.

7. E. Moen, "Social Problems in Energy Boom Towns and the Role of Women in Their Prevention and Mitigation," in J. and J. Davenport, *The Boom Town: Problems and Promises in the Energy Vortex* (Laramie: University of Wyoming Department of Social Work, 1982), 5.

8. *Summary Report: Community Leadership and Development* (Trinidad, Colo.: Trinidad Community College, 1994), 3.

9. Ibid.

10. *National Policy Study on Rural Tourism and Small Business Development*. Prepared for United States Travel and Tourism Administration by Economics Research Associates. U.S. Department of Commerce, Washington, D.C. (1989), 5.

11. As presented by Winthrop P. Rockefeller, chairman, President's Council on Rural America, National Rural Tourism Development Conference, Kansas City, Missouri, April 1992.

12. C. Kuralt, *On the Road with Charles Kuralt* (New York: Random House, 1985), 171.

13. *Tourism Works for America* (Washington, D.C.: Travel Industry Association of America, 1997), 1.

14. Ibid., 2.

15. "Outdoor Recreation in America 1996, Executive Summary" (prepared by Roper Starch Worldwide for The Recreation Roundtable in cooperation with the Bureau of Land Management, New York, August 1996).

16. Ibid., 9.

17. P. Long and J. Nuckolls, "Organizing Resources for Rural Tourism Development: The Importance of Leadership, Planning and Technical Assistance," *Tourism Recreation Research* 19, no. 2 (1994): 19–34.

18. L. Addison, "An Approach to Community-Based Tourism Planning in the Baffin Region, Canada's Far North: A Retrospective," in *Practicing Responsible Tourism*, ed. Lynn Harrison and Winston Husbands (New York: John Wiley & Sons, 1996), 296–311.

19. W. McLaughlin, C. Black, and P. O'Connell, "The Tweed Shire Tourism Strategy: Implications of a Local Tourism Planning Process" (paper presented at the Benefits and Costs of Tourism conference, Port Stephens, NSW, Australia, October 1991).

20. J. Ap and J. Crompton, "Residents' Strategies for Responding to Tourism Impacts," *Journal of Travel Research* 32, no. 1 (1993): 50.

1. California's majestic Mt. Shasta provides the backdrop for this image of the California and Oregon Stage Company. Louis McLane, head of Wells Fargo and Company, privately observed in 1865 that riding aboard a stagecoach may have "looked very well to the lithographer," but that to passengers "it was the devil in reality." The overland stagecoach has become a symbol of the Wells Fargo Bank. (Courtesy Wells Fargo and Company)

2. Trains portaged steamboat passengers and freight around a wild stretch of whitewater on the Columbia River known as the Cascades. Photographer Carleton Watkins preserved this meeting between the side-wheeler *Oneonta* and the portage train in 1867. Probably the first tourism in the Pacific Northwest consisted of steamboat excursion travel by residents of Portland, Oregon. (Courtesy Oregon Historical Society, OrHi21112)

3. Sinclair Lewis's novel *Free Air*, a classic of the early-twentieth-century transcontinental auto travel narrative genre, was published in 1919. The book draws on the experiences of Lewis and his wife, Grace, on their 1916 trip to tell the story of Claire Boltwood, a high-society Brooklyn Heights girl, her father, an overworked business magnate, and Milt Daggett, a mechanic from Minnesota, as they tested old social conventions in new western settings. (This item is reproduced by permission of The Huntington Library, San Marino, California.)

HOW'S THE ROAD?

BY

KATHRYN HULME

"Now the joys of the road are chiefly these:
A crimson touch on the hardwood trees;
A vagrant's morning wide and blue,
In early fall when the wind walks, too;
A shadowy highway cool and brown,
Alluring up and enticing down . . ."

BLISS CARMAN

PRIVATELY PRINTED
SAN FRANCISCO, CALIFORNIA
1928

4. Kathryn Hulme's *How's the Road?* privately published in 1928, chronicles an auto tour from New York to San Francisco taken by the author and a woman friend, "Tuny," who during the course of their journey distinguish themselves from the stereotypical "girls" of the twenties. They were "good mechanics, capable of making any repair of the car"; they rejected the conventional gender restrictions of the age more and more the further west they went. (This item is reproduced by permission of The Huntington Library, San Marino, California.)

5. Still photograph from *The Tourists* (New York: Biograph Company, 1912). Mabel Normand, as the tourist Trixie, buys souvenir pottery in front of the Fred Harvey Indian Building, Albuquerque. (From the collections of the Library of Congress Moving Image Section)

6. Photograph depicting Nampeyo and members of her family during their stay at Hopi House in 1905. (Special Collections, The University of Arizona Library, Photograph, "Roof Garden Party, Hopi House" (1905); neg. no. 11,027)

7. Cover of *The Great Southwest*. Frank P. Sauerwein's *The First Santa Fe Train* appeared as a postcard as early as 1908. On the back of the postcard version of this image the caption reads, in part: "Indians watching the first Santa Fe train crossing the continent, whose advent meant so little to their minds, and so much to the white man."

8. Fred Harvey postcard, "Pueblo Indians Selling Pottery" (Detroit: Detroit Publishing, 1902). (Special Collections, the University of Arizona Library)

9. *Land of Enchantment*, by Woodrow Crumbo (1946); watercolor on paper; 17 3/4 x 23 1/2 in. (The Philbrook Museum of Art, Tulsa, Oklahoma)

10. Mural by Kenneth Adams, located in the Zimmerman Library at the University of New Mexico, commissioned by President Zimmerman in 1937. The mural plaque reads:

a. The Indian, showing his work as the artist (opposite, top).
b. The Spanish, giving a general idea of their contribution to the civilization in the area in the fields of agriculture and architecture (opposite, middle).
c. The Anglo, with scientific contributions (opposite, bottom).
d. The union of all three in the life of the Southwest (above).

The mural elicits regular protests from Chicano students at the University of New Mexico. Sylvia Rodriguez analyzes the mural's meaning in her essay "Tourism, Whiteness, and the Vanishing Anglo." (Courtesy of the Zimmerman Library)

Chapter Five

Shedding Skin and Shifting Shape: Tourism in the Modern West

Hal Rothman

Tourism is a devil's bargain, not only in the twentieth-century American West, but throughout the nation and the world. Despite its reputation as a panacea for the economic ills of places that have lost their way in the postindustrial world or for those that never previously found it, tourism typically fails to meet the expectations of communities and regions that embrace it as an economic strategy. Regions, communities, and locales welcome tourism as an economic boon, only to find that it irrevocably changes them in unanticipated and uncontrollable ways. From this one enormous devil's bargain, the dilemma of a panacea that cannot fulfill its promise and alters instead of fixes, flows an entire collection of closely related conditions that complement the process of change in overt and subtle ways. Tourism transforms culture, making it into something new and foreign; it may or may not rescue economies. As a viable option for moribund or declining places, tourism promises much, but delivers only a little, often in different forms and ways than its advocates anticipate. Its local beneficiaries come from a small segment of the population, "the growth coalition," the landowners, developers, planners, builders, real estate sales and management interests, bankers, brokers, and others.[1] The capital that sustains these interests comes from elsewhere, changing local relationships and the values that underpin them, along with their vision of place.

100

Others flounder, finding their land their greatest asset and their labor lightly valued. With tourism come unanticipated and irreversible consequences, unexpected and unintended social, cultural, economic, demographic, environmental, and political consequences that communities, their leaders, and their residents typically face unprepared. This coupling of promise and problem defies the typical mitigation processes of American society, the planning, zoning, and community sanction that historically combine to limit the impact of change.

The embrace of tourism triggers an all-encompassing contest for the soul of a place. As amorphous as this concept is, it holds one piece of the core of the devil's bargain of tourism as a form of living. All places, even untrammeled prairies or rugged deserts, have identities; people see and define them, they have intrinsic characteristics, and they welcome or repel as much based on people's definitions of them as on their innate characteristics. Human-shaped places, cities and national parks, marinas and farms, closely guard their identities, their people located within these constructions in ways that give them not only national, regional, and local affiliation but also a powerful sense of self and place in the world. That identity depends on the context of the place—is linked to its social shape as well as its economy, environment, and culture—and challenges to it threaten the status quo, especially when those challenges pull on the bonds of community by pitting different elements, elements that previously shared alliances, against one another. As these bonds fray, sub-rosa tension—there all the time but buried in the fictions of social arrangements—comes to the surface as the impact of change throws the soul of the place, any place, up for grabs.

In the twentieth-century American West, tourism initiates this contest as it regenerates myriad patterns that challenge the existing structure of communities and regions and reshape them. The initial development of tourism often seems innocuous and harmless, "beneath the radar" of outside interests, lucrative but not transformative. As places acquire the cachet of desirability with travelers, they draw people and money; the redistribution of wealth, power, and status follows, complicating local arrangements. When tourism creates sufficient wealth, it becomes too important to be left to the locals. Power moves away from local decision-makers, even those who psychically and socially invest in the ways of the new system tourism creates, and toward outside capital and its local representatives. This redistribution changes internal relations over time as it consolidates into a new dominant template or overlay for the places it develops. The new shape disenfranchises most locals as it makes some natives and most "neo-natives"—those who are attracted to the places that have become tourist towns by the traits of the transformed place—economically better off and creates a place that becomes a mirror image of itself as its identity is marketed. A series of characteristic and oft-repeated consequences results from this scenario, leaving all but a few in tourist communities questioning whether they were better off in the economic doldrums in which they lived before tourism came to town.

In this sense, tourism is the most colonial of colonial economies, not because of the sheer physical difficulty or the pain or humiliation intrinsic in its labor, but as a result of its psychic and social impact on people and their places. Tourism, and the social structure it provides, makes unknowing locals into people who look like themselves but who act and behave differently as they learn to market their place and its, and their, identity. They change every bit as much as did African workers in the copper mines of the Congo or the diamond mines of South Africa, men from rural homelands who became industrial cannon fodder. Unlike laborers in these colonial enterprises, who lived in obscurity as they labored, tourist workers face an enormous contradiction: who and what they are is crucial to visitors in the abstract; who they are as service workers is entirely meaningless. Tourist workers quickly learn that one of the most essential traits of tourist service is to mirror onto the guest what that visitor wants from you and your place in a way that affirms the visitor's self-image.

Here begins a dilemma, a place where locals must be what visitors want them to be in order to feed and clothe themselves and their families, but also must guard themselves, their souls, and their place, from those who less appreciate its special traits. They negotiate these boundaries, creating a series of "boxes" between themselves and visitors, rooms in which locals encourage visitors to feel that they have become of the place but where these locals also subtly guide visitors away from the essence of being local. The Sugar Cane Train in Maui nods in this direction as the conductor tells us his story; tourists do not much care about the stories of the cane-cutters outside the train window.[2] In this process, the visited become something else, somehow different from who they were before as they exchange the privilege of their identity. This offer to share an image of their sense of belonging for coin becomes a far more comprehensive and often more perplexing bargain than merely exchanging labor and the assets in their ground or on it for their sustenance.

This process of scripting space, both physically and psychically, defines tourist towns and resorts. All places have scripted space; the scripting of space is part and parcel of the organizing of the physical and social world for the purpose of perpetuation. Like commercial space, tourist space is specially scripted, to keep visitors at the center of the picture while simultaneously cloaking, manipulating, and even deceiving them into believing that their experience is the locals' life, reality, and view of the world. "Wasn't it wonderful here [in Hawaii] before Captain Cook showed up," a friend said to me over dinner at an exquisite shoreside restaurant in Ma'alea Bay, Maui, thoroughly swallowing the fiction of the scripted space of tourism.[3]

Despite often seductively quaint and romantic settings, seeming harmlessness, and a reputation as a "clean" industry, tourism is of a piece with the modern and postindustrial, postmodern worlds; its social structures and cultural ways are those of an extractive industry. While its environmental by-products are not the tailings piles of uranium mining, in the West, they include the spread of real estate development, the gobbling up of open space in narrow mountain valleys, the traffic and sprawl of expansive suburban communities, and the transformation of the physical environment into roads and reservoirs that provide activity and convenience for visitors. Tourism offers its visitors romanticized visions of the historic past, the natural world, popular culture, and especially of themselves. The sale of these messages, even in their least trammeled form, is what iconoclastic author Edward Abbey called "industrial tourism," the packaging and marketing of experience as commodity within the boundaries of the accepted level of convenience to the public.[4]

The most postmodern of such devices, the ones that meld the technologies, attitudes, and styles of the Age of Information, the era of the global transmission of knowledge that followed 1980, go even further. They purposely create another level of experience that masquerades or prepares for so-called authentic experience, blurring any line that may remain and often making the replica more seductive than the original. Using experience to script space in another way, to design artificial controls that seem natural and ordinary as they highlight the activity by subtly persuading the visitor that the activity is their own, this postmodern form shatters historical distinctions between the real and the unreal by producing faux replicas of experience independent of the activity from which they derive.

Las Vegas has best defined this reality in its redefinition of space, time, and meaning into constructs that serve the visitor, but this form has become ubiquitous. The climbing gym, which offers indoor "mountain climbing" and training for the initiated and uninitiated alike, also fuses these concepts. A seventy-five-foot-high climbable rock face, called Surge Rock and sponsored by Coca-Cola as a way to promote its newest soft drink, Surge, at Sega Gameworks in the Showcase Mall, a prototype upscale entertainment and commercial development that opened in 1997 on the Las Vegas Strip, took this experience to new heights. As the project debuted, Showcase developer and entrepreneur Barry Fieldman climbed the rock face; family and friends arriving at his six-year-old's birthday party watched him ascend as they rode the elevator down to the first floor, where other climbers assembled.[5]

With the varieties of experience available in the postmodern world, all tourism, from Surge Rock to the Eiffel Tower to an African safari, and even backpacking in the Bob Marshall Wilderness in Montana or following in the footsteps of proto-archaeologist Heinrich Schliemann, is scripted industrial tourism. The wealth of industrial society, its transportation technologies, its consumer goods, its emphasis on convenience, and the values of a postmodern, postconsumption culture create the surplus that allows people to select any experience they choose. Its goal is not experience, but fulfillment—experience that makes the chooser feel important, strong, powerful, a member of the "right" crowd, or whatever else they crave. Those determined to leave mainstream society in search of an individual sense of non-tourist travel are scripted into believing that backpacking in the Bob Marshall makes them unique or at least part of a rare breed, somehow intellectually and morally above other tourists. This conceit is common among elites—academics and environmentalists among them—who believe they know better than the rest of humanity. The embrace of the inherently fraudulent "ecotourism," a mere code word for an activity that so parallels the colonial tourism of Theodore Roosevelt in Africa, in the hopes of creating a better world, reveals a stunning naïveté. Finding the little out-of-the-way inn in rural Ireland no more "invents" a unique experience than does a bus tour of Las Vegas or the Universal Studios tour in Los Angeles. It merely offers a wrapper that promises certain sensibilities a self-affirming "authentic experience" in the viewer's terms. The delusion of distance from their society and the superiority of spirit and sometimes skill it connotes exists even for the climbers of Mount Everest. Even as Rob Hall, the vaunted New Zealander guide of the Himalayas, recognized his death was imminent during a tragic May 1996 ascent, he spoke to his eight-months-pregnant wife and through her, his unborn child, on a satellite phone, diminishing the idea that any form of tourism can be other than that of the global market. The expedition took place so that people who could afford it could feel personally satisfied; a total of eight people died as a result.[6] "Bagging trophy," as some caustically refer to the status side of postmodern tourism, can be dangerous as well as exhilarating.

For Americans, the geographic and cultural landscapes of a mythic American West hold these psychic trophies. The West is the location of the American creation myth, the national *sipapu*, the figurative hole in the earth from which Pueblo Indian people emerged in their story of the beginning of the world. The image of the West, especially in the conquest that occurred between 1848 and 1890, serves that same mythic purpose for Americans. The Revolutionary War has distant meaning, but in the late twentieth century, the West holds mythic sway. In the post–Civil War West, the United States emerged anew and reinvented itself, shedding slavery, sectionalism, and states' rights and becoming the American nation that persisted until its post-Watergate fragmentation. The new nation embodied in the West transcended the inherent flaws of the first republic, impaled on its own inconsistencies by the shelling of Fort Sumter; the West healed the hole in the heart of the nation born anew after its epic and cataclysmic tragedy. The revised national creation myth gave the West primacy in American life and thinking that grew from innocence and the potential for reinvention, a cachet that further marked the region's importance in a postindustrial world that increasingly depends on tourism. When Americans paid homage to their national and nationalistic roots, they did not look to Independence Hall; they went west as they believed their forefathers did, to find self and create society, to build anew from the detritus of the old.[7] This need for redefinition explains the historic and modern fixation with the West in the United States and even in Europe.

Western tourism stands at the heart of the American drama precisely because it occurs on the same stage as the national drama of self-affirmation; to Americans the West is their refuge, the home of "last best places," as writers William Kittredge and Annick Smith touted the region at the end of the 1980s, home to the mythic landscapes where Americans become whole again in the aftermath of personal or national cataclysm. This virtue and incredible burden makes tourism in the West more tantalizing and tempting, more fraught with tension and anxiety, and more full of text, subtext, and depth than anywhere else in the nation. The same activity in the West means more than elsewhere; the myth of exceptionalism has a life of its own as the Rockies rise in front of westward-bound travelers even as late as Jack Kerouac's adventures in the 1950s.[8] That peculiar standing makes western tourism a crucible in which the forces that drive American capitalism collide with growing and increasingly disparate and random forces, economic, social, cultural, and political, that shake the foundations of the modern world.

Different parts of the American West react to tourism in disparate ways. One West, urban and rural, is tourist-dependent; in states such as Nevada and Hawaii, which depend on tourism to the exclusion of other economic strategies, tourism has become an extension of state government. In both, tourism has paid the bills as it framed a postindustrial economy and postmodern culture; both also show traits of being plantation economies, run by outside capital and local overseers at the expense of the local public.[9] The identity of such places became what they marketed. Tourism there was studied, measured, and surveyed in an attempt to balance its impact with the profits it brought without alienating visitors. In another West, rural, rooted, and increasingly challenged by changing economic conditions, tourism has long been a by-product, a shadow economy to which few gave much credence. It seemed to many, especially those possessed of the myths of individualism that permeate American culture, ephemeral and unimportant, not as substantive as making things, growing food, or raising animals. In places such as 1920s

Jackson Hole, Wyoming, or southern Utah at the proclamation of the Grand Staircase–Escalante National Monument in 1996, the outright dismissal of its significance as well as its amorphousness allowed tourism to develop with little input, to function autonomously, apart from other more thoroughly measured parts of the regional economy. A third West, urban, more affluent, and more cosmopolitan, regarded tourism as an integral part of the regional mix, an essential sector of the economy that was not categorically different from the industrial sector or other service endeavor. Los Angeles and San Francisco reflexively cater to tourism as just another economic endeavor. Almost without the recognition of larger regional society, both visitor and visited, tourism acquired distinct forms in such places.

As different as they are in geography and activity, the forms of tourism create similar patterns of life. In origins, economic structure, hierarchical organization, dependence on corridors of transportation, and transformative impact on existing communities, a diverse range of places, from the Grand Canyon to Las Vegas and Disneyland, offer numerous parallels. Tourism is barely distinguishable from other forms of colonial economies. Typically founded by resident proto-entrepreneurs, the industry expands beyond local control, becomes institutionalized by large-scale forces of capital, and then grows to mirror not the values of the place, but those of the traveling public of the various moments of the twentieth century. The malleability of the industry makes the places that engage it more pliable, creating pockets of prosperity within localities that are typically limited to incoming neo-natives. Existing elites find themselves facing a trade-off. They can accept profitable but diminished status or fight with all their energy against outside forces. For ordinary people who typically limped along in many of these locales, tourism offered the promise of panacea but delivered far less. Many gave up long-standing patterns of life with the expectation that tourism would provide better material sustenance without diminishing their sense of self or place. Often it did not, leaving people who had once accepted their position in the structure of their world in an unsettled mood and economically only barely better off. As a salvation for social, cultural, and economic problems, tourism has typically fallen short; success with it can be even more devastating than failure. Tourism's economic results range from good to disastrous, but from a social perspective, no one it touches remains as they were. Its changes are powerful, profound, and typically unexpected.

The selection of tourism is a sequence of imperfect choices that muddies understanding with its promise of prosperity. It is not inherently bad for people, communities, or regions; it is a choice. But as nineteenth-century social critic William Dean Howells once observed, choice can be a curse. For many places in the contemporary American West of the 1990s, tourism offers the best available economic strategy to maintain community fabric, but places that seek it forget that the places that embraced tourism earlier in western history chose it because they had few other economic options. Tourism's greatest danger is its image as panacea for places. Community leaders hurry to imperfect choices derived from insufficient information without recognizing the potential consequences. Only the benefits, only the successes, only the flow of revenue to state, county, and local coffers, and not the increase in expenditures and the changing social picture, occupy their thoughts. The economist's fallacious dream of rational choice based on perfect information collapses as unanticipated consequences overwhelm expectations in tourist communities.[10]

Tourism is where modern capitalism ends and its postmodern equivalent, a compelling rendering of the post-1980s cultural and economic landscape, begins. The view of the shore from Lahaina Bay offers a legible geography that operates within a series of conventions that appear intelligible to inhabitants of an industrial sociocultural and economic landscape, but are really quite different. On Maui, experience is the commodity for sale; viewing the whales both epitomizes and is at the same time irrelevant to this process. Maui connotes relaxation and renewal, the respite from the clawing of the modern; its scripting is designed to promote comfort, convenience, and security. Simultaneously it emphasizes the experience of being over the comforts it offers. In this it is postmodern script, placing the visitor at the center of the picture and encouraging concern with the self far and away above any interaction with the world. The physical world is not the catalyst for experience; on Maui, it is backdrop to the self.

Postmodern capitalism is new terrain, largely unrecognizable except to those who experience it. It is not the capitalism of Andrew

Carnegie, J. P. Morgan, Henry Ford, Armand Hammer, or J. Paul Getty, but more that of Walt Disney, Bill Gates, and gaming impresario Steve Wynn. It is not national or nationalistic, but transnational and global. Its emphasis is not on the tangible of making things, of ever larger assembly lines and production processes, but in the marketing of images, of information, of spectacle. It creates information and information-processing systems and the accouterments that turn regional and national economic endeavor into a global commodity. Of equal significance, postmodern, postindustrial capitalism produces images that convey emotions, hope and contentment chief among them, as well as conduits through which information can travel. It is a form at once substantial and inconsequential, crucial yet trivial, meaningful yet ephemeral. Its sociocultural impact is vast; in its ability to move information, and as a result to move more traditional forms of economic endeavor such as assembly-line work, postmodern global capitalism is truly revolutionary. Postindustrial capitalism has changed the very meaning of economic endeavor, providing new ways to produce wealth in a transformation as profound as the industrial revolution.

Industrial capitalism began in a productive ethos, a work ethic rightly or wrongly labeled "Protestant," and an ideal of making things large and small with an ebullient joy that helped make consumption of these goods an afterthought. Pragmatism permeated the production phase of American capitalism, that great expansion of productivity associated with the years between 1865 and 1914. It focused on the transformation of raw material into usable commodity such as steel or finished product such as a sewing machine or telephone. The shelves of goods available in the "palaces of consumption," the department stores, were the signature of the age. Utility defined this phase of capitalism, manifesting in the time and motion studies of Frederick Winslow Taylor and the subsequent invention of the assembly line, as well as in transportation systems, such as railroads and electric street cars, that utilized industrial technologies.[11]

Intimately connected to production was consumption, the dominant feature of the stage of industrialization that gathered momentum following World War I. The spectacular consumption of the late nineteenth century, labeled "conspicuous" by social critic Thorstein Veblen, triggered an emphasis on the status rather than the utility of goods. This continued with the advent of mass technologies such as the radio, the moving picture, and later television, and reached its pinnacle in the refinement of details that marked the planned obsolescence built into the graciously lined and finned vehicles of the immediate post–World War II era. Consumption became first a means to an end in American society and later an end in itself; before collecting toys took hold, consumption fueled production. Consumption was about using and enjoying the largesse of American economic development, a concept that was foreign as industrialization began in the United States, but that grew in significance in fits and starts until it gathered full force during the 1920s. That enjoyment made desirable, or commodified, went hand-in-hand with the rise of advertising, the widespread availability of credit, and the increased social importance of the self. It reached a pinnacle during the American cultural revolution of the 1960s, articulated with a razor-sharp edge by social observer and wag Tom Wolfe in his famed essay from the 1970s, "The Me Decade."[12] In this world, the needs of the individual ruled, without social checks upon them. The ethic of tangible consumption became the dominant feature in the transformation of the nation from one that avowed deferred gratification to one that collectively and individually sought fulfillment in an instant.

First industrial-age Americans made things; then they bought them. In the postindustrial world, Americans became consumers of more than tangible goods, of the spirit and meaning of things rather than of their physical properties. What Americans of a certain class could touch and hold no longer exclusively granted the security and importance to which its possessors were accustomed; when anyone could lease a BMW, the elite needed more: the control of feelings, emotion, identity, and modes of understanding that signified status, a way to differentiate themselves from the increasingly luxurious mass cultural norm. In a world short on time, in which only the very rich and the very poor possessed it and only one of those two groups had the means to utilize it, a new way to define the self as special came to the fore. In turn, this created a new form of commodification that came to dominate the American and international landscape. Corporations packaged and people purchased what they felt granted them identity, but that identity ceased to follow traditional iconography and became a product of the international culture marketplace.[13] Modernism had been about finding the individual's place in the world of machines; the mergers and downsizing of postindustrialism rendered the individual irrelevant as postmodernism made the self the only meaningful reference point. Ultimately, this affirmed a series of trappings, tangible and shapeless, that proclaimed an identity of the self, a far cry from the national identity of the production ethos. Adorning the self became a goal, but adorning not only with jewelry and clothing. An intangible dimension gained great significance.

Tourism, in which people acquire intangibles—experience, cachet, proximity to celebrity—became the successor to industrial capitalism, the endpoint in a process that transcended consumption and made living a function of accouterments. It created a culture, languid and bittersweet, and as writer Mark Edmundson put it "very, very self-contained . . . [with] little fire, little passion to be found," that had as its object participation in consumption.[14] Yet even the young recognized that this culture was equally post-tangible, not about consuming things but about possessing experience. Material goods no longer fulfilled and created status in the United States and Europe. Only a very few products were so elite that they could not be widely owned, and even those few could be suitably copied. Goods were not sufficient; status became a function of time spent, of context, of address, of place, of table in a restaurant. Although the water was the same and the towels no softer and only marginally fluffier at the Grand Wailea's pool than at any other, the pool contained a trained aestheticism that Americans, and world citizens, mistook for better. The pilfered wristbands there provided entrée into this world, the look of prosperity and status, wrapped around the intangible of presence in the "right" places. In the postindustrial, postmodern world, people collect the difference embodied in travel experience as some once collected Fabergé eggs. The act of travel, especially on terms dictated by the self, has come to mark the self-proclaimed well-rounded person and has allowed individuals to define themselves as unique. Travel as defining experience has become a new form of religion, a harbinger of a new way in which to believe and especially value the self. Bumper stickers will soon sport sayings like "she who has been the most places and stayed in luxury in all of them wins" instead of the more passé "he who dies with the most toys wins."

Tourism is the archetype of the service economy, the market of the future. Its form resembles that of the industrial world and derives wealth from it, but tourism is new, postindustrial in the way it competes economically and in the transnational global patterns of capital distribution it reveals. The seemingly nondescript Sunnyside Inn lodge and restaurant on the shores of Lake Tahoe appears certain to be a one-owner lodge, an old-time resort. Here in a home built by Captain Kendrick of the Schlage Lock Company early in the century, visitors receive an elegant and relaxing experience, real hospitality like the captains of industry received. A close look at the walls reveals a line of photos of peer restaurants, other members of the T S Restaurant chain—in Kaanapali, Lahaina, Malibu, and Huntington Beach.[15] The Sunnyside Inn has not belonged to family operators since 1986, when San Francisco restauranteurs bought the inn and restored it to its former elegance. Sunnyside Inn was one of more than one dozen restaurants, all scripted to offer unique experience, to obviate in the place of each in one management group. This faux chain, precisely unlike chain restaurants such as Denny's in the diversity of ambience, but adhering to the formula, shows the ways in which activities packaged as distinct have structural parallels. These too are networks, shaped by the scripting of space, formed of capital, of influence, of power, of attraction, but they outwardly deny their association with each other in a way that industrial networks never did.

Nor is participation in this economy the same as in its industrial counterpart. Selling ambience, experience, and identity has little in common with selling durable goods except for the physical act of selling. Little that can be touched and handled changes hands in the tourist transaction; the souvenirs are big business, but they are emblems of the point, not the point itself. What occurs is more complicated and ambiguous than a typical material sales transaction in American society. A feeling is transmitted and perhaps shared; a way of living is expressed; a mode of behavior, be it the ethos of skiing, the appreciation of the Mona Lisa, or the way to hold your cards at the blackjack table, is offered and recognized if not always understood. These markers of belonging, of being part of the fashionable, the exciting, the new, become critical in a world where most earlier indicators of status have become easily attainable, and as a result have lost their ability to differentiate from the masses. In this new form of exchange, something meaningful but not tangible, typically the identity, way of life, or feel of a place and its people, seems to be offered up for a price. But not always.

A view of tourism from the perspective of the visited and not the visitor highlights a different set of relationships in the transaction between visitor and visited. For locals and incoming "neo-native" workers, people who embraced the constructed ethos of a place and generally become willing to be underemployed there to imbibe its essence, the embrace of tourism leads to significant changes. A world in which people do what appears to be the same thing but in a different way, with a different feel, becomes first characteristic and then overwhelming. Sun Valley, Idaho, native and writer John Rember cogently describes this situation; "There are worse lives than those lived in museums," he mused about his own fate, "worse shortcomings than a lack of authenticity."[16] As problematic as is the concept of authenticity, Rember's definition holds much weight. "Authentic" to him is a world that serves its residents ahead of outsiders, that grows crops, hunts animals for the table instead of sport, and is tuned to the rhythms of the land; it is agricultural and industrial, the forms called first and second nature by noted thinker William Cronon.[17] The tourist world inverts that principle, opening a new realm of existence, a third nature, much to the distress of Edward Abbey (who made a living writing about experience without acknowledging his own role in creating change) and locals who remember a time before tourism descended upon them and altered their lives.

The world Rember recalls and eloquently describes contains Cronon's first and second nature. First nature, the prehuman landscape, and I would add, its organization by humans for subsistence purposes, contained essentially hunting and gathering, herding, and small-scale agrarian regimes. It is not devoid of humans, for that would render it meaningless and abstract, a time beyond time for the human race; instead first nature describes hundreds of centuries of relationship between a species and their world, which they typically could affect only in small ways. The prototype for second nature became Cronon's Chicago, a place apart from first nature but intrinsically tied to it, its utility transformed by proto-industrial and later heavy industrial processes, forms of organization, and physical and intellectual structures and symbols.[18] If first nature was organized to feed and clothe the self and the family, second nature's forms were designed to market to the world.

This "third nature," like postindustrial economies and postmodern thinking, focuses not on what can be touched, but on what can be felt in a personal and emotional sense. It is a natural world organized to acquire intangibles—experience and cachet, to grant identity, to regard nature not as source of food, but instead as fount of psychic energy and emotion. Faux or real, scenery evokes powerful emotions. The *fin de siècle* tourist understood the Grand Canyon as an affirmation of the nation. The postmodern tourist sees it not as external untrammeled nature, but in its impact on the self. Surge Rock is real to people who do not see El Capitan as more than a climbing rock; it provokes similar respect because for the self, it shares the same purpose with El Capitan. Third nature is intangible, ungrasped by the hands. It is ethereal; only in the mind and maybe even the heart can its significance exist.

Yet even those who remember a world before the tourism of third nature and sometimes resent the present cannot live without tourism, for it provides them a promise of permanence in place, a kind of importance, and income. Where Rember's ways of making a living never existed or have become tenuous, where the power of social structure has weakened and frayed, where many or even most have little to look forward to except the drudgery of poverty and irrelevance, the promise of tourism, and often the physical changes and attendant growth it creates, provide hope and the glimmer of a future. Tourism begins as panacea for real problems but becomes addictive. Its promise of vitality appears to offer a way to do better than survive, merely to bump along near the bottom in eternal mind-numbing stasis, a way to dream of better in a reality much the same. It is as seductive as is a tourist's view from a Zodiac in Lahaina harbor.

These multiple tensions play in ambiguous and multifaceted ways in the development of a tourist economy. The selection or acceptance of tourism as a strategy forces a new characterization of the virtues of place, different from its previous shape. When AMFAC developed Kaanapali as a resort, it evaluated the area differently than it did for sugar production. Tourism also illuminates a working description of the local power structure, soon to change as a result of the industry. These two features define place, often to the consternation of people who perceive their position in a manner different from which it becomes ascribed. Here John Rember's fictional characters live, here the "real" of the local world separates from the perceived real that visitors are encouraged to embrace as locals deftly guide them away from their own essence. At this location, the tension between the various polarities of these different world views finds its manifestation.

Tourism turns place and people into something different, but few can do without its benefits. It brings new neighbors, who often do not share existing values, but those newcomers are a source of prosperity. In the West, tourism encourages the marketing of something different than the beef grazed on local grass, the timber in nearby forests, or the riches buried deep in the ground. While these too can be exercises in colonialism that impress a structure upon the town, they require only local backs, not their hearts or minds as well. In tourism, the very identity of place becomes its economic sustenance, and in that transformation is a complicated and paradoxical situation for the people of a place.

In the post–World War II era, the basic three overlapping and intertwined forms of tourism—heritage or cultural tourism, recreational tourism, and entertainment tourism—melded into images of their earlier incarnations.[19] Heritage and recreational tourism in the West, historically linked by geography, developed closer ties as the tastes of the American public changed. Entertainment tourism eventually included both recreational and heritage tourism within its broad dimensions, packaging experience in resorts and national parks and mimicking what these forms offered in the packaged unreality of Disneyland, theme parks, and even Las Vegas. The result was an industry that was sufficiently malleable to weave straw into gold. As in the children's fairy tale about the miller's daughter, there was a steep price to pay for the trick: the cultural, environmental, and psychic transformation of place. Tourism made new places that looked like their predecessors and occupied the same geography, but ultimately all the past and future shared in such places was the physical attributes of the place.

The approach of tourism also frayed the bonds of community. Ties within communities exist on two levels: actual bonds of connection and agreed-upon fictions of community. In this latter category, people paper over the differences between them in an effort to maintain the semblance of community. They stipulate that their disagreements are matters of conscience and belief that divide people of good character and intent. The embrace of tourism shattered such fictions, pitting different elements against each other, those who stood to benefit from the changes against those whose economic status would be driven downhill as a result. Such tension is not unusual in any kind of community; especially in small tourist or resort towns, the destruction of the fiction that all have the best interests of the community at heart led to a rending of the social fabric. Those who stood to benefit, the members of the growth coalition, embraced the new, sometimes with terrifying alacrity; those whom this economic change left in stasis or decline seethed, resented, and sometimes resisted.

These elements banded together and developed a range of strategies to halt, slow, deflect, or reverse the changes that tourism brought. A continuum of response among those threatened evolved, taking all forms from resistance to negotiation to acceptance to denial, as places defined themselves in terms of their past, which often seemed far more palatable than the present and future. In highly educated and sophisticated communities, filled with neo-natives from the elite groups in American society, such resistance could be powerful and all-encompassing. The loosely defined rubric of "quality of life" served as the concept behind such efforts. In communities with greater affinity to accept power from above, with fewer people who felt control over the fate of their place, such actions often consisted of grumbling disguised as social critique. In all cases, the right to challenge change was conveyed through self-identification rituals that had social, cultural, and sometimes economic traits. These rituals, ranging from photographs of the people of Aspen lined up on the local rugby field next to markers connoting the year they arrived to commercials reminding Las Vegans of "how it used to be before the volcano, before the pyramid," proved local and neo-native identity and strengthened ties within the wide group that was no less than ambivalent about the changes tourism caused.[20]

As a solution to the social and economic problems of the colonial status inherited from the nineteenth-century West, the industry has vast limitations. The "sink" of economic strategies, the last resort of moribund communities and states, the bottom to which all economies flow, tourism is employed by local leaders as a solution to the problems of places with declining industries. Tourism required no special skill of its employees save a willingness to be gracious and attentive. Operators of tourist enterprises rarely required tax abatements and local dollars to support the industry, and the retail trade generated by tourism filled the coffers of most western states with sales tax revenue. Tourism often became a response to economic desperation. It served as a replacement economy for declining industries. Viewed through the rosiest of lenses, it promised that a community could retain its fabric and character as it brought prosperity.

Unlike traditional industries, which often brought a labor force that became socialized to local norms, tourism came replete with transient newcomers. Labor followed tourism, as did managers and other supervisory personnel. So did neo-natives, people drawn to tourist destinations for their charm and amenities, for their *mise èn scene*, who found themselves embracing a fixed moment in local time. The tourists themselves became a strong influence, objects of contempt and gratitude, but harbingers of a range of experience beyond that of most locals. The need for tourists to experience something that they defined as real but that they could quickly understand compelled change. Locals who expected to be who they were became who their visitors wanted them to be; increasingly these purveyors of local service ceased to be local at all. Neo-natives replaced locals, creating the oddly postmodern spectacle of newcomers imitating locals for visitors to give those outsiders what they were paying for: reality as the tourist understood it.

A paradox resulted: local communities that embraced tourism expected that they would be visited by many people but that mostly their lives would remain the same. They did not anticipate, nor were they prepared for, the ways in which tourism would change them, the rising cost of property in their town, the traffic, the self-perception that the work they did was not important, the diminishing sense of pride in work and ultimately in community, and the tears in the social fabric that followed. Many found selling themselves more complicated than selling the minerals in their ground or the beef raised on their ranches. With diminishing options, tourism was sometimes all there was.

Western tourism typifies the impact of the industry in places that rely on it throughout the world. With the exception of the belt from Seattle to San Diego, the West remains an economic colony, supported by federal and outside dollars, subject to both extraregional and intraregional influences, seeking to assert independence and to control its destiny, that finds itself with the economic structure and sociocultural issues of a colony hardened beyond transfiguration. The structure of these communities and their evolution, the way they utilize transient and semipermanent labor, and their constant reinvention as new forms of themselves highlights the problems of tourist-based economies. Identity becomes malleable as national chains, many of them resort-based, replace local businesses. These stores become ubiquitous, obscuring local business and culture to a traveling public that is seeing just what it saw at home in a different setting—in the process, affirming home, travel destination, and self. This homogenization and increasing uniformity reflect rather than foreshadow transformation. Although the arrival of such businesses illustrates the increased economic importance of tourist communities, it also spells the end of existing cultures. Often this arrival amounts to "killing the goose that laid the golden egg." The inherent problem of communities that succeed in attracting so many people is that the presence of those very people destroys the cultural and environmental amenities that made the place special.

This is the core of the complicated devil's bargain that is twentieth-century tourism in the American West. Success creates the seeds of its own destruction as more and more people seek the experience of an "authentic" place transformed to seem more "authentic." In search of "lifestyle" instead of life, these seekers of identity and amenity transform what they touch beyond recognition. Things that look the same are not the same; actions that are the same acquire different meaning. In the process, tourists validate the transformations they cause; local will must bend to them as it deflects them, all the while fostering a grumbling social critique often indistinguishable from nostalgia for the world they have demolished. The tensions of industrial capitalism take on new shape. Third nature, nature as spectacle, develops an ethos that claims similarity to first nature rather than to the industrial second nature that provides its wealth. Tourism complicates; it defines and redefines life after industrialization. It is different yet the same. Western tourism sells us what we are, what we as a nation of individuals need to validate ourselves, to make us what we want to be. In that process, we as tourists change all that we encounter. Making us what we want to be means shaping other places and people along with ourselves. This is the fault line of tourism, its Grand Canyon.

Notes

1. John R. Logan and Harvey L. Molotch, *Urban Fortunes: The Political Economy of Place* (Berkeley: University of California Press, 1987); Karl Kim, "Tourism on Our Terms: Tourism Planning in Hawaii," (Western Governors' Association, 1991), 14.

2. Dean McCannell, *The Tourist: A New Theory of the Leisure Class* (New York: Schocken Books, 1976), 91–98.

3. I owe the concept of scripted space to Norman M. Klein, "The Politics of Scripted Space: [Las] Vegas and Reno" (keynote address, Nevada Historical Society Fifth Biennial Conference on Nevada History, May 20, 1997); Cynthia Weiss, conversation, February 1993; Mike Davis, *City of Quartz: Excavating the Future in Los Angeles* (New York: Verso, 1991).

4. Edward Abbey, *Desert Solitaire* (Tucson: University of Arizona Press, 1968, 1988), 54–70.

5. I attended this party; many thanks to Michael P. Cohen for unpacking the paradigm of climbing gyms as he explained his unpublished paper, "The Climbing Gym: An Environmental History."

6. Jon Krakauer, *Into Thin Air: A Personal Account of the Mt. Everest Disaster* (New York: Villard, 1997).

7. Pauline Maier, *American Scripture: Making the Declaration of Independence* (New York: Alfred A. Knopf, 1997); Alan Taylor, "Pluribus," *New Republic* 216, no. 26 (June 30, 1997): 34–38.

8. William Kittredge and Annick Smith, eds., *The Last Best Place: A Montana Anthology* (Helena: Montana Historical Society, 1988; reprint Seattle: University of Washington Press, 1991); David Wrobel, *The End of American Exceptionalism: Frontier Anxiety from the Old West to the New Deal* (Lawrence: University Press of Kansas, 1993).

9. Kim, "Tourism on Our Terms," 8–9.

10. William Dean Howells, "The Problem of the Summer," in *Literature and Life* (New York: Harper Brothers, 1902), 216–17; Gary S. Becker, *Accounting for Tastes* (Cambridge: Harvard University Press, 1996); Patrick Long, "Win, Lose, or Draw?: Gambling with America's Small Towns" (Washington, D.C.: Aspen Institute, 1994).

11. Daniel T. Rodgers, *The Work Ethic in Industrial America, 1850–1920* (Chicago: University of Chicago Press, 1978); William Leach, *Land of Desire: Merchants, Power, and the Rise of a New American Culture* (New York: Random House, 1993); T. J. Jackson Lears, *Fables of Abundance: A Cultural History of Advertising in America* (New York: Basic Books, 1996).

12. Leach, *Land of Desire;* Stuart Ewen, *Captains of Consciousness: Advertising and the Social Roots of Consumer Culture* (New York: McGraw-Hill, 1976); Tom

Wolfe, "The Me Decade and the Third Great Awakening," in *Mauve Gloves and Madmen, Clutter and Vine and Other Stories, Sketches, and Essays* (New York: Farrar, Straus, and Giroux, 1976); David Halberstam, *The Fifties* (New York: Villard Books, 1993).

13. Christopher Lasch, *The Revolt of the Elites: And the Betrayal of Democracy* (New York: W. W. Norton, 1995).

14. Mark Edmundson, "On the Uses of a Liberal Education: As Lite Entertainment for Bored College Students," *Harper's* 295, no. 1768 (September 1997): 40–41.

15. Sunnyside Inn 50th Anniversary Menu, Summer 1997; n.a., T S Restaurants, Hawaii and California, copy possession of the author.

16. John Rember, "On Going Back to Sawtooth Valley," in William Studebaker and Rick Ardinger, eds., *Where the Morning Light's Still Blue: Personal Essays about Idaho* (Moscow: University of Idaho Press, 1994), 88; on the problems of the idea of authenticity, see James Clifford, *The Predicament of Culture : Twentieth-Century Ethnography, Literature, and Art* (Cambridge: Harvard University Press, 1988), and Clifford, *Routes: Travel and Translation in the Late Twentieth Century* (Cambridge: Harvard University Press, 1997).

17. William Cronon, *Nature's Metropolis: Chicago and the Great West, 1848–1900* (New York: W. W. Norton, 1991); xvii, 56–57.

18. Cronon, *Nature's Metropolis*, 265–67.

19. For more on this typology of tourism see Hal Rothman, *Devil's Bargains: Tourism in the Twentieth-Century American West* (Lawrence: University Press of Kansas, 1998), "Introduction," 10–28.

20. Douglas C. Comer, *Ritual Ground: Bent's Old Fort, World Formation, and the Annexation of the Southwest* (Berkeley: University of California Press, 1996); Andrés Résendez, "Caught between Profit and Ritual" (Ph.D. diss., University of Chicago, 1997); many thanks to Tom Latousek for alerting me to the existence of this ritual; Palace Station commercial aired on Las Vegas local television, January–April, 1997.

Processes: Tourism and Cultural Change

The essays in Part II offer insights into the ways in which tourism in the West has changed and developed and the effects that those processes have had on tourists and on the people they visit. The essays return us to some of the themes explored in Part I's essays on perceptions of tourists and the toured upon. Historians Carlos Schwantes and Marguerite Shaffer, literary scholar Leah Dilworth, and anthropologist Sylvia Rodriguez provide case studies of tourism's development and impact.

In "No Aid and No Comfort" Schwantes surveys the linkage between transportation development and tourism development in the northern West—the state of Oregon, and the territories of Washington, Idaho, and Montana—from the mid to the late nineteenth century. While stagecoaches may be steeped in frontier romance, those who ventured in them experienced extreme physical and even, in some cases, mental discomfort. Early western steamboat travel was perhaps a little less physically taxing, but mentally more so, as passengers worried constantly about boiler explosions. With the arrival of railroads in the northern West came easier travel and massive advertising campaigns to promote tourism. Successful western tourism promotion involved offering the public a semblance of frontier wildness and wilderness, but with an accompanying abundance of real comfort and safety—things the steamboats and stagecoaches were less able to offer. A century later, improved transportation has rendered the northern West even more accessible and the comfort levels are far greater; yet the passion for returning to wildness, reentering "frontier environments," but without "frontier concerns," is still at the heart of tourism in the region. It is worth mentioning, too, that the "virtual West," the celluloid West that has graced movie and television screens for a century now, is the most instant, and ever more facile means of transportation to a region rich in movement and mythic imagery.

While Schwantes explores part of the physical infrastructure of tourism (the vehicles that transported tourists to sites) and the advertising efforts of stagecoach, steamboat, and later railroad companies to present places in the northern West in the second half of the nineteenth century, Dilworth focuses more squarely on the early-twentieth-century efforts of the Fred Harvey Company and the Atchison, Topeka and Santa Fe Railroad (AT&SF) to present the native peoples of the Southwest. Dilworth's "Tourists and Indians in Fred Harvey's Southwest" focuses on the tourists, too, and the ways in which a region and some of its inhabitants were marketed to them. She notes that the Fred Harvey Company and the AT&SF presented a version of southwestern Indian life that actually said very little about the inhabitants of that region, but one that speaks volumes about the desires, expectations, and anxieties of the white, middle-class American tourists who visited.

By promoting Indians as "lost cultures," subdued and dying races, tourist promoters effectively undermined the possibility of meaningful cultural exchanges between the visited and their visitors. Apache Indians and Hispanic people were not a part of the picture presented to the touring public by the Fred Harvey Company. Those groups did not fit into the popular Anglo image of the Southwest's resident peoples as peaceful, primitive folk. The prescribed boundaries of the touristic exchange could not be broken, and, as a consequence, little of true cultural value was exchanged between Anglos and Indians.

In "Seeing America First" Shaffer examines various early-twentieth-century efforts to generate interest in the nation's own natural wonders and cultural treasures over those of Europe. Adopted by the Great Northern Railway in 1910, the "See America First" slogan became the watchword of western tourist promotion for the following two decades or so. Shaffer focuses particularly on how various promoters of western tourism sought to define the meaning of sites for tourists. Yet, for all these efforts, the tourists, while inspired by the slogan, demonstrated a good deal of individual initiative. Transcontinental auto tourists were introduced to a culture of the road at automobile camps along the way and came to appreciate the nation more as they "discovered" what they perceived to be "true Americans." They did, in fact, experience the openness, freedom, and friendliness of the West that the promoters emphasized. They also contrasted those qualities with the over-civilization and urban claustrophobia of the East. A good number of the cross-country automobilers were women and, as Shaffer notes, their frequent breaks with accepted social convention and their entry into masculine worlds belied their presumed "refinement."

Rodriguez, like Dilworth, focuses on the Southwest and on the Anglo-Indian touristic exchange. In "Tourism, Whiteness and the Vanishing Anglo" she explores how "whiteness" has served as a deeply invisible or unmarked racial category and how the search for ethnic and racial "otherness"—that is, ethnic tourism—has nurtured Anglo hegemony in the region. She explains that as the Anglo population has expanded in southwestern tourist towns such as Taos and Santa Fe, Anglos have increasingly disappeared from the art, sculpture, and other forms of cultural representation in the region. She illustrates this process by which "material reality is reversed or inverted through symbols" through an examination of southwestern art, sculpture, and cultural iconography.

Like Dilworth, Rodriguez notes that the tourist has begun to emerge as a satirical figure in southwestern folk art. But this is the undercurrent; the prevailing trend has been one of Anglo dominance and utilization of the theme of the "ethnic other," from the efforts of the Fred Harvey Company in the early twentieth century up to the present. Anglos may be vanishing from the Southwest's cultural imagery, yet at the same time they are expanding their presence and control over the region through the selective representation of its other peoples.

Taken together, these four essays highlight how tourism promoters have created highly specific and selective images of western peoples and places. The essays also stress that tourism has real cultural, economic, and political effects on both the visited and visitors. What's more, the essays emphasize that these processes of historical and cultural change are complex ones that do not lend themselves to easy generalizations.

Chapter Six

No Aid and No Comfort: Early Transportation and the Origins of Tourism in the Northern West

Carlos A. Schwantes

Travel was not new to the northern West in the 1880s, but tourists from outside the region were still a rarity. The state of Oregon and the hinterland territories of Washington, Idaho, and Montana were so geographically remote from Anglo population centers of the East Coast and Europe that they remained well beyond the reach of all but the most venturesome sightseers. Even after through passenger trains first threaded their way across the northern West on a daily basis in 1883, most tourists from the East still preferred to vacation in California or Colorado because of the considerable extra time and money required to travel to the far Northwest—not to mention the lack of good tourist accommodations.

Regional foodways and homespun dress styles—even the way the scattered residents of the far Northwest reckoned the passage of time—must have seemed rustic to visitors. Back in mid-1865 the *Idaho World,* a newspaper published in a mining town north of Boise, had observed (on what must have been an exceedingly slow news day) that "the difference in time between Idaho City and New York is about two hours and forty minutes; between San Francisco and this place about thirty-five minutes. When it is 12 o'clock at Idaho City it is about twenty minutes to 3 o'clock in New York and twenty-five minutes past 11 o'clock in San Francisco." The curiosity was not the odd fractional differences. Until railroads divided North

America into modern time zones in the mid-1880s, dozens of local standards prevailed. Rather, it was the newspaper's repeated use of the word "about." Until railroads insisted on accurate time measured to the minute, standards were less precise, and "about time" was good enough for the scattered communities of the far Northwest. Space too acquired a new meaning, especially in terms of how much of it separated the northern West from cities of the East and Midwest until completion of a northern transcontinental railroad in 1883.[1]

Beginning in the 1850s on the lower Columbia River and in the 1860s on the upper Missouri River, the first of many steamboats churned across the inland waters of the Northwest. From river landings a growing network of stagecoach lines extended reliable transportation to mining and military outposts that lay well beyond the reach of the region's navigable waterways. Pioneer settlers saluted both the steamboat and stagecoach as symbols of modern civilization, though seldom did they equate those two early modes of transportation with tourism.

For instance, in the spring of 1861 the first steamboat battled its way up the Columbia and Snake rivers to reach the site of what is now Lewiston, Idaho. The new settlement, a merchant outpost that sprang up almost overnight to supply Idaho and Montana gold camps during the greatest mining rush the Pacific Slope had experienced since California in 1849, was located more than seven hundred feet above sea level and more than four hundred miles from the Pacific Ocean. For steamboats to regularly penetrate that far inland without the aid of a canal or locks was an amazing accomplishment. It prompted one journalist to observe that not fifteen years earlier the Clearwater Valley above Lewiston "was a howling wilderness, and a white man carried his life in his hands, who dared to venture in these parts," but traveling now by steamboat, "gentlemen seated on the forward guard view the scenery, smoke Havana cigars, and quaff Champagne cock-tails. The daily papers penetrate here, and St. Louis news is read here in seventeen days after date." It was a strange feeling, "that of whirling along by steam where so few years before the Indian and the trader had toiled through the virgin forest, bending under the weight of their canoes." The new transportation technology delighted travelers accustomed to the rigors of travel by horseback or canoe, yet a journey of any substantial distance across the northern West in the 1860s and 1870s still meant a slow, tedious, and often dangerous ordeal that held little appeal for most tourists.[2]

The region's first commercial transportation links dated from the late 1840s and early 1850s, when travel between the far Northwest and the rest of the United States invariably entailed a long and circuitous odyssey. Upon leaving Oregon's Willamette Valley, for instance, a traveler bound for the East Coast had to sail first west and then south before finally heading in the logical direction to reach Boston, Baltimore, or any other population center located east of the Rocky Mountains. In other words, passengers, mail, and express had to first journey down the Columbia River and south along the Pacific Coast to make steamship or stagecoach connections in San Francisco. For better or for worse—and even for the most seasoned travelers it was unquestionably for worse—anyone who entered or left the Oregon Country by commercial transportation had to choke back their fears of the entrance to the Columbia River. Dangerous sandbars and currents caused much dread then; and even at the beginning of the twenty-first century, with modern aids to navigation, dredging, and Coast Guard protection, the area still commands respect from masters of small and medium-size vessels, who must carefully calculate winds, tides, and currents to predict the best time to cross the Columbia bar safely.

Not until 1860 did stagecoaches at last link Portland and California; and not until 1864 did a union of steamboats and stagecoaches provide travelers with a shortcut east from Portland along the Columbia River and Oregon Trail to a connection with overland stagecoaches in Salt Lake City. Until then, just about the only long-distance travelers able to avoid the Columbia bar were settlers in scattered villages along Puget Sound and in the Rogue River gold country just north of the Oregon-California border.

The travail of travel was likewise a burden weighing on settlers on the opposite side of the Rocky Mountains in future Montana, where in 1860 the first steamboat reached the head of navigation on the Missouri River at Fort Benton to offer commercial transportation between there and Saint Louis. Again, few people who made the trip could recommend it to any but the most venturesome tourists. A steamboat journey from Saint Louis to central Montana was simply too long (two months or more each way) and the daily discomforts too many. The alternative, long-distance travel by stage-coach, had even less to recommend it.

On the Central Overland route connecting the Missouri River with the Pacific Coast, stagecoaches were strictly utilitarian vehicles. They did not normally advertise for or attempt to cater to tourists, and most tourists would have found several weeks of stagecoaching along dusty trails crossing Kansas, Nebraska, Colorado, Wyoming, Utah, Nevada, and California to be unbearable. Stagecoaches later became popular, even romantic, vehicles providing day trips within national parks like Yellowstone and Yosemite, and even today they haul tourists around Yellowstone. The overland stagecoach has become the symbol of Wells Fargo Bank, but it is well to remember that when Louis McLane, general manager and later president of Wells Fargo, wrote his wife in 1865 about artistic depictions of travel by coach, he said, "I thought staging looked very well to the litho-grapher, but was the devil in reality."[3]

Lithographic images, Hollywood, and popular fiction have romanticized stagecoach travel across the frontier West. True, when the daily or tri-weekly stagecoach reached a typical settlement in the sagebrush, an enthusiastic crowd of townspeople invariably awaited it. Stage time was often the highlight of the day. Drivers enjoyed the public attention and delighted in making a dramatic entry. They took great personal pride in both the appearance of their coach and its well-groomed horses. But as McLane understood, the passengers themselves seldom found much that was romantic or glamorous about stage travel, except when viewed from hindsight. Rarely was a trip of any length without its trials and discomforts. "One of the most tedious journeys that can be made is that in a stage-coach, if one is compelled to be a cramped denizen of its hard seats for several days and nights at a time."[4]

In addition to the crowding and intense jolting that caused passengers to complain bitterly of aching bones and bruised flesh, there were the occasional torments of rain and dust that seeped through the ill-fitting side curtains. Not surprisingly, it was claimed that many a seasoned veteran of stagecoach travel preferred to carry his twenty-five-pound allotment of personal luggage in bottles and flasks, the contents of which dulled the miseries of the journey. One traveler from the East wrote that until he went by stage to California, "I had always considered the physical essentials to be food and drink, but soon I learned they were drink and food."[5]

Winter weather so increased operating difficulties that some of the smaller stage lines simply quit running for the duration. Others struggled through: "All night long we rode, slapping our hands and stomping our feet to keep the blood circulating, gradually ascending the mountains [Siskiyous], and keeping the great dipper always before us." In summer a coach might be traveling constantly within a cloud of dust raised by the horses' hoofs, and the searing heat inside might rise to one hundred and ten degrees. Drivers and their horses were often cloaked in gray dust from the sagebrush plains, and after scarcely more than an hour's ride on a dry, hot day, passengers looked like coal miners following a hard day's work. "From head to foot they were covered with grime, their faces streaked with rivulets of mud from trickling sweat or tears from dust-inflamed eyes." Alkali made passengers' skin sore and rough and burned their eyes and noses.[6]

On occasion a passenger might become suddenly ill or, as happened in March 1866 on the Overland stage, turn violently insane. The crazed pilgrim stabbed a fellow traveler several times, killed another man with a pistol, and injured a third before he himself was finally shot and mortally wounded. When a passenger used whiskey too freely to clear his throat of dust, he might become drunk enough to create excitement among his fellow travelers. It is no wonder that Overland passengers relished the opportunity every ten or twelve miles to get out and stretch a minute or two while the horses were changed.

As for a nighttime journey by coach, most travelers recalled only the overwhelming fatigue it induced. That was when the long day of lumbering along dusty and rutted roads frayed passengers' nerves and caused tempers to flare. A good night's sleep was out of the question. After darkness fell the best any harried traveler could expect was to doze in his place or, space permitting, to curl up like a dog in an empty seat corner. Passengers forced to ride upright with an elbow resting in the window strap, or a leg extended across a bulky mail sack, or a shoulder supporting the head of a snoring companion were likely to remember an all-night trip as an ordeal. To add to their discomfort, in the dead of night one of the coach's big wheels might drop into a deep rut or hole and cause the coach to lurch suddenly forward on its flexible suspension. Half a dozen drowsy travelers might tumble together into one heap on the floor. "Get used to it," was the advice given by veteran stagemen. Travelers had plenty of time to adapt to these hardships because a stagecoach journey from the Missouri Valley to the far Northwest usually took as long as thirty days *each way.*

By comparison, travel aboard a river steamboat was usually far more comfortable than that aboard a jostling stagecoach. For people eating in the salon, steamboat meals were filling and usually served on time. Best of all, they were included in the price of passage, unlike travel by stagecoach, during which a hungry traveler had to pay for each meal separately. One more advantage of boat travel was that a ticket holder could ship considerably more free baggage than was usually allowed aboard a stagecoach. The reason, incidentally, why a traveler might prefer one mode of transportation over another depended less on income levels than on the time of travel (because low water caused big trouble for Missouri River steamboats during the late summer and fall seasons) and the location of one's final destination—not to mention such personal concerns as fear of drowning while aboard a steamboat.

As for safety: on the Columbia River, where for two decades the Oregon Steam Navigation Company maintained a fleet of seaworthy and well-staffed boats, no passenger ever lost his or her life in an accident involving one of its vessels. No such claim could be made for the wild waters of the Missouri River, where, unlike the Columbia, snags abounded to impale an unwary vessel.

The long steamboat trip from Saint Louis to Fort Benton could not be labeled a pleasure cruise, except perhaps by comparison to an overland stage journey. E. W. Carpenter, who made a journey in 1865 aboard the *Deer Lodge,* recalled it this way: "Two months of life on a 'mountain steamer,' with cracked roofs and warped decks, especially adapted to the broiling of passengers in fair weather and drenching of them in foul; two months of life between a double wall of muddy bluffs bounding the river on either side and cutting off whatever scenery might lie beyond, was naught but tedious in the experience, and could not prove entertaining in the description." As often happened aboard a long-distance stagecoach, some boat passengers dealt with boredom by downing a considerable quantity of whiskey at night and then sleeping off their liquor-induced haze during the following day.[7]

Compared to oceangoing vessels, the structure of a river steamer often appeared as light and fragile as theater scenery, and if it caught fire, it burned as hot and fast as well-seasoned kindling. Most passengers feared explosion far more than a shipboard fire, yet it was the ubiquitous snag that posed the greatest danger for travelers along the Missouri River. Statistics suggest that snags were at least thirty times more likely than boiler explosions to destroy any steamboat regularly plying the the muddy waters of the Missouri. Perhaps because such explosions were likely to be horrific disasters, many a passenger grew alarmed when the "steamer groaned and gasped, and moaned and sighed continually. The cabin floor rose visibly at each pulsation of the engines as they drove the frail vessels," wrote newspaperman Henry M. Stanley. "I fear there will be a 'fine bust-up' some of these days."[8]

This brief description of the rigors of travel across the northern West, which did not improve appreciably even after completion of a transcontinental railroad across the central West in 1869, illustrates why most tourists avoided that remote corner of the United States. A few hardy journalists went there in the 1860s and 1870s and reported what they saw, but for the typical tourist a trip to the northern West still demanded too much time and effort.

Steamboat excursion travel by residents of Portland, Oregon, was perhaps the earliest example of Anglo tourism in the northern West, and it began as a response to local needs, not national trends. Two routes, in particular, became popular as excursion runs, and these attracted boats and services that catered primarily to the pleasure seekers who resided in the largest metropolitan center in the entire region (a town of only 17,500 people as late as 1880). From Portland up to the Cascade Mountains went tourists who wanted to spend a leisurely day touring the Columbia Gorge; downriver to Astoria steamed people who desired to spend a few days, or the entire season, at the seashore. Both routes attracted pleasure riders almost from the beginning of steamboating on the Columbia River in the 1850s, but the Astoria run was the first to evolve into a popular excursion trip, since more vacationers used it.

Randall V. Mills in his classic *Stern-Wheelers up Columbia* (1947) provided an evocative account of early-day steamboat tourism in the Pacific Northwest. He noted that every summer during the 1860s and 1870s a growing number of tourists from the Willamette Valley traveled to Astoria and the ocean beaches of Oregon and Washington. The sawmills and canneries of Astoria itself held little appeal for excursionists, but south from the Columbia River stretched the Clatsop Plains, fronted by the ocean and wide, sandy beaches, and backed by tranquil woods and the quietly flowing Lewis and Clark River that paralleled the Pacific coast for miles and sometimes came within the sound of the breakers coming ashore not more than two or three miles to the west. Disembarking near the remains of Lewis and Clark's old Fort Clatsop, travelers could hire horses or carriages for the short trip through the forest to the beach, or walk the distance themselves. The area first became popular with campers in the 1860s, when a few Portland families took time for a summer holiday at the coast.[9]

Far from Portland and the popular appeal of nearby mountains or coast lay another of the northern West's earliest tourist attractions. That was Shoshone Falls, which for a few years enjoyed a measure of national prominence. This natural curiosity on the Snake River near the site of future Twin Falls, Idaho, though concealed in the Great Basin desert miles from the nearest population outpost, was easily reached by stagecoach from Kelton, Utah, a station on the recently completed transcontinental railroad. As the *Pacific Tourist* informed its readers in 1884:

> Tourists will also bear in mind, that this is the station nearest to the great Shoshone Falls. These falls are 110 miles from Kelton. Passengers from the east will arrive at about 10 o'clock P.M., and stay all night. Passengers from the west will arrive at about two o'clock A.M. The next morning they will take the stage run by the North-western Stage Company, 100 miles to Rock Creek Station, which are made over good roads in twelve hours. Here you will stay over night, and take a team the next morning for the falls.

The road threaded its way across a landscape of lava rocks dotted with stunted sagebrush. "No sight of the great falls is seen, until you reach a point one mile from them, when they suddenly burst upon the eye with a grandeur and magnificence truly bewildering."[10]

As early as 1886 the Union Pacific Railway issued a booklet called *Inter-Mountain Resorts*, which directed readers' attention to Salt Lake City, Ogden Hot Springs, Yellowstone National Park, and three southern Idaho destinations: Soda Springs, Guyer Hot Springs, and, of course, Shoshone Falls. Each of these places offered tourists a chance to ponder curiosities of nature or society or the opportunity to improve physical and mental health, two of the driving forces behind tourism in the late-nineteenth-century West.[11]

Tourism in the northern West really boomed when completion of a northern transcontinental railroad, the Northern Pacific in 1883, at last linked Saint Paul and points east with Portland and Puget Sound. Never before had it been so easy to make the trip. It is at that time too that tourist travel to Alaska first became popular. Regular tourist voyages up the Inside Passage probably dated from 1881, when Henry Villard, who at that time headed the Northern Pacific and numerous other transportation enterprises of the northern West, took the first large excursion party north and excited growing popular interest in the Great Land. His eighty guests, who included General Nelson Miles, then in command of the army on the Pacific Coast, and a military band, cruised aboard the well-equipped steamer *Idaho*.

Villard's 1881 excursion was the result of rising American fascination with Alaska since its purchase fourteen years earlier, a fascination roused by a growing number of writers, including naturalist John Muir, who inspired would-be travelers with their glowing descriptions of Alaska sights and dispelled the notion that it was nothing but a "Polar Bear Garden" festooned with icicles. From the comfort of deck chairs, tourists could follow the ever changing panorama of native villages, verdant forests, snow-capped mountains, and glaciers, and, because their vessels were but briefly exposed to the open sea, none need suffer the discomfort of protracted seasickness. As Muir summed it up, "No other excursion that I know of can be made into any of the wild portions of America . . . at so cheap and easy a price."[12]

Ease of travel made all the difference in promoting tourism in the northern West. Of course, Yellowstone National Park, established in 1872 and easily reached in comfort and style via the luxury accommodations of Villard's Northern Pacific Railway after the early 1880s, became an ever more popular attraction. So too did the mountain lakes of northern Idaho and the region's numerous hot springs.

Unlike the early overland stagecoach and steamboat companies, transcontinental railroads promoted tourism as an end in itself, beginning with basic announcements by the Union Pacific and Central Pacific lines in the late 1860s and multiplying in the 1880s with all types of beautifully illustrated brochures and posters.

Transcontinental railroads, and even some regional carriers, funded elaborate advertising campaigns to sell the northern West to prospective tourists and settlers, but operators of stagecoach and steamboat lines did so only rarely, if at all. That was true even for large carriers like the Oregon Steam Navigation Company or Ben Holladay's Overland Mail stagecoaches.

Perhaps it had been difficult enough to maintain reliable transportation and communication to communities scattered across the West. When steamboat and stagecoach lines advertised their services, they typically did so by posting simple notices in newspapers or in public places. They relied almost exclusively on blocks of black and white type. Only rarely did they use illustrations or even a splash of color. Their images seldom consisted of more than small, decorative woodcuts or engravings that profiled a generic steamboat or stagecoach. The general lack of visually arresting material was, of course, consistent with the printing technology of the nineteenth century. By contrast, during the era of steamboat excursions in the early twentieth century, a few companies prepared elaborate tourist brochures similar to those issued by railroads.

Apart from listing the settlements it served and giving the approximate length of the trip—"Through in Six Days to Sacramento!"—a stagecoach company might direct public attention to the advantages it offered. "Travelers avoid Risk of Ocean Travel," boasted an 1866 broadside for Henry Corbett's "Overland Mail Route to California." Listed almost as an afterthought and in the smallest type on the entire poster was one section that anticipated the kind of regional boosting that railroads did so well in later years: "This portion of the Pacific Slope embraces the most BEAUTIFUL and attractive as well as some of the most BOLD, GRAND and PICTURESQUE SCENERY on the Continent. The highest snow-capped mountains (Mt. HOOD, Mt. SHASTA and others) deepest ravines and most beautiful valleys." Devoting even this limited amount of attention to the countryside traversed by stagecoach passengers would have been unthinkable only a decade earlier, when the bold landscape of the West was viewed mainly as an impediment to travel.[13]

During the pioneering phase of steamboat and stagecoach travel across the northern West, neither new mode of passenger transportation advertised for tourists as such. These vehicles were intended mainly to haul passengers, goods, and express from one point to another. Any visual pleasure a traveler might derive from the scenery along the way was wholly incidental. Elaborate color posters advertising the West to tourists would wait until well after completion of the first transcontinental railroad. The same was true for elaborate promotional brochures designed to lure settlers west.

Steamboats and stagecoaches provided basic transportation in exchange for payment, but provided no special inducements for people from outside the region to travel west. Precious metal was apparently enough to do that. It might be said that the railroads created a new regional landscape, while steamboat and stagecoach pioneers struggled to adapt their respective technologies to the prevailing natural landscape. If they physically altered that landscape in any way, it was incidental to facilitating the movement of people and goods.

For railroads of the northern West, the tourist trade quickly formed an important part of their business. Hunting of a sort had always been an informal part of any long steamboat or stagecoach journey across the northern West, and gradually it evolved into an integral part of railroad tourism. For example, the sight of a herd of antelope or buffalo seldom failed to bring bored travelers to the rail of a steamboat on the upper Missouri River. "At about 10 o'clock the sudden reversion of the engines and sharp whistling proclaiming 'Something Up,' I dropped an abstract of mining property which I was engaged in copying in the dining room and, rushing on deck, found the entire force of the boat engaged (such as had guns) in shooting buffalo," wrote James Knox Polk Miller in his diary for June 6, 1867. Four youthful bison, attempting to cross the river, found themselves directly in front of the steamboat.

They were terribly frightened and endeavored to reach the shore, which they did. But the banks were so steep that they were unable to ascend them. They were accordingly butchered without any difficulty although many shots were fired before the desired result was obtained. It made me pity them to see their frantic efforts to escape and the storm of bullets with which they were saluted. After they were killed, or badly wounded, the steamer's yawl was lowered and rowing to the sides of the enormous carcasses, towed them to the side of the steamer where they were hoisted aboard and duly skinned & cleaned for the table.

Later as the boat tied up for the evening, Miller saw a passenger shoot at a beaver but miss.[14]

It was all too common for steamboat travelers to treat the abundant wildlife they saw along the banks of the Missouri River as convenient targets on which to test their marksmanship. Steamboater Charles Bailey once recalled the "frenzy of excitement" when passengers spotted a herd of about fifty antelope that plunged into the Missouri and swam for the other shore. "There were plenty of guns and ammunition on board, and every man of the crew and passengers was shooting into that herd. I was 'on watch,' but I grabbed the rifle and rushed forward on the hurricane deck and shot one, and by that time four had been killed and were floating down the river with the current." Bailey estimated that nearly five hundred shots were fired into the herd.[15]

The urge to shoot something was no less compelling for stagecoach passengers. The journalist John Mortimer Murphy observed that in passing through the dense forests of Oregon's Blue Mountains "we caught glimpses occasionally of a timid deer, an inquisitive wolf, and coveys of the dusky or mountain grouse, which seemed to take no notice of the human foes firing at them with revolvers."[16]

Making casual targets of game animals lost none of its popularity after the coming of the railroad. Wallis Nash observed that when he crossed Nebraska's Great Plains by train in 1877, the antelope seemed "too tame for their own comfort. Often they were within range of the train and there was a perfect fusillade from the rifles and revolvers with which a good many of the passengers were armed." For more civilized hunters the Worcester Excursion Car Company operated a special car on the Northern Pacific line during the 1880s. Built expressly for hunting and fishing parties of wealthy tourists, these cars came complete with cook and porter, and the Northern Pacific would park them on sidings along its right-of-way for up to six weeks. Thus in addition to being identified with good health or the beauty of nature, the northern West emerged as a "sportsman's paradise" by affording tourists unusually good opportunities for hunting and fishing. "Days and weeks are passed in fishing, boating, loafing, drinking in new life and strength and hope and ambition in every breath."[17]

But the times were changing, along with the nature of tourism. Later in the 1880s the Northern Pacific Railroad terminated special carload rates on wild animal meat traveling to eastern markets. After hauling tons of buffalo hides and meat from the Great Plains, the railroad became a convert to conservation when it realized that tourism was a much more profitable and enduring business than the wholesale slaughter and ultimate extinction of the West's game animals. General passenger agent Charles S. Fee noted in *Forest and Stream* in 1888:

To a very considerable portion of the traveling public, the game and fish of the region traversed by the Northern Pacific Railroad constitute its chief attraction. This large and ever increasing class of travelers are well-to-do people who have money to spend, and are thus desirable patrons of the road. Any course which will decrease the supply of the game which they seek will tend to reduce the travel over the road by this class, who will go where they believe game to be most abundant.[18]

What Fee suggests here is that the West could become too tame, too devoid of its wild attractions, to attract tourists from the East, who demanded comfortable and civilized accommodations but who still desired to survey a relatively uncivilized landscape from their train windows. This became the trick for many a community across the northern West in the early twentieth century: to balance comfort with sufficient wildness to lure tourists, particularly people from outside the region. For example, in 1900, the Great Northern Railway noted that "There is an impression in the East that the people of the Western States are disposed to be lawless. The West is a child of the East. . . . There is as little disorder and frontier rowdiness in Montana as in any state of the Union."[19] It is notable that the publication did not deny the existence of frontier lawlessness and rowdiness, but merely asserted that it was no more extensive than in any other place in the country.

The Northern Pacific took a similar approach in 1910 when it reminded easterners that "the old West still lives in the mountains, but it has taken on alluring ways for Eastern folks who want to be perfectly safe, sane, comfortable and happy. Sacrifices gladly made by pioneers that they might enjoy the scenic glories and health-giving opportunities of the rugged old West are no longer required."[20]

Tourism of the northern West evolved in a number of stages. The first involved building a basic network of public transportation, admittedly very crude at times. Then a few adventuresome journalists wrote books that made it possible for would-be tourists to travel the northern West from the comfort of their own armchairs. When local excursionists ventured out of Portland and other early settlements on a Sunday outing or a week's vacation at the seashore, they pioneered early tourism on the waterways of the northern West. The scope of tourism in the northern West expanded along with the network of railroad passenger service. Finally, the coming of the automobile democratized tourism as never before.

Automobiles were admitted to Mount Rainier National Park for the first time in 1908, Crater Lake in 1911, Glacier in 1912, and Yellowstone in 1915. Wonderland would never be the same. When in 1927 railway travel to national parks increased by 5 percent, that by automobiles grew by 9 percent. The noticeable switch from vacation travel by boat or passenger train to private automobiles increasingly worried railroad executives.

Railway Age speculated that an increasing number of people of modest income took vacation trips by automobile because they felt uncomfortable when traveling by railway Pullman cars and being confronted with the custom of having to give tips. "They would much prefer to sidestep this fearful and wonderful experience and knock around in their own cars, living in tourist camps, where they need not put on any sort of front and can behave naturally." One observer believed the "up-to-date motor camp to be the finest melting pot of our democracy."[21]

Budget-conscious tourists felt out of place in any resort where guests were expected to change their clothes three times a day, which was typical for some posh hotels. The formality of a railroad outing was captured by these words: "Provision will be made at Yellowstone station for the care of ladies' hats, and for cleaning and pressing clothing while passengers are en route through the Park. A nominal charge is made for the service." Moreover, even a two-week vacation in Montana was far too expensive for most households, especially when the railroad fares and hotel bills for four or five family members were combined. However, traveling by car and camping out at night, a family could significantly reduce those expenses.[22]

Western railroads had for years encouraged travel to vacation centers in the northern West by advertising their scenic beauty or recreation advantages, but a new development in western winter travel during the 1930s was the ski resort. Prior to this, winter was a time of diminished tourist revenues. The demands of tourism would literally redefine the seasons in the northern West, just as an earlier era of tourism had meant transforming landscapes widely considered unappealing into veritable wonderlands.

Consider only how tourism has heightened the value of the West's considerable empty space, places that pioneer settlers scorned. It is with good reason that Idaho only recently sold itself to tourists as "The Great Getaway." The Frank Church River of No Return Wilderness is the largest such area in the lower forty-eight states. Capitalizing on nature's abundance, Idaho lures visitors from the city to sample the hinterland charms of its dude ranches, whitewater rafting, and mountain trails; and an increasing number of these people are electing to stay on as residents.

In the northern West today, tourism ranks either first or second as the most important source of state revenues. For that reason the work of attracting a steady stream of tourists to Oregon, Washington, Idaho, and Montana remains a big and important business. In some instances it involves fabricating something appealing from a declining natural-resource-based town that formerly lay well beyond the beaten path for most tourists. The communities of Leavenworth and Winthrop, Washington; Sisters, Oregon; and Kellogg, Idaho, are all examples of places that have sought to project the ambiance of a movie set, their urban motifs being either the old West or old Bavaria, in an effort to lure tourists. If anything, tourism has become the single most powerful force in shaping the popular image of the northern West at the dawn of the twenty-first century.

In retrospect, it is clear that the several transcontinental railroads extended across the northern West between 1883 and 1909 laid the foundation for tourism as it exists today, the early steamboat excursion traffic on the lower Columbia River notwithstanding. The railroads did that by making a journey to the northern West both comfortable and relatively brief, especially compared to the rigors of long-distance travel by steamboat or stagecoach, and fostering the construction of lodges and hotels that catered to tourists. With the cost of their tracks, stations, locomotives, and other support structures and machinery being enormous when compared to steamboat or stagecoach operations, railroads had an added inducement to advertise widely for tourists as well as all other types of passenger and freight business. As the Milwaukee Road phrased it, "But the building of a railroad is one thing, and the development of traffic is quite another. Long before our rails crossed the Dakota-Montana line we had a force of experienced immigration agents in the field prospecting, not for gold, nor silver, nor copper, but for business." That business included prospecting for tourists.[23]

The Union Pacific at the turn of the century offered the public no fewer than twenty attractive booklets, and its subsidiary companies listed still more titles. Most could be obtained for the cost of a postage stamp. Some of the brochures were travel guides, and some dealt with acquisition of irrigated lands. The northern transcontinental railroads set in motion a process of promotion that continues to the present time, even if railroads themselves are no longer the direct beneficiaries of the crowds of tourists who visit the northern West each year.

Notes

This chapter derives from my books *The Pacific Northwest: An Interpretive History*, 2nd ed. (Lincoln: University of Nebraska Press, 1996); *Railroad Signatures across the Pacific Northwest* (Seattle: University of Washington Press, 1993); and *Long Day's Journey: The Steamboat and Stagecoach Era in the Northern West* (Seattle: University of Washington Press, 1999).

1. *Idaho World,* June 17, 1866.
2. *Oregonian,* June 8, 1861; Fitz-Hugh Ludlow, "On the Columbia River," *Atlantic Monthly* 14 (December 1864): 703–5.
3. This quotation comes from the McLane letters at Wells Fargo and Company headquarters, San Francisco.
4. John Mortimer Murphy, *Rambles in North-Western America from the Pacific Ocean to the Rocky Mountains* (London: Chapman and Hall, 1879), 173.

5. Henry L. Wells, "Staging at Night," *West Shore* 10 (January 1884): 5.

6. Ibid., 6; Ralph Moody, *Stagecoach West* (New York: Thomas Y. Crowell, 1967), 244.

7. *Overland Monthly* 2 (April 1869): 378–86.

8. Henry M. Stanley, *The Autobiography of Henry M. Stanley*, ed. Dorothy Stanley (Boston: Houghton Mifflin, 1909), 100–101.

9. Steamboat tourism is discussed at length in Randall V. Mills, *Stern-Wheelers up Columbia: A Century of Steamboating in the Oregon Country* (Lincoln: University of Nebraska Press, 1977; previously published Palo Alto, Calif.: Pacific Books, 1947).

10. Frederick E. Shearer, ed., *The Pacific Tourist: The 1884 Illustrated Trans-Continental Guide of Travel from the Atlantic to the Pacific Ocean* (New York: Bounty Books, 1970; reprint of *The Pacific Tourist: Adams and Bishop's Illustrated Trans-Continental Guide of Travel from the Atlantic to the Pacific Ocean*, 1884), 187.

11. This theme is developed in Earl Pomeroy, *In Search of the Golden West: The Tourist in Western America* (New York: Alfred A. Knopf, 1957).

12. An excellent introduction to Alaska tourism is Ted Hinckley, "The Inside Passage: A Popular Gilded Age Tour," *Pacific Northwest Quarterly* 56 (April 1965): 67–74.

13. Advertisement for "Overland Mail Route to California," issued in Portland, July 19, 1866. Copy in the Bancroft Library, University of California, Berkeley. After its Grand Consolidation, Wells Fargo on April 1, 1867, promoted overland coaches between Omaha and Sacramento with these words: "The route passes through the celebrated silver regions of Nevada, the valley of Great Salt Lake, the beautiful scenery of the Rocky Mountains and the GREAT PLAINS, and is the cheapest and most expeditious route to the Atlantic States."

14. Andrew Rolle, ed., *The Road to Virginia City: The Diary of James Knox Polk Miller* (Norman: University of Oklahoma Press, 1960), 97–98.

15. *Kansas City Star*, January 9, 1925.

16. John Mortimer Murphy, *Rambles in North-Western America from the Pacific Ocean to the Rocky Mountains* (London: Chapman and Hall, 1879), 166.

17. Wallis Nash, *Oregon: There and Back in 1877* (Corvallis: Oregon State University Press, 1976; previously published London: Macmillan, 1878); Great Northern Railway, *Public Timetable* [ca. 1901], 36.

18. Charles S. Fee, *Forest and Stream*, as quoted in *Wonderland Junior* [1888], 21.

19. *General Information about Montana* (St. Paul: Great Northern Railway, 1900), 11.

20. *Rocky Mountain Vacations* (St. Paul: Northern Pacific Railway, [ca. 1910]); *The Missoula and Blackfoot Valleys, Montana* ([Chicago: Chicago, Milwaukee & St. Paul Railway, 1914]), 6.

21. *Railway Age*, October 29, 1927, 842; Frank E. Brimmer, "Vacationing on Wheels," *American Magazine* 102 (July 1926): 56–57, 172–6.

22. Where *Gush the Geysers* (Salt Lake City: Oregon Short Line, 1910).

23. *Milwaukee Railway System Employees' Magazine*, September 1914.

Chapter Seven

Tourists and Indians in Fred Harvey's Southwest

Leah Dilworth

In 1912 the Biograph Company released a Mack Sennett short called *The Tourists,* starring Mabel Normand. In the film Miss Normand plays a tourist named Trixie who disembarks from a Santa Fe train at Albuquerque with three tourist friends. She gets so involved in buying souvenir pottery from the Indian women in front of the Fred Harvey Indian Building (Fig. 5) that she and her companions miss their train and have to wait for the next one.

Making the best of an inconvenient situation, Trixie decides to go sightseeing at a nearby pueblo. There she attracts the attentions of "Big Chief" (a white actor in a war bonnet), who squires her around the pueblo. Trixie has such a good time seeing the sights with Big Chief that she gives her tourist beau the brush-off. But "Mrs. Big Chief" (an Anglo woman in a wig) gets jealous, which puts the "Indian Suffragettes on the War Path." Mrs. Big Chief and a crowd of Indian women (most of whom appear to be Native Americans) determine to chase the offending tourist from the village. Trixie temporarily eludes them by hiding in an Indian blanket, but eventually Mrs. Big Chief and the other women chase Trixie and the three tourists back to the train, which they beat on with clubs. As the train pulls out and recedes into the middle distance, the tourists smile and wave handkerchiefs.[1]

142

This film accurately represents—even as it parodies—the main features of ethnic tourism in the Southwest between the turn of the century and the First World War. To begin with, the setting of the film, in and around the Fred Harvey Indian Building, adjacent to the Santa Fe depot at Albuquerque, is quite appropriate. The Fred Harvey Company, in its relationship with the Atchison, Topeka, and Santa Fe Railway (AT&SF), was the most powerful agent of tourism in the region. During this period, the company, through its tourist attractions and publications, fostered a remarkably coherent—and persistent—version of the Southwest as a region inhabited by peaceful, pastoral people, who were "living ruins," survivals from the childhood of civilization. Presumably, what lured Trixie and her tourist friends to the Southwest was the promise of an encounter with these living relics of the past. This encounter, which was thoroughly mediated by the Santa Fe Railway and the Fred Harvey Company, was a kind of reenactment of the Columbian discovery narrative. The tourists in the film journeyed out from "civilization" via the Santa Fe Railway and discovered the peaceful, welcoming natives at the Fred Harvey Indian Building. The Indians sold them objects of native manufacture, and, having engaged in a satisfying exchange and seen the sights (albeit after an unusually "close encounter"), the tourists returned home to civilization with souvenir evidence of that encounter and tales of the region's wonders.

Fred Harvey's representation of the Indian Southwest spoke to what Renato Rosaldo has called "imperialist nostalgia," a sense of longing for what one is complicit in destroying or altering, in which the feeling of nostalgia is "innocent" and what is destroyed is simply rendered as "lost."[2] The cultural and economic incorporation of the Southwest, in which the Harvey Company and the AT&SF were primary agents, caused profound disruptions and changes among Native American communities. At the turn of the century, these processes were carried out in the name of progress, with the recognized cost being the necessary destruction of primitive ways of life. Even as the AT&SF conquered the region, it and the Harvey Company set about preserving the vanishing Indian. To expand on Rosaldo's idea, I would argue that Fred Harvey and the AT&SF were nostalgic not for what was actually destroyed but for an Indian that never existed; in the interest of selling tickets and hotel accommodations in the region, the two corporations constructed a version of Indian life that reflected and spoke to American middle-class desires and anxieties.

The Fred Harvey Company and the AT&SF created and coordinated touristic desires by rendering southwestern Indian life as a "spectacle," a cultural discourse that constructed epistemological and social relations between tourists and Indians as primarily visual; subjectivity resided with the touristic gaze, and Indians were objectified as culturally "blind" and static, available for touristic consumption.[3] Whatever anxieties might have accompanied touristic desires (e. g., the fear that Indians might resist economic and cultural exploitation) were defused in the spectacle by the representation of Indians as "living ruins," simultaneously appearing from the past and disappearing from the present.

By rendering Indians as "lost" and as objects of consumption or exchange among tourist subjects, the spectacle of tourism made the experience available for the production of tourist narratives but shut down the possibility of dialogue between Native Americans and tourists. *The Tourists* works as a comedy in part because it opens up the threat of real communication. The comic misunderstanding occurs because Trixie crosses the boundary between Indian and tourist. Her mistake is to stray too far from the train and to get too close to the natives. As a parable, the film teaches that in the encounter with the primitive other, it is best to keep one's distance and not to "go native," to stick to one's own side of the tracks, so to speak. But Trixie's transgression reveals more about the implications of that warning. Even though the tourist is presented as innocent and simply overenthusiastic, her interest in the Indian man threatens a sexual liaison. This potential connection across the touristic divide is threatening, because it would admit and display the Indians' full subjectivity. The film winds up representing this subjectivity in another way: the liaison between Trixie and Big Chief is derailed by the intervention of the Pueblo women, who strenuously resist the tourist's incursions into their territory. The image of the women beating the Santa Fe train with clubs would never appear in Fred Harvey's Southwest.

The Rise of the Fred Harvey Company

The story of how Fred Harvey, with his dining facilities along the AT&SF and his Harvey Girls, civilized the West has become something of a frontier legend.[4] Beginning in 1876 with a single Topeka, Kansas, lunchroom, the English immigrant Harvey went on to found a virtual empire of eating establishments and hotels in the Southwest. Although the Algeresque myth of Fred Harvey would have it that his company was the vision of one man with a single-minded devotion to quality, what is often glossed over is the Harvey Company's relationship with the Santa Fe Railway. It was a thoroughly modern and corporate success story; Harvey's operations were deeply embedded in the structures and massive capital of the Santa Fe Railway. From the beginning it was a symbiotic relationship, based on the railroad's providing the transportation and infrastructure to make Harvey able to deliver standardized, high quality services. The Santa Fe built and owned the hotels, and the Harvey Company furnished and operated them as well as dining cars, newsstands, and other shops along the railroad's route.[5]

In 1895, after nearly going bankrupt, the AT&SF decided to step up efforts to promote tourism in the region.[6] To publicize the attractions of the Southwest, the AT&SF began in the mid-1890s to commission ethnographers, artists, and photographers to depict Indian life in the region. Following the Santa Fe's lead, in 1902 the Fred Harvey Company formed its own Indian Department, which bought and sold Indian-made objects, coordinated the display of these objects as well as actual Native Americans, and published postcards, souvenir books, and pamphlets. After Fred Harvey's death, his son Ford Harvey took over the company and appointed his brother-in-law, John Frederick Huckel, to head the Indian Department. Huckel selected Herman Schweizer, a former news agent for the Harvey Company, to manage the operation in Albuquerque.[7] Huckel, Schweizer, and another Harvey employee, Mary Elizabeth Jane Colter, were largely responsible for creating the Fred Harvey image of the Indian Southwest. While the Santa Fe handled the advertising for both the railway and Harvey, Huckel oversaw the publication of several souvenir books and hundreds of postcards, which often used AT&SF artists, paintings, or photographs.

Schweizer's job was mainly buying and selling Indian objects, and Colter designed several hotels as well as shops and attractions and arranged their interiors.[8]

Over the next three decades the Harvey Company and the AT&SF continued to market and display aspects of Indian cultures and in the process helped to create a regional identity based on an aesthetic appreciation of Indian cultures. Not only did these practices promote tourists' desire to visit the region, they also provided a corporate image for the Harvey Company and the AT&SF. Symbols of "Indianness" spread all along the railway line, through the hotels, into the decoration of the trains themselves, and into the promotional literature and corporate imagery. The Santa Fe named one of its first-class trains the *Chief*, and the corporation's emblem, a cross within a circle, came into use in 1901 and was described as "a symbol descended from pre-historic man." Likewise, the Fred Harvey Company adopted as its emblem the thunderbird, which the company claimed was part of the mythology of many of the Indians of North America.[9] Thus these two modern corporate entities, which were paragons of efficiency and service marketing, wrapped themselves in an Indian blanket, so to speak, and used Indians to "naturalize" their activities.

The Spectacle of Fred Harvey's Southwest

Fred Harvey's representations of Indian life in the Southwest took two basic forms: the museumlike display of "live" Indians and their material culture and written and graphic representations of Indian life. Displays of Indian life organized by the Santa Fe and the Harvey Company appeared at world's fairs and regional expositions as well as in Harvey hotels and shops. Graphic and written representations of Indians appeared in the Santa Fe's ads, calendars, timetables, and pamphlets, in Harvey postcards, souvenir books, and lantern-slide lectures. These representations circulated images of and information about Native Americans within the region and throughout the nation in order to induce tourists to visit Fred Harvey's Southwest.

In forming display attractions in the region, the Harvey Company used the strategies employed by ethnographers at expositions and fairs. At the core of the Harvey display attractions were collections of Indian-made objects, exhibited in museumlike settings with the occasional presence of actual Native Americans to demonstrate crafts and dances. Herman Schweizer was instrumental in forming the collections of Indian material culture for the Harvey Company. Most of the objects Schweizer purchased were sold to tourists, collectors, and scientists collecting for museums. At the turn of the century all of the institutional collections of Indian material culture were in the East and Chicago, and the Harvey Company was an important supplier. Between 1903 and 1918 Schweizer's clients included George Dorsey, who purchased for the Field Museum; the National Museum in Washington; the Carnegie Museum; the Berlin Museum; and George Heye.[10]

What Schweizer didn't sell to scientists, tourists, and collectors, the company kept for display. As the AT&SF collected paintings, so the Harvey Company built a collection of Indian material culture. The company's ties to museums and scientists gave its collection scientific authority: in 1904 at the Louisiana Purchase Exposition in St. Louis, the Harvey Company won an award for "Aboriginal Blanketry and Basketry," and the company to some extent imitated museum methods of keeping records, documenting sources, establishing a library, and interviewing Indians.[11] The importance of building a collection for display was made clear by Herman Schweizer in a 1905 letter to William Randolph Hearst. Hearst, a prodigious collector, was interested in Navajo blankets and was one of Schweizer's most important customers. Even so, Schweizer had to inform Mr. Hearst that not all the company's "exhibit rugs" were for sale: "[T]he first object in establishing this exhibit was to furnish an attraction for the Santa Fe and I believe you realize it has been a most remarkable success in that direction. That was the reason it was not considered proper to send away some of our choicest things for obviously it was intended to bring people who wanted to see or purchase them over the Santa Fé."[12]

This mixture of the business interests of tourism and the scientific credibility that allowed a claim of authenticity and authority pervaded the Harvey display strategies, especially the permanent display attractions in the Southwest, the most important of which were the Indian Building at Albuquerque (opened 1902) and Hopi House, next to the Grand Canyon hotel, El Tovar (opened 1905). The Indian Building was the first big display attraction created by

Harvey, and it combined very effectively the two "regions" of the world's fair model, offering both ethnographic authenticity and pleasure.[13] The building was located between the Alvarado Hotel and the Santa Fe depot along an arcade two hundred feet long. This complex was designed in the mission style, with tile roofs, stucco exterior, arches, and bell towers reminiscent of a Spanish mission. Mary Colter designed the interiors of the Indian Building; it was her first job for Harvey, and she would later design many hotels and attractions for the company.[14]

Tourists' experience at this attraction was fully mediated by the railway and Fred Harvey in a kind of train-hotel complex. Santa Fe trains stopped at Albuquerque for from twenty-five minutes to an hour, and the Indian Building was constructed so that from the depot, passengers would pass first between Indians displaying their wares in front of the Indian Building, then through the Indian Museum with its ethnographic displays, then to the workroom with Indians weaving or making other crafts, and then to the curio shop, where they could purchase objects similar to those they had just seen.

These displays were organized to manipulate tourists' desire to possess the objects. The visitor moved through a kind of hierarchy of desire, from museumlike displays to the shop. Upon entering the Indian Building the visitor was transformed into the collector; he or she was educated in connoisseurship and authenticity and then was provided with an opportunity to buy Indian-crafted objects. The desire to possess these objects was also promoted in the arrangement of the Main Room of the Indian Building. Designed by Mary Colter, it strongly resembled a domestic interior and seemed to suggest how one could live with these objects. The collection on display seemed to belong to a knowledgeable collector-connoisseur, perhaps even the legendary Fred Harvey himself. The room's arrangement combined the abundance and eclecticism of the Victorian interior with the ethnographic exhibit, like a curiosity cabinet writ large. This style of interior decoration was a great success, and the AT&SF and the Harvey Company continued to use this combination of Indian and Hispanic motifs in their hotels, trains, and attractions for the next forty years.

Indian artisans were central to Harvey display attractions:

At Albuquerque in the Indian Building are a number of Navahos spinning and dyeing wool, weaving blankets, braiding
quirts, and making primitive silver ornaments with their crude
tools. Among them is Tsonsi-Pah, a girl of six years, whose
mother instructs her when the pattern becomes too intricate.
Pottery makers, apart by themselves, are moulding and decorating, and Indians from other tribes—Santo Domingo, Isleta,
Laguna and San Philipe—are lounging around in their picturesque costumes.[15]

In this description Indians do three things: they make things to sell,
they sell things, and they "lounge" picturesquely. This sort of Indian presence is a hallmark of Harvey literature and representations
of Indians. Indians were conceived of as making objects for tourist
consumption or as objects of visual consumption themselves, both
as sights to be seen and as photo opportunities.

The Harvey Company promoted two artisans as celebrities: Elle
of Ganado, a Navajo weaver, and the Hopi-Tewa potter Nampeyo.
In the tourist literature they were virtually the only Native Americans known by name; they appeared in many tourist display
settings, and their images were widely reproduced. In Harvey literature, Elle was continually referred to as "the most renowned
weaver among the Navahos," and she was one of the main attractions at the Indian Building.[16]

Nampeyo was the star of Hopi House, which was built near the
Harvey hotel, El Tovar, at Grand Canyon and opened in 1905. Mary
Colter designed Hopi House as a place where Hopi Indians would
live and make craft objects that could be sold. The house was designed to look like a Hopi dwelling and, like the Indian Building,
contained ethnographic displays and objects for sale. A photograph
of Nampeyo and her family at Hopi House in 1905 appeared in the
Harvey pamphlet *El Tovar by Fred Harvey: a New Hotel at Grand Canyon of Arizona*. It is titled "Roof Garden Party, Hopi House" and
depicts a thoroughly domesticated scene (Fig. 6). The accompanying text describes the Indian life on display there:

Here are Hopi men, women, and children—some decorating
exquisite pottery; others spinning yarn and weaving squaw

dresses, scarfs, and blankets. Go inside and you see how these gentle folk live. The rooms are little and low, like their small-statured occupants. The floors and walls are as cleanly as a Dutch kitchen. The Hopis are making "piki," twining the raven black hair of the "manas" in big side whorls, smoking corn-cob pipes, building sacred altars, mending moccasins—doing a hundred unAmerican things. They are the most primitive Indians in America, with ceremonies several centuries old.[17]

As a tourist spectacle, Hopi House claimed to reveal authenticity by letting the tourist in on the back regions of Hopi life, but it was what Dean MacCannell has called staged authenticity.[18] While actual Hopi domestic life looked very different from what was staged at Hopi House, the display presented as "natural" (because it was primitive) a self-contained domestic economy. These "at home" Hopis are defined by their "unAmerican" activities, which are preindustrial and exotic, but also familiar in their artisanal industriousness.

In addition to the displays of Indians and their material culture at the Indian Building and Hopi House, the Santa Fe Railway and the Fred Harvey Company organized displays at many national and international expositions, including the World's Columbian Exposition in 1893, the 1904 Louisiana Purchase Exposition in St. Louis, and the United States Land and Irrigation Exposition in Chicago in 1910.[19] In 1915 the company participated in two expositions in California celebrating the opening of the Panama Canal and the anticipated economic benefits to the West Coast: the Panama-California Exposition was held in San Diego, and the Panama-Pacific International Exposition was in San Francisco.[20] At all of these events the AT&SF and the Harvey Indian Department worked in conjunction with scientists to make displays that promoted the Southwest through its aboriginal inhabitants.

The entry of the United States into the First World War in April 1917 resulted in the nationalization of the railroads in December of that year. Until 1920, the railroads were run by the U. S. Railroad Administration, during which time there was no luxury train service. Accordingly, the AT&SF and Fred Harvey's tourist business slowed, and all plans for new hotels were shelved.[21] After the war, the Santa Fe was faced with the increasing presence of automobiles and a diminishing number of railway passengers. The Santa Fe—

Harvey response to this threat was the Indian Detour. This joint venture provided a way for the Santa Fe to extend its control over tourists through the automobile. On May 15, 1926, the first Indian Detour made all of northern New Mexico accessible to thousands of tourists. Touring cars run by the Harvey Company met railroad passengers at either Albuquerque or Las Vegas, New Mexico, and took them on one-, two-, or three-day tours of Indian pueblos, ruins, and artists' studios, and then returned them to the train to continue their journey.

As Harvey had brought southwestern Indian life to tourists at display attractions such as the Indian Building and Hopi House, on the Indian Detours, Harvey took tourists directly to the Indians. The attractions on the detours included ruins, scenic landscapes, and pueblos where detourists could witness dances or buy pottery. The "Harveycars" were driven by men dressed in a sort of Tom Mix riding costume, and the tour guides, or "couriers," were all women, modeled on the successful Harvey Girls. The couriers wore a Navajo-style costume consisting of a skirt, velveteen shirt, concha belt, and "squash blossom" necklace.[22]

The Indian Detour was relatively short-lived—the Depression put a stop to much of the tourism in the region—but it held the promise of even more authentic encounters with Indians. The promotional literature promised that the Indian Detours would "open up this little known territory to the discriminating traveler" by taking the tourist "off the beaten path" of the railroad.[23] Meanwhile, as with the railroad attractions, the Indian Detour encounter was thoroughly mediated through the "thunderbird" car, the "cowboy" driver, and the "Indian maiden" guide.[24]

Appearing and Disappearing
in Fred Harvey's Southwest

The Harvey spectacle of Indian life presented images of Indians that seemed to render them entirely understandable and easily classifiable. In Harvey representations, ethnographic groupings of Indians hardened into types, determined by bundles of a few characteristics, and arranged along an implicit evolutionary scale, from utter savagery to a primitive version of American middle-class life. This was a moral as well as evolutionary scale, which rated Indian groups "good" or "bad" according to their hostility to civilized life. At the bottom were the Apaches, a conquered people who remained unregenerate savages; then came groups like the Mojave and Pima Indians who were very primitive but harmless and doomed to disappear; then the Navajos, whose nomadic ways made them somewhat suspect, but whose industriousness redeemed them; and finally the Pueblo Indians, peaceful and settled agriculturalists who lived in houses. Among the Pueblos, the Hopis retained the attribute of being the "most primitive," meaning the most isolated and culturally "pure."

The Harvey spectacle represented the Southwest as a peaceful and fully domesticated region. It was not the wild, manly, cowboys-and-Indians West represented by Frederic Remington's mounted Plains warriors. *First Families,* a compendium of typical Harvey images, presented picture after picture of Indian domestic life. Men were shown doing masculine things like hunting and riding horses, and women, when they were not depicted as mothers with children or "olla maidens" carrying water, were making baskets, pots, or blankets or preparing food. This book presented a fantasy of Indian society reduced to its simplest social unit, the family, and it conceived of a rural, village utopia, with simplified, familial social relationships.

Native American rituals were also an important part of the Harvey spectacle. Ceremonial dances, as exotic performances, were perfect tourist attractions. The Hopi snake dance was the ritual most often represented, but other ceremonial dances, such as the Santo Domingo corn dance, the harvest dance at Isleta, and the Hopi kachina dances made their appearances in postcard images.

The central icon of Fred Harvey's Southwest was the Indian artisan. The crafts of weaving, pottery making, basket making, silversmithing, and turquoise drilling were prevalent in Harvey publications. In the tourist market, the crafts that Indians made were important commodities, and the tourist literature promoted them for obvious reasons. Like the typology of Indian "tribes" in the Southwest, primitive crafts were codified in a few, strict ways: basketry and pottery making were presented as the most primitive crafts, and these were solely the province of women, especially

Pueblo women, although the Pima and Apaches were sometimes shown as basket makers. Weaving appeared to be the occupation solely of Navajo women (although it was occasionally acknowledged that Hopi men also wove) and was considered less primitive than basketry or pottery. Finally, silversmithing was what Navajo men did. Even though silversmithing was not strictly a "primitive" craft, since the Navajos had learned the skill from the Spanish, it came in for a lot of attention, because the Harvey Company bought and sold Navajo silver. The iconography of these artisan images seemed to urge a commercial transaction. The images usually presented a lone artisan at work with several examples of completed craft objects arranged around him or her; the artisan seems to be offering the objects for sale to the viewer, who, as a tourist, was also a potential customer.

These representations of Indian domestic life, artisans, and rituals spoke to Americans' anxieties about generational continuity, the changing social roles of women, the value of labor, and spiritual "weightlessness."[25] The spectacle of these "good Indians" amounted to a premodern, edenic fantasy; they seemed to represent a time before modernity and all its attendant problems, when "tradition" prevailed, when the authority of the father was unquestioned, when men were men and women were women, when people knew the value of an honest day's work, and when spiritual values were immanent. Furthermore, the positioning of these bourgeois values as primitive, or premodern, seemed to provide evidence of their universality and naturalness.

Although images of the good, peaceful, domesticated Indian dominated the Harvey literature and displays, a parallel strain of "bad Indian" imagery persisted. Images of olla maidens, mothers and children, and contented craftspersons existed alongside representations of the "aged squaw," the snake dance, and the wild Apache. While icons of the "good Indian" may have suggested that the Southwest was a kind of American Eden, the bad-Indian imagery suggested aspects of the primitive that were threatening, unassimilable, and ultimately doomed to extinction. These representations carried an exotic, frightening, or grotesque appeal that had been part of the tourist spectacle since the exposition midways of the late nineteenth century, but there was an implicit guarantee that because these Indians were tourist attractions, they were harmless. They had been captured, framed, and tamed within the tourist spectacle.

These positively and negatively charged representations constructed Indians, on the one hand, as objects of desire and, on the other hand, as objects of fear. Indians in the tourist spectacle became a locus for these emotions, which were themselves a result of imperialist social relations. The subject under imperialism desires what the other possesses *and* fears the other's subjectivity, which represents a potential threat. Constructing the other as dichotomous, splitting it in two, renders it powerless. The two Indians, one noble, the other savage, are both marginalized figures, existing in the past of the bourgeois imagination; neither is a full subject position. The process of dichotomizing also defuses the fear and the desire of the subject by seeming to universalize or naturalize the ideology that is their source. The fears and desires that arise out of inequitable social relations are rewritten as repulsion and nostalgia, emotions that are indulged in the marginalized realm of the touristic spectacle.

If what *appeared* in the Harvey spectacle of the Southwest were either entirely good or entirely bad Indians, there were a number of aspects of Indian life that did *not appear*. For example, contemporary Apache life, for the most part, was not depicted. When images of Apache people did appear, they showed their "warlike" past, which were images that spoke about the power of the conqueror; the Apaches were a worthy foe, but now they were defeated. Images of the consequences of that defeat, however, were not included in the spectacle; the defeated Apaches held no romantic or exotic appeal for the Harvey Company and its tourists. In this regard, it is significant also that Geronimo made no appearance in the Harvey literature. Even though he appeared at world's fairs, the company chose not to capitalize on his notoriety, perhaps because as a living Apache warrior, he might still represent a threat to tourists.

If the Apaches were a kind of "present absence" in the tourist spectacle, in the 1910s and 1920s, depictions of Hispanic life in the Southwest were virtually absent from it. While Hispanic crafts were sold in Harvey curio shops during this period, Hispanic artisans were nowhere apparent.[26] The disappearance of Hispanic culture was gradual. The early Harvey and AT&SF literature was much more likely to feature images of Hispanic life. For example, when it opened in 1902, the Indian Building was called the Indian and Mexican Building. The 1904 souvenir picture book, *The Camera in the Southwest*, contained photographs of a bullfight, burros, Hispanic beggars, a horse and cart, as well as views of El Paso, but the book's text prefigured the disappearance of Hispanic subjects by claiming that "[t]he Spanish civilization never took hearty root in this land. It resulted only in a rude and inharmonious grotesquerie. It was earnest, and not brutal, but it failed. These pictures reveal that it pursued a course of 'benevolent assimilation,' and that the effort affords no historical encouragement to such a course. Degeneration seems to be the only lesson it clearly teaches."[27] The last two sentences offer a clue as to why Hispanos did not make picturesque subjects: miscegenation. Indians were characterized as pure primitives, but people of Hispanic descent were "figures who simultaneously perverted both the purity of Indian savagery and that of European civilization."[28] Hispanos were perceived as combining the savagery of the Indian with the bad traits of the Spanish—for example, Catholicism.

The stereotypes of Hispanic men and women as lazy, carefree, and dirty, with no thoughts of the future, was already well established. Early travel literature about the region is full of them. David Weber suggests that the negative stereotypes were in place by 1820 and that they descended from the anti-Spanish-Catholic stereotype that was present since colonial times. The "Black Legend" of the Spanish conquest insisted that unlike the English, who came to the new world to make a safe home for their families, the Spanish came to exploit the natives as slaves and to live in luxury.[29] This anti-Catholicism is also apparent in the absence of depictions of Catholic processions, which occurred in many of the Pueblo villages.

In fact, many Hispanos, like many Native Americans, participated in the area's economy as wage laborers; the railroads were built and maintained with Hispanic labor, and Hispanic workers were in high demand as agricultural laborers beginning in about 1900, when big irrigation projects were underway. But Hispanic peons, peasants defined by their labor, were not exotic. Unlike Indians, Hispanos did not qualify as a primitive folk worth preserving; they were not about to disappear, and anthropologists did not study them. Their presence in the tourist spectacle threatened to reveal the actual infrastructure of massive capital and exploited labor that lay behind the spectacle. Furthermore, unlike Native Americans, Hispanos were numerous, and boosters for statehood in Arizona and New Mexico (granted in 1912) tried to downplay the fact that most of the inhabitants of these territories were Hispanos, not Anglos.[30] The spectacle of potential Hispanic voters was not picturesque. As a result of these stereotypes and prejudices, since the turn of the century in New Mexico Hispanos have found themselves in what Sylvia Rodríguez has called a "tri-ethnic trap," caught between hegemonic Anglo economic and political power and the "tourism-engendered Anglo glorification of Indian culture."[31]

The Machinery of the Tourist Spectacle

The touristic desire to experience the Columbian moment is redolent of imperialist nostalgia. A telling example of the rhetoric of this "emotion" is the introduction to *The Camera in the Southwest*, which maintains a distinctly elegiac tone even as it praises the agents of progress:

> The ruins of an ancient civilization and the beginnings of a new and higher one in "The Sad Southwest, the Mystical Sunland," that is the compass of the story—the historical romance—related by the series of vivid and interesting pictures contained in this book. It is a story told to the swift eye and not to the slower ear. But to such as are able to interpret the series of pictures with historical understanding, illuminated by imagination, what a tragic fascination the book will possess—what numberless centuries of human history, of life and love, of hope and despair, of endeavor and achievement, are covered by one glance of the eye, from that picture of the light, airy, frail-looking steel bridge by which the Santa Fe railroad leaps the deep, dark chasm of the Cañon Diablo, to the rude ruins of the Cliff-Dweller's castle on another page—but geographically near-by. The one fairly stands for the new civilization of the country, the other probably as fairly for a civilization whose history has vanished in the midst of centuries—never to be recovered, or recovered only in doubtful fragments painfully patched together by the persevering archeologist.[32]

By juxtaposing an image of a train trestle with one of a ruin, the loss that this passage insists on seems inevitable in the face of progress as represented by the railroad. The violence of conquest is erased and replaced by loss or "vanishing," and the response to this process is rendered as nostalgia or "tragic fascination."

The passage also reveals the centrality of the railroad and photography in apprehending and understanding the region. In the tourist spectacle, the train and the camera were the coordinating machinery that reconciled the seemingly contradictory aims of progress and preservation. Together the Santa Fe Railway and the representations (many of them photographic) produced by the Fred Harvey Company embodied the forces of imperialism and nostalgia, erasing and preserving at the same time.

Images of the encounter between trains and Indians appeared frequently in Harvey publications, and they inscribed the history of the conquest of Native Americans as inevitable. A powerful example is *The First Santa Fe Train,* by Frank P. Sauerwein (Fig. 7). The introduction to the Harvey souvenir picture book *The Great Southwest,* which reproduced this painting on its cover, depicted the history of the Southwest as waves of European conquest: the conquistadors, the Jesuits and Franciscans, the Americans, and the railroad: "Finally came the railroads—the greatest open trails—and with their coming time alone was required to reclaim the wilderness."[33] In conjunction with the Sauerwein painting, this sentence compressed that history: the train conquered the Indians. The conquest was easy because Indians were perceived as ruins, already gone. In the simple juxtaposition of train and Indian, the power relationship is clear; the Indian could not comprehend, much less resist, the transforming energies of the railroad.

The train was also important in mediating the encounter between tourist and Indian and thus figured prominently in Harvey images. A widely reproduced image is the postcard "Pueblo Indians Selling Pottery," which depicts a train, a tourist man and girl, railroad employees, and a group of Pueblo women (Fig. 8). The caption on the back of this postcard emphasizes the primitiveness of Pueblo culture:

Comely Indian maidens, and aged squaws, meet the train and sell their wares. This pottery is made by hand in their crude

way, moulded without a wheel, and often decorated with geo-
metrical or symbolical designs. The Pueblo Indian is a true
Pagan—superstitious, rich in fanciful legend, and profoundly
ceremonious in religion. His gods are innumerable—gods of
war, and gods of peace; of famine and of plenty; of sun and of
rain.

Standing in for the *Niña,* the *Pinta,* and the *Santa Maria,* the train has
brought the tourist to an encounter with an absolutely primitive
other. In Harvey's Southwest, the uncomprehending but friendly
natives greet the tourists, who learn from this postcard that the civilization and beliefs of the natives are embodied in the simplicity of
their pots, which the tourists can buy and carry away. The technology of the pot is implicitly contrasted with the train, as are the Indian women with the tourists and railroad employees.[34]

As a cultural practice within capitalism, tourism remakes the
world into a spectacle through which the tourist moves freely, as a
consumer of goods. In Fred Harvey's Southwest, the combination
of the subjective gaze and the mobility of the train afforded tourists
the freedom to choose the objects of consumption. The tourist subject is mercurial and mutable; he or she is at once a spectator and an
actor, able to assume numerous roles. In the spectacle, the tourist plays
the role of tourist, but the Indian, supposed to be authentic, does not
play a role.[35] The tourist can escape into the panopticon of the train,
but the Indian is always caught in the trap of visibility. The tourist is
always the subject, the receiver of information; the Indian is always
the object of the gaze, a commodity to be consumed visually.

As presented in its publications, the Harvey Southwest was
to be apprehended at a glance in a proliferation of colorful, picturesque images. Writing served in Harvey publications mainly as
captions to visual representations of Indian life and provided
anecdotal ethnographic information. According to *The Camera in
the Southwest,* the modern way of understanding is through sight
rather than through the words of the storyteller; the "swift eye" is
superior to the "slow ear." The reader of the souvenir picture book,
the armchair tourist, understood that the region was presented as
a spectacle, a story readable by turning the pages and interpreting with the eye.

The Touristic Exchange

The exchange between tourists and Native Americans did not produce mutual communication. Mutual communication occurred
back home between the tourist and his or her audience. As Indian-
made objects (or representations of Indians) traveled out from the
region, they became benign sources of knowledge, valuable but not
destructive or threatening. Removed from the site of the touristic
encounter and taken home, souvenirs—be they postcards, snap-
shots, or a pot purchased from an Indian artisan—became objects
loaded with meaning, sources for narratives of the region. The tourist narrative is a story of a quest for contact with authenticity and
gains its authority from the journey into and return from the realm
of the other. As vehicles for touristic narratives, the Harvey postcards, playing cards, and picture books made especially appropriate
souvenirs. They recapitulated the spectacle of the Indian Southwest
as a series of attractions and could function as "museums of Human
nature" that constructed meaning and organized knowledge of the
other.[36]

What the spectacle of Indian life in Fred Harvey's Southwest
offered was not a connection with authenticity that would bring an
end to nostalgia and longing but the maintenance and celebration
of difference and distance, which produced nostalgia and longing.
Ethnic tourism is a discourse that demands that tourists make meaning out of the disjunction between the tourist subject and the other.
Out of this distance and the desire or nostalgia it creates, interpretation is required; the distance creates a space within which the tourist can establish his or her authority. What the tourist narrates is not
only a story of "discovery," with souvenirs perhaps metonymically
prompting the narrative, but also the narrative of the tourist's own
subjectivity. Thus the touristic encounter becomes an event through
which one establishes one's subjectivity in relation to an other.

Sightseeing and collecting souvenirs might seem to satisfy the
imperialist nostalgia that motivated ethnic tourism in the Southwest.
But ironically, the past (or simplicity or authenticity) that the primitive represents and that is so desired always slips from one's grasp;
tourism constructs authenticity in such a way that it is never attainable. Sightseeing is doomed; the very presence of the observer spells

the end of the authenticity of the observed. The same is true of the collector, whether ethnographer or tourist; in the act of collecting, the collectible disappears from the world of its origin, and the experience of collecting is no longer available. Collecting brings about a literal depletion of the culture one desires so desperately, which makes one desire it all the more—a process similar to the erasing and preserving powers of the train and the camera. The unfulfillable desire that drives collecting may be why it is often referred to as a pathology. Similarly, tourism is a kind of pathology in that the touristic journey must be enacted time and time again.

The touristic economy of desire also speaks about the energies of capital. Just as capitalism needs natural and human resources, so it needs cultural otherness to maintain its own cultural practices. Ethnic tourism is one of the mechanisms by which capitalism, as it eliminates different systems of production, incorporates cultural difference as otherness—as primitive, old-fashioned, or quaint.[37] But only difference that is perceived to be disappearing is celebrated. Other differences, such as class inequalities in modern cities, are in no danger of disappearing—or being preserved as tourist attractions. To continue to function, ethnic tourism in the Southwest has had to maintain a constant Indian disappearing act. So far it has been very successful; for the past one hundred years tourists have been hurrying to the region to see authentic Indian culture before it disappears.

Re-presenting the Touristic Encounter

The tourist spectacle of Fred Harvey's Southwest denied the subjectivity of Native Americans by representing them as vanishing, silent, and blind to modernity. But of course, Native Americans are aware of and have a very great interest in the "outside" world, and Indian artists and artisans have long depicted tourists in their work.

Land of Enchantment, a 1946 watercolor by Woodrow Crumbo, a Creek-Potawatomi artist, reimagines the Fred Harvey version of the touristic encounter and comments on it in terms of the spectacle and exchange (Fig. 9). In the painting, all three tourists wear eyeglasses and intently inspect a Navajo woman and girl, who do not return their gaze but peer obliquely from lowered faces. In contrast to the tourists, the woman and girl are covered up; the little girl is enfolded in a blanket, and the woman stands behind the one she is selling. They seem to be trying to deflect the tourists' gaze, which suggests an attempt to resist the inequitable social relations present in the encounter.

This painting recalls other depictions of the touristic encounter, such as Trixie's in *The Tourists*. In these representations women tourists usually predominate or are the most active participants in the exchanges with natives: in *The Tourists* Trixie selects the souvenir pots to buy (her tourist beau pays for them), and in *Land of Enchantment* it is the female figure who most closely inspects the rug. Her husband stands back, presumably preparing to pay. The touristic encounter might recapitulate the masculine discovery narrative, but the exchange—the purchase of souvenirs—inscribed the gendered nature of consumerism on this narrative. The humor of *Land of Enchantment* hinges on the woman's role as primary consumer. Her largeness, the profusion of her accessories, and the smallness of her costume, call attention to her as a consumer and an object of display. Tourist women are not simply observers of the spectacle of Indian life but, like the Indian women they purchase souvenirs from, are part of what is on display. Even though they are the primary consumers, they too become consumed by the spectacle.

The question of what exactly is for sale here is also interesting: it is surely blankets, but because the girl and the woman are so closely covered by the blankets, they are almost part of the merchandise. Thus, viewing the Indians through their "spectacles," the tourists can hardly distinguish Indian from commodity. Furthermore, the broken "Land of Enchantment" sign indicates that the land is not inherently mystical or wondrous but is in fact under the spell of the tourist spectacle and commodification.

Finally, although the exchange of blankets for tourist dollars seems impending, the painting indicates that another exchange has already taken place. A doll, apparently representing a white cavalry officer, peeks out from the little girl's blanket.[38] There are a number of ways to interpret the presence of this doll. It could be seen as a "trifle" like the beads traded for Manhattan and thus a harbinger of the destruction the girl's culture. But the fact that she possesses a representation of the other culture opens up a crack in the hegemony of the exchange. It suggests that she might be creating her own narratives, that she is not simply an object of exchange but is also a subject, capable of creating meaning. The image stops short of suggesting the possibility of dialogue, but it does seem to open up the possibility of meaningful interpretive activity on both sides of the encounter.

Crumbo's image rewrites the Columbian encounter to reveal its commercial underpinnings. An exchange may be taking place, but the Navajo woman and girl are not available for objectification. In resisting the touristic gaze, they will not become objects of desire; they, and the Land of Enchantment, are not accessible or possessible. Instead, it is the tourists who are curiosities available for inspection; they are what is "discovered" in this version of Fred Harvey's Southwest.

Notes

This chapter is derived from "Discovering Indians in Fred Harvey's Southwest" in *Imagining Indians in the Southwest: Persistent Visions of a Primitive Past* by Leah Dilworth, Smithsonian Institution Press, © 1996 by the Smithsonian Institution.

1. Mack Sennett, *The Tourists* (New York: Biograph Co., 1912), paper print.
2. Renato Rosaldo, "Imperialist Nostalgia," *Representations* 26 (1989): 107–22.
3. Guy Debord, *Society of the Spectacle* (Detroit: Black and Red, 1983), 5.
4. For mythologies of Fred Harvey, see Keith L. Bryant Jr., *History of the Atchison, Topeka and Santa Fe Railway* (New York: Macmillan, 1974), 106–22; Lesley Poling-Kempes, *The Harvey Girls: Women Who Opened the West* (New York: Paragon House, 1989); Mary Lee Spence, "Waitresses in the Trans-Mississippi West: 'Pretty Waiter Girls,' Harvey Girls and Union Maids," in Susan Armitage and Elizabeth Jameson, eds., *The Women's West* (Norman: University of Oklahoma Press, 1987), 219–34; and Diane Thomas, *The Southwestern Indian Detours: The Story of the Fred Harvey–Santa Fe Railway Experiment in "Detourism"* (Phoenix: Hunter Publishing, 1978). See also George Sidney, *The Harvey Girls* (Los Angeles: MGM, 1946), film.
5. Bryant, *History of the Atchison, Topeka and Santa Fe Railway*, 118.
6. Bertha P. Dutton, "Commerce on a New Frontier: The Fred Harvey Company and the Fred Harvey Fine Arts Collection," in Christine Mather, ed., *Colonial Frontiers: Art and Life in Spanish New Mexico, the Fred Harvey Collection* (Santa Fe: Ancient City Press, 1983), 93.
7. James David Henderson, *"Meals by Fred Harvey": A Phenomenon of the American West* (Fort Worth: Texas Christian University, 1969), 29.
8. Virginia L. Grattan, *Mary Colter: Builder upon the Red Earth* (Flagstaff, Ariz.: Northland Press, 1980), 1–9; Marta Weigle, "Exposition and Mediation: Mary Colter, Erna Fergusson, and the Santa Fe/Harvey Popularization of the Native Southwest, 1902–1940," *Frontiers* 12 (1991): 120–30; Helen Pinion Wells, "The Fred Harvey Fine Arts Collection," *American Indian Art* 1, no. 2 (1976): 32.

9. Merle Armitage, *Operations Santa Fé* (New York: Duell, Sloan, and Pearce, 1948), 118–19; John F. Huckel, *First Families of the Southwest* (Kansas City: Fred Harvey, [1913], reprint 1920), n. pag.

10. For more on Schweizer's collecting practices, see John Adair, *The Navajo and Pueblo Silversmiths* (Norman: University of Oklahoma Press, 1944), 25–27; Byron Harvey III, "The Fred Harvey Collection 1899–1963," *Plateau* 36, no. 2 (1963): 33–53; and Byron Harvey III, *The Fred Harvey Company Collects Indian Art* (Phoenix: Heard Museum, 1981), 9–10.

11. Harvey, "The Fred Harvey Collection," 36–37.

12. Schweizer to Hearst, 31 December 1905, Fred Harvey Papers, Heard Museum, Phoenix, Ariz. Schweizer eventually capitulated and sent the coveted objects to Hearst, because, well, he was William Randolph Hearst, and he was a regular traveler on the Santa Fe. Schweizer to Hearst, 5 February 1906, Fred Harvey papers, Heard Museum Library, Phoenix, Ariz.

13. Marta Weigle, "From Desert to Disney World: The Santa Fe Railway and the Fred Harvey Company Display the Indian Southwest," *Journal of Anthropological Research* 45 (1989): 133.

14. The development of a "Santa Fe style" in architecture and interior design has been well documented. See Marcus Whiffen and Carla Breeze, *Pueblo Deco: The Art Deco Architecture of the Southwest* (Albuquerque: University of New Mexico Press, 1984), and Carl D. Sheppard, *Creator of the Santa Fe Style: Isaac Hamilton Rapp, Architect* (Albuquerque: University of New Mexico Press, 1988). Mary Colter is recognized as one of the style's main promoters. She worked for the Harvey Company from 1902 to 1948 and designed Hopi House, the Watchtower, and the Lookout at the Grand Canyon, as well as Bright Angel Lodge, La Posada at Winslow, and El Navajo in Gallup. See Grattan, *Mary Colter*, and Wiegle, "Exposition and Mediation,"120–30.

15. *The Indian and Mexican Building* (Albuquerque: Fred Harvey, 1904), n. pag.

16. Huckel, *First Families*, n. pag.

17. William H. Simpson, *El Tovar by Fred Harvey: a New Hotel at Grand Canyon of Arizona* (N. p.: Santa Fe Railway, [1905?]), 21–23.

18. Dean MacCannell, *The Tourist: A New Theory of the Leisure Class* (New York: Schocken Books, 1976), 91–107; Weigle, "From Desert to Disney World,"125.

19. Barbara Kramer, "Nampeyo, Hopi House, and the Chicago Land Show," *American Indian Art* 29, no. 1 (1988): 47; Robert A. Trennert, "Fairs, Expositions, and the Changing Image of Southwestern Indians, 1876–1904," *New Mexico Historical Review* 62 (1987): 142.

20. For more information on the Santa Fe Railway's and Harvey's involvement in the expositions, see "The Grand Canyon of Arizona at Panama-Pacific Exposition," *Santa Fe Magazine* 8, no. 8 (1914): 49–50; Phoebe S. Kropp, "'There Is a Little Sermon in That': Constructing the Native Southwest at the San Diego Panama-California Exposition of 1915," in Marta Weigle and Barbara Babcock, eds., *The Great Southwest of the Fred Harvey Company and the Santa Fe Railway* (Phoenix: Heard Museum, 1996), 36–46; Michael Miller, "New Mexico's Role in the Panama-California Exposition of 1915," *Palacio* 91, no. 2 (1985): 13–17; "Museum and School Share in San Diego's Triumph," *Palacio* 2, no. 2 (1914): 2; Sheppard, *Creator of the Santa Fe Style*; and "Sidelights on the Panama-California Exposition," *Santa Fe Magazine* 9, no. 4 (1915): 25–27.

21. Grattan, *Mary Colter*, 32.

22. Nancy Fox, "Margaret Moses: Collector and Courier," *Palacio* 90, no. 3 (1984): 29–31.

23. *Harveycar Motor Cruises off the Beaten Path in the Great Southwest* (Kansas City: Fred Harvey, N. d.), n. pag.

24. Weigle, "From Desert to Disney World,"130.

25. T. J. Jackson Lears, *No Place of Grace: Antimodernism and the Transformation of American Culture 1880–1920* (New York: Pantheon, 1981), 220.

26. Herman Schweizer bought and sold objects of Hispanic manufacture for Harvey shops and displays, and there was some demand locally for Hispanic crafts, but it was not until the 1930s that there was a national market for them. See Dutton, "Commerce on a New Frontier," 98. For more information on the preservation of Hispanic culture in New Mexico, see Sylvia Rodríguez, "Ethnic Reconstruction in Contemporary Taos," *Journal of the Southwest* 32 (1990): 541–55 and Suzanne Forrest, *The Preservation of the Village: New Mexico's Hispanics and the New Deal* (Albuquerque: University of New Mexico Press, 1989).

27. *The Camera in the Southwest* (Kansas City: Fred Harvey, 1904), n. pag.

28. Raymund A. Paredes, "The Mexican Image in American Travel Literature, 1831–1869," *New Mexico Historical Review* 52 (1977): 23.

29. David Weber, "'Scarce More than Apes': Historical Roots of Anglo American Stereotypes of Mexicans in the Border Region," in David Weber, ed., *New Spain's Far Northern Frontier* (Albuquerque: University of New Mexico Press, 1979), 299.

30. See Mark Reisler, *By the Sweat of Their Brow: Mexican Immigrant Labor in the United States, 1900–1940* (Westport, Conn.: Greenwood Press, 1976).

31. Sylvia Rodríguez, "Land, Water, and Ethnic Identity in Taos," in Charles L. Briggs and John R. Van Ness, eds., *Land, Water and Culture: New Perspectives in Hispanic Land Grants* (Albuquerque: University of New Mexico Press, 1987), 321.

32. *The Camera in the Southwest*, n. pag.

33. *The Great Southwest along the Santa Fe* (Kansas City: Fred Harvey, [1911] 1921), n. pag.

34. Karen Seger and Joseph Wilder have discovered that a later version of this postcard was radically altered. In the later version, the two trainmen in the center have been transformed into Pueblo women, one of whom carries a child on her back. (These two women were lifted from another Harvey postcard.) In addition, two of the Pueblo women have had their black stockings and leather shoes painted over to appear as moccasins and leggings. See Karen Seger and Joseph Wilder, "Publishing the Southwest," *Journal of the Southwest* 32 (1990): 377–80.

35. Deirdre Evans-Pritchard, "How 'They' See 'Us': Native American Images of Tourists," *Annals of Tourism Research* 16 (1989): 102.

36. Michel Foucault, *Discipline and Punish: The Birth of the Prison* (New York: Pantheon, 1977), 202, and Donna Haraway, "Teddy Bear Patriarchy: Taxidermy in the Garden of Eden, New York City, 1908–1936," *Social Text* (Winter 1986): 23.

37. Judith Williamson, "Woman Is an Island: Femininity and Colonization," in Tania Modleski, ed., *Studies in Entertainment: Critical Approaches to Mass Culture* (Bloomington: Indiana University Press, 1986), 112.

38. Thanks to Sally Stein for suggesting this identification of the doll and for her helpful interpretation of this image.

Chapter Eight

Seeing America First: The Search for Identity in the Tourist Landscape

Marguerite S. Shaffer

In the fall of 1905 Fisher Sanford Harris, secretary of the Salt Lake City Commercial Club, coined the phrase, "See Europe If You Will, But See America First," in an effort to promote tourism in the United States. Shortened to "See America First," the slogan quickly captured the imaginations of western boosters and businessmen interested in developing the tourist industry in the intermountain West. Although Harris gathered representatives from cities across the West to establish a voluntary "tourist trust," lack of resources and cooperation doomed his promotional scheme to failure.[1] The slogan, however, endured. In 1910, the Great Northern Railway adopted "See America First" as its corporate logo and motto to publicize the development of Glacier National Park. No longer just a regional booster slogan, "See America First" gained the status of a corporate trademark. The Great Northern's wide-scale publicity efforts popularized the slogan; and as World War I closed Europe to American tourists, "See America First" was adopted by a variety of organizations, including Good Roads associations, the Panama Pacific International Exposition, the National Park Service, as well as by touring advocates and travel writers, to advocate domestic tourism. Through this process "See America First" was transformed, during the ensuing decades, into a popular and patriotic touring emblem.[2]

165

Although a unified movement with clearly defined and articulated aims never emerged around the slogan, "See America First" did express the diverse and popular ideas that united entrepreneurs and individuals interested in the development of tourism in the United States. Scattered throughout popular periodicals, touring ephemera, and advertisements, promoted by commercial clubs, railroad companies, automobile manufacturers, touring organizations, and travel writers, and appropriated by a number of tourists, "See America First" signified not only the emerging possibilities for touring in the United States, but also an ongoing dialogue concerning American identity and American nationhood.[3] Tourist industries used the slogan to create and market quintessentially American landscapes, defining tourism as a patriotic ritual of citizenship.[4] Reciprocally, tourists embraced the slogan in an effort to define their tourist journeys, situating themselves as individuals within the tourist landscape. Personal touring narratives and travelogues reveal how tourists consumed the idealized images of America associated with "See America First" and made them their own.

In 1919 Sinclair Lewis published *Free Air*, which recounts the possibilities and the perils of early automobile touring. Growing out of a transcontinental trip Lewis took in 1916 with his wife, Grace Hegger Lewis, the novel traces the physical and social distances traversed through the experience of automobile touring.[5] Claire Boltwood, a high-society Brooklyn Heights girl, and her father, an overworked business magnate, set off on a transcontinental automobile tour in the hopes that fresh air and the adventure of the open road will relieve Mr. Boltwood of his "nervous prostration" brought on from overwork. Their first day on the road they meet up with a mechanic, Milt Daggett, from Schoenstrom, Minnesota, who abandons his garage and his midwestern roots and takes to the road in pursuit of Claire and the possibilities she represents. Traveling from Minneapolis to Seattle in a Gomez-Deperdussin roadster, Claire descends from the exclusive, overly civilized world of Brooklyn Heights into the "real" America. For the Boltwoods this is a "voyage into democracy." For Milt Daggett this is an opportunity to remake himself, leaving behind his provincial and unsophisticated midwestern roots. He skitters and jounces behind the Boltwoods in his Teal Bug, always available to rescue them from the uncertainties of road and automobile, and in the meantime he educates himself about the social graces of proper etiquette and rhetoric.[6]

The novel hinges on the possibilities of the road—the tourist landscape. In motoring through small western towns and windswept prairies, over gleaming mountains and along stretches of open road, Claire discovers not only the "real" people and places of America, but also her own power and independence. Meanwhile, Milt Daggett escapes the confines of small-town, middle America and learns the ways of urbanity and sophistication. In the tourist landscape Claire and Milt are not defined or restricted by their respective social settings. Claire is no longer of Brooklyn Heights and Milt is no longer of Schoenstrom. They inhabit a "nonordinary" setting, in many ways liminal space, a place of re-creation and social fluidity where they are outside of the social as well as the physical confines of home and work.[7] In the tourist landscape Claire and Milt transcend the boundaries of class status and reinvent themselves so that they can be partners on an equal basis. In detailing the adventures of automobile touring Lewis aptly describes the imaginative possibilities embedded in the tourist experience. He celebrates both Claire and Milt as individuals rather than products of their environments, underscoring the potential of American democracy, but at the same time he exposes the possibilities of touring. He reveals the tourist landscape—in this case the open road—as a place outside or beyond everyday life and social conventions where the tourist can refashion him or herself and escape the restrictions of occupation, class, and family background.

Free Air represents one of many narratives, both fictional and documentary, that detailed the experiences of American tourists. From its inception in the early nineteenth century, touring in the United States resulted in a literature of social and cultural commentary. Early transcontinental railroad tourists and pilgrims to natural, historic, and literary shrines set down their experiences, thoughts, and reactions in letters to home newspapers, essays in popular magazines, and travel books.[8] However, during the nineteenth century the touring public remained relatively small. Consequently, early touring narratives focused less on the experience of touring and more on social commentary facilitated by the touring experience.

With the emergence of the automobile, touring became increasingly popular among upper- and middle-class Americans. Unlike the railroad, where rigid schedules and established stops limited passengers to preplanned final destinations, the automobile provided a much more suitable means of transportation for the individual tourist.[9] The word *tour*, coming from the Latin *tornus*, which came from the Greek word signifying "a tool for describing a circle, a turner's wheel," expressed the ideal of a circular journey—a movement away from home, going from site to site at one's leisure, and then returning home.[10] The automobile, catering to the whims of the individual driver, fostered this type of experience. In essence, the automobile shaped and defined the popular touring experience explicitly as a personal journey. As a result, the novelty and the expanded possibilities that came with automobile touring spawned a myriad of publications commenting on and detailing the popular touring experience. As historian Warren Belasco has noted, the early twentieth century witnessed the publication of a vast number of articles, touring journals, pamphlets, diaries, manuals, accounts, and novels. Some tourists kept touring logs and privately published chronicles of their tours. "Freelance writers with a keen eye for a potential fad wrote accounts of transcontinental journeys for newspapers and magazines, while more serious essayists probed the long-run implications for society as a whole."[11] Belasco argues that despite their diversity in form, this eclectic literature shared the desire to celebrate the individual experience of touring, and in the process, represented the popular touring experience.

Just as Sinclair Lewis revealed the social fluidity and the possibilities of the tourist landscape, so other tourist literature and touring narratives commented on the ways in which tourists experienced the tourist landscape and appropriated the marketed tourist experience. Tourists did not thoughtlessly consume the images of America promoted by prescriptive touring literature and objectified by tourist attractions. Many of the touring narratives published during the early twentieth century reveal that tourist responses ranged widely from trite notations to thoughtful meditations about their travels. In many of these narratives, individual journeys of self-realization are set in the context of prescriptive ideals about touring. Some upper- and middle-class tourists bought into the marketed tourist experience without question. Others, self-conscious about their status in an increasingly modern society fraught with working-class unrest, urban vice, ethnic and racial conflict, and overseas foes, revealed their ambivalence by celebrating an idealized and nostalgic image of America in which they, as spectators, remained in control of their own and the nation's destiny. Still others used the experience of tourism to reinvent themselves as independent individuals rejecting or stretching the social and cultural boundaries of early-twentieth-century American society. Overall these narratives shared a common theme. Written by and for upper- and middle-class white Americans, they all participated in and expanded the discourse of national and individual identity defined by "See America First."

Many tourists took to the road explicitly to discover America. As Lewis presents it, the Boltwoods' transcontinental automobile tour was not simply a therapeutic journey; this was a voyage of discovery. Claire was traveling to the "real" America. On the morning of the Boltwoods' second day out on the road, after a particularly harrowing first day of touring in which the Gomez-Dep got stuck in the mud, followed by an uncomfortable night at a run-down drummer's hotel in Gopher Prairie, Minnesota, Claire stopped at a garage to take on gas. While waiting for the car she had a revelation: the people she had met at the hotel the night before were not rude as she had originally assumed. It was her own air of eastern exclusiveness that had made these people seem offensive and intrusive. In a moment of epiphany she exclaimed, "Why, they aren't rude. They care—about people they never saw before. That's why they ask questions! I never thought—I never thought! There's people in the world who want to know us without having looked us up in the Social Register!" This moment of realization introduced a central theme in the novel. While Claire stood there waiting for her car, she noticed a sign on the air hose at the garage that said "Free Air." "There's our motto for the pilgrimage," she declared. The narrator noted, "Thus Claire's second voyage into democracy."[12]

As the title, *Free Air*, drawn from a pun on the gas station air pump, reveals, the Boltwoods' tour was a journey away from the exclusive and sheltered environment of the East represented by Brooklyn Heights and into the open spaces of America, a place of democratic openness and infinite possibility, according to Lewis. In developing this theme of discovery, Lewis suggests that the experience of tourism offered a way to learn about America, and in seeing

America to become an American. As Claire says later in the tour while sitting with Milt around a camp fire at Yellowstone Park, "There is an America! I'm glad I've found it!"[13]

Many tourists revealed in their narratives that, like the Bolt-woods, they too took to the road to "See America First." Their narratives suggest that the prescriptive literature promoting "See America First" was successful in shaping the ways in which tourists imagined and experienced their tours. Some narratives simply chronicled the events of touring day by day, noting the sights seen, the mileage covered, and the condition of hotels. They bespoke an uncritical acceptance of "See America First" promotional literature that encouraged them to consume the sacred landscapes of America and thus become better citizens. In one of the earlier transcontinental touring narratives, Emily Post informed her readers that the "advertisements" prompted her to take a transcontinental automobile tour to the 1915 San Francisco expositions. Very early in the description of her tour she commented, "One thing that we have already found out; we are seeing our own country for the first time!"[14] Vernon McGill, in his *Diary of a Motor Journey from Chicago to Los Angeles,* chronicled the journey his family took in a Willys Knight motor car. Detailing the route between McPherson and Garden City, Kansas, McGill noted, "In 'seeing America first' along this route, one passes many points of historical interest. Today we passed the stamping ground of the famous scout, Kit Carson, and at another point a sign called our attention to a place where General Custer battled with the Indians."[15]

Like McGill's, some tourist narratives simply ticked off the popular attractions tourists visited. Others celebrated the experience of the road and the people encountered along the way. Beatrice Massey in her account of a transcontinental motor trip from New York City to San Francisco counseled readers that touring offered "the only way to get a first-hand knowledge of our country, its people, the scenery, and last, but not the least its roads—good, bad, and infinitely worse."[16] Similarly, Mary Crehore Bedell, who took a circular tour around the United States with her husband, noted, "There is no better way of discovering the fine traits of our fellow countrymen than by packing up a kit and going-a-gypsying."[17] In addition, Effie Price Gladding, celebrating her tour from the Pacific to the Atlantic via the Lincoln Highway, wrote, "We have a new conception of our great country; her vastness, her varied scenery, her prosperity, her happiness, her boundless resources, her immense possibilities, her kindness and hopefulness. We are bound to her by a thousand new ties of acquaintance, of association, and of pride."[18] In a similar vein, Maria Letitia Stockett encouraged her readers, "By all means see America First and then see it again. Don't miss the rangers. See the National Parks—it will restore your faith in democratic government—almost—but I do not wish to exaggerate."[19] Dallas Lore Sharp, the nature writer, recounting his transcontinental tour from Massachusetts to California, perhaps most eloquently explained that the purpose of crossing the country by motor was to see, feel, and understand America: "that so we might have faith and love for this broad land, its forms and terms and manners, its habitable soil, its cheerful sky, its many and mighty cities, its multitongued, multi-millioned, but not amorphous, people."[20] These narratives reveal that tourists stopped to admire natural scenery, historic sites, and technological wonders, just as the prescriptive literature instructed them to, and in doing so they sought to discover the "real" America.[21]

As the divergent "See America First" literature prescribed, in seeing the sights of American history and the landscapes of the nation, tourists experienced firsthand the character and nuances of the nation, and their narratives overflow with references to the various America types and the distinct American places they surveyed. However, the sites they saw and the people they met did not always correspond to the official images of America prescribed by "See America First." Individual tourists constructed their own images of America as they traveled through the tourist landscape. At times, those images were just as idealized as those presented in the prescriptive literature; at other times, tourists presented a seemingly more realistic view of the landscape they traversed. On the whole, however, tourist narratives appear less concerned with constructing an image of national unity and more concerned with discovering a place in which they felt "at home." These narratives reveal a diverse series of underlying anxieties that suggest that individual tourists took to the tourist landscape not only for pleasure but also to discover or invent an America in which they, as white, upper- and middle-class citizens, threatened not only by increased immigration, labor unrest, and racial diversity, but also by a sense of powerlessness and "weightlessness" manifested in modern urban-industrial living, could regain some sense of security and self-control.[22]

Frederic F. Van de Water, a journalist and freelance writer famous for his adventure stories, mysteries, travel writing, and essays, wrote in his introduction to a touring narrative describing his family's transcontinental tour that after "five weeks and two days, three originally smug New Yorkers underwent a slow and amazing transformation . . . at the end of the ordeal they were no longer New Yorkers, but Americans, which, they learned, is something surprisingly and heartenly different." Van de Water's narrative, *The Family Flivvers to Frisco*, tells the story of the Engineer, the Commodore, and the Supercargo—a husband and wife and their six-and-a-half-year-old son—who drove from the suburbs of New York City to San Francisco in a Ford touring car they called Issachar, auto-camping all the way. Written primarily to direct others who might wish to make a transcontinental automobile tour, the book describes the experience of automobile camping: the necessary equipment and clothing, the life and social character of auto-camps, and the pleasures and hazards of the road. Beyond its prescriptive tone, the narrative also chronicles what the family discovered out on the road. Writing about the benefits of the tour, Van de Water noted, "As for the engineer, much has come to him in the way of knowledge. . . . For the first time in thirty-five years, he has been able to visualize the American nation." He went on to conclude, "To us 'America' no longer is an abstract noun, or a familiar map of patchwork, or a flag, or a great domed building in Washington. It is something clearer and dearer and, we think higher. It is the road we traveled." Van de Water proclaimed, "You cannot comprehend America unless you go and see it."[23]

Like Claire Boltwood, Van de Water's crew left New York in a cynical and snobbish frame of mind, ignorant and dismissive of an America outside of their exclusive milieu. They arrived in San Francisco, "thin" and "tanned, brown as Indians," transformed into "native" Americans not only by the scenery and the historic sites and shrines they witnessed, but also by the friendly, democratic Americans they encountered along the way. In auto-camps across the continent they met the common people of America, touring, working, and tramping. Van de Water noted that days spent in camp revealed the community of makeshift automobile camps. He commented on "the warming friendliness of neighbors who rested." He went on to explain, "By grace of the fact that they were all there, the campers regarded each other as acquaintances. They squatted together in the shade and debated many things. They compared equipment. They sought information regarding the roads ahead. The camp was filled with lazy, pleasant talk all day long." Tourists shared in the community of the road seemingly free of the boundaries of social class and family background. For Van de Water the community of the auto-camp represented an ideal democratic community, with an "unguardedly friendly, almost family-like air"; a community not unlike an idealized version of the nineteenth-century rural small towns that were being rapidly supplanted by large urban centers and a national commercial and technological network.[24]

In witnessing the landscape of America firsthand, in communing with "real" Americans, Van de Water suggested that he and his family came to be better citizens. "Traveling, as we traveled, through the heart of the nation," he mused, "brought us a new definition of what constitutes nationality." He explained that the urban dweller who lived in an apartment rarely knew his neighbor: "In streets where one hurries, severely intent upon his own affairs, life is individualistic and egocentric." In this atmosphere one "never savors the full flavor of what citizenship in the republic means." Only by traveling in the "open land," he argued, could one begin to comprehend "the advantages of being an American." He concluded, "gradually, it dawns upon him that citizenship by itself, that existence in these regions untouched by the blight of New York is the faint equivalent of membership in a brotherhood, the due guard and sign of which is a word of greeting and a smile."[25] Beyond the details of auto-camping lore, his story suggests that touring really was about discovering the "real" America, but the America he discovered was clouded by nostalgia.

The nation he described was a homogeneous America composed of courteous, generous, friendly people always willing to lend a helping hand in times of trouble. It was an America of open spaces, rural landscapes, and sublime scenery. Celebrating the tour, Van de Water wrote:

We have seen the background of the nation's birth roll past us on either hand as Issachar rattled West. We know America and

Americans as only those who go motor camping can learn to know them. We have discovered a people and a land whose existence the average New Yorker never even suspects. The scenery, the vast extent of America have awed and thrilled and lifted us up, but its people have stirred us the most—its dear, kind, friendly people.[26]

Van de Water suggested that, just as advocates of "See America First" promised, touring stimulated patriotism by revealing through firsthand experience not only the physical wonders of the nation, but also the democratic spirit of the American people.

As Warren Belasco has noted in his study of automobile touring, the America that tourists celebrated extended from the community of other automobile tourists met along the road. Like Van de Water, many touring narratives noted that the community of the road was a democratic melting pot reflecting a wide geographical mix and a broad cross-section of middle-class tourists.[27] For many tourists, according to their narratives, the experience of automobile touring reaffirmed their faith in the democratic principles on which America was founded. On the road they encountered a regionally diverse cross-section of American society and a sense of brotherhood, community, family. Over and over touring narratives commemorated the democratic community of the road. In essence these narratives idealized the America they discovered while touring, constructing a mythological image of America that more accurately reflected their dissatisfaction with and their fears about the status of democracy in an urban-industrial America than it did the realities of American life.

In reality, the America of automobile camps, tourist attractions, and the open road comprised a relatively homogeneous community of upper- and middle-class, urban, white Americans. Although occasionally auto tourists met up with traveling salesmen, migrant workers, and tramps, automobile touring took time and money. During the late teens and the early twenties it was a pastime enjoyed by a select few of the upper and upper-middle class.[28] To say that this select community reflected the diversity and democracy of America denied the ethnic and racial conflicts and concerns that characterized the Progressive Era, as well as the increasingly urban and corporate character of American society. The America these tourists saw and eulogized nostalgically looked back to a Jeffersonian ideal of an American society composed of independent yeoman landholders living in a pastoral setting—a middle landscape.[29] Through the power of the tourist gaze, automobile tourists imagined themselves and their fellow tourists as independent citizens enjoying the bounty of the American land and existing self-sufficiently with the help of their fellow "citizens." Just as proponents of "See America First" constructed and promoted an idealized image of America for tourists, tourists themselves took to the road in search of an ideal America that might negate their feelings of powerlessness. Although the images of America promoted by "See America First" advocates varied and did not always match the ideals celebrated by tourists, both promoters and participants took part in the discourse surrounding an ideal America that resulted from a growing uncertainty and dissatisfaction with the realities of urban-industrial life.[30]

Many of the touring narratives expressed this anxiety about the status of American society by looking for and finding an America of democratic, rural, small-town communities primarily associated with an idealized West. The West became the antithesis of the northeastern industrial core. Tourists associated it with democracy, freedom, friendliness, and community. They saw only a land of farmers, ranchers, cowboys, and friendly Indians—people who lived close to the land. Over and over again touring narratives idealized the West as the "true" America in opposition to the overly civilized, urban East. As Letitia Stockett exclaimed in her chronicle of a cross-country tour, "To see the real America go west."[31] Similarly, Katherine Hulme noted in her touring narrative, How's The Road? that after crossing the Mississippi River, "something within us that had been taut, suddenly loosened. We actually felt ourselves expanding in the genial sunshine and we seemed to take up more room in the seat."[32] Rather than depicting the realities of western society, this idealization of the West implicitly revealed the anxiety felt by upper- and middle-class tourists about the seeming failure of democracy, the anonymity, and the bureaucracy associated with modern, urban-industrial society. In idealizing the West, tourists blatantly ignored not only the ethnic diversity of the West but also its increasingly urban and industrial character.[33]

Like other commemorative events and activities, tourism was multivocal. It brought together, as historian John Bodnar has explained of other acts of commemoration, "powerful symbolic expression—metaphors, signs, and rituals—that give meaning to competing interpretations of past and present reality." The range of touring narratives suggests that the personal as much as the prescriptive shaped the tourist experience. Prescriptive touring literature explicitly and implicitly celebrated an ideal of national unity. Touring narratives, on the other hand, did not concern themselves so much with national unity as with finding some personal understanding of what America represented and where the tourists as individuals fit within that America. In their search to discover America, tourists embraced the values of the official culture expressed by prescriptive literature, and they simultaneously altered the official image of national unity with their own concerns and anxieties.[34] Many touring narratives presented thoughtful meditations of self-discovery in which tourists measured their lives and their identities in both positive and negative ways. They used the landscape of tourism as a venue to consider their role, place, and purpose in American society and in the larger context of life. They also challenged the realities of their contemporary society by imagining a more nostalgic ideal of America. Political concerns and social status, as well as gender identity, influenced the ways in which individual tourists conceived and presented these journeys of self-exploration.

In *Free Air* Milt Daggett used the social fluidity of the open road and automobile camps to escape his small-town roots and refashion himself as a more cultured and urbane young man. Seeing the world and seeking out new possibilities embodied the potential of self-transformation. While on the road he observed the behavior of traveling salesmen, whom he called "pioneers in spats," so that he might learn the ways of the city, and he bought a book of rhetoric so that he might improve his speech. By the time he reached Seattle he had set his sights on going to school and becoming an engineer, rather than settling for owning a small-town garage in which he was "all but one of the working force." In the process of his tour, he traversed geographical and social space so that he might win the hand of Claire Boltwood. On the road, Milt became an individual unfettered by his social background, his small-town roots, his high school education, and his provincial manners. He could rely on his own skill and intelligence to solve the problems that confronted him. The appearance of Milt's old friend Bill McGolwey, the proprietor of the

Old Home Lunch place in Schoenstrom, at his flat in Seattle revealed the extent of Milt's transformation. Milt wondered to himself, "Was this the fellow he had liked so well? These the ideas which a few months ago he had taken as natural and extremely amusing?"[35] In essence, the freedom of the tourist experience allowed Milt to actualize the myth of the self-made man. Through Milt's transformation, Lewis presents the landscape of tourism as a special place—a place beyond the restrictions of work and home—where one was freed from the confines of occupation, social class, and family background. In essence, this was a place where the American dream still had meaning.

As sociologist Dean MacCannell has explained, tourist attractions are best understood as cultural productions. As staged representations of various aspects of life, tourist attractions conveyed a totality that was increasingly absent from urban-industrial life.[36] The tourist gaze transformed the built and the natural environment into scenery and spectacle.[37] Through the experience of touring, individuals became spectators, surveying a variety of scenes and sites that represented nature, work, history, art, other—the totality of modern life. Anthropologist Nelson Graburn has defined tourism as "a special form of play involving travel." Looking at the tourist experience as the antithesis of the experience of everyday work and routine, Graburn suggests that through the tourist journey the individual is transported to a "nonordinary state wherein marvelous things happen."[38] Like the experience of going to the theater, an amusement park, or the movies, the experience of tourism provided a setting in which individuals could refashion themselves.[39] By going on vacation, "vacating" the workaday routines, tourists moved beyond both the physical and the imaginary boundaries of home and work that shaped and defined their everyday identities. They entered a realm of fantasy, they communed with strangers, they witnessed the foreign. In this liminal environment, tourists, as anonymous spectators, surveyed the tourist spectacle from the outside, and yet only from their perspective did that spectacle have meaning. As outsiders they were free to adopt any role. As strangers they experienced a kind of "privacy in public," where they could act spontaneously without fearing the judgments of their quotidian milieu of family, friends, coworkers, and acquaintances.[40]

In their narratives, many tourists spoke of the transformative possibilities embedded in the tourist landscape. Nature writer Dallas Lore Sharp and his wife Daphne took to the road in search of "a better country." Recounting their experience in his book, *The Better Country*, Sharp detailed not only his perceptions about America but also his own personal transformation on the road. The Sharps had reached their middle fifties, their four boys had all gone off to college, and the house was empty. In allegorical terms Sharp wrote, "Daphne and I found ourselves at the top of the long hill up which for so many years we had been climbing." If they followed the main road they descended to "Pension Place . . . Cemetery beyond. End of Road." So, instead they decided to turn off on "an old trail, unimproved, unposted, and utterly untraveled."[41] Their goal was to motor cross-continent from their home in Hingham, Massachusetts, to Los Angeles and begin a new life in California.

In his narrative Sharp mused at each stopping point about whether they had reached the "better country." Through his journey he discovered that "the better country" was not a place so much as a state of mind, signifying an escape from the responsibilities of home and work. It embodied the meaning of Sharp's retirement. It stood for the potential of the golden years of their married life, when the obligations to children and success were past and only the possibilities of leisure, pleasure, and self-realization remained. Driving out of Dodge City he resolved, "I would break training now . . . I would never utter another epoch-making word to anybody, nor consult another time-table, nor own another alarm clock, nor care what day of the week it is, what hour of the day." From the perspective of the open road he began to escape from the restrictions that his ordinary life had imposed upon him. He went on to explain, "I knew that at last I had actually left Hingham and was even now entering . . . that Better Country of whose reality I had been persuaded, and toward which, a stranger and a pilgrim, I had been always on the road."[42] It was on the road—through the experience of tourism itself—that Sharp achieved the state of mind embodied by his quest for "the better country."

This "better country" that the Sharps went in search of manifested all the possibilities of the tourist landscape. For the tourist, it provided a place where one could discard the social self and actualize the personal self. It represented both a public and a private space where the individual—the tourist—had the opportunity and the power to define what was meaningful and what was not. For some the tourist landscape embodied a place of self-fulfillment and self-expression removed from the strictures that defined acceptable social behavior in everyday society. Writer Hoffman Birney linked this sense of freedom and authenticity to the experience of the strenuous life. His narrative detailing a tour of the Southwest is filled with tales of sleeping under the stars and exploring Indian ruins and desert landscapes, scavenging for Indian pottery and arrowheads, and photographing the sights and scenes of the desert landscape. Writing of a pack trip to Rainbow Bridge, Birney challenged his readers: "If you have in you a love of the true solitudes, if you can find a thrill in penetrating lands that have not changed since the cliff-dwellers built their homes in the red walls of the Tsagi, if the silent, calm, beautiful, savage, treacherous desert means more to you than all the wildernesses of steel and brick that men call cities— then you will revel in that ride to Teas-ya-toh, [the Cottonwood Water, on the way to the Rainbow Bridge]!" The difficulties of a pack trip—managing the mules, negotiating dangerous trails, and camping outdoors—and the experience of viewing the "wonders" of a country where "nature has run riot," effected a profoundly moving personal experience, according to Birney. He could respond only that God had been very good to him for allowing him to witness these wonders. In conclusion he admonished his readers, "Go there; and if you do not come away a little better for the experience, a little more closely in tune with the Infinite, I'll pay for your trip!"[43]

As historian Harvey Green has explained, the early decades of the twentieth century witnessed a great upsurge of interest in the strenuous life—a movement perhaps best represented by Theodore Roosevelt and his quest for health, athleticism, and action. Advocates of the strenuous life presented physical exercise of all sorts as a curative for the nervousness or neurasthenia that seemed to be overwhelming the middle classes of urban-industrialized America. Just as bicycling was seen as a reinvigorating exercise, so touring narratives suggest that automobile touring offered the necessary adventure and action for personal regeneration.[44] Birney's narrative revealed that touring offered more than just the challenge of physical adventure and intense experience. As a retreat into nature, it also held the promise of spiritual renewal. Although the framework of the market defined the landscape of tourism, individual tourists used this landscape to transcend the social boundaries of urban-industrial society. Ironically, in seeking to actualize the self in this liminal environment, tourists adopted the desires of the therapeutic, anonymous individual central to the consumer society they thought they were fleeing.

As historian T. J. Jackson Lears has written, "Throughout the twentieth century, a recoil from overcivilized qualities of modern existence has sparked a wide variety of quests for more intense experience ranging from fascist fascination with death, to the cult of emotional spontaneity of avant garde artists to popular therapies stressing instinctual liberation." In some ways the experience of tourism might best be understood in this context. Touring narratives celebrated the strenuous life out in the open, overcoming the hazards of poorly constructed and ill-marked roads, camping out, confronting nature. They also celebrated the quest for self-realization. In this way, touring embraced both risk and physical exertion, promising intense experience and self-fulfillment.[45] From this perspective, touring reflected the larger cultural concerns expressed by the therapeutic ethos: the desire for vigorous health, the desire for authentic experience, and the desire for self-fulfillment. Touring narratives suggest that as a voyage of self-discovery, tourism promised "temporary escape to a realm of intense experience far from the stiff unreality of bourgeois culture."[46] Many tourists used the language of the therapeutic ethos to define their tours. For men this language reflected an anxiety about their own powerlessness as individuals in a corporate, urban-industrial society. For women, this language suggested that the desire for self-fulfillment embodied specifically gendered meanings in a society still wed to the ideology of separate spheres.

In *Free Air* Claire Boltwood not only discovered the "real" America, but she also discovered power, independence, and adventure in touring the West. As a member of the exclusive social world of Brooklyn Heights, Claire was "used to gracious leisure, attractive uselessness, [and] nut-center chocolates." She personified the ideal of a refined young woman. As the narrator explained, she knew very little about the life that existed beyond her social set of Brooklyn Heights and Manhattan, and she had had to do very little for herself throughout her life. The first day out after leaving Minneapolis, hopelessly stuck in thick Minnesota gumbo, Claire realized that her life would be different on the road. When her father finally told her to go get someone to help them out of the mud, she responded, "No. One of the good things about an adventure like this is that I must do things for myself. I've always had people do things for me." She added, "I suppose it's made me soft." Instead of seeking help, she scavenged in the wet mud for brush to provide footing for the tires, and she reveled in being wet and dirty. She became like a "pioneer woman," the narrator explained, "toiling" on the land. On that first day out Claire had her first experience of real physical work. Once out of the mud hole and back on the road, her hands became "sturdy," her eyes "tireless," and she was ready to "drive forever." The next morning she rolled out of bed, tired and stiff, but she soon realized that "she was stronger than she ever had been, that she was a woman, not a dependent girl."[47]

In setting out on a tour alone with her ill and helpless father, in negotiating muddy, rough roads, in checking radiator water and tire casings, Claire assumed an air of authority, responsibility, and independence, which would have been symbolically unacceptable and unattainable in the social structure of Brooklyn Heights. In the tourist landscape she transcended the ideological boundaries of the upper- and middle-class cult of domesticity, escaping the class-defined confines of separate spheres. She not only ventured out into the landscape, a landscape of dangerous roads and potentially dangerous strangers, she also entered into predominantly masculine spaces. Midway into her tour, talking low by a campfire in Yellowstone, she asked Milt Daggett, "Will I get all fussy and ribbon-tied again, when I go back [to Brooklyn Heights]?" His response revealed the gendered possibilities of the tourist experience. "No. You won't," he said, "You drive like a man."[48]

In experiencing the strenuous life, in searching for self-realization, touring took on added meaning for women measured against (judged by) the standards of the cult of domesticity. The landscape of tourism offered women a venue outside of the domestic sphere in which they could reimagine themselves as independent, self-sufficient, active members of society. As drivers, women challenged the restrictions placed on them by the ideal of the upper-middle-class woman who stayed at home, outside of the public sphere, and cared for her family, letting her husband deal with the demands of getting a living.[49] Interestingly, a majority of the published touring narratives were written by women who set out on the road to find freedom and independence. And many of these narratives expressed a gendered understanding of the tourist landscape.

In 1928, Katherine Hulme privately published *How's The Road?* which chronicled a tour from New York to San Francisco taken by the author and a woman friend, "Tuny." "Ashamed of [their] woman's heritage of fickle fancy," Hulme and her friend Tuny took to the road to see America because they were "hungry for the outdoors," and as Tuny explained, "because we'd rather drive our own car than be driven by a ship."[50] In many respects their decision to make a transcontinental tour represented a declaration of independence. They named their roadster Reggie, in opposition to the men that "name their cars Sally or Lizzie," not only referring to the medieval tradition of knighthood but also implying the feminine control of the masculine machine.[51] From the start they asserted their rights as women to enjoy the public sphere defined by the road and the automobile, despite the disapproving looks of "motherly" women who frowned on their queries about the location of hotels after dark. Versed in the basics of auto mechanics and the regimen of camping, Hulme and Tuny were more than self-sufficient and had few fears about traveling alone.

The pair tackled thick prairie gumbo, worn tires, mechanical problems, dirty hotels and lunch rooms, and collapsing tents in the drenching rain with the same skill and fortitude as their male counterparts. Despite the understated tone, it is clear from the narrative that they understood their touring experience in gendered terms as a challenge to standard assumptions and expectations about the woman's place and role in American society. Hulme represented Tuny and herself as embodiments of the New Woman of the twenties—educated, single, economically independent, and socially equal to men.[52] On the road they became the companions of traveling salesmen, college boys, cowboys, and farmers. As tourists, they gained access to the male-dominated public sphere—the drummer's hotels, the blacksmith shops, the town garages, and the great outdoors.

In the narrative, Hulme was careful to distinguish Tuny and herself from the stereotypical "girls" of the twenties. Early on, she recorded her amazement at the "elaborate toilettes" of two young women in a communal bathroom at the auto-camp in Pierre, South

Dakota. She remarked that their "cheap little faces were rather effective with their layers of unreal pink and white, if one didn't look beyond the face." As "the girls" left, Tuny's only comment was "Hell's Bells," a subtle pun on the established social standards of feminine beauty and the realities of an American society that idealized restricted roles for women. In contrast, Hulme and Tuny wore "utterly disreputable" outfits of "dingy" tweed knickers, wash-streaked shirts with mud-blackened oxfords. And they paid little attention to make-up or hair "that had been smoothed down with a bacony hand, that had ridden bare through dust storms and hung over smoke and had sometimes been rudely jammed up against the black greasy housing of Reggie's underside during various tinkerings."[53]

Rejecting the standards of feminine beauty and behavior, Hulme and Tuny embraced the adventures of automobile touring and camping. They braved thick prairie mud where others feared to cross. They traversed the Big Horn Mountains in Montana despite warnings that "no one [had] made it so far this year." And they traveled through "practically uninhabited" country "tast[ing] a little of the exultation of the soul and the despair of the body that the early pioneers must have felt when they first looked upon that glorious barrier, [the Rockies] shimmering like white heat under its covering of eternal snow." Recording a triumph in South Dakota, Hulme wrote about an episode where the road had been washed away and a group of automobile tourists were forced to take to the open prairie, "every man for himself and his car." Resorting to irony, Hulme noted that she and Tuny—two women—were the first who dared to cross the stream that would take them back to the road. Hulme subtly drew attention to their success and self-sufficiency as two lone females in a society that valued the action of "every man for himself."[54]

Not only were they able to negotiate the adventures of difficult driving and treacherous roads, but they were also "good mechanics, capable of making any repair of the car." Although few of the men they met on the road had faith in their skills, they could change tires, flush the crankcase, and grease the grease cups as well as any garage mechanic. Hulme explained that they had to begin "tinkering [on their car] in lovely lonely spots," because they had "many experiences with the 'assisting' man camper who thinks that when a woman gets anything more complicated than an egg-beater in her hand, she is to be watched carefully."[55] Celebrating their ability to manage not only the intricacies of the machine but also their own work, Hulme used the masculine images of machinery and work to underscore the possibilities of the tourist experience for women.

The further west they traveled, the further they retreated from the conventions of eastern society and the associated gender restrictions. The wide-open landscapes and small towns of the West reflected not only the absence of eastern cities and urbanity but also the seeming disappearance of the social restrictions of urban and suburban life. Hulme noted when they neared the Mississippi River that they were "anxious to get out of the shadow of cities to the broader spaces," where they could camp and enjoy the outdoors. She linked their new-felt freedom and independence with the West. In this land of cowboys, ranchers, and farmers the pair abandoned the refinements of "lady-like" behavior and enjoyed their experiences with an unaffected pleasure. Hulme recalled sharing meals with the cowboys at a small western inn: "In the shadow of their famished onslaughts upon the food, Tuny's and my voracity went unheeded. We wallowed through second and third 'helpings' and after meals we slept off the effects of our gorgings, like so many stuffed pythons." She went on to remark, "It was disgraceful, but it made us one of them. After the second meal they ceased referring to us as the 'two young ladies from the East' and called us 'the girls.'"[56] This new label was in no way connected to the two young women they had met in the bathroom in Pierre, South Dakota. Rather than reflecting their distinctly feminine characteristics, in Hulme's mind, this label identified them as fellow westerners and fellow cowboys, freed from the restrictions of eastern and feminine refinement.

In abandoning feminine refinements and adopting the guise of self-sufficient tourists, Hulme and Tuny gained admission to places that had been predominantly associated with men.[57] They mixed with the traveling salesmen at drummer's hotels and followed their lead on difficult roads, negotiating chuckholes, rocks, and gumbo like professional travelers.[58] They camped on the open prairie alone and entertained two cowboys who stopped to greet them. When stopping in towns, they haunted garages and blacksmith shops, purchasing supplies or overseeing repairs. The blacksmith in Choteau, Montana, invited the pair in to watch him work his forge. "He found a rod, scanned it critically, seeming to see through its rusty stiffness, the curving bracket he could make of it. Then he thrust it into the live coals of his forge. He pumped the bellows and a spurt of red sparks shot up the chimney. And while the rod heated, he led us around his shop, exhibiting specimens of his wrought-iron work-manship," wrote Hulme.[59] He even went so far as to show the pair his bulging biceps. The sexual undertones of Hulme's description ironically reinforce the symbolic importance of their female presence in this masculine space. As tourists Hulme and her companion were thus able to vicariously experience this traditionally masculine work. Sociologist Dean MacCannell has suggested that the tourist view of various aspects of work allowed tourists to comprehend the total-ity of work in a modern society where the experience of work was completely fragmented and seemingly meaningless.[60] However, for upper- and middle-class women this comprehensive tourist view had added meaning. At least in the early twentieth century it legitimately admitted these women into the realm of masculine work, from which they had been ideologically excluded, without the stigma attached to lower-class women laborers.

Many other women tourists wrote of their tours in a similar vein, celebrating their sense of power, individuality, and indepen-dence. Emily Post, Winifred Hawkridge Dixon, and Letitia Stockett, to name only a few of the women tourists who published touring narratives during the teens and twenties, all commented in one way or another about the gendered experience of being on the road.[61] An early transcontinental motorist, Post traveled from New York to San Francisco for the California expositions with her son and a female relative in the summer of 1915. Her son did all of the driving, the party stayed at the best hotels along the way, and Post commented primarily on the quality of accommodations, the condition of the roads, and the sights to be seen. She recounted, however, that from the start people responded to the news of her trip with incredulity. In many ways, her narrative, which she had arranged to publish serially with *Collier's,* offered proof that a woman could comfortably make a transcontinental automobile tour. Winifred Dixon and her friend Toby toured throughout the Southwest admiring the Indian ruins, witnessing Indian ceremonies, and viewing the dramatic desert land formations. Although they frequently encountered skepticism about their ability—as two lone women—to brave the dangers and uncertainties of road and car, Dixon's narrative reveals that they succeeded at traversing the West from Texas to Montana on their own. The experience of managing steep mountain passes, muddy roads, and necessary car repairs gave them "courage to meet new contingencies" and to overcome all feelings of "helplessness."[62] Similarly, Letitia Stockett occasionally noted the disparaging comments made by skeptical men in her touring narrative that recounted the adventures of a transcontinental tour taken by three Wellesley girls. Like the others, her story revealed the gendered significance of the touring experience for women.

These narratives suggest that many of the upper- and middle-class women who took to the road found added meaning in the freedom and adventure of the touring experience. Women writers used the imagery of self-realization and renewal that characterized the therapeutic ethos to express the gendered possibilities of the tourist landscape.[63] Despite the fact that they sometimes worried about the dangers and uncertainties of the road or had to rely on the help of a passing man, women represented themselves in their narratives as independent, self-sufficient, and responsible, in contrast to the overly civilized, refined young ladies they left behind. Just as women took advantage of the opportunities presented by the theater, the amusement park, and the dance hall to escape the confines of patriarchal domination, so they used the experience of tourism to liberate themselves from the ideal of the refined, soft-spoken lady, who stayed at home, nurtured her family, and submitted to the will of her husband. In the tourist landscape upper- and middle-class white women were able to transcend the expectations—the limitations—of the domestic ideal, thus paving the way for the New Woman, who embraced an ideal of heterosexual interaction within the public sphere, where men and women could come together as equals. Ironically, many of the touring narratives written by women connected this sense of liberation with a mythological ideal of the West, representing themselves as modern-day pioneers and looking back nostalgically to an earlier ideal of women as domestic producers.

The diverse array of prescriptive material disseminated by advocates of "See America First" to encourage Americans to tour America presented a complex assortment of images of the nation. Businesses and organizations used "See America First" to construct and promote their own ideal of America. Although the resulting visions differed, reflecting the divergent concerns of the individuals and organizations who created them, they all shared in the desire to construct and promote official, marketable images of a unified and united American nation. In part, this desire reflected an attempt to transform a diverse American public into a unified group of tourists or consumers—to provide a coherent subject or object—America—for tourists to see, understand, and consume. However, the construction and promotion of America as a unified national entity on the part of tourist industries and advocates also reflected a pervasive apprehension about the emergence of a modern, urban-industrialized nation-state. "See America First" was part of a larger discourse that revolved around the changing meaning of America as the forces of industrialization, urbanization, incorporation, and immigration reshaped the political, the economic, the social, and the cultural boundaries of American society.[64]

Touring narratives reveal that tourists also participated in this discourse. Many tourists took to the road to discover America. However, the America they found did not always conform to the images presented by prescriptive touring literature. Many tourists followed the directive of "See America First" and frequented the sacred landscapes promoted by tourist industries and advocates, but the America they saw not only reflected the desires and interests of promoters but also expressed the concerns and ideals of white upper- and middle-class Americans anxious about their own status and identity in a modern, urban-industrial society. Through their touring narratives tourists celebrated a nostalgic image of America that referred back to a nineteenth-century society of small towns, middle landscapes, and face-to-face interaction objectified by a mythological West. In this idealized landscape, outside the confines of everyday life, tourists sought to define themselves. As an adventure into the nonordinary, touring provided an opportunity for intense experience, spiritual renewal, and self-realization. This experience had different meanings for men and women. However, for both men and women, this quest for self-discovery was integrally connected to the discourse of national identity manifested through "See America First." As historian John Higham has written, "We are well aware of the aggressive nationalism that sprang up after 1890. We do not so often notice analogous ferments in other spheres: a boon in sports and recreation; a revitalized interest in untamed nature; a quickening of popular music; an unsettling of the condition of women."[65] Anxieties about finding the "true" self implicitly expressed apprehensions about the bureaucracy, the anonymity, the "weightlessness" of modern American life. These same concerns on a social level provoked the larger dialogue concerning issues of nationality and nation and the true meaning of America. On different levels, with different intentions, promoters or producers of the "See America First" idea and tourists or consumers of the "See America First" experience shared a common desire to invent a unified and united ideal of America as a nation. The dissonance between their versions of "See America First" reveals the struggle, the conflict, and the dialogue that took place behind the myth of national unity.

Notes

1. Marguerite S. Shaffer, "'See America First': Re-Envisioning Nation and Region through Western Tourism," *Pacific Historical Review* 65 (November 1996): 559–82.

2. Marguerite S. Shaffer, "Negotiating National Identity: Western Tourism and 'See America First,'" in Hal K. Rothman, ed., *Reopening the American West* (Tucson: University of Arizona Press, 1998), 122–51.

3. For an examination of the relationship between "See America First" and national identity see Marguerite S. Shaffer, "See America First: Tourism and National Identity, 1905–1930," (Ph.D. diss., Harvard University, 1994).

4. For example, see Marguerite S. Shaffer, "Seeing the *Nature* of America: The National Parks as National Assets, 1914–1929," in *The Development of Mass Tourism: Commercial Leisure and National Identities 19th and 20th Century Europe and North America*, ed. Shelly Barnowski and Ellen Furlough (Ann Arbor: University of Michigan Press, forthcoming).

5. Despite the vast amount of scholarship on Sinclair Lewis and his fiction, there has been relatively little scholarship on *Free Air*. For a brief discussion of *Free Air* as one of Lewis's serialized novels, see Martin Bucco, "The Serialized Novels of Sinclair Lewis," in *Modern Critical Views, Sinclair Lewis*, ed. Harold Bloom (New York: Chelsea House Publishers, 1987), 63–70. For an overview of the biographical circumstances behind the narrative, see Mark Schorer, *Sinclair Lewis: An American Life* (New York: McGraw-Hill, 1961), 235–39 and 253–61.

6. Sinclair Lewis, *Free Air* (Lincoln: University of Nebraska Press, 1993; reprint of 1919 ed.), 13 and 45.

7. Nelson H. H. Graburn, "Tourism: The Sacred Journey," in *Hosts and Guests: The Anthropology of Tourism*, 2nd ed. Valene L. Smith (Philadelphia: University of Pennsylvania Press, 1989), 21–36. See also Victor Turner and Edith Turner, *Image and Pilgrimage in Christian Culture: Anthropological Perspectives* (New York: Columbia University Press, 1978).

8. Earl Pomeroy, *In Search of the Golden West: Tourism in Western America* (Lincoln: University of Nebraska Press, 1990), 15. Although there is no schol-

arly monograph detailing the history of the literature of travel and tourism as it developed in the United States, a number of works on the history of tourism in America provide a selective overview of some of that literature. In addition to Pomeroy, see Warren James Belasco, *Americans on the Road: From Autocamp to Motel, 1910–1945* (Cambridge, Mass.: MIT Press, 1979); Dona L. Brown, *Inventing New England: Regional Tourism in the Nineteenth Century* (Washington, D.C.: Smithsonian Institution Press, 1995); John A. Jakle, *The Tourist: Travel in Twentieth-Century North America* (Lincoln: University of Nebraska Press, 1985); and John F. Sears, *Sacred Places: American Tourist Attractions in the Nineteenth Century* (New York: Oxford University Press, 1989).

9. See Belasco, *Americans on the Road*, 19–39, for the differences tourists found between travel by train and travel by automobile.

10. *The Oxford English Dictionary*, 2nd ed., vol. 18 (Oxford: Clarendon Press, 1989), 304, and Daniel J. Boorstin, "From Traveler to Tourist: The Lost Art of Travel," in *The Image: A Guide to Pseudo-Events in America* (New York: Atheneum, 1980), 85.

11. Belasco, *Americans on the Road*, 7–8.

12. Lewis, *Free Air*, 38, 46, and 47.

13. Ibid., 140.

14. Emily Post, *By Motor to the Golden Gate* (New York: D. Appleton, 1917), 6 and 23.

15. Vernon McGill, *Diary of a Motor Journey from Chicago to Los Angeles* (Los Angeles: Grafton Publishing Corp., 1922), 31.

16. Beatrice Massey, *It Might Have Been Worse: A Motor Trip From Coast to Coast* (San Francisco: HarrWagner Publishing Co., 1920), foreword.

17. Mary Crehore Bedell, *Modern Gypsies: The Story of a Twelve Thousand Mile Motor Camping Trip Encircling the United States* (New York: Brentano's, 1924), 262.

18. Effie Price Gladding, *Across the Continent by the Lincoln Highway* (New York: Brentano's, 1915), ix.

19. Letitia Stockett, *America: First, Fast and Furious* (Baltimore: Norman-Remington Co., 1930), vi.

20. Dallas Lore Sharp, *The Better Country* (Boston: Houghton Mifflin Co., 1928), 36.

21. For a selection of touring narratives addressing at various levels the issues of seeing America, see also Myrtle Barrett, *Our Wondrous Trip* (Author, 1914); Hoffman Birney, *Roads to Roam* (Philadelphia: Penn Publishing Co., 1930); Daniel Smith Crowningshield, *The Jolly Eight: Coast to Coast and Back* (Boston: Richard G. Badger, 1929); Winifred Hawkridge Dixon, *Westward Hoboes: Ups and Downs of Frontier Motoring* (New York: Charles Scribner's Sons, 1921); Theodore Dreiser, *A Hoosier Holiday* (London: John Lane Co., 1916; reprint, Bloomington: Indiana University Press, 1997); James Flagg, *Boulevards All the Way—Maybe* (New York: Doran, 1925); Katherine Hulme, *How's the Road?* (San Francisco: Author, 1928); Caroline Rittenberg, *Motor West* (New York: Harold Vinal, 1926); Gula Sabin, *California by Motor* (Milwaukee: Author, 1926); Ted Salmon, *From Southern California to Casco Bay* (San Bernardino, Calif.: San Bernardino Publishing Co., 1930); Frederic F. Van de Water, *The Family Flivvers to Frisco* (New York: D. Appleton, 1927); Paul E. Vernon, *Coast to Coast By Motor* (London: A. and C. Black, 1930); Clara Walker Whiteside, *Touring New England on the Trail of the Yankee* (Philadelphia: Penn Publishing Co., 1926); and Andrew Wilson, *The Gay Gazel: An Adventure in Auto Biography* (Author, 1926).

22. For a discussion of the origins of these feelings of powerlessness, weightlessness, and anonymity and the reactions to these feelings see T. J. Jackson Lears, *No Place of Grace: Antimodernism and the Transformation of American Culture, 1880–1920* (New York: Pantheon Books, 1981).

23. Van de Water, *The Family Flivvers to Frisco*, 5–6, 8, 9, and 173. For a biographical sketch of Van de Water's writing career, see Stanley J. Kunitz, ed., *Twentieth Century Authors, First Supplement* (New York: H. W. Wilson Co., 1955), 1023–24.

24. Van de Water, *The Family Flivvers to Frisco*, 293, 71, and 137. For a discussion of the values and ideals associated with the small town, see Robert Wiebe, *The Search for Order, 1877–1920* (New York: Hill and Wang, 1967).

25. Van de Water, *The Family Flivvers to Frisco*, 45.

26. Ibid., 240.

27. Belasco, *Americans on the Road*, 92–103.

28. For an overview of the development of automobile touring see Belasco, *Americans on the Road*. Although Belasco implies, as do the tourists' narratives that he analyzes, that touring was a democratic pastime, the time and expenses demanded for an automobile tour suggest that it remained a relatively exclusive pastime into the 1920s and beyond. In 1921 an estimated 20,000 Americans out of a population of 100 million Americans, approximately .02% of the total population, made transcontinental tours. (For estimated number of transcontinental tourists see Belasco, 72. For population estimates in 1921 see *Historical Statistics of the United States, Colonial Times to 1970*, part 1 (Washington, D.C.: Government Printing Office, 1975), 9.) Granted a transcontinental motor tour was the most expensive and time-consuming type of tour, and thus drew only a limited number of tourists. When compared to the number of people estimated to have traveled abroad in 1921—294,000 people—the exclusivity of automobile touring becomes more apparent. (For the number of people traveling abroad see *Historical Statistics*, part 1, 404.) Although Belasco notes that in 1919 there were 6.7 million cars registered in the United States, which increased to 17.5 million in 1925, arguing that "It seems reasonable that the number of autocampers increased proportionally," with some agencies suggesting that during the 1920s there were between 10 and 20 million auto-campers on the road each year, what one needs to consider is that all those who might have used automobile camps were not tourists. (See Belasco, 74.) Many of the touring narratives published suggest that auto tourists took to the road for a month or sometimes more, with daily costs per person ranging between $1.00 and $5.00, not including repairs, and initial costs of equipment. Thus, a month-long tour at the least might cost between $30.00 and $150.00, which accounted for between 2% and 10% of the average clerical worker's yearly income of $1,505. Even Belasco notes that "a $100.00 trip was beyond the range of the average family with an annual income under $1,500." (For the cost of touring, see Belasco, 42–43. For the average yearly income of clerical workers, see *Historical Statistics*, part 1, 321.) In addition, a depiction of the class of people who toured also depends on how the idea of touring is defined. I believe that the experience of touring meant much more than just spending the night on the road with an automobile. It was a vacation of more than one day or night spent on the road and directed toward the leisure possibilities offered along the road. Although automobile touring was presented as a much more democratic form of leisure, it was not until after World War II that this became a reality.

29. For a discussion of the agrarian myth and the ideal of the middle landscape, see Henry Nash Smith, *Virgin Land: The American West as Symbol and Myth* (New York: Vintage Books, 1957), and Leo Marx, *The Machine in the Garden: Technology and the Pastoral Ideal in America* (New York: Oxford University Press, 1964).

30. Note that some narratives were even more blatant in their fear of the mongrelization of American society. For example see Whiteside, *Touring New England on the Trail of the Yankee*. Theodore Dreiser on the other hand offers an alternative vision in his touring narrative *A Hoosier Holiday*, commenting on the widespread Americanization and commercialization of American society.

31. Stockett, *America: First, Fast, and Furious*, 44.

32. Hulme, *How's the Road?*, 9.

33. For a broad overview of the social, ethnic, and racial realities of the West, see Patricia Nelson Limerick, *The Legacy of Conquest: The Unbroken Past of the American West* (New York: W. W. Norton, 1987). For a discussion of the urban character of the West, see Earl Pomeroy, *The Pacific Slope: A History of California, Oregon, Washington, Idaho, Utah, and Nevada* (New York: Knopf, 1965).

34. John Bodnar, *Remaking America: Public Memory, Commemoration and Patriotism in the Twentieth Century* (Princeton, N.J.: Princeton University Press, 1992), 15. As Bodnar has explained, "Ordinary people . . . react to the actions of leaders [and the images of official culture] in a variety of ways. At times they accept official interpretations of reality. . . . Individuals also express alternative renditions of reality" (Ibid., 16).

35. Lewis, *Free Air*, 87, 50, and 338–39.

36. Dean MacCannell, *The Tourist: A New Theory of the Leisure Class* (New York: Schocken Books, 1976), 24.

37. For a discussion of the tourist gaze in contemporary Western culture see John Urry, *The Tourist Gaze: Leisure and Travel in Contemporary Society* (London: Sage Publications, 1990).

38. Graburn, "Tourism: The Sacred Journey," 22 and 25.

39. George Lipsitz has noted that "theater attendance enabled individuals to play out fictive scenarios of changed identities, to escape from the surveillance and supervision of moral authorities and institutions." He argues, "The fantasy world of the theatrical stage encouraged audiences to pursue personal desires and passions at the expense of their socially prescribed responsibilities." George Lipsitz, *Time Passages: Collective Memory and American Popular Culture* (Minneapolis: University of Minnesota Press, 1990), 8. For additional discussion of the freeing possibilities of leisure activities, see Kathy Peiss, *Cheap Amusements: Working Women and Leisure in New York City, 1880 to 1920* (Philadelphia: Temple University Press, 1986), and Roy Rosenzweig, *Eight Hours for What We Will: Workers and Leisure in an Industrial City, 1870–1920* (New York: Cambridge University Press, 1983); in relation to amusement parks, see John F. Kasson, *Amusing the Million: Coney Island at the Turn of the Century* (New York: Hill and Wang, 1978); in relation to movie theaters, see Lary May, *Screening Out the Past: The Birth of Mass Culture and the Motion Picture Industry* (New York: Oxford University Press, 1980).

40. For a discussion of the idea of "privacy in public," see Kasson, *Amusing the Millions*.

41. Sharp, *The Better Country*, 6.

42. Ibid., 113.

43. Birney, *Roads to Roam*, 268–69, 287, and 295.

44. Harvey Green, *Fit For America: Health, Fitness, Sport and American Society* (New York: Pantheon Books, 1986), 219–58. See also John Higham, "The Reorientation of American Culture in the 1890s," in *Writing American History: Essays on Modern Scholarship* (Bloomington: Indiana University Press, 1970), 73–102.

45. Lears, *No Place of Grace*, 32 and 98–139. Although Lears does not actually address the wilderness experience as an antimodernist phenomenon, his analysis of the martial impulse suggests that touring and the possible wilderness experience it encompassed embodied similar antimodernist desires and anxieties.

46. T. J. Jackson Lears, "From Salvation to Self-Realization: Advertising and the Therapeutic Roots of the Consumer Culture, 1880–1930," in *The Culture of Consumption: Critical Essays in American History, 1880–1980*, ed. Richard Wightman Fox and T. J. Jackson Lears (New York: Pantheon Books, 1983), 11.

47. Lewis, *Free Air*, 11, 14–15, 33, and 45.

48. Ibid., 143.

49. For a discussion of the gendered experience of driving, see Joseph Anthony Interrante, "A Moveable Feast: The Automobile and the Spatial Transformation of American Culture, 1890–1949" (Ph.D. diss., Harvard University, 1983), and Virginia Scharff, *Taking the Wheel: Women and the Coming of the Motor Age* (New York: Free Press, 1991).

50. Hulme, *How's the Road?* 1.

51. Ibid., 2. See Belasco, *Americans on the Road*, 35–36 for a discussion of the medieval connotations of Reggie, Hulme's car.

52. For a discussion of the image of the New Woman, see Carol Smith-Rosenberg, "The New Woman as Androgyne: Social Order and Gender Crisis, 1870–1936," in *Disorderly Conduct: Visions of Gender in Victorian America* (New York: Knopf, 1985), 245–96; Estelle Friedman, "The New Woman: Changing Views of Women in the 1920s," *Journal of American History* 61(1974): 373–93; and Ellen Wiley Todd, *The "New Woman" Revised: Painting and Gender Politics on Fourteenth Street* (Berkeley: University of California Press, 1993), 1–38.

53. Hulme, *How's the Road?* 16, 96, and 97.

54. Ibid., 35, 43, and 19.

55. Ibid., 13.

56. Ibid., 9 and 40–41.

57. For an overview of the gendered spaces of small-town, middle America, see Lewis Atherton, *Main Street on the Middle Border* (Bloomington: Indiana University Press, 1954), 33–64.

58. For a history of the traveling salesman and his symbolic significance in American culture, see Timothy B. Spears, *One Hundred Years on the Road: The Traveling Salesman in American Culture* (New Haven: Yale University Press, 1995), and "'All Things to All Men': The Commercial Traveler and the Rise of Modern Salesmanship," *American Quarterly* 45 (December 1993): 524–55.

59. Hulme, *How's the Road?* 63.

60. MacCannell, *The Tourist*, 56–76.

61. Post, *By Motor to the Golden Gate*; Dixon, *Westward Hobos*; Stockett, *America: First, Fast, and Furious.* For other examples, see Barrett, *Our Wondrous Trip*; Bedell, *Modern Gypsies*; Caroline Rittenberg, *Motor West*; Sabin, *California By Motor.* Note that some women traveled with their husbands, and many did

not comment specifically on their experience in gendered terms. However, the mere number of published narratives written by women suggests that touring offered a particularly novel experience for women, traditionally hemmed in by the ideology of the domestic sphere.

62. Dixon, *Westward Hobos*, 87. See Scharff, *Taking the Wheel*, 135–64.

63. See Smith-Rosenberg, "The New Woman as Androgyne," for an interesting discussion of how some women novelists of the twenties borrowed male language to define the identity of the New Woman.

64. For a broader discussion of these issues, see Wiebe, *The Search for Order;* Lears, *No Place of Grace;* Alan Trachtenberg, *The Incorporation of America: Culture and Society in the Gilded Age* (New York: Hill and Wang, 1982); and John Higham, *Strangers in the Land: Patterns of American Nativism, 1860–1925* (New York: Atheneum, 1985).

65. Higham, "The Reorientation of American Culture in the 1890s," 79–80.

Chapter Nine

Tourism, Whiteness, and the Vanishing Anglo

Sylvia Rodriguez

Tourism has shaped the character of race-class relations in northern New Mexico, particularly Taos and Santa Fe, in profound and complex ways that warrant a sustained project of critical analysis focused upon the ideological workings of the state's "enchantment industry." Capitalism in any form, of course, shapes race-ethnic, class, and gender relations everywhere in the world. But while pervasive and relentless, capitalism is neither uniform nor monolithic. It comes in numerous forms that evolve through stages and that assume a multiplicity of global and local faces. The modern racial order of north central New Mexico would have evolved differently if, for example, smokestack industry, oil, or agribusiness had been its economic mainstay instead of tourism. It is debatable whether tourism represents the only viable economic trajectory for the region or historically a form of underdevelopment.[1] But in any case, the peculiar configuration of racial and cultural politics seen in New Mexico bears the distinctive signature of tourism. The approach to tourism pursued in this essay concurs with Dean MacCannell's observation that tourism is anthropologically interesting as an expression of modernity, and also with his claim that the controlling power of white culture is based on the social construction of ethnic others.[2]

A connection between the tourist gaze and whiteness can be demonstrated through an analysis of art in New Mexico as racial inscription. This refers to the fact that most if not all art in New Mexico is heavily inscribed, or to put it another way, saturated, with ethnoracial meaning, as will be discussed below. But instead of the white construction of ethnic otherness or the ethnic internalization of the tourist gaze, my focus here will be upon what I call the phenomenon of the Vanishing Anglo.[3] On the one hand this "vanishing" is consistent with the invisibility or transparency of whiteness in general. As the unmarked category in the U.S. racial order, whiteness is by definition invisible. This invisibility is a product of white privilege, which involves the collective power to name or mark who is "colored," "ethnic," "racial," or nonwhite. It implies that to be white is none of the above and synonymous with what is normal and thus unmarked. Whiteness is usually referred to in the "new whiteness studies scholarship" as a category, but it also involves practice or sets of practices, of which ethnic tourism, or tourism in search of ethnically exotic others, is a prime example.[4] Whiteness has been invisible but at the same time organizationally central to the construction of art and romantic representations of New Mexican society as ethnic and exotic for the purpose of promoting Southwestern tourism. Yet Anglos were previously more visible in New Mexico's public discourses of cultural history than they are today. Their disappearance from the public stage coincides, ironically and significantly, with "Anglo" (or "non-Hispanic white") demographic expansion in tourist towns like Santa Fe and Taos. As so often seems the case, material reality is reversed or inverted through symbols.

The following discussion will examine some examples of "Anglo" signifiers and their gradual disappearance from public cultural, especially visual, discourse. The erasure of Anglo whiteness among amenity migrants (former tourists who take up residence in the region in order to enjoy on a more permanent basis the "amenities" that attracted them in the first place) will then be juxtaposed to the historical claim to whiteness enunciated by Spanish Americans. The contrast between these two varieties of local whiteness serves to "de-essentialize" the category of whiteness by showing that it does not consist of a single homogeneous essence, but rather, like nonwhite categories, is multifaceted and internally differentiated. The plurality of whiteness is as complex as the plurality of color, and no less important to a critical analysis of how the tourist gaze constructs race in New Mexico and the Southwest.

The tourist gaze constructs its object according to the social positionality, including the class and racial status, of the gazer. In short, what one sees and wants to see, as a tourist engaged in sightseeing, depends in part on one's position in the larger social order. John Urry has proposed that the tourist gaze is structured by class, such that a middle- and a working-class gaze can be distinguished, which he refers to as the romantic and the collective gaze respectively. The romantic gaze, he argues, seeks an experience of "solitude, privacy, and a personal, semi-spiritual relationship with the object of the gaze," in contrast to a working-class "collective" gaze, which strives toward common experience.[5] Transfixed from the start by what Charles Lummis called "sun, silence, and adobe," the tourist gaze in New Mexico has always been of the romantic, middle-class variety. It is moreover a white gaze in its desire to behold ethnic others, particularly Indians. It focuses on a threefold visual semiotic or set of visual meanings composed of Indians; a vast, empty, arid landscape; and adobe architecture. The ideological construction of the American Southwest in the North American touristic imagination is the premier case of "domestic" Orientalism, with the same colonizing motive.[6] Its cornerstone is art, beginning with the promotional productions of the Taos art colony and continuing through successive generations of photographic, ephemeral, literary, and fine and folk art forms. The core whiteness of this gaze lies not only in imperialist nostalgia or anti-modern escapism but, most importantly, in the selectively racialized landscape it projects.

Bourgeois whiteness is the organizing principle behind the yearner sensibility, which seeks transcendence and redemption through union with a spiritually suffused Indian other, located within a pristine, empty, geologically monumental landscape. This framing of a primordial, nonwhite ethnic other within a stark desert-mountain wilderness is both modernist and privileged. It is also antimodernist because it flees the alienation and corruption of industrial civilization, just as Taos's art colony salonier Mabel Dodge did, and as hundreds of amenity migrants attempt to do each year in New Mexico's gentrifying tourist towns. Its privilege entails the power to construct a fanciful racial order in which the downtrodden Indian is elevated to a quasi-supernatural position of spiritual superiority, while Mexicans are relegated to the unclean lower class. Anglos are either exoticized or omitted from this scenario altogether.

Yet the enduring and endearing cliché of New Mexico as a tourist mecca is tricultural harmony, which surely implies the presence of Anglos.

Early art-colony art included Anglos within the Indianist-yearner landscape of enchantment only as cowboys or mountain men. Modern everyday Anglo figures, whether as tourists, businessmen, or everyday working citizens, are not part of the visual vocabulary of Southwest art. Nor, for that matter, are the contemporary, everyday lives of Indians or Mexicans. Romantic, premodern images are preferred. The mountain man is historically distant and the cowboy removed by class and rurality from the artist, tourist, or migrant who relocates to New Mexico for its aesthetic and "lifestyle" amenities. Both represent "ethnicized" versions of rural, working-class whiteness: the mountain man or leather-stocking is indianized, whereas the cowboy derives from borderland *vaqueros* but becomes the quintessential gringo hero. Both do physical work close to nature, at preindustrial forms of labor. Both served as guerrilla warriors in frontier racial battles. Only the exotic or "culturally otherized" ethnics and déclassé, ethnicized whites populate the enchanted landscape sought out by tourists and others drawn to New Mexico.

Commodification is both process and outcome in capitalist development. The commodification of New Mexico and the Southwest is based upon an aesthetic transmutation of the regional and local racial orders, in addition to the more straightforward aesthetization of the landscape. The former is of concern here. Ethnicity is objectified, sanitized, and sold, signified through a seeming infinitude of manufactured images and objects. It is a cherished truism that "true art" transcends race, ethnicity, and other social difference to express what is universal. But in New Mexico, what we call art is about little other than race and ethnicity. This is a function of the commercialization or commodification of ethnic symbols along with the natural resources. In a word, art has become a form of racial inscription, which enacts and bears the mark of stratification.

Consider the fact that just about any painting, sculpture, or other artifact on display in any given art gallery or museum or shop window in downtown Taos or Santa Fe makes some kind of implicit or explicit statement about ethnicity or ethnic identity, including that of the artist. Indeed, it is very difficult to find a work of art, much less any curio or tourist trinket, that does not make some kind of ethnic, pseudoethnic, or metaethnic (reflexively, sometimes ironically, ethnic) statement. This is not to claim that ethnicity or ethnic identity is necessarily the original subject matter of the art or artifact in question, but instead to emphasize that the contemporary context within which the object is viewed, interpreted, and valued imbues it with fundamental and inescapable ethno-racial meaning. This is as true for a Georgia O'Keefe landscape as it is for a santo, rug, pot, or kachina doll, or paintings by Joseph Sharp, Bert Phillips, R. C. Gorman, Michael Martinez, Tavlos, or Fritz Scholder. Each of these may be "about" ethnicity in a somewhat different way, and the positionality or vantage point and social location of each artist reveals a different aspect of the totality. But ethnicity is central to its contemporary meaning and appeal.

The gaze within which such ethnic meanings are arrayed marks them as other and different from the perceiver. This implies an embodied consciousness that is pervasive but unmarked. The landscape it sees is empty, grand, and populated by savages. The imagery of enchantment is modernist, racialist, and masculinist all at once, as forthcoming examples will show. The aesthetic panorama of a Nature unspoiled by humans is a creature of modernist nostalgia. Whereas the early art-colony painters populated their landscapes with exotic premodern ethnics, O'Keefe carried the vision to its logical conclusion and left people out altogether. Gender differentiation in this vision seems probable, but cannot be considered here. The sensibility behind these variations is nonetheless much the same. White, Anglo, bourgeois consciousness organizes this gaze, supposing itself to be universal and alone. Its historic precursor is the imperialist gaze that subjugated and extracted and collected from the subaltern "tribal" world of "people without history."[7]

The driving question behind this essay is, Why are there no— or so few—white people depicted in art-colony art? This is another way of asking why the art dwells so much on Indians and to a lesser extent on Mexicans—in short, the ethnic, colored other. Because so few paintings or other forms of colony art depict bourgeois Anglos, those few pieces that do are well worth looking at. Two examples, one obscure and the other infamous, will suffice to illustrate why Anglos have kept themselves out of the paintings. The first, *Lunch at Lone Locust*, painted in the 1920s by Taos art colonist Walter Ufer, shows an Indian man in braids waiting table for an Anglo family of outdoor diners seated under a ramada, against the distant backdrop of Taos mountain.[8] This unusual painting openly depicts the master-servant relationship normally never shown in colony art. It moreover shows Anglos as tourists, a subject returned to later. This is one of Ufer's least known or reproduced paintings. Quite simply, inclusion of the master spoils the magic.

The second example is the infamous mural by Kenneth Adams located in the west wing of Zimmerman library at the University of New Mexico, commissioned by President Zimmerman in 1937 while Adams was an artist in residence (Fig. 10). The mural's four panels depict New Mexico's social and cultural history and future aspiration from the ideological standpoint of the New Deal. Thus they represent the progressive thinking of the day, something to keep in mind when interpreting the murals through the lens of the present. The four panels show the cultural progression of the three ethnic groups, culminating in their "futuristic" union. The first panel shows stylized Pueblo and Navajo Indian figures, mostly in profile: a basket maker, potters, and a weaver. The central figure is female and presented full-face, seated before a loom. Her eyes are closed, and she has no mouth. The profiled figures have no facial features either. The second panel shows Hispanic men and women plowing and plastering adobe buildings. Most are shown from behind, but those in profile lack eyes and mouths. The third panel shows a central Anglo figure, a blond, male doctor in a surgical mask, holding a newborn blond baby. He is flanked by white male and female figures, shown in profile without facial features, peering into microscopes. The fourth panel shows a central blond, white male presented full face with gazing blue eyes and a mouth, shaking hands on either side with an Indian male in profile and Hispano male also in profile, neither with eyes or mouth. A small plaque near the last panel relates the history of the painting, and quotes the following from President Zimmerman's original grant application for the mural:

1. The Indian, showing his work as the artist;
2. The Spanish, giving a general idea of their contribution to the civilization in the area in the fields of agriculture and architecture;

3. The Anglo, with scientific contributions; and
4. The union of all three in the life of the Southwest.

Every year or so, ever since the student movement of the 1960s, almost like a rite of spring, Chicano students denounce these murals and call for change in the institutional racism and sexism they express and appear to celebrate. The mural was vandalized at least once, and over the years protesters have demanded that it be destroyed or removed, or at least labeled in a reflexive, critical manner. Historian Ramon Gutiérrez cites the Zimmerman mural as a negative inspiration for the revisionist view of New Mexico colonial history he pursues in *When Jesus Came the Corn Mothers Went Away.*[9] But criticism notwithstanding, the mural perdures in this prominent institutional venue, there for all to behold, a glowing testimony of the official, Anglocentric, androcentric, New Deal (pre-nuclear, pre–civil rights) era view of New Mexico's tricultural history and destiny. It remains because the touristically appealing triethnic paradigm still prevails in civil discourse.

To contemporary critical eyes, the mural is blatantly racist and sexist. A critical (and presentist) reading of the painting or other public cultural forms does not necessarily impute conscious or malevolent intent to their creators. On the contrary, such an analysis proceeds on the presumption that the cultural values being expressed are normative for their time and place, and therefore tacit, and largely unexamined by those who hold them. The meaning such cultural productions have for those who participate in them is thus quite different from the interpretation arrived at through ethnographic or social analysis. To put it another way, observer's and actor's models are not the same.

From the standpoint of contemporary critical analysis, the Zimmerman-Adams mural is racist because it seems to prescribe a social order and division of labor in which Indians make crafts, Mexicans do backbreaking labor, and Anglos control scientific technology. Indians and Mexicans are rooted in and symbolize the premodern past, Anglos signify and control the present and the future. The Anglo also directs and mediates interaction between the Indian and Mexican. To a feminist perspective, the androcentrism and misogyny of the last two panels are inseparable from their racialism. What the mural's ultimate vision of futuristic-utopian New

Mexico amounts to is a world cleansed of women—the only kind, by the way, in which miscegenation can never occur.[10] The races come together but remain separate and pure. The very act of giving birth is appropriated by a self-cloning white male scientist, who comes to mediate "harmony" among equal (they are there together) but unequal (the Anglo in control, the only one who looks ahead and wears a white shirt) men. It could be retitled, "When Science Came All the Mothers Went Away."

Another more recent example of public art reveals the same social order laid out in the Zimmerman mural. This is Glenna Goodacre's sculpture entitled "Sidewalk Society" (1990) located in Civic Plaza in downtown Albuquerque. The piece features a superficially updated assortment of the familiar stereotypes. It shows an Anglo boss in a suit directing a Mexicano laborer posed with hardhat held against his chest in a deferential manner. A young Anglo female executive strides by. Nearby a young collegiate-looking Anglo couple with a toddler gaze upon and converse with (or interrogate) a traditionally attired Navajo woman holding onto her little girl. The assembly is rounded out by a young (Anglo) boy on a skateboard. Here the agent of progress appears in the form of a female executive instead of the male scientist found in Zimmerman, but both are unambiguously Anglo. The relation among the ethnic groups is the same: the Anglo male is in charge of the present and the future (he points to the distance), the Mexican does manual labor, and the Indian is object of the tourist gaze. Significantly, the touristic couple face the Indian with their backs to the classic patron-peon interaction. Once again, this underscores the paradox of Anglo whiteness in the Land of Enchantment: the whole enterprise depends on an Anglo-dominated racial hierarchy that must somehow be erased from touristic view. The romantic gaze is ruined by the presence of other tourists or modern urban figures and by direct visible evidence of the social inequality that underpins the entire system.

So while the ethnic figures in the Zimmerman mural or Goodacre sculpture continue to recycle endlessly though myriad variations of New Mexico's artistic-touristic landscape, the Anglo male so central in these exceptional works has all but vanished from the sphere of public cultural representation. Without doubt he remains the least reproduced member of the great New Mexican all-male iconic racial trinity. According to Chris Wilson's excellent history of Santa Fe architecture and public pageantry, this erasure began after World War I and was well entrenched by the 1930s:

> In the mid-1920s, as the promotion of Pueblo and Spanish culture geared up, the immigrant population that has been known as "Americans" took a step down from the pinnacle of public rhetoric and became "Anglos." The adoption of the term, made Anglos into one ethnic group among others, with no special claim to superiority. American era scenes not only disappeared from public ceremony but also public murals.
>
> Although Anglos had played prominent roles in the city's history for a century, in fact owned most of the real estate by the 1890s, the logic of tourism promotion and the romantic yearnings of transplanted residents required their removal from public history. While the architectural revival emphasized Pueblo form, the Fiesta increasingly focused on the Spanish heritage of Santa Fe, and from the 1930s to the early 1950s, the Spanish-speaking population assumed control.[11]

Thus, as Wilson effectively notes, Anglos began to retire from the "cavalcade of enchantment" as soon as they were named.

The same process occurred in the Taos fiesta parade, although with about a twenty-year time lag behind Santa Fe. The Taos summer fiesta was invented in the late 1930s by Anglo boosters in order to promote plaza business during the height of the tourist season. Originally the historical-hysterical parade included Kearny's Army of the West on horseback, but after 1940 only Coronado's conquistadors remained. Mountain men, pioneers, and artists stayed part of the pageantry for longer, but had effectively vanished from parade discourse by the 1970s. Today the Taos fiesta parade contains virtually no symbolic reference to Anglo culture as such, past or present, although signifiers of the American state are plentiful (such as a military color guard, or even Smokey Bear, cuddly mascot-icon of the U.S. Forest Service). Instead, the symbolic emphasis is upon an expanded spectrum of Hispanic ethnoracial identities, ranging from *Genizaros* (hispanicized, detribalized Indians of the colonial period) and Aztec dancers through Mexicans (folk dancers, *mariachis*, equestrian *charros*, etc.) and Chicano lowriders, to Spanish rulers, explorers, and flamenco dancers. The banishment of Kearny from the symbolic discourse of New Mexico's public history was reaffirmed again in 1996 when no sesquicentennial (150th anniversary) was proposed to commemorate the 1846 American occupation of Santa Fe. Newspaper columnist Larry Calloway tried in vain to provoke debate about this resounding public silence, but it remained a nonissue.[12]

The expression par excellence of Anglo symbolic annihilation is found in the Santa Fe fiesta figure of Zozobra. Zozobra, or Old Man Gloom, is a giant paper effigy immolated on the first night of the Santa Fe fiesta. It was invented in 1926 by artist Will Schuster and quickly caught on as a permanent feature, to become probably the signature icon of the event. Although the figure has undergone various stylistic modifications over the decades, its fundamental features have remained pretty much the same. The giant puppet now stands about forty feet tall, has large ears and movable eyes, mouth, and arms, and groans and howls while burning. Its shaggy hair has been blond, green, or orange, and during World War II his face merged the features of Hitler and Hirohito. Today Zozobra has heavy red lips and sports a bow tie, buttons, and cummerbund, as well as cuffs on his jointed, movable arms. Both hands have prominently extended index fingers that seem to scold. Two constant, unmistakable features of Zozobra are that he is white and male. To have made him otherwise would never have worked. Yet his whiteness is as taken for granted as his gender.

The history of Zozobra is well documented, and Ronald Grimes has correctly described the ritual burning as the most dramatic and cathartic event of the fiesta.[13] But Grimes has trouble integrating the image of Zozobra into his Jungian analysis of Santa Fe's Hispanic-Catholic symbolism. The overall ethos of the burning seems oddly secular yet "pagan," while its open expression of collective sadism creates a deeply disquieting, if cathartic, effect. Zozobra thus remains entirely disassociated from the explicitly Catholic religiosity as well as the civil officialdom of the other public ceremonies that make up the fiesta. Nor would anyone confuse its ostensible "pagan" character with Native American religious ritual. In a public cultural discourse pervaded by symbols of Hispanic and Indian ethnicity, Zozobra represents the unmarked yet core Anglo tradition of the

Santa Fe fiesta. Indeed, it is one of only two fiesta activities in which Anglos make up a clear majority of organizers.[14]

So who is Old Man Gloom? From one critical standpoint, he embodies the white, urban, capitalist, patriarchal order that so many middle- and upper-middle-class amenity migrants are fleeing when they relocate to places like Santa Fe and Taos. Zozobra has become the symbol of Anglo whiteness itself, in all its unbearable experiential ambivalence. Joseph Traugott has suggested that Zozobra originally represented a self-portrait of its creator, who symbolically immolated his past, pre–Santa Fe life by torching the puppet.[15] This may well be true, but the portrait also transcends the personal. For Shuster, like so many urban refugees who migrate to New Mexico, coming to Santa Fe represented the start of a new life. This new life constitutes a repudiation of the evils of modernity: a flight from alienation, from hierarchy, and from capitalist materialism, into a fantasy community of multicultural brotherhood that nurtures spirituality and creative individual freedom.

But ambivalence inescapably inheres in the structural positionality of whiteness. Privilege precludes equality. As Karen Brodkin puts it:

> Ambivalence is part of the experiential structure of whiteness itself, and that structure has played a powerful role in making it near impossible to conceptualize a viable way of life outside the double binds that are part of living white. . . . Like double binds in general this construction of whiteness seems like a certifiable formula for keeping people reproducing whiteness in their efforts to escape its contradictions. Please note, I am not making a case for "poor little white folks, we too are oppressed." Whiteness wouldn't be an effective double bind if the privileges it brings weren't real, if white folks had nothing to lose but their chains. Privilege, however unacknowledged, is key to its experiential structure.[16]

Zozobra is Santa Fe's ritual symbol of this dilemma. My critical observer's interpretation is not meant to preclude or negate myriad and diverse individual interpretations by actors who participate in the event. Indeed, it is offered as a proposition to be tested through further inquiry.

The satirical image of the tourist is the single exception to the vanishing Anglo trend just outlined. The tourist is the only image of Anglo cultural whiteness whose incidence has increased rather than diminished since the 1920s, although it still remains comparatively rare, particularly in fine art. This increase is not surprising given the proliferation of the real thing, but it is nonetheless significant that such representations tend to be vernacular, occurring mostly in the form of wood carvings (such as "wooden tourists" that mimic wooden Indians) and cartoons (such as Jerome Milord's spoofs on Santa Fe Style). The satirical figure of the tourist may well have surfaced first in Pueblo ritual clowning. It is important to note that Anglo "white-out" is not confined to Anglo artists. Consider, for example, the fact that painters R. C. Gorman and Miguel Martinez never portray Anglo women, nor do white people appear in the paintings of popular New Mexico artists Edward Gonzales or Anita Rodriguez. To point this out, of course, is to state the obvious. As one art collector quoted in the *Santa Fe Reporter* put it, "The thing that makes Santa Fe interesting is not Anglos."[17] It is precisely this claim I wish to problematize.

Cultural politics in New Mexico are fraught with poignant ironies. The one to turn to next concerns the fact that whereas Kearny's soldiers are no longer palatable images in New Mexico's public discourses of self-representation, Coronado's or de Vargas's conquistadors still very much are. The conquistador image is of interest here because its whiteness is so ambiguous. On the one hand, the conquistador, like other New Mexican Spanish imagery, remains part of the official cavalcade of enchantment insofar as it is deemed exotic, other, ethnic, and thus not white. On the other hand, from the internal standpoint, it constitutes nothing less than a claim to whiteness. So here is a situation in which at least some of the "real" white folks don't want to be acknowledged or represented as such, while the "off-white" folks, or at least some of them, do.

That it is some, but not all, "Hispanic-Mexican-Nuevomexican-Chicanos-Raza" (etc.) who want to be considered white is important and significant. This plurality arises from more than class differentiation, because in addition to "old family" Hispano elites, there are plenty of poor, rural, genetically mestizo New Mexicans who call themselves "Spanish." "Spanish" can mean white or not white depending on the context, including the implied or explicit other side of the slash mark, as well as the positionality of the speaker-designator. The context is moreover historically conditioned. Thus "Spanish" in one context and point in time means, first and foremost, not-Indian; in another it means not-Mexican or, as Nuevomexicanos say, not *surumato*.[18] In each of these cases it signifies a relatively superior position along the whiteness continuum. But it automatically loses altitude on the whiteness scale once Anglos enter the picture—albeit never absolutely. The fragility of Spanish-American whiteness was demonstrated during the 1998 Oñate Cuartocentenary celebration in Albuquerque, when Hispano proponents of a commemorative statue to Juan de Oñate, the leader of the first Spanish colonial settlement colony, were obstructed by a vocal coalition of Native Americans, Chicanos, and a few Anglos, who objected because of Oñate's infamous brutality toward the people of Acoma Pueblo.

The purpose of dragging the Spanish skeleton out of the Chicano closet is to show that there are many whitenesses. There is whiteness modified or even marked by class (e.g., "white trash") and there are varieties of post-ethnic whiteness achieved through class mobility, such as Jews, Italians, Irish, Poles (see note 4). There is the "unbearable whiteness [read Nordic] of skiing," as nicely put by Annie Coleman in her discussion of the largely monoracial ski industry in the American West.[19] Then there is the nouveau Crypto-Jewish whiteness, which for Jewish amenity migrants is a flight from whiteness but for Hispanics another step, ironically, toward whiteness. Popular interest in New Mexico's Crypto-Jews has been aroused by Stanley Hordes's and other scholarly research into the hidden and suppressed history of *conversos,* or converted Jews, in Spanish colonial America. In effect this history provides a kind of hispanicized, pre-American, "spiritual genealogy" or "place charter" for Jewish amenity migrants in New Mexico. For some Hispanos, this history allegedly awakens forgotten memories of covert ritual practices, fragments of a buried legacy of secrecy, dual identity, and artful duplicity. Reclaiming a Crypto-Jewish identity, for someone of self-identified Spanish-American or mestizo heritage, implies a claim to whiteness. But this may or may not correlate with a rejection of Catholicism on the one hand or of Indianness and *mestizaje* on the other.

In showing that there are many whitenesses, the plurality of color is simultaneously evoked. With all these pluralities arrayed before the analytic eye, the phantasm of separate, bounded, pure essential identities, marked or unmarked, is called into question and begins to dissolve. The hegemonic, inherently masculinist ethnic triad of New Mexican tourist art and official civil discourse asserts separate, essential, racial identities and destinies. The strategy of tourism's symbolic transmogrification of the southwestern racial order was to selectively commodify color and simultaneously erase whiteness from the visual field. The tourist gaze freezes and commodifies alterity or difference against a field of disappeared whiteness. But whiteness must be marked in order analytically to see more clearly the structures of power as well as the contingent, hybrid, tension-filled processes and practices of racial and ethnic/non-ethnic identity formation. This undoes the tourist gaze, if only for a moment.

Notes

I wish to thank Chris Wilson and editors David Wrobel, Pat Long, and Brad Johnson for their critical comments on earlier versions of this chapter.

1. Tourism needs to be analyzed in relation to other economic correlates in any given setting, such as, for example, the pervasive and powerful role of the federal government in New Mexico, including ownership and control of a large proportion of land and natural resources.

2. Dean MacCannell, *The Tourist: A New Theory of the Leisure Class* (New York: Schocken Books, 1976); Dean MacCannell, *Empty Meeting Grounds* (New York: Routledge, 1992), 121–46, especially "White Culture."

3. "Internalization of the tourist gaze" refers to a process in which the ethnic objects of the tourist gaze come, as ethnic subjects, to believe in and perform according to the idealized image projected onto them by tourists, art colonists, and other yearners after the exotic. This can result in a kind of split consciousness, between the scripted, performed self and the "backstage," "real" self. See Sylvia Rodriguez, "Tourist Gaze, Gentrification, and the Commodification of Subjectivity in Taos," in *Essays in the Changing Images of the Southwest*, ed. Richard Francaviglia and David Narrett (Arlington: Texas A & M University Press, 1994), 105–26.

4. The new "whiteness studies" scholarship on race posits whiteness as an analytic construct, an unmarked category, a set of practices, a structure of privilege. It shifts analytic focus away from the races to the structures and operation of white privilege and implicit or naturalized definitions of whiteness against which all color is located and assigned meaning. A variety of theo-

retical approaches are emerging within this general framework. Some examples of recent works include MacCannell, *Empty Meeting Grounds;* David Roediger, *The Wages of Whiteness: Race and the Making of the American Working Class* (New York: Verso, 1990); Toni Morrison, *Playing in the Dark: Whiteness and the Literary Imagination* (Cambridge: Harvard University Press, 1992); Ruth Frankenberg, *White Women, Race Matters: Social Constructions of Race* (Minneapolis: University of Minnesota Press, 1993); also R. Frankenberg, ed., *Displacing Whiteness* (Durham, N.C.: Duke University Press, 1997); Theodore Allen, *The Invention of the White Race* (London: Verso, 1994); Vron Ware, *Beyond the Pale: White Women, Racism, and History* (London: Verso, 1992); Karen Brodkin Sacks, "How Did Jews Become White Folks?" in *Race,* ed. Steven Gregory and Roger Sanjek (New Brunswick, N.J.: Rutgers University Press, 1994), 78–102; Karen Brodkin, *How Jews Became White Folks and What That Says about Race in America* (New Brunswick, N.J.: Rutgers University Press, 1998); Noel Ignatiev, *How the Irish Became White* (Cambridge, Mass.: Harvard University Press, 1995); Ian F. Haney Lopez, *White by Law: The Legal Construction of Race* (New York: New York University Press, 1996); David Stowe, "Uncolored People, The Rise of Whiteness Studies," *Lingua Franca* 6 (September–October 1996): 68–77; Mike Hill, ed., *Whiteness, A Critical Reader* (New York: New York University Press, 1992).

5. John Urry, *The Tourist Gaze* (New York: Sage Publications, 1990), 45; Rodriguez, "Tourist Gaze," 109.

6. Edward Said, *Orientalism* (New York: Vintage Books, 1979); Barbara Babcock, "By Way of Introduction," and "'A New Mexican Rebecca': Imaging Pueblo Women," *Journal of the Southwest* 32, no. 4 (Winter 1990): 383–99; 401–37); Marta Weigle, "Southwest Lures: Innocents Detoured, Incense Determined," *Journal of the Southwest* 32, no. 4 (Winter 1990): 499–540.

7. See, for example, Mary Pratt, *Imperial Eyes: Travel Writing and Transculturation* (New York: Routledge, 1992); Caren Kaplan, *Questions of Travel: Postmodern Discourses of Displacement* (Durham, N.C.: Duke University Press, 1996). The term "people without history" was applied, with a certain irony, by anthropologist Eric Wolf to the so-called primitive, tribal peoples encountered and subjugated through European exploration, conquest, and colonization of the non-Western world. See Eric Wolf, *Europe and the People without History* (Berkeley: University of California Press, 1982).

8. Walter Ufer's "Lunch at Lone Locust" is reproduced in black and white at plate 197 in P. J. Broder, *Taos: A Painter's Dream* (Boston: New York Graphic Society, 1980).

9. Ramon Gutiérrez, *When Jesus Came, the Corn Mothers Went Away* (Palo Alto: Stanford University Press, 1991). Gutiérrez referred to the mural as a catalyst for his work in a public address at the University of New Mexico on November 18, 1993.

10. This is because unlike maternity, biological paternity is intrinsically uncertain; so the guarantee of paternal descent rests on stringent (male) control over female sexuality. The social boundaries that demarcate purity of race are maintained through regulation of women's sexual behavior and accessibility. Because the possibility of transgression nevertheless always exists, the only way to eliminate risk altogether would be to preempt the female gestative function. This is the technological solution actually depicted, no doubt quite innocently, in the mural. It is the deeper meaning embedded in an already quite unconsciously sexist, racist, and seemingly "natural" vision of an all-male utopian future.

11. Chris Wilson, "Tourist Commodification and Ethnic Polarization in Santa Fe (A Newcomer's Narrative)" (paper presented at the American Studies Association meeting, Kansas City, October 16, 1996), 5–6; also see Chris Wilson, *The Myth of Santa Fe* (Albuquerque: University of New Mexico Press, 1997).

12. See Larry Calloway in the *Albuquerque Journal*, August 6, 1996; August 17, 1996; *Albuquerque Journal North*, August 22, 1996. Calloway attributes the noncelebration of Kearny's Army of the West's 'bloodless' occupation of Santa Fe to the current mood of "political correctness" fostered by revisionist educators. "New Mexico," he writes, "seems, on the official level to be part of the United States. . . . In the opinion of many New Mexicans, the conquest, even if it was non-violent, doesn't call for celebration. Many cutting-edge historians see the Mexican American war and the doctrine of Manifest Destiny as shameful. Many see the concluding Treaty of Guadalupe Hidalgo as fraudulent. And they teach this attitude in the schools." *(Albuquerque Journal, August 6, 1996).* A response from UNM Professor Felipe Gonzales argued that many ambivalently regarded historical events, subject to conflicting interpretations, are not commemorated nationally, such as the Civil War and the Vietnam war *(Albuquerque Journal, August 17, 1996).* Calloway responds that this "theory of conflicting interpretations" does not explain why the 1996 state legislature appropriated $210,000 in advance to support the 1998 Cuarto Centennial of the Spanish colonization of New Mexico, despite the fact that "Pueblo Indians and non-Catholics aren't likely to dance in the streets over this one." *(Albuquerque Journal North, August 22, 1996).* He sees it as simply a matter of ethnic politics in a state where Hispanics make up a substantial portion of the electorate. While this is true, neither Calloway nor Gonzales considers the enchantment factor, which had managed to remove Kearny from public view well before the Chicano movement or revisionist historiography.

13. Ronald Grimes, "Symbol and Conquest: Public Ritual and Drama," in *Santa Fe, New Mexico* (Ithaca: Cornell University Press, 1976); Donna Pierce, ed., *Vivan Las Fiestas!* (Santa Fe: Museum of New Mexico Press, 1985); Joseph Dispenza and Louise Turner, *Will Shuster: A Santa Fe Legend* (Santa Fe: Museum of New Mexico Press, 1989); Wilson, *The Myth of Santa Fe.*

14. Anglo cultural "ownership" of the Zozobra "tradition" is enunciated, for example, by participants recorded in the excellent but controversial video documentary "Gathering Up Again: Fiesta in Santa Fe," by Jeanette DeBouzek and Diane Reyna (Santa Fe: Quotidian Independent Documentary Research, 1992). The crowd Zozobra draws is, however, very mixed. The other mostly Anglo-organized fiesta event is the Melodrama, which satirizes city politics and current events (see Grimes, "Symbol and Conquest," 201–7). Zozobra and the Pasatiempo parade were part of the "counter fiesta" invented by members of the post–World War I art-colony generation in reaction to the commercialism and militaristic themes propounded by the "old guard" (Edgar Lee Hewitt and company) at the Museum of New Mexico, who had invented/revived the Santa Fe fiesta in the late teens (see Wilson, *The Myth of Santa Fe,* 211–15). The Melodrama appears to be an offshoot of the Pasatiempo parade.

15. John Villani, "Zozobra Created as Self-Portrait," *Albuquerque Journal,* September 8, 1996.

16. Karen Brodkin, 1996 manuscript version of *How Jews Became White Folks,* ch. 3, p. 48. This particular passage has been deleted from the published work (1998), but I quote it here with permission of the author.

17. Ann Constable, "Hidden Treasures," *Santa Fe Reporter*, February 9–15, 1994.

18. *Surumato* is a term Nuevomexicanos use to refer to (usually lower-class) Mexican nationals.

19. Annie Gilbert Coleman, "The Unbearable Whiteness of Skiing," *Pacific Historical Review* 64 (November 1996): 583–614.

11. This picture appeared on page 98 of *Searching for Yellowstone*. Their drivers decked out in matching full-length "dusters," a line of stagecoaches prepares to depart from the National Hotel, Mammoth Hot Springs, about 1890. (National Park Service photo)

12. This picture appeared on page 94 of *Searching for Yellowstone*. The immense National Hotel was constructed at Mammoth Hot Springs by the scandal-ridden Yellowstone Park Improvement Company in 1883. Occasionally modified and modernized, it served visitors well into the twentieth century. (National Park Service photo)

13. President Chester A. Arthur (front row, center), an enthusiastic outdoorsman, made the first presidential visit to Yellowstone in 1883. The media coverage of this visit brought greater public attention to the young park. His party, shown here in camp in the Upper Geyser Basin near Old Faithful, included (front row, left to right) Montana governor Schuyler Crosby, General Phil Sheridan, the president, Secretary of War Robert Lincoln, and Missouri senator George Graham Vest. (F. J. Haynes photo courtesy of the National Park Service)

14. A carefully staged picnic scene in the Upper Geyser Basin, about 1880, shows off the camping finery of an early tourist party. Photograph by Bozeman, Montana, commercial photographer Henry Bird Calfee. (Courtesy of the National Park Service)

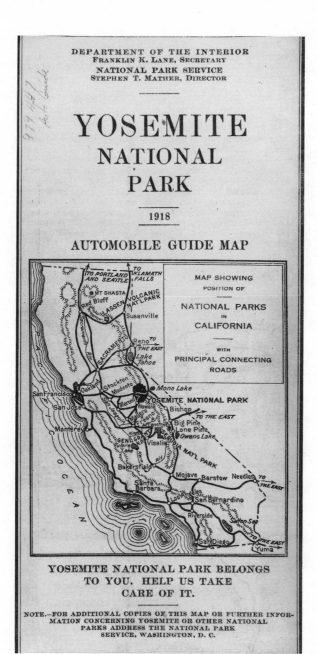

15. National parks and a new highway geography. Beginning in 1916, the National Park Service issued guide maps for auto tourists. Besides serving the needs of park promotion, the maps displayed the spatial relationship between parks and cities in the motor age. (Courtesy of Yosemite National Park)

16. View from the road. In parks like Yosemite, 1915, park planners designed roads to present the parks' natural beauty to motorists in an unfolding scenic narrative. (Photo courtesy of Yosemite National Park)

17. Knowing nature through machines. The appearance of cars in parks did not necessarily herald the demise of nature. Instead, it raised the potential for harmony between technology and the natural world. Roads and cars enabled tourists to have intimate encounters with nature. Along Mount Rainier's "Road to Paradise," circa 1915, auto tourists passed the snout of Nisqually Glacier. (Photo courtesy of Mount Rainier National Park Archives)

18. Park gates not only welcomed auto tourists but also symbolized the transition to a special landscape for cars in nature. Circa 1915. (Photo courtesy of Mount Rainier National Park Archives)

19. Another view from the road. Mount Rainier, 1915. (Photo courtesy of Mount Rainier National Park Archives)

20. To promote the fortunes of its Utah Parks Company subsidiary, the Union Pacific produced an extensive body of advertising matter characterized by dramatic images of southwestern scenery such as Zion National Park's Great White Throne. (Image number 1-160, reproduced courtesy of the Union Pacific Museum Collection)

21. Tourists who patronized the services of the Utah Parks Company found many ways to see and be seen, such as this horseback excursion at Angel's Landing in Zion National Park. (Image number 8646, reproduced courtesy of the Union Pacific Museum Collection)

Photograph by J. E. Haynes, St. Paul   *OLD FAITHFUL*

YELLOWSTONE
NATIONAL PARK

22. Various examples of promotional literature urging travel to the national parks relied upon certain highly familiar images to spark an instant recognition from their readers. Few images could have been more immediately recognizable than Yellowstone's Old Faithful Geyser. (Reproduced from *National Parks Portfolio*, 1931).

GLACIER

NATIONAL

PARK

23. Beyond the alluring scenic magnificence of its mountains, the promotion of Glacier National Park often included reference to the romantic history of the region's Blackfoot Indians, as envisioned by many white Americans. (Reproduced from *National Parks Portfolio*, 1931)

ROCKY MOUNTAIN
NATIONAL PARK

24. National park advertising frequently blended the portrayal of pristine wilderness with the promise of accessibility for a wide array of tourists, as seen, for example, in this photograph of visitors in Rocky Mountain National Park. (Reproduced from *National Parks Portfolio*, 1931)

25. The Merced River flooded the Yosemite Valley in Yosemite National Park in January 1997, flowing through lodging and campgrounds like the Lower River Campground in this photograph. (Photo courtesy of Yosemite National Park Archives)

Part III

Parks: Tourists in Western Wonderlands

The national parks are the West's greatest tourist attractions and are the source of the imagery through which many nonwesterners and westerners define the West. Since much of the West's most spectacular natural scenery, many of its most fragile ecosystems, some of its endangered species, and some of its most prized mineral and timber resources lie within park boundaries, it is not surprising that the parks have been contested sites. In some cases, the forced relocation of Indian peoples prefaced or accompanied the creation of parks; native peoples were removed or restricted to render nature's wonders accessible to white Americans. The story of tourism in the parks is much messier than its promoters have suggested.

The authors of all four of the essays in this concluding section emphasize that the tension at the very heart of so much of the controversy surrounding tourism in the national parks is inherent in the Organic Act of 1916. This famous piece of legislation tried to balance the seemingly irreconcilable goals of preservation and public pleasure. From the establishment of the first parks in the late nineteenth century until well into the twentieth, the concept of the parks as national treasures, wilderness havens—sites of spiritual, mental, and physical rejuvenation—had to be sold to the public. The National Park Service (NPS) needed to create a demand for the parks, and it ended up doing such an effective job that tremendous strains were placed on the supply. How, in the face of such demand, could the parks still offer a pleasurable experience, an escape into nature, a sojourn with the wilderness?

The four essays move chronologically from writer and Park Service employee Paul Schullery's overview of early tourism in Yellowstone, through historian and Park Service employee David Louter's exploration of automobile tourism in the parks in the early twentieth century and historian and curator Peter Blodgett's overview of park promotion from the teens to the early 1930s, to chief historian of the NPS Dwight Pitcaithley's analysis of the pleasure-preservation conundrum in more recent decades.

Schullery's "Privations and Inconveniences" surveys the wanton excesses of early park concessionaires and the comparative lack of comforts and conveniences for early tourists. He then offers a critical examination of the common critique of the development of tourism in Yellowstone and other places as a pre-designed, packaged, and standardized experience. Schullery wonders how else, given the circumstances, "public use of Yellowstone might have proceeded" at all. Furthermore, Schullery notes that had utilization of Wonderland proceeded along the path preferred by the early concessionaires, things could have been considerably worse. He reminds us, too, of the experience of the resident Sheepeater Indians, who were moved to reservations in Idaho and Wyoming in 1877, and the famous flight of Chief Joseph's Nez Percé Indians through the park that same year. Schullery also emphasizes that the scale of privations and inconveniences associated with Yellowstone is a broad and varied one.

David Louter's "Glaciers and Gasoline" addresses the common perception of automobiles in the parks as something akin to the serpent in Eden. He suggests that the matter is rather more complex than this simple juxtaposition of machine and garden; indeed, the auto has been a fundamental part of the parks, rather than something fundamentally apart from them, since 1908, when Mount Rainier became the first park to admit autos. Louter focuses on Mount Rainier as "a flagship park for the motor age." A 1912 pictorial describing Mount Rainier as a meeting of "Glaciers and Gasoline" suggests that the automobile in the early twentieth century, far from being the antithesis of nature's garden (the carrier of Edward Abbey's "Industrial Tourists"), was thought of as being more akin to Leo Marx's machine in the garden: a technological innovation that enhanced access to nature and was thus a vital part of nature.

Blodgett, in "Selling the Scenery," emphasizes the tremendous impact of a pair of individuals, Stephen T. Mather and Horace M. Albright, on the promotion of the parks. Blodgett demonstrates that while the Park Service often worked closely with the railroads in publicizing the parks, it was not by any means a pawn of the railroads. Similarly, the Park Service collaborated effectively with automobile associations and city commercial clubs and tourist bureaus. Mather's and Albright's success in promoting tourism in the parks proved a catalyst to the entire western tourist industry. Given their goals—primarily, the vital need to generate public enthusiasm for the parks in order to prove their viability and thereby earn political support for their preservation—the two were incredibly successful. But, as Blodgett concludes, and as Pitcaithley emphasizes in the volume's concluding essay, "A Dignified Exploitation," when it came to self-promotion the parks were probably too successful for their own good.

Pitcaithley briefly surveys the ground covered by Schullery, Louter, and Blodgett, then explores some of the excesses that might have accompanied park promotion, including a cable car across the Grand Canyon, proposed in 1919, and an elevator next to the Great Falls of the Yellowstone. In striving to maintain the delicate balance between public enjoyment and park preservation, the exploitation of the parks remained, for the most part, relatively dignified. Pitcaithley, like Schullery, reminds us that there were paths that could have led toward considerably less dignified exploitation.

Nonetheless, with the development of visitor facilities funded by Mission 66, the debate over the purpose of the parks and the role of the Park Service resurfaced. But even the most ardent critics of park development, such as Edward Abbey, actually had the effect of promoting public visitation while celebrating the isolation of certain parks (Arches, in Abbey's case). Still, as Pitcaithley notes, Abbey would be pleased with the Park Service's recent plans for implementing an even more dignified exploitation of the West's Wonderlands. Those plans will require a little more effort (more privations and inconveniences) on the public's part to enjoy the scenery, and are likely to both enhance the visitation experience and better preserve the parks, although the number of encounters between glaciers, geysers, and gasoline is likely to diminish.

Chapter Ten

Privations and Inconveniences: Early Tourism in Yellowstone National Park

Paul Schullery

Right from the start, we called it Wonderland. Countless early guide-books, tour brochures, and promotional articles used the term, which became common among park visitors as well. To the Northern Pacific Railroad (NPRR), the park's most tireless and effective promoter, the name Wonderland sometimes applied rather vaguely to the whole northwestern United States, but the name stuck most determinedly to Yellowstone, probably because there really was more wonder here.[1]

In the 1870s, only a few hundred people reached the park each year, but they were vocal in their amazement. Because many of them were also influential or prominent citizens, word spread quickly of the glories of what at the time was formally known as "the Yellowstone National Park" (once there were other national parks, the "the" was dropped). Until the 1880s, most visitors were from nearby states, but after about 1883, as the NPRR publicity campaign geared up, the park began to attract the attention of more and more long-distance visitors. President Chester A. Arthur's visit in 1883 is seen as something of a milestone in this process; the visit was exhaustively reported in the world press.

Nathaniel Langford, self-advertised hero of the park's creation (he was fond of joking that his initials, N. P., stood for "national park"), became its first superintendent in 1872. With no budget, no facilities, and little public support, he accomplished very little and may have even intended it that way. Aubrey Haines has suggested that Langford's inaction, besides being the result of no funding, was also caused by his continuing association with the railroad. Langford's lack of activity may have been aimed at "preventing the development of strong concession interests in the Park until such time as the Northern Pacific pushed its tracks close enough to dominate the development of visitor facilities."[2]

Langford visited the park only twice during his five-year administration. His one annual report, produced in 1873, outlined the problems facing not only the manager but also the visitors, explaining that the park could be reached only by pack train, "a mode of travel attended with many privations and inconveniences."[3] What visitors found when they arrived was as wild as it was wonderful.

By 1879, there were still only eighty-nine miles of what might generously be called roads. Travelers had also established more than two hundred miles of passable or recognizable trails that took them to the major attractions (no doubt some of these trails followed pre-existing Indian trails). Travel writer Carrie Strahorn described the roads in 1880 as having been "cut through the timber over rolling ground, with stumps left from 2 to 20 inches above the ground, and instead of grading a hill it went straight up on one side and straight down on the other."[4] Some of these original grades can still be seen, faintly making their way through the forests of northern Yellowstone. They often do just grind right straight up the hill (wagons and coaches must have unloaded the passengers on those grades, or the horses couldn't have made it); others wind hopefully back and forth across the slopes, as if looking for a gentler path but never really finding it.

If Wonderland was to become a resort matching its name, as its promoters hoped, it would need much more than tolerable roads. It would have to provide pleasant accommodations, trustworthy places to eat, and good transportation. Someone had to decide where people should stay, what they should eat, and how they should travel. Thus began the often uneasy but entirely necessary three-way relationship between the federal government, the public, and the park concessioner.

Today, with an increased awareness of the ecological effects of any development in a national park and an ever intensifying scrutiny of all government management of natural resources, commercial enterprises of any sort in national parks are distrusted, or seen as merely a necessary evil. Former Yellowstone superintendent Robert Barbee has referred to this suspicion as the "money-changers in the temple" mentality, suggesting that it takes a comfortably simplistic view of what concessioners do. Yellowstone has provided us with the full spectrum of case studies, from the very worst to the very best, in commercial hospitality in a park.

One of the many differences between the way we perceive the park today and the way its first visitors did is in this very issue of concessioners and their role in parks. Every historian who has written about the early days in Yellowstone has taken the side of those people who wanted less development rather than more, and some have argued the case with an almost embarrassing level of emotion. I certainly have done so. We are accustomed to a certain level of development in Yellowstone, and anything more jars our sensitivities.[5]

At first, there were practically no comforts for tourists. James McCartney, Harry Horr, and Matthew McGuirk had established modest (according to some early accounts even that adjective was too flattering) facilities centered on the thermal pools in the Mammoth Hot Springs area, McCartney and Horr at the springs themselves and McGuirk down along the Gardner River to the east. They provided a rude sort of shelter in a cabinlike hotel, a bathhouse or two for those seeking the "healing" waters, and rough but ample fare in the form of locally shot game. Slowly others arrived who were willing to risk their energy and resources on the chance that the park would eventually attract enough money to justify the effort.[6]

Some of these early concessioners were scoundrels or worse, but many were genuinely fond of the park and conscientious about providing good service. As the years passed, the reliable ones were usually sorted out from the fly-by-night schemers, so for most of the time, at least after the very rocky first decade or two, tourists felt passably well served.

There were essentially two types of concessions. The first was the outfitter or manager of a single little operation. In the park's administrative archives, these are represented on some odd piece of hotel stationery, requesting permission, in a pinched script, to bring in a party of tourists on such-and-such a date, begging the honor of an early reply and all of that wonderful formal language now vanished from our customs. The other type was the larger corporation, generally favored by early National Park Service managers after 1916, if only because it was easier to watch over a few big businesses than many small ones or because the big ones seemed better able to provide consistent service.

My favorite scoundrel among the small operators was E. C. Waters, who from 1889 until 1907 ran a steamboat tour business on Yellowstone Lake. Even on paper Waters is instantly dislikable. He wrote stacks of long, simpering, obsequious letters to the various superintendents, responding to the many complaints and accusations that flew his way. He used his political influence to help get rid of a superintendent he especially disliked, he was implicated in at least one attempt at poaching, and he generally behaved in the manner of the worst stereotypes of the sleazy park concessioner. The nadir may have come when he established a small zoo on Dot Island in Yellowstone Lake, where one visitor reported seeing an elk so hungry that it actually ate meat. Apparently Waters was feeding them only garbage.[7]

But the real risks to the park's overall welfare were not from those individual small concessioners. To the extent that the park's resources and the tourists' visits could be really ruined, only a big concessioner could do it right. The first such to emerge was the Yellowstone Park Improvement Company (YPIC). Today even the name would make most park defenders nervous; we would object that the last thing nature needs is "improvement." But at the time the term did not necessarily bode ill, because at the time to "improve" a property might mean only to build a few necessary structures on it. Like many of the political-economic stories of Yellowstone, the tale of the YPIC is convoluted enough to be a short book in itself—a greed-and-graft potboiler of the Gilded Age, with silk-vested entrepreneurs directing their nefarious plot from elegant eastern drawing rooms. The YPIC was the corporate front for a group of businessmen, most noteworthy of whom was C. T. Hobart, superintendent of a planned branch of the NPRR that would run from the main line up the Yellowstone River Valley to the park.[8]

The NPRR was always a presence in the more important deliberations of this sort. Clark City, some fifty-two miles north of the park on the Yellowstone River, renamed itself Livingston in the early 1880s in honor of an NPRR official. About the same time the miners

just outside the northeast corner of the park named their community Cooke City in honor of NPRR's Jay Cooke, so hopeful were they
of his attention and eventual investment in a branch line to their
area—a branch line running, if at all possible, through the park.

Of course the money for concessions development had to come
from somewhere, and most western citizens couldn't wait for more
railroads to be built in more places; the boosterism of a recently
settled region had little sympathy with anything that slowed progress
toward more settlement. I suspect that if a poll had been taken in 1880
asking Americans if railroads should be run to the major attractions
in Yellowstone, an overwhelming majority would have said yes. To
them the railroad was the very soul of the future; what could be wrong
with swift, efficient travel around Wonderland?

However, if polled about the YPIC, those same Americans might
not have reacted so affirmatively, not because they feared the dam-
age the concessioner might do to Yellowstone (most could not have
cared), but just because the company was such a blatant scam. Even
in those days the terms the YPIC wanted were outrageous. Through
its agreement with the secretary of the interior, the company sought
to acquire exclusive rights to cheap rental of a *square mile* of land
surrounding each of the seven biggest visitor attraction areas. It was
allowed to cut timber elsewhere at will, rent other lands as needed,
and exercise a variety of other extremely generous freedoms in the
new park.

The public, politicians, and scientists protested, but the outcry
did not stop the YPIC from constructing the first of the several huge
hotels that would eventually appear in the park. This was National
Hotel at Mammoth, four stories high and more than four hundred
feet long. Laborers worked through the winter of 1882–1883, using
local lumber (the stumps are still visible on the lower slopes to the
southwest), and living on game meat from the park. They completed
enough of the giant building for the hotel to open for the summer.
But when the YPIC could not pay them, the builders staged a sit-in
(still living on park game) in an unsuccessful attempt to force their
employer to pay them their back wages. Instead YPIC went bankrupt, and the National Hotel ended up in the hands of the NPRR.

Such was the start of the serious hotel business in Yellowstone.
Less pretentious hotels were established at Mammoth Hot Springs
and near the Lower Geyser Basin in the mid-1880s, and tent-camps

also began to flourish. The NPRR became ever more visible and active in setting up concession operations to serve its railroad passengers, and it was merciless in forcing out competition. For many years writers would tell hilarious and appalling stories of the strange service found in park concession operations. By the 1890s it was entirely possible to find your way around the park in fair comfort, with every hope of encountering at least a rude sort of hospitality, and often much more.

If the 1870s was the decade of Yellowstone's greatest ecological disruption, the 1880s might be seen as the decade of the greatest risk from wholesale development. In its development of the Yellowstone tourist trade, the NPRR, an aggressive and extraordinarily powerful American corporation, followed the business impulses of the day and the example of almost every other resort area in America. The railroad's leadership long attempted to lay tracks clear to the geyser basins, and well into the 1890s Cooke City residents hoped that tracks might reach them as well, through the park up the Lamar Valley and along Soda Butte Creek. It's hard to imagine these railroads in the park today without wincing, and even then there were quite a few people who did not think the park needed quite so much improvement. The resistance the NPRR met in these goals, which no doubt its leadership saw as entirely honorable consequences of the creation of the park, must have surprised them. The NPRR track reached its terminus near the north entrance of the park in 1883, and the Union Pacific reached the west entrance in 1901, but no tracks ever reached the park's big attractions.

Opposition to wholesale development of the park came from many quarters. Key legislators, most notably Missouri senator George Graham Vest; well-placed journalists, especially George Bird Grinnell; and others fought to contain development and protect the park from being reduced in size in the 1880s and early 1890s. In fact, without the "park grab"—actually a series of moves over more than a decade, all designed to consolidate or enlarge NPRR's control—by the YPIC and its descendent corporation, much that was accomplished in the rapid evolution of park management probably would not have been possible. Without Grinnell's dozens of editorials and articles in *Forest and Stream* and continual public pressure from other sources, the campaign to protect Yellowstone's wildlife would certainly have had less urgency and public exposure.[9] The

specter of wholesale development horrified enough of our forefathers to prevent the park from taking that direction.

It is entertaining, in a perverse sort of way, to imagine what the
park would be like if it had been developed like the busier portions
of the Poconos or the Adirondacks: a patchwork of private holdings,
ski slopes, lodges, condominiums, mini-malls, and pretty lakes lined
with "camps" and cabins. Driving through the park and looking at
it with a realtor's eye gives one a different feel for the landscape. The
Antelope Creek drainage of Mount Washburn is a fabulous ski hill,
Hayden Valley is an obvious golf course. It is less entertaining, but
very instructive, to realize how close the park came to that fate. The
battle was fought early enough in the park's history that the stakes
were still largely hypothetical; had visitation already been heavy and
clamoring for more services and amenities, development would
have been much harder to fight off.

But Yellowstone was as undefined for visitors as it was for the
developers and the legislators. The matter of what people should
do once they got to the park was no little problem. From the first,
some visitors displayed the behavior that has made the word "tourist" a worldwide term of derision. They left campfires burning, care-
lessly starting fires. They took axes to the delicate sinter formations
in the geyser basins, hauling off tons of fragments. They abused the
geysers and hot springs in many other ways, laundering their clothes
in them, jamming an incredible assortment of junk down the vents,
and provoking geysers to erupt by "soaping" them. As already described, they slaughtered the animals, blazing away at everything
they saw.

But, as Aubrey Haines has observed, what should we have expected of them?

Captain Ludlow typified them as prowling about "with shovel
and axe, chopping and hacking and prying great pieces of the
most ornamental work they could find. Men and women alike
joining in the barbarous pastime." Perhaps this is unfair, for how
were those plain country people . . . to know how they should
act? No one had told them. Indeed, it was only in the rudeness
of their action that they differed from the scientific visitor who
used his hammer to break off a piece of exquisite hot-spring
filigree for his specimen sack. These people were vandals all,

whether their trophies served a parlor knick-knack cabinet or a museum exhibit case.[10]

Ludlow wasn't the only traveler to express exasperation with the insensitivity of the average tourist. One especially galling practice was the scratching of names in the delicate geyserite of the thermal basins. Owen Wister, who first visited the park in 1887, asked, "Why will people scrawl their silly names on the scenery? Why thus disclose to thousands who will read this evidence that you are a thoughtless ass?"[11]

Wister also captured the conflict that confronts all parks, of just how much development was necessary to allow for the "benefit and enjoyment of the people." In a conversation he had in 1891 with a woman who favored a then-active proposal to build an elevator to the foot of the Lower Falls of the Grand Canyon, the woman criticized him for elitism:

> "But why should your refined taste," objected a lover of the multitude to whom I told this, "interfere with the enjoyment of the plain people?"
> "Have the plain people told you or anybody that the one thing they lie sleepless craving for is an elevator to go up and down by those falls the way they do in hotels?"
> "They would like it if it was there."
> "Of course they would. Is that a reason to vulgarize a supreme piece of wild natural beauty for all time? How are the plain people to learn better things than they know if you lower to their level everything above it?"[12]

And there you have one of the greatest challenges of national parks: striking a balance between catering to public taste and elevating it, always in the hope that those in charge of the parks actually know what good taste is.

Yellowstone required us to stretch our awareness in many ways, for the legislation creating Yellowstone Park did not tell people how to act. At every step along the way, the public, the park managers, and the resource itself would have to resolve what was and was not appropriate. The creation of the park in 1872 launched the American public, indeed the world public, on a search for Yellowstone in the grandest sense: not just to learn what was there and enjoy it, but to make sense of it in the context of their times.

Historians of travel have emphasized the tourist industry's requirement that major destinations provide a highly standardized experience, but these historians have given an unrelievedly sinister tone to what happened in Yellowstone as the visitor experience became defined and institutionalized. As one recent historical study commented, "the same socioeconomic and cultural currents which have dictated events on the balance of the American landscape—that is, the command and control of nature to serve an industrial market economy based on acquisition and possession—also transformed the feral Yellowstone wilderness into a packaged, consumable product."[13] Another historian, speaking more broadly, summed up the irony of tourism in a world where travel is hardly the adventure it once was: "Travel as tourism has become like the activity of a prisoner pacing a cell much crossed and grooved by other equally mobile and 'free' captives. What was once the agent of our liberty has become a means for the revelation of our containment."[14]

There is no question that Yellowstone tourism was the product of effective, highly organized marketing, that the park was "packaged as an object of cultural desire."[15] And it took only a few years for the park tour to firm up along a single route, with predictable stops at the best-known features. There is, however, a great deal of question about what that packaging meant to the average visitor experience and about what the alternatives were. Statements about the packaging of the park clearly imply that this was a regrettable if not tragic sacrifice of Yellowstone's true potential as a source of enjoyment, but it never becomes clear what the alternative experience should have been. Historian John Sears has complained that "despite the vast natural areas of the park that remained unvisited by the average tourist, Yellowstone was curiously artificial. . . . Its natural wonders were theatrical and the impact of these curiosities as elements in a show was reinforced by the trappings of the tourist culture which sprang up around them."[16] These are important points, but traditional academic historians are perhaps a little too comfortable in their hindsight, and are ignorant of the fragility of "the vast natural areas of the park that remained unvisited."

I have often thought how much fun it would be to be able to go back in time, knowing what I know now, and take one of the standard tours of the park in the early days. Perhaps I would react as did Rudyard Kipling, who began his account of an 1889 visit with the lament that "Today I am in the Yellowstone Park, and I wish I were dead." Kipling was appalled by the attitudes of the tour group he encountered at Cinnabar, the rail terminus near the north entrance: "It is not the ghastly vulgarity, the oozing, rampant Bessemer-steel self-sufficiency and ignorance of the men that revolts me, so much as the display of these same qualities in the women-folk."[17] Or would I, like Frederic Remington on an 1893 visit, marvel at the park's most adventurous stretch of road, over the newly constructed Golden Gate trestle, and then reflect on how its wonder was reduced because "as the stages of the Park Company run over this road, every tourist sees its grandeur, and bangs away with his kodak."[18]

It is true that the park's promoters were fairly successful in selling Yellowstone, not only to those who would buy train tickets, hotel rooms, and all the other services but also to a distant populace who found even knowing of such a strange place to be worthy recreation. We have not adequately considered the extent to which public knowledge of the young park was the result of photography and artwork; the combination of pictures and words reached far in acquainting the world with Yellowstone's wonders. In 1897, *Harper's* editor Charles Dudley Warner was not exaggerating when he wrote that "all the world knows, from the pens of a thousand descriptive writers and from the photographs, the details of these marvels."[19]

Today, there is widespread concern among conservationists that Yellowstone is "overcrowded," a condition that affects not only the well-being of the resources of the park but also the quality of the experience. I am convinced those concerns are valid; some time, perhaps about forty years ago, perhaps longer, we became so numerous in Yellowstone that we crossed some threshhold of use that resulted in an unacceptable diminishing of the experience.[20] From that perspective, it is easy to view the aggressive promotion of the park in earlier times as a harmful thing. But from the perspective of the people who wanted to visit the park, who yearned for whatever combination of its features they found rewarding, the promotion of Yellowstone must have seemed entirely good and appropriate.

The trivialization of a spectacular natural area's real beauty and power through the standardization or "packaging" of the visit is always regrettable, but it is hard to imagine how else public use of

Yellowstone might have proceeded. Visitors during the park's first decade, often relying on their hunting skills to feed themselves and following their own judgment about where to go, how to acquire firewood, and how to treat the park's fragile thermal features, amply demonstrated that Yellowstone could not long afford highly individual approaches to its enjoyment, at least by people with the values of late-nineteenth-century Americans. It is both naive and absurd to imagine that unmanaged people at that time would display the environmental awareness needed to develop a landscape-sensitive visitation system whereby any number of visitors could travel the park without serious impact on the landscape. The only way to move large numbers of people through Yellowstone and allow them the opportunity to view the recognized geological and geothermal "wonders" was through industrial tourism.

Indeed, we may be grateful that it worked out that way. For all the now-regrettable things that early managers and concessioners did, their development of a recognized Yellowstone experience did serve to protect John Sears's "vast natural areas of the park" from random and uninhibited use until attitudes relating to those areas matured to the point that managers understood the risks and how to handle them.

What may be most remarkable about the Yellowstone tour is how quickly it achieved a stable form that in many ways has not changed. It may have taken a trapper or prospector months to reach the Yellowstone Plateau from St. Louis or farther east; a great learning occurred in that process that later visitors would not share. But by 1883, when the NPRR Park Branch Line reached Cinnabar, it was possible for a family in New York City to board a train and reach the park in about the same time as it would take to drive that distance today in a car. Yellowstone was abruptly and universally available and would need all the organization and standardization it could get.

The visit, whether it took five days, seven days, or several weeks, contained the same elements. Depending upon where a visitor entered the park, the starting and ending points varied, but the classic "grand tour," as it was portrayed most commonly by visitors and writers, began with the hot-spring and geyser basins and concluded with the canyon, the scenic finale. The loop road, essentially complete in its present form by 1905, has dictated the terms of the typical visit ever since. Early independent travelers in their own conveyances (labeled "sagebrushers" for their habit of camping at will along the roads) had the opportunity to vary the pace and route, but few departed from the main roads.[21] The road itself guides almost all visitors around the park today.

The shortcomings of the view that the commercialization of the Yellowstone experience simply victimized the tourist can be seen in visitors' reactions to the experience. Certainly the average tourist, knowing essentially nothing about what Yellowstone had to offer, depended heavily on park managers and commercial services to lead the way to the "attractions." John Sears has said that directions to all the tourist attractions were quickly spelled out: "The raw material of nature was rapidly transformed into a cultural commodity by reproducing and marketing verbal descriptions and pictorial representations of these places, by building roads and bridges so that tourists could reach them, by constructing facilities to accommodate the tourists, even by the act of naming their features (a process which in important ways defined their cultural meaning)."[22]

There is a good bit of hyperbole here. The raw material of nature, unless it was smashed into oblivion by souvenir-hungry tourists or shot to death by poachers, remained as raw as ever. We now know that roads and bridges can have all kinds of effects on ecological processes, effects that weren't understood by early park managers, but even at its height, Yellowstone development didn't cover one percent of the park. Decisions *were* made about which of the "raw materials" were required stops on a park visit; in that decision-making process, the raw materials may indeed have become conceptually different than they had been prior to the park's establishment, but the difference is not as simple or as easy to measure as Sears seems to believe.

It is true, though, that once there were professional guides and guidebooks, tourists were directed not only to where they should go, but also to what they should *feel* about what they saw. This process, too, has been portrayed as fairly sinister and manipulative, but again it seems to have been precisely what the visitors most wanted and needed. The quality of the guidebooks and other sources of information was often quite high, considering the limitations of the available information in the late 1800s and early 1900s; the sentiments promoted in the standard park guides were often as lofty as they were lamely expressed. The "homogenization" of the visitor experience could just as easily be viewed as an essential educational process.

In these early days, the search for Yellowstone led us to what has been called a "personality of place." Yellowstone was being given an image; its character was being defined and institutionalized. With the benefit of hindsight we can see that by 1900 the park already had a complex personality, however shallow the commercial portrayals of it might seem to us. Besides its obligation to protect geological wonders, the park was quickly given a bundle of additional informal responsibilities. It served as a repository of a stylized western experience (stagecoach rides, campfire cookouts and talks), as a protective forest covering on the headwaters of some of the West's most important watersheds, as a refuge of wildlife no longer welcome in settled areas, and as a resort where universal vacation activities, from swimming to riding to dancing, could be enjoyed. Some of these uses were widely known, some were familiar only to a few. The Yellowstone experience, in fact Yellowstone itself, was being defined not just by the promoters or the managers, but by the visitors themselves. Visitors, as much as the tourism industry, were the ones who passed the word of Yellowstone to many others, who might never visit but who would now have some idea of its personality. And at the same time as the personality became known, so did the visitor's awareness of the recreational experience being offered here and of how best to enjoy it. People were learning how to act.[23]

To assume that most, or even many, visitors responded precisely as the guidebooks implied they should is to sell human nature short. The early accounts of Yellowstone—whether diaries, articles, promotional brochures, guidebooks, or scientific reports—may not be reliable indicators of what most visitors really got from the experience. These accounts were written by professional journalists and travel writers, a self-conscious and untypical crowd if ever there was one. Such accounts may be a rich and important source of information about the early visitor experience, but even today public attitude surveys reveal surprising and unexpected reactions to Yellowstone.

We did not create Yellowstone National Park one day early in 1872. Instead, on that day we embarked upon an ongoing process—a work in progress—based upon our always growing knowledge of the park and upon our changing attitudes about our relationship with nature. We will always be establishing Yellowstone. Every visitor participates in the search for Yellowstone; each first-timer sets out on a journey of discovery, no matter how many times the place has been discovered by others. The vehicles of that discovery—whether television travelogues, received wisdom of other visitors, published materials, a road system, a hotel and campground network, a stagecoach, a mule, a pair of hiking boots—are modified over time, but they are at last only vehicles for each person's search. The intellectual and esthetic resources of the individual come into play and provide the Yellowstone experience with endless permutations, no matter how regimented the trip may seem or be on the surface. We may lament the limitations that commerce and culture place on the Yellowstone experience, but we must never underestimate the resourcefulness of each individual visitor in finding his or her way to the wonder of the place.

Once the tourist industry took hold and the park visit was standardized, the personal journey of discovery succeeded or failed only as a matter of degree. The experience quickly became very well defined and achievable. Except in the most unlikely circumstances, such as during the fires of 1988, when portions of the park sometimes could not even be reached, hardly anyone could fail to view Old Faithful in eruption, or the Grand Canyon from Artist Point. Almost any visit met the minimum standard of a "good" visit as defined by our culture. But even in the first years of the park, from that minimum standard rose a galaxy of opportunities, from the brief glimpse of a mule deer fawn from a stagecoach at dusk, to the unique combination of events occurring each evening at the old bear-feeding grounds, to a brief romantic interlude along the rim of the Grand Canyon.

The experience of our ancestors, decked out in full-length dusters and thumbing their guidebooks, may have fallen short of our own hopes and expectations for a Yellowstone visit, but we must judge our forebears gently, for they found much in Yellowstone. If the place had not lived up to its unofficial name, "Wonderland," and if these people had not carried home such lively stories of its marvels, no amount of commercial promotion could have succeeded in making it the goal of one of American life's foremost pilgrimages. If Yellowstone had not been an authentic global wonder, it would have settled into a regional recreational role, more on the scale of the New York Catskills or the Wisconsin Dells.

We cannot leave our early visitors without checking in on the people who had been visiting and even inhabiting Yellowstone for ten thousand years: the Indians. In 1879, Superintendent Norris, who frequently expressed concern over hostile Indians, built an imposing blockhouse on a small hill adjacent to the Mammoth Hot Springs. He was fearful of Indian attack through much of his administration, and knew that such fears on the part of potential visitors would hurt the park's status as a vacation destination. Park administrators before 1900 did not see Indians the way later generations of tourism professionals would, as potentially an added "attraction" to bring visitors to an area. Throughout the 1880s, complaints were published in the national press of Indians hunting or traveling in the park, and they were blamed for any number of fires that occurred there, some of which they may have set.[24] But even before Norris's arrival in 1877, the resident Sheepeaters were moved to reservations in Wyoming and Idaho. In 1878 the Bannocks were stopped, by military force, from moving around so much. The disenfranchisement of Indians from their traditional uses of the Yellowstone Park area made some headlines, but was generally accomplished with little fanfare, and with no sense of loss on the part of early visitors.

The most famous episode in the park's Indian history was the flight of the Nez Percé tribe in 1877.[25] About 750 of the Nez Percé, a very patient group of people who lived in eastern Oregon, refused to settle on a reservation as required by the U.S. government. They set out from their homeland in the spring of 1877, hoping to reach the lands north and east of the park. Along the way, they engaged the U.S. Army quite successfully several times, but eventually they were caught and defeated near the Canadian border in Montana Territory, as they attempted to reach the Canadian Sioux lands. Some did escape into Canada, but more were placed on reservations. This whole "war" is now seen as one of the most tragic episodes in the sordid history of the subjugation of Native Americans, and it made one of their leaders, Chief Joseph, a folk hero for his wisdom and eloquence in the face of the losses and hardships his people endured.

The Nez Percé passed through the park in late August and early September, pursued by General O. O. Howard and six hundred soldiers. They entered from the west, traveled up the Madison River, kidnapped some tourists (leaving one for dead) in the geyser basins, crossed the Central Plateau to the Yellowstone River just north of the outlet of Yellowstone Lake, then followed Pelican Creek up to the upper Lamar River, and eventually left the park across the Absarokas. They did not know the way, and the time they lost in the park was time they couldn't afford. Though the leaders preferred not to harm anybody, some younger warriors were not so discreet; in various skirmishes and attacks two other tourists were killed, and a few others were taken prisoner and forced to act as guides.

Oddly enough, it was during this period, even after the forced settlement of various native groups who used the park regularly, and after the even better known episode of the Nez Percé war, that perhaps the most intriguing perceptual legacy of Native American–Yellowstone history was firmed up. This was the belief held by many people, including many early historians and park managers, that Indians were afraid of the park area.[26] By 1877, when Norris became superintendent, it was widely believed that Native Americans held the geysers and hot-spring areas in "superstitious awe" and were afraid to venture near them. It isn't clear what the people who believed this theory made of all the Indians, including the Nez Percé, who seemed to have no qualms about coming into the park to hunt or otherwise move around.

It would be easy to see this theory as a conscience-soothing justification generated by the whites for taking the land from the Indians—"We can have it because they never wanted it in the first place"—but I doubt that such motivations had much to do with it; at the time, whites seemed to feel no need to justify the massive relocation and destruction of Indians throughout the West. More likely, people fell for this story because it fit nicely with the prevailing stereotypes of Native Americans as simple savages. More recent study has shown that many of the tribes that used the Yellowstone area had, in fact, a reverential attitude toward the land and its geothermal features. The idea that they were afraid may have come from accounts of Christianized Indians, who had been introduced to the concept of hell and saw in Yellowstone a spooky resemblance to the whites' descriptions of the place.

The privations and inconveniences of the early tourists were gradually replaced by more and more comfort and a nearly suburban level of convenience. After 127 years, the search for Yellowstone goes on: many parts of the visit, such as the joy of watching a geyser erupt, have not changed, but others, such as doing one's laundry in a quiet hot spring, are blessedly gone. Changes like these are always a matter of scale and perspective. Today's complaints about privations include occasionally weak television reception in recreational vehicles in campgrounds, and inconveniences include poor cell-phone performance in some parts of the park. Nonetheless, the typical park visit is still in good part a reflection of decisions made in the 1870s about what was worth seeing and therefore worth building a road to. The biggest change may be that instead of the park having too few admirers and friends anxious to spend time among its wonders, it now may have too many, and the very quality of the experience may be at risk. But even here, on any given day, few people visiting Yellowstone are in a position to judge, because the changes take a long time. The parents of today's visitors saw and enjoyed a different Yellowstone, one with significantly fewer people but also one with rampant bear feeding, poorer hotel service, and even poorer fishing; but forty years ago Old Faithful still seemed very crowded on a July weekend, and traffic snarls were probably more common than they are now. We would have to search the memories of grandparents to encounter really grand changes in the pace and mood of the typical visit.

For the Indians, the ten-thousand-year experience of a free Yellowstone that ended by 1880 was replaced by other experiences. Local tribe members soon began to visit the park as part of the visitor flow, quietly continuing some of their less noticeable gatherings and spiritual activities here and there, and eventually becoming part of the occasional special events of the early National Park Service. When we see photographs of some park ceremony with an Indian or two in traditional dress on the dais, uneasy feelings of tokenism are stirred, though it is difficult to know precisely what relationship of respect might have existed among the white and Indian individuals involved. But it seems plain that after 1900 or so, in the eyes of many tourists, local Indians in Yellowstone were part of the Wild West show, like the geysers and the bears, and their culture and presence were put to use in the marketing of the region for tourism. Even today, among the park professionals I know, the foremost symbol of the cheap, tasteless Yellowstone souvenir is not a T-shirt or an ashtray with a picture of Old Faithful or a bear on it; it is the rubber tomahawk (though these are actually very hard to find today in park stores and gift shops, they will probably be invoked for many years because they capture so much that is silly, misdirected, and yet publicly appealing about the souvenir business).

It has been interesting and encouraging to watch the Indian relationship with Yellowstone change over the past two decades. The involvement of many western tribes in the deliberations over management of greater Yellowstone bison herds, for example, signals a kind of re-enfranchisement of the people who have known those animals best and longest. We are not all searching for the same Yellowstone, nor do we all have the same fundamental notion of what is a privation, or what is an inconvenience.

Notes

1. Aubrey L. Haines, *The Yellowstone Story: A History of Our First National Park* (Yellowstone Park: Yellowstone Library and Museum Association, 1977; reprint, Yellowstone National Park: Yellowstone Assn. for Natural Science, History and Education, and Niwot: University Press of Colorado, 1996), 2:354, attributes the source of the name "Wonderland" to imitation of Lewis Carroll's (Charles Dodgson) book *Alice's Adventures in Wonderland* (1866). He further notes that "the little girl Dodgson [Carroll] wrote his story for visited Yellowstone National Park as a grownup and seemed almost as thrilled as if she had really gotten into that peculiar place through the rabbit hole." See also Lee Whittlesey, *Yellowstone Place Names* (Helena: Montana Historical Society, 1988), 166, for the earliest known use of the term "Wonderland" in reference to the park—A. Bart Henderson's diary for July 24, 1871: A. Bart Henderson, "Journal of the Yellowstone Expedition of 1866 under Captain Jeff Standifer . . . Also the diaries kept by Henderson during his prospecting journeys in the Snake, Wind River and Yellowstone Country during the years 1866–1872" (ms. no. 452, Beinecke Library, Yale University; typescript in manuscript collection, Yellowstone Park Research Library, Yellowstone National Park). I have discussed this with Lee Whittlesey, and we are not certain that Henderson's mention of "Wonderland" can be regarded as a reliable first use of that term in reference to Yellowstone. There are some places in Henderson's diary that were clearly written after the date given, and his use of the term "Wonderland" might have been one of those retrospective additions.

2. Haines, *The Yellowstone Story*, 2:31.

3. Nathaniel Langford, *A Report of the Superintendent of the Yellowstone National Park for the Year 1872* (Washington, D.C.: Government Printing Office, 1873), 2.

4. Carrie Strahorn, *Fifteen Thousand Miles by Stage* (New York: G. P. Putnam's Sons, 1911), 268. The best and most detailed summary of the early visitor expe-

rience in Yellowstone is Lee Whittlesey, "Yellowstone's Horse-and-Buggy Tour Guides: Interpreting the Grand Old Park, 1872–1920" (manuscript in preparation for publication, used with permission of the author, February 1996). See Haines, *The Yellowstone Story*, and Bartlett, *Yellowstone: A Wilderness Besieged* (Tucson: University of Arizona Press, 1985), for more on the early tourist experience, as well as Bartlett's excellent overview of the park's first decade of tourism in "Will Anyone Come Here for Pleasure," *American West* 6, no. 5 (September 1969): 10–16.

5. Concerning the issue of value judgments by historians of early park opponents and threats, I am especially indebted to H. Duane Hampton, "Opposition to National Parks," *Journal of Forest History* 25, no. 1 (January 1981): 36–45.

6. Haines, *The Yellowstone Story*, I, 196–98, and Bartlett, *Yellowstone: A Wilderness Besieged*, 116–17.

7. Bartlett, who described Waters as "probably the most difficult concessioner who ever operated in Yellowstone Park," told his story superbly in *Yellowstone: A Wilderness Besieged*, 189–93. For a well-researched and entertaining account of the park interior's first hotel keeper, George Marshall, see Lee Whittlesey, "Marshall's Hotel in the National Park," *Montana, the Magazine of Western History* 30 (Fall 1980): 42–51. Marshall started his hotel service on Fountain Flats near the junction of Nez Perce Creek and the Firehole River in 1880.

8. Besides the detailed treatments of the YPIC by Haines and Bartlett, see also Chris Magoc, "The Selling of Yellowstone: Yellowstone National Park, the Northern Pacific Railroad, and the Culture of Consumption, 1872–1903" (Ph.D. diss., University of New Mexico, 1992).

9. H. Duane Hampton, *How the U.S. Cavalry Saved Our National Parks* (Bloomington: Indiana University Press, 1971), 53–80.

10. Haines, *The Yellowstone Story*, I, 200.

11. Owen Wister, as reprinted in Paul Schullery, ed., *Old Yellowstone Days* (Boulder: Colorado Associated University Press, 1979), 74.

12. Ibid., 75–76.

13. Magoc, "The Selling of Yellowstone," 4.

14. Eric Leed, *The Mind of the Traveler, from Gilgamesh to Global Tourism* (New York: Basic Books, 1991), 286.

15. Magoc, "The Selling of Yellowstone," 5.

16. John Sears, *Sacred Places, American Tourist Attractions in the Nineteenth Century* (New York: Oxford University Press, 1989), 181.

17. Rudyard Kipling, as quoted in Schullery, *Old Yellowstone Days*, 87.

18. Frederic Remington, as quoted in Schullery, *Old Yellowstone Days*, 119.

19. Yellowstone superintendent Robert Barbee and I, in a presentation given by him to the Arts for the Parks annual awards meeting in Jackson, Wyoming, September 26, 1992, suggested that in fact the artwork may have been the most important influence on public impressions of the park at a time when very few Americans had actually seen the place; just as important, they led the way in establishing much of the esthetic standards by which later visitors viewed the park:

In Yellowstone, of course, the name we all think of first is Moran. His field sketches helped Congress to create Yellowstone National Park; when in recent times has an artist wielded that kind of power in the real world of legislative negotiation? And yet, what may be most impressive about Thomas Moran, and about William Henry Jackson, the pioneering photographer who traveled Yellowstone with him in 1871, is not what they achieved politically, but what they achieved esthetically. What impresses me is how often they got it right—how often they established the standard for the rest of us. They had the vision needed to take a whole new world and define its artistic possibilities for all the generations that followed. There were no signs or boardwalks leading them to the best vistas; they just knew them when they saw them. And we, standing figuratively on the esthetic shoulders of these giants, look from the same vistas and find all the wonder they did so long ago. (manuscript in author's files)

Historian Judith Meyer, in her fascinating study *The Spirit of Yellowstone* (Lanham, Md.: Rowman and Littlefield, 1996), has made a point similar to mine here regarding the visitor experience, emphasizing that standardization of the basic trip did not necessarily equate with uniformity of experience:

People have always come—and probably always will come—to Yellowstone "preprogrammed" to encounter, interpret, and describe the park in particular ways. However, such expectations do not preclude fascination and surprise. Even today, when so much as been written, painted, photographed, even filmed about the park, most tourists still find something about the Yellowstone which is a surprise. (74)

The statement about the park being well reported is from Charles Dudley Warner, as quoted in Schullery, *Old Yellowstone Days*, 160. Whittlesey, "Yellowstone's Horse-and-Buggy Tour Guides," pointed out that "by 1895, there were numerous national, regional, and local lecturers" on Yellowstone Park, and provides abundant evidence of their extraordinary reach in American culture.

The importance of art, folk art, and such commercial combinations of art and photography as postcards, is apparent in Richard Saunders, "Graphic Images and Publisher Exploitation of Yellowstone Park in Postcards: 'Viewing the Marvelous Scenes in Wonderland,'" *Popular Culture in Libraries* 3, no. 2 (1995): 121–39. As Saunders points out in describing the postcard industry of Niagara Falls, Washington, D.C., and Yellowstone National Park, "There are hundreds of images from each place and even before mid-century literally tens of millions of cards were produced and sold." Imagine the reach of millions of small images of Yellowstone working their way into the homes of Americans.

20. Unfortunately, like the holders of all other positions in this issue, I am unable to provide quantification for this position in terms of undeniable proof of the degradation of the experience. It is almost as difficult to provide incontrovertible proof that the Yellowstone resource has been degraded by the heavy visitation, though it seems obvious that the *Greater* Yellowstone resource is losing ground steadily.

21. Haines, *The Yellowstone Story*, II, 100–159, is a chapter entitled "On the Grand Tour," which fully describes the variety and process of the early tourist experience in Yellowstone.

22. Sears, *Sacred Places*, 123.

23. A very helpful case study of changing attitudes among managers, concessioners, and visitors in one portion of Yellowstone is Karl Byrand, "The Evolution of the Cultural Landscape in Yellowstone National Park's Upper Geyser Basin and the Changing Visitor Experience, 1872–1990" (M.S. thesis, Montana State University, 1995).

24. Joel C. Janetski, *The Indians of Yellowstone Park* (Salt Lake City: University of Utah Press, 1987). The pages of *Forest and Stream* magazine contained a number of reports of such Indian-set fires. The almost laughable irony in these complaints is that today many people look upon those same Indian-set fires as having been a part of Yellowstone's ecological and cultural landscape for thousands of years—perhaps in some parts of the park, such as northern grasslands, an important part. Changing values among the park's white protectors are as important an element of the search for Yellowstone now as they ever have been.

25. Haines, *The Yellowstone Story*, I, 216–39.

26. See especially Janetski, *The Indians of Yellowstone Park*, 77–83, and Joseph Weixelman, "The Power to Evoke Wonder: Native Americans and the Geysers of Yellowstone National Park" (M.A. paper, history department, Montana State University, July 19, 1992).

Chapter Eleven

Glaciers and Gasoline: The Making of a Windshield Wilderness, 1900–1915

David Louter

Sometime in the late 1960s, my family piled into our big blue Buick and headed for my grandparents' home in Vancouver, B.C. We left behind L.A. and the smog alerts of summer, and drove north on that great river of concrete, Interstate 5, for the mild Northwest. Part of that journey included a trip to Crater Lake National Park. I remember vividly rising up through forests on a steep road, emerging into the open, stopping at the rim above a lake that seemed part of the sky, or at least as big and unbelievably blue. In the rarified air, even with the din of the parking lot, it seemed quiet. It was as if sound had been drawn into the crater. We didn't stay long. Most likely we took a bathroom break, ate a snack, and headed on our way. We were Ed Abbey's "industrial tourists."

In recent years, I've returned to the park for work, and despite my academic detachment, I have reactions similar to those of my youth. It all seems so familiar. Driving here seems normal. There are no signs telling me otherwise; there are no barriers to drive around. I am welcomed with open gates and splendid scenery. The road around the lake skirts the rim when possible, and places the lake at the center of my view. Framed in my windshield, the lake's image passes in and out of sight with each turn of the road, like poetry. With curves that follow the topography and guard walls of stone, the road seems to belong to the landscape. And as the container for my car, it is how I see the park; it is how I know nature in this place.

I offer this as a story of "nature as we see it" in the late twentieth century, an experience with a national park that I would venture reflects how many—millions—of Americans encounter their national parks. Now, I'm not so naive as to think that the road is "natural." A great deal of thought has gone into making it appear this way, particularly through landscape architecture. Still, what impresses me is that I am willing to forget, albeit temporarily, that the road intrudes on, or is harmful to, the environment because it appears to fit the scene so well and reveals the lake to me. I find Crater Lake and other parks attractive for these reasons. They intrigue me with their natural beauty. Yet I'm left wondering why automobiles seem so familiar in an otherwise primitive landscape. And what does this say about the meaning of national parks?

I make sense of automobiles in national parks by thinking of this as a story about space and time. Like my memory as a child, the distance between the city we left and the park we arrived in disappears. Memory, the mental maps we create of our world, is a selective and inexact process. In memory the city and the park, the places we live and the natural places we visit, merge. They become part of the same mental as well as physical geography. Automobiles and the highways they travel have shortened the distance and time it takes to reach national parks. They have brought them closer together. Autos and highways have made it possible to think of national parks—to understand their meaning—not as wild places reserved from progress but known because of it. Although this notion began early in the century and has changed over time, it is still with us. It is a legacy of knowing nature through machines.

The introduction of automobiles in national parks helped foster a new principle of preservation in which it was possible to commune with nature in a car. Americans in the twentieth century would encounter parks primarily through autos; they would interpret the park landscape from a road and through a windshield. A twentieth-century phenomenon, the automobile helped reinvent the nineteenth-century idea of national parks as products of America's cultural achievements and vestiges of the nation's disappearing wilderness for a modern, mobile audience. For Americans of the Progressive Era (1890–1920), this could be positive. The presence of autos in a national park embodied the hopeful notion that nature and technology could be blended into a new kind of aesthetic, one which would solve the social dilemma brought forth by our ambiguous relationship with the natural world. Thus, coming to terms with the automobile, like coming to terms with technological progress itself, redefined the meaning of national parks as places of *windshield wilderness*, where it was possible for machines and nature to coexist without the same industrial transformation affecting other parts of the nation. One made it possible to appreciate the other.

The national park idea is a flexible notion; we "dispossess" parks of native peoples to protect them as wilderness, and we allow native peoples to "inhabit" parks to protect them as wilderness. Notions about the ways we know nature through work and leisure are also flexible.[1] Perhaps the greatest example of this conceptual flexibility is the way automobiles have shaped our perceptions of parks as wilderness reserves (open to cars). Early in the twentieth century (and perhaps, still today) automobiles provided Americans with the authentic experience they desired from the natural world. Automobiles supplied not only the vehicle by which middle-class Americans got back to nature but also the vehicle by which they knew nature itself. Granted, the relationship between nature and autos (and the roads developed for them) was delicate, but through regulated use and thoughtful development parks seemed to offer a way to control the advance of modern life that so often came at the expense of wild places. What evolved, then, was a model of national parks in which automobiles and highways were a part of nature. Ideally, they helped create national parks for a modern audience. The model was, and remains, visible in the rustic architecture and landscape design of parks like Crater Lake and Mount Rainier. Though it has changed in response to new social conditions and expectations about wild lands, it continues to have a powerful hold on how we imagine national parks.

This optimistic notion is most commonly associated with the management of parks under the National Park Service in the 1920s, as it responded to the growth of auto tourism and mass ownership of automobiles. But the seeds were planted well before then. The rise of auto use and auto interest groups appeared early in national parks. Between 1900 and 1915, automobiles first entered national parks, and by 1915 all parks were open to autos. It was during this period when park patrons and managers responded to the presence of automobiles and began to consider the meaning of national parks within the context of the motor age. Rather than viewing the presence of machines as incompatible with a wilderness experience, they began to fashion a new set of mental perceptions about national parks in which automobiles made the experience seem possible.

The coming of the automobile to national parks was a reflection of the way Americans generally embraced the auto as a way to return to nature. After 1910, thanks to Henry Ford, the auto increasingly became more affordable and more reliable for middle-class Americans. Although greeted with some apprehension about modern life and industrialization, the automobile provided a way for Americans to encounter nature on their own. As the rise of auto touring and auto camping in the 1910s demonstrated, finding "primitive" nature by the road with a modern machine was not only possible, it became a national pastime. In the new social order, middle- and upper-class Americans perceived that they were becoming more removed from the natural world in their daily lives. At the same time, they enjoyed steadily more leisure time for visiting nature, and increasing mobility that enabled them to visit nature. However contradictory it seemed, in the emerging consumer culture of the day, automobiles offered the means to escape their problems and reclaim a firsthand experience with nature.[2]

The automobile, the very symbol of technology destroying an older way of life, offered mobility and freedom. It promoted individualism and a closer and more "intimate" experience with the natural world. It was a world lost to industrial capitalism, now represented by the railroad, the nineteenth-century symbol of technology and change. Freer to move or stay where they pleased, and go where they could pilot their machines, motor campers were engaging in a more democratic version of the back-to-nature movement of the late nineteenth century.[3] They found an authentic experience in an age that seemed to many made "unreal" by technological advances. And national parks, more than any other public lands, represented the ideal of the auto as an enabling technology. Parks may have been vestiges of American wilderness, but they were also vestiges of nature by the road.

Popular interpretations of automobiles and national parks, however, overlook this point. Instead, they emphasize the coming of autos as inevitable. The rapidity with which automobiles were adopted by Americans and their mass use were simply too overwhelming to stop. Other treatments of automobiles in parks rightly underscore their acceptance as a twentieth-century reality; without the constituency automobile owners represented, national parks would not have had a strong voice for their protection in the nation's new political and social order.[4] While these interpretations are informative, they have a tendency to view the appearance of autos in parks as negative—the serpent in the garden—or as an unfortunate political compromise that has contributed to the erosion of the wilderness values of parks. But our appreciation of national parks increases if we consider the park road as the container for the automobile.[5] The introduction of autos into national parks, then, represented an attempt to reconcile these machines with nature, so that automobiles became part of an experience that made the landscapes they crossed feel more authentic.

Roads, physically and conceptually, paved the way for the transformation of parks into special spaces for automobiles and nature. At the turn of the century, roads were shaped to be appropriate for parks, but parks also shaped roads, and were even identified as ideal settings for laying them out. Roads symbolized a form of modernity, in that their construction altered the primitive to make way for human use of nature, and employed the technology of an industrializing society. Roads also provided access to parks and satisfied the democratic notion embedded in the national park idea. The justification for and design of roads are telling of an ideal of preservation through development that considered roads as not intrusions but enhancements.

Within the context of nineteenth-century ideas of nature, advanced by park designers such as Frederick Law Olmsted, roads were expressions of the natural world as "scenery," artistic compositions of the picturesque and sublime, and not nature as wild and unpredictable. In this sense, roads provided a scenic narrative; they organized and selected views for park visitors. They also protected these reserves by regulating use—concentrating people in specific areas—and presenting nature. Without roads, visitors would not have been able to encounter a national park. Army engineers constructed roads in Yellowstone and Mount Rainier, for example, that conformed to these standards. Routed like paths in a garden, roads did not disturb a park's primeval setting. Roads, in effect, "produced" a space we know as a national park.[6]

We can think of the appearance of autos with that familiar saying, "if you build it, they will come." And they did. In 1908, Mount Rainier was the first park officially to admit automobiles. It did so shortly after construction began on the park's first road, the "Road to Paradise," which reflected the basic design philosophy noted above. The road, also known as the "Government Road" and "Nisqually Road," provided access to the popular subalpine meadow called Paradise on the mountain's southern shoulder over a route intended to display the park's sublime and picturesque scenery.[7]

But roads alone could not reconcile cars to wilderness. As machines of the modern age, autos were greeted initially with displeasure at worst and uncertainty at best in park settings. Park officials worried that autos would disturb visitors and threaten their safety when autos and horses met on the same roads—roads designed with horses and not four-wheeled machines in mind. In 1900, for instance, when the first car chugged into Yosemite, park officials banned automobiles primarily for these reasons.[8] Bowing to pressure from automobile clubs, though, the secretary of the interior allowed autos into Mount Rainier, but only after drafting a long list of regulations containing rules restricting hours of operation, speeds, and general conduct.[9]

Mount Rainier's regulations were adopted in varying forms in other parks. They were prescriptive measures that characterized the Progressive era's approach to problems initiated by technological innovations; they offered a sense of control about a changing relationship with nature, and even improved opinions about the value of autos in parks. After one season, Mount Rainier's superintendent, who had previously objected to autos in the park, announced that the regulations "protected motorists from considerable danger," that visitors derived "a great deal of pleasure" from driving into the park, and that the machines were generally accepted by the public.[10]

Roads and regulations aided but did not complete the process of reconciliation. Regulations, for example, emanated from deeper concerns over the best method of seeing parks and understanding their true essence as horses were replaced by machines. They were concerns that would not be answered immediately. With its ability to shatter older barriers of distance and travel time, the automobile not only changed people's lives outside of parks and the way people got to parks, but also reconfigured the way they toured the parks. It reordered the spatial relationships within them and fostered new kinds of expectations about encounters with nature.[11]

One of the main concerns was that motor touring focused attention on specific sites rather than the whole landscape. At the first national parks conference held at Yellowstone in 1911, for example, Louis W. Hill, Great Northern Railway president and chief promoter of Glacier National Park, complained that autos turned national parks into mere day-trips. Tourists could reach points of interest faster than by horse and spend more time there and less time on a stage. Hill said that he would be "embarrassed" to drive his car into Yellowstone. The trip would occur too quickly, the pace too fast. "I could take the car, make the trip, and be back for lunch," Hill noted. "Now, what kind of trip would that be?" Hill, who carried his machine around on his train, could only justify driving a private auto into Yellowstone if it were part of a longer tour of the West, a rather facetious comment considering the poor quality of the region's roads.[12] What really bothered Hill and those who catered to tourists was the threat autos posed to the hegemony of the railroad-supported concessions in Yellowstone as well as other western parks.

Others warned that autos cheapened the park experience. By whizzing along a park road, visitors would lose touch with nature. In 1912, hearing of the recent debates over admitting autos into parks, especially Yosemite, Lord James Bryce warned against it. "If Adam had known what harm the serpent was going to work," Bryce wrote, "he would have tried to prevent him from finding lodgement in Eden; and if you stop to realize what the result of the automobile will be in that wonderful, that incomparable valley, you will keep it out." Bryce, the British ambassador to the United States, was making an argument for national parks within the tradition of the English garden and its American counterpart in the nineteenth-century public park. At higher rates of speed, he observed, the "focus is always changing, and it is impossible to give that kind of enjoyment which a painter, or any devotee of nature, seeks if you are hurrying past at a swift automobile pace." In other words, the automobile wasted scenery.[13]

Bryce's comments, often cited for their great foresight, spoke to the romantic and nostalgic responses many Americans felt with the coming of automobiles to national parks, particularly with their displacement of horse and wagon travel. Curiously, those who waxed poetic about horse coaches selectively overlooked complaints by passengers about the choking dust and jarring discomfort of a drive over rutted park roads. More importantly, Bryce's views misread another component of reconciling machines with parks: the democratizing influence that automobiles would have. Cars transformed parks into places not for the select elite who could afford to travel by train to parks and spend days in them, but places open to the greatest number of Americans to whom they belonged. According to Robert M. Marshall, chief geographer of the U.S. Geological Survey, people should have the right to choose when and how they toured the parks. These reasons alone, he suggested, merited granting the privilege of autos in parks.[14]

By their actions, Americans in general agreed. By the early 1900s, railroads brought tourists within less than fifteen miles (and a short stage ride) of Mount Rainier and Yosemite, but within a few years, automobiles surpassed this and other forms of transportation to and into the parks. As auto ownership soared (from a half million in 1910 to 1.3 million three years later), motorists became a formidable force in national park affairs; they developed a well-formed coalition of special interest groups, including auto clubs as well as business and political leaders, all supporting the use of autos in parks. In 1912, for instance, Seattle and Tacoma formed a park advisory committee that would be highly influential in Mount Rainier's administration and development, especially its accommodations for the motoring masses.

Perhaps the most widely known example was the pressure auto enthusiasts exerted to open Yosemite to cars. At the national parks conference held at Yosemite in 1912, Secretary of the Interior Walter L. Fisher recognized that automobiles had come to stay in national parks. His comments were influenced by the presence of well-organized automobile clubs, automobile manufacturers and agents, good-roads boosters, and commercial organizations at the conference. Their representatives had been inundating his office with telegrams and letters requesting that the machines be admitted to Yosemite. They spoke a language politicians understood. Economically, the appearance of automobiles in Yosemite was free advertising and would boost car sales; auto travel to the park would promote the construction of better roads, and increase tourism in the immediate area and around California as a whole. Moreover, auto enthusiasts and their organizations represented a powerful voting bloc. Senator Frank Flint, for example, testified that the Automobile Club of Southern California, with 4,500 members, was the largest in the nation. His state had the second highest ownership of automobiles, next to New York; there were approximately 84,000 cars on the road, and in California there were more cars per capita than in any other state. All of this added clout to his club's keen interest in opening Yosemite to automobiles.[15]

In 1913, Secretary of the Interior Franklin K. Lane, when he lifted the ban on autos in Yosemite, acknowledged the importance of cars in the administration of national parks and in making them "as accessible as possible to the great mass of people."[16] Lane was a Californian who had replaced Fisher, and his decision is often cited as the turning point for the presence of autos in parks, while the early acceptance of autos in Mount Rainier generally goes unnoticed. Nevertheless, Lane's decision refined the meaning of national parks in the auto age and underscored how cars would justify their protection as economic engines for tourism. The debates over autos in Yosemite occurred around the same time that scenic preservationists, led by J. Horace McFarland, president of the American Civic Association, and John Muir, president of the Sierra Club, were fighting to protect national parks from consumptive uses, the ravages of logging, water-power projects, and grazing. The most flagrant instance, of course, occurred when Secretary Lane approved San Francisco's proposal to dam the park's Hetch Hetchy Valley in 1913. Coincidently, his decision came in the same year that he lifted the ban on autos in Yosemite.[17]

While the introduction of cars into Yosemite may have highlighted the importance of roads, regulations, democracy, and tourism in the way Americans came to terms with machines in wild landscapes, Hetch Hetchy raised the adjustment to cars in parks to another level. The battle over Hetch Hetchy may have been the clarion call for scenic preservation nationally, but the juxtaposition of automobiles and a dam in a national park setting usually goes unnoticed. However, it provides a way of thinking about parks as places where one could commune with nature in an automobile.

The naturalist John Muir and his Sierra Club embraced the automobile as a way to expand the political support of parks and meet utilitarian arguments with their own that auto tourism to national parks would promote economic growth.[18] But Muir was also a complex thinker who valued nature as well as technology. He may have preached the value of nature over civilization, but like Ralph Waldo Emerson a half century before, Muir entertained the possibility for harmony between nature and machines. As Emerson reasoned, the machine in the landscape (which in Emerson's time was the train) was not an unresolvable conflict, at least philosophically. How could it be, if technology was a product of man and man was a product of nature? Evidently, Muir saw automobiles the way Emerson saw trains. Cars seemed to present a lesser menace than grazing sheep in Yosemite or flooding one of its valleys. In fact, the presence of autos seems to have assured the ascendancy of a new preservationist norm that accommodated nature and automobiles. It excluded the industrial extraction of natural resources, but incorporated the modern machine into the enjoyment of the natural world through outdoor recreation and nature tourism. In this light, parks were a kind of national commons for nature and machines.[19]

This strain of thought casts the introduction of automobiles into national parks in a different light. The automobile brought people to nature in national parks, where the possibility of an accord between the machine and wilderness outweighed the potential for destruction. Viewed in this way, national parks were ideally suited for automobiles, the only question being under what conditions parks could make the adjustment. For parks like Yellowstone, which finally admitted cars in 1915, the transition was difficult because they had to break free of railroad hegemony over travel to the park and its tourist facilities. In addition, remote parks like Yellowstone would not see more auto tourists until road and automobile improvements after World War I made long-distance motor travel inviting to a larger audience. Yosemite, on the other hand, made the transition more easily, because despite its age, it did not have a major railroad patron and was poorly developed for tourism. Moreover, Yosemite was attractive to auto users because, as one historian noted, "it was the only major western park located within easy driving distance of two major urban centers—Los Angeles and San Francisco."[20]

Of all the early parks, however, Mount Rainier displayed best the ideal qualities for automobiles in a national park. It stands out as a flagship park for the motor age. On the one hand, Mount Rainier National Park, created in 1899, fits the model for a park as it was envisioned in terms of the nineteenth century—a cultural icon. Its roughly square boundaries enclose a relatively small area and focus attention on the principal feature: the volcano dominating the skyline of Puget Sound in western Washington. But on the other hand, Mount Rainier set the pace for knowing nature through machines in national parks. By the time the National Park Service was created (1916) and embraced the auto as its savior, Mount Rainier had not only allowed the first autos into a national park but also provided access by road and car in a way that emphasized the view from the road, and the road as part of a scenic narrative.

Mount Rainier was also important because it made the transition to automobiles with great celerity and with little conflict, primarily because of the park's proximity to Tacoma and Seattle. Like Yosemite, it lacked a railroad patron. And if Yosemite was within "easy driving distance" of Los Angeles and San Francisco, then by contrast Mount Rainier was but a brief errand into the wilderness for residents of the Puget Sound cities. The majority of visitors who came to Mount Rainier by car or other means of travel resided in nearby cities. Even though there was train service to the park by 1904, the automobile quickly dominated as the mode of travel to the park and within the park by 1910. That year, of the nearly eight thousand visitors to the park, almost twice as many came by auto as by train or stage.[21] As the Seattle photographer and conservationist Asahel Curtis remarked, the main reason for the automobile's acceptance was that the national park's "short distance" from Seattle and Tacoma made it "possible for many to make the trip to the mountain parks in their own machines."[22]

Both cities had energetically supported the park's establishment and later promoted its development and participated in its administration, especially its improvements for automobile tourists, through the Seattle-Tacoma Rainier National Park Advisory Committee (later known as the Rainier National Park Advisory Board). In a sense, the formation of the joint committee evolved from the claims each city made to the mountain as a symbol of its community's scenic beauty, quality of living, and regional superiority in the late nineteenth and early twentieth centuries. The Puget Sound cities displayed an interest not only in promoting Mount Rainier for tourism but also in incorporating the region's spectacular mountain scenery into the amenities each city offered. As the automobile and improved roads made Mount Rainier a short motor drive from each city, these conditions opened new opportunities for tourism in the nearby Cascades. Seattle also incorporated the mountain and other surrounding mountain ranges into its plans for a series of parks and boulevards, designed by John C. Olmsted as early as 1903, and featured Mount Rainier prominently in the Alaska-Yukon-Pacific Exposition in 1909. For its part, Tacoma laid claim to the mountain and tried to change its name to Mount Tacoma, setting off a feud with Seattle. In addition, the city's local "good roads movement" brought together an array of interests, represented by automobile owners, bicycle clubs, boosters, and businessmen, who concentrated on improving the county road, the Mountain Highway, from Tacoma to Mount Rainier. By 1913, the state legislature had passed a bill to turn the county road into a state highway, to be designated as the "National Park Highway."[23]

At the beginning of the century, the influence of Seattle and Tacoma typified the way western cities exerted an influence well beyond their boundaries, whether exploiting surrounding hinterlands for natural resources or for their appeal to tourists. Denver residents, for example, laid claim to the Estes Park country several hours north of the city. Denverites boosted their town as the place from which auto tours of the West began, and their promotion of Estes Park for motoring popularized the area and played a major part in the establishment of nearby Rocky Mountain National Park in 1915.[24] More importantly, the patronage of the Puget Sound cities illustrated a trend for national parks in the motor age. Mount Rainier may have been a park in the nineteenth-century sense of the word, with its emphasis on scenic grandeur. But at the same time it was a new version of the national park ideal, primarily because its audience represented a new generation of park visitors: twentieth-century urban, middle-class tourists. It was an audience that "got back to nature" in its own machines, on its own terms and its own schedule. Unlike their nineteenth-century counterparts, these visitors sought experience in nature that emphasized recreation and self-fulfillment over contemplation of the mountain's deeper cultural significance.[25]

Their perception of the park was mediated by their machines. The auto not only framed their understanding of Mount Rainier as a national park, it strengthened their sense of what national parks should be.

These conditions suggest why Mount Rainier was treated as an anomaly at the national parks conferences. As assistant secretary of the interior Carmi A. Thompson observed in 1911, Mount Rainier possessed conditions that were "entirely different" from other more remote and often older national parks, and automobiles were "entirely advisable." The park contained but "one point of interest," Thompson argued, "that great mountain standing there as it does a lofty citadel, snow capped and bordered with glaciers." Tourists were interested primarily in seeing and climbing "that lofty mountain, so there can be no possible objection to taking them to the base of the mountain as quickly as possible and as comfortably as may be."[26] After a visit to the park that year, Thompson appeared to be carried away with the potential of the new machines. He promised to support a road all the way to Mount Rainier's summit. Impressed with the park's new road and the accessibility of such natural wonders as its glaciers, he exclaimed to a Tacoma audience, "I, like the average man, like to climb mountains in an auto." "Yours," he added "is the only one obliging enough to let me."[27]

Although the assistant secretary's plans never materialized, they demonstrated the way automobiles transformed people's perceptions of national parks, especially in terms of the spatial relationships between the park and its visitors. As the time and effort it took to reach the park decreased, people began to think of Mount Rainier within the context of their new automobility. As early as 1909, Milnor Roberts, from Seattle, noted that one could look at pictures of snow-mantled mountains and polar regions in magazines, but "the remoteness of these scenes lessens our chances of ever seeing them." Mount Rainier, on the other hand, was close at hand, "a wonderland of glaciers and snow in our own country." It was so easily reached by automobile that its reputation was spreading. A party "leaving Seattle or Tacoma in the morning," he wrote, by evening could pitch camp at timberline in "the shadow of that great peak" and with a view of "the vast forest wilderness."[28]

Moreover, the automobile seemed to enhance rather than diminish tourists' perceptions of the national park. Passing through the park's portal, they were forced to slow down, to leave behind the "exhilaration of speed" in exchange for the "calmer glories of nature." Throttled down, their high-powered machines transported them over a "perfect road" winding through a dense forest and then up the mountain past waterfalls and glaciers.[29] If anything, the automobile compelled tourists to recognize that when they entered a national park, they were in a special landscape. The contrast of machines in such a setting alone, it seems, triggered this response. A new set of metaphors appeared to describe the experience. A *Sunset* pictorial published in 1912, for example, enthusiastically described motoring in Mount Rainier as an encounter between "Glaciers and Gasoline."[30]

When thrown together in national parks, primeval nature and modern technology could even elicit reactions of wonder that bordered on the spiritual. The following year, Carpenter Kendall observed that the "new-fangled dynamics" of the automobile enabled him to go "motoring on the mountain" and delight in its ageless mysteries. Ascending Mount Rainier by automobile, as Kendall noted, transported him through "a deep cathedral wood" with air "heavy with silence, as of prayer," past the "anthem of the river," and within reach of the "glistening peak which lifts its shining crest into the heavens." Far from being a disruptive influence, his machine and the wild surroundings made the experience seem entirely "natural." As Kendall concluded, "If a landscape architect with his very best degree under his arm had planned these choice bits, they could not have been more perfectly set."[31]

Increasingly, automobiles helped to satisfy middle-class desires to seek restorative encounters with the natural world found in national parks and other scenic landscapes. Because most middle-class Americans could afford to be away only for short periods of time, the automobile expanded the range and opportunities for their vacations, all of which added to its popularity. Meanwhile, western communities and boosters, like those of Seattle and Tacoma, touted scenic grandeur as a drawing card for tourists and supported auto tourism and national parks as essential parts of their economic development. For these reasons, the automobile was a preferred means of transportation in national parks; it not only brought people into closer contact with nature but tended to tighten the bonds between urban centers and these wild landscapes. Enos Mills, who was the chief advocate for Rocky Mountain National Park, went so far as to say that autos were better than horses for seeing the outdoors. Horses were more destructive of scenery than automobiles; horses required too much attention, trampled and overgrazed meadows, and needed too many facilities for their care. Cars, on the other hand, made camping inexpensive and comfortable. For these reasons, the automobile was a preferred means of transportation in national parks; it not only brought people into closer contact with nature but tended to tighten the bonds between urban centers and wild landscapes.[32]

This new orientation expanded upon the original concept of seeing a national park from a road, as espoused by nineteenth-century park designers and engineers, to include automobile travel. Motoring was a means of knowing nature that also embraced the park within a new geography created by the highway and automobile. The greatest expression of this new orientation was the interest in building a road encircling Mount Rainier. Army engineers had proposed a road around the mountain during the construction of the government road to Paradise (1904 to 1910). In 1911, for example, John Williams suggested that with the completion of the first park road, the next phase in opening the park to public use would be to fulfill the Army's "fine plan." Williams's illustrated tourist guide, entitled *The Mountain That Was "God,"* included the Army's revised map of the park, which showed the proposed route around the mountain of some eighty to one hundred miles. The route branched off from the Paradise road and worked its way around the mountain, providing access to as many of the "great 'parks'" as possible and reaching the "snout of each glacier" before returning to the Paradise Valley.[33] Although Williams argued that a road around the mountain was essential, in part, to its "proper policing" and "its protection from forest fires," he underscored the importance of the road for understanding the mountain as a whole and for providing better access to the mountain for other parts of the region.

In 1912, the Seattle-Tacoma Rainier National Park Advisory Committee presented a similar proposal as a key component of its plan for the "development and exploitation" of the national park. Concerned chiefly with improving the park's road system, the new joint committee described the road proposal in terms similar to those of John Williams. However, the group also stressed its relationship to other road projects that would increase the number of park entrance roads, namely in the park's three undeveloped corners. These areas were more than "natural entrances" for "an encircling road system." They were avenues that would eventually bring the park closer to the Puget Sound country's "two principal cities."[34]

The committee's involvement illustrated why the automobile played such a central role in the park's development and meaning. Without a railroad patron for Mount Rainier, the group considered its role in park policy as a practical matter of regional and commercial interest. Ultimately, it expected the federal government to protect and improve the national park for public enjoyment. It also expected the government to share its interest in building the roads in and to the park. The committee's interest also displayed a more compelling reason: Mount Rainier was not an isolated wilderness beyond the influence of modern life, but a wilderness that was there because of it, and growing more connected all the time to urban areas through roads and automobiles.[35]

In their responses to public pressures and the increased mobility of park patrons, park administrators aided in the process. They began to portray the park differently in their annual reports. In 1913, they no longer described the park—its geography, natural features, and amenities for visitors—as in isolation from, but rather in relation to, the Puget Sound cities. Administrators began to include the park's orientation to Seattle and Tacoma in their descriptions of the park's physical setting. They emphasized the distance from the Puget Sound cities to the park's main entrance, and the "thoroughfare" leading to the park and its connection with the road to Paradise. They continued to document who traveled to the park by horse and wagon or on foot and how many people came to "camp." But they paid closer attention to the type of automobile tourists entering the park, whether in a private car or auto stage, and for a time stopped reporting the number of mountain ascents.[36]

They also initiated surveys for a road system to encircle the park, reflecting the interests of groups like the Seattle-Tacoma park committee. As envisioned by both park administrators and park supporters, the park, county, and state road systems, both existing and proposed, would advance together. In doing so, roads would further incorporate the park into the surrounding region; they would form networks not only for economic growth but also for inspiration. The relationship was not lost on supporters of Crater Lake National Park. As William G. Steel, founder of the park and president of Crater Lake Company, observed in 1911, the automobile "was our only means of salvation."[37] Without the auto and a system of good roads, the rather remote park would not have drawn a national audience. And, as a park brochure announced a few years after the government completed a road encircling the lake, driving along the crater rim was not a "joy ride, but a pilgrimage for devotees of Nature." Touring the lake by car was "a spiritual experience—nothing less."[38]

Although roads would make the park accessible from every direction, the goal of the road system was to bring the park closer to residents of Seattle and Tacoma. Of particular interest was a road up the Carbon River, located in the northwestern corner of the park. It had long been assumed that this would be the next area developed after the southwestern corner; it lay closer to Seattle. Moreover, some considered the northwest side of Mount Rainier to contain the park's "grandest" scenery, characterized by the mountain's steep north face, dense lowland forests, broad alpine parks, and terminus of the Carbon Glacier.[39]

In 1915, however, the distance between the park and these cities was shortened more conceptually than physically. That summer, Stephen T. Mather visited Mount Rainier as part of his tour of national parks. Mather, then director of national parks under the secretary of the interior, would become the first director of the National Park Service when the agency was established the following year. He hoped his trip would dramatize the purpose of national parks and the need for their management by a federal bureau. Members of the Seattle-Tacoma park committee joined him on a pack trip around the rugged west side of the mountain, ending at Carbon River. Mather's presence foreshadowed the alliance he would forge with local business leaders in the management of national parks. His tour to the northwest corner also would prove valuable for acquiring funds to develop other facilities here once he became director of the new park bureau. In his mind, the Carbon River Road was the first leg in a road system around the mountain, including its north side, that would be essential in the completion of Mount

Rainier as a national park.[40] More importantly, the system reflected his larger conception of national parks as intimately related to public highways, a notion that would inform his approach to the management of the nation's parks and be one of his most enduring legacies.

By 1915, though, there was only one road, the road to Paradise Valley, in Mount Rainier National Park. Still, the introduction of autos—controlled through regulations, conveyed over a road designed for scenery—popularized the park and enabled modern Americans to experience it and to know the nature it preserved in a novel way that was central to our understanding of national parks in the early twentieth century. Perhaps more than any other park of its time, Mount Rainier represented this ideal. The introduction of autos into the park provides a valuable perspective on the meaning of parks in the motor age. Mount Rainier's urban patrons considered the mountain a symbol of their region's and cities' scenic beauty and a source of tourist revenue. They also thought of the park in terms of their new mobility. The automobile not only brought the park closer to them physically, it also altered how they thought of it conceptually. Their road proposals suggested how they interpreted the park within the context of the nation's urban industrial order in which business and nature preservation coexisted. They also suggest a way of mapping out the park in a new kind of mental geography. The park was not an isolated reservoir of wilderness preserved from progress, but known because of progress.

Most of all, the acceptance of autos in national parks in the first fifteen years of the twentieth century embodied the optimistic belief that nature and technology were mutually beneficial. It fostered a new preservation ideal of communing with nature by car that would fully blossom with a federal agency dedicated to their care in 1916. National parks, illustrated by Mount Rainier, were cultural constructions of nature, abstract notions made real through use. In the nineteenth century, those notions centered on parks as symbols of America's cultural achievements, selections of the western landscape's most sublime natural icons, which were to be viewed and contemplated. In the early twentieth century, those notions centered on parks increasingly as places for outdoor recreation, enclaves of nature to be reached by and known through machines.

Notes

I explore this idea of knowing nature through machines further in David Louter, "Windshield Wilderness: The Automobile and the Meaning of National Parks in Washington State" (Ph.D. diss., University of Washington, 2000). I would like to thank the National Park Service for the use of photographs to illustrate this chapter (see Figs. 15–19). I would also like to extend my appreciation to John M. Findlay and David Wrobel, whose thoughtful criticism made this chapter better.

1. See, for example, Mark D. Spence, *Dispossessing the Wilderness: Indian Removal and the Making of the National Parks* (New York: Oxford University Press, 1999); Theodore R. Catton, *Inhabited Wilderness: Indians, Eskimos, and National Parks in Alaska* (Albuquerque: University of New Mexico Press, 1997); William Cronon, "The Trouble with Wilderness; or, Getting Back to the Wrong Nature," in William Cronon, ed., *Uncommon Ground: Toward Reinventing Nature* (New York: W.W. Norton, 1995), 69–90; Richard White, "'Are You an Environmentalist or Do You Work for a Living?': Work and Nature," in Cronon, ed., *Uncommon Ground,* 171–85; Paul Sutter, "Driven Wild: The Intellectual and Cultural Origins of Wilderness Advocacy during the Interwar Years" (Ph.D. diss., University of Kansas, 1997).

2. Warren Belasco, *Americans on the Road: From Autocamp to Motel, 1910–1945* (Boston: MIT Press, 1979); John Jakle, *The Tourist: Travel in Twentieth-Century North America* (Lincoln: University of Nebraska Press, 1985), and "Landscapes Redesigned for the Automobile," in Michael P. Conzen, ed., *The Making of an American Landscape* (Boston: Unwin Hyman, 1990), 293–310; John B. Rae, *The Road and Car in American Life* (Cambridge: MIT Press, 1981); T. J. Jackson Lears, *No Place of Grace: Antimodernism and the Transformation of American Culture, 1880–1920* (New York: Pantheon Books, 1981); T. J. Jackson Lears and Richard W. Fox, eds., *The Culture of Consumption: Critical Essays in American History, 1880–1980* (New York: Pantheon Books, 1983); Hal K. Rothman, *Devil's Bargains: Tourism in the Twentieth-Century American West* (Lawrence: University Press of Kansas, 1998), 50–112.

3. Warren Belasco, "Commercialized Nostalgia: The Origins of the Roadside Strip," in David L. Lewis and Laurence Goldstein, eds., *The Automobile and American Culture* (Ann Arbor: University of Michigan Press, 1980), 105–22.

4. See, for example, Richard G. Lillard, "The Siege and Conquest of a National Park," *American West* 5 (January 1968): 28–32, 67–71. For a more scholarly treatment, see Neil Maher, "Auto Tourism, Wilderness, and the Development of Great Smoky Mountains National Park," in David Harmon, ed., *Making Protection Work: Proceedings of the Ninth Conference on Research and Resource Management in Parks and on Public Lands* (Hancock: George Wright Society, 1997), 47–54. For a standard treatment of automobiles as a political necessity now out of control, see Alfred Runte, *National Parks: The American Experience* 2nd ed., rev. (Lincoln: University of Nebraska Press, 1987), 156–61, 167–68, 170–77. Richard W. Sellars, *Preserving Nature in the National Parks: A History* (New Haven: Yale University Press, 1997), provides a broad overview of the ways in which autos and roads have shaped Park Service culture and management.

5. I borrow this concept offered by John Jakle in "Landscapes Redesigned for the Automobile."

6. Frederick Law Olmsted, "The Yosemite Valley and the Mariposa Big Trees," reprinted in Larry M. Dilsaver, ed., *America's National Park System: The Critical Documents* (Lanham, Md.: Rowan and Littlefield, 1994), 22–24; Alfred Runte, *Yosemite: The Embattled Wilderness* (Lincoln: University of Nebraska Press, 1990), 31; Laura Wood Roper, *FLO: A Biography of Frederick Law Olmsted* (Baltimore: Johns Hopkins University Press, 1973), 70, 137–38; Ethan Carr, *Wilderness by Design: Landscape Architecture and the National Park Service* (Lincoln: University of Nebraska Press, 1998), 29; Linda Flint McClelland, *Building the National Parks: Historic Landscape Design and Construction* (Baltimore: Johns Hopkins University Press, 1998), 18–47; Barbara Novak, *Nature and Culture: American Landscape and Painting, 1825–1875* (New York: Oxford University Press, 1980); Mary Shivers Culpin, *The History of the Construction of the Road System in Yellowstone National Park, 1872–1966: Historic Resource*, vol. 1 (Denver: National Park Service, 1994), 26–27. See also Henri Lefebvre, *The Production of Space*, trans. Donald Nicholson-Smith (Oxford: Blackwell, 1991), 77–78, 94. Lefebvre argues that "space" reflects a set of historical social relationships. This is not to say that the natural forces preserved within the political boundaries of Yellowstone and Mount Rainier national parks do not exist outside of human knowledge and experience, but that we conceptualize those forces and the park itself through culture. David E. Nye, *American Technological Sublime* (Cambridge: MIT Press, 1994), xiii, 70–78. Nye is speaking more about the presence of the transcontinental railroad in the western landscape in the late nineteenth century, and I have adapted his observations to illustrate my argument.

7. For a comprehensive history of the road to Paradise, see Richard H. Quin, "Nisqually Road (Government Road), Mount Rainier National Park" (Historic American Engineering Record No. WA-119, Library of Congress, Washington, D.C., 1992), 1–54.

8. Anne F. Hyde, "From Stagecoach to Packard Twin Six: Yosemite and the Changing Face of Tourism, 1880–1930," *California History* 65 (Summer 1990): 164; Robert Shankland, *Steve Mather of the National Parks* (New York: Alfred A. Knopf, 1951), 63–66.

9. Chester Thorne to Secretary of the Interior, April 8, 1907, Record Group 79, Records of the National Park Service, Entry 1—Records of the Secretary of the Interior, box 38, National Archives, Washington, D.C. "Annual Report of the Acting Superintendent of the Mount Rainier National Park, 1908," in *Annual Report of the Secretary of the Interior, 1908* (Washington, D.C.: Government Printing Office, 1908), 477–78. In 1908, 117 auto permits were issued, and more than 2,800 people visited the park. Above Longmire, for example, automobiles were limited to use between 9:00 and 11:00 A.M. and 3:30 and 5:30 P.M. The speed limit for automobiles was six miles per hour, except on straightaways when no horse teams were in sight, where the speed limit was fifteen miles per hour. The rules of the road also dictated that teams always had the right of way over automobiles, and when approached by teams, the automobile driver was to pull to the outer edge of the road and stay there until teams could safely pass.

10. *Annual Report of the Acting Superintendent of the Mount Rainier National Park, 1906* (Washington, D.C.: Government Printing Office, 1906), 7; *1908 Annual Report*, 471.

11. Virginia Scharff, *Taking the Wheel: Women and the Coming of the Motor Age* (New York: Free Press, 1991); Jakle, *The Tourist*; Jakle, "Landscapes Redesigned for the Automobile"; Joseph Interrante, "A Movable Feast: The Auto-

mobile and the Spatial Transformation of American Culture, 1890–1940" (Ph.D. diss., Harvard University, 1983), and "You Can't Go to Town in a Bathtub: Automobile Movement and the Reorganization of Rural American Space, 1900–1930," *Radical History Review* 21 (Fall 1979): 151–68.

12. Department of the Interior, *Proceedings of the National Park Conference Held at Yellowstone*, 30. Hill's comments, however, anticipated the park-to-park highway dedicated within a decade.

13. "National Parks—The Need and the Future," in *University and Historical Addresses* (New York: Macmillan, 1913), 393–94, 397–401, reprinted in David Harmon, ed., *Mirror of America: Literary Encounters with the National Parks* (Boulder: Roberts Rinehart, 1989), 126–27.

14. Department of the Interior, *Proceedings of the National Park Conference Held at Yellowstone*, 34.

15. Department of the Interior, *Proceedings of the National Park Conference, 1912*, 61.

16. Shankland, *Steve Mather of the National Parks*, 6–7. Lane quoted in Richard Lillard, "Siege and Conquest," 69.

17. Stephen Fox, *John Muir and His Legacy: The American Conservation Movement* (Boston: Little, Brown, 1981), and Roderick Nash, *Wilderness and the American Mind*, 3rd ed. (New Haven: Yale University Press, 1982). The Hetch Hetchy decision is reprinted in the "Annual Report of the Secretary of the Interior, 1913," in Department of the Interior, *Reports of the Department of the Interior, 1913*, vol. 1 (Washington, D.C.: Government Printing Office, 1914), 90–93.

18. Department of the Interior, *Proceedings of the National Park Conference, 1912*, 137.

19. Fox, *John Muir and His Legacy*, 127–28, 352; Robert Athearn, *The Mythic West in Twentieth-Century America* (Lawrence: University Press of Kansas, 1986), 196–98. See also William H. Goetzman and Kay Sloan, *Looking Far North: The Harriman Expedition to Alaska, 1899* (New York: Viking, 1982), and Michael L. Smith, *Pacific Visions: California Scientists and the Environment* (New Haven: Yale University Press, 1987), for the complex social and professional composition of the scientific community around the turn of the century. Muir was often considered to be a western transcendentalist, a voice for wilderness, whose ideas could be traced back to Concord transcendentalists Ralph Waldo Emerson and Henry David Thoreau. Although Thoreau and other New England intellectuals grappled with the burgeoning industrial order, Emerson's insights are quite useful for understanding how Americans of another generation made sense of modern life and fashioned a new aesthetic. It was not that nature was either pristine or defiled, Emerson suggested. Technological innovations created new landscapes, which needed to be considered within a larger perspective. Everything was part of the same great "Order" of being and possessed its own beauty and value. For insights on Muir's debt to Emerson and transcendentalism, see Leo Marx, *The Machine in the Garden: Technology and the Pastoral Ideal in America* (New York: Oxford University Press, 1964), 227–42, esp. 242.

20. Hyde, "From Stage Coach to Packard Twin Six," 164. This point was not lost on Stephen Mather when he became director of national parks in 1915. That year thousands of visitors were expected for the world's fairs in San Diego and San Francisco. Many people would come by automobile and would want to see the fabled wonders of Yosemite. Mather wasted little time in using the expositions as a reason for improving the park for motorists and as a way to

stimulate park travel. (For similar reasons, Mather ordered Yellowstone open to cars that year, though under a complex system to appease concessionaires.)

21. *Annual Report of the Acting Superintendent of the Mount Rainier National Park to the Secretary of the Interior, 1910* (Washington, D.C.: Government Printing Office, 1910), 7–9. There were 4,413 visitors who came in cars, compared to 2,620 who came by stage.

22. Asahel Curtis to Enos Mills, July 3, 1912, Asahel Curtis Papers, box 1, file 23, University of Washington.

23. Padraic Burke, "The City Beautiful Movement in Seattle" (master's thesis, University of Washington, 1973); William H. Wilson, *The City Beautiful Movement* (Baltimore: Johns Hopkins University Press, 1989); Arthur D. Martinson, "Mount Rainier or Mount Tacoma? The Controversy that Refused to Die," *Columbia* 3 (Summer 1989): 10–16; Genevieve E. McCoy, "'Call It Mount Tacoma': A History of the Controversy over the Name of Mount Rainier" (M.A. thesis, University of Washington, 1984); Edward S. Hall to Secretary of the Interior, February 28, 1913, Record Group 79, Entry 6, box 135, file 12–7–2, "Roads, Trails, and Bridges," National Archives, Washington, D.C.

24. Shankland, *Steve Mather,* 78–79.

25. Rothman, *Devil's Bargains,*143–67. For an extensive history of Mount Rainier and its relationship with the Puget Sound cities, see Theodore R. Catton, *Wonderland: An Administrative History of Mount Rainier National Park* (Seattle: National Park Service, 1996).

26. Department of the Interior, *Proceedings of the National Park Conference, 1911,* 33.

27. "Favors Road up Mountain," *Spokane Review,* December 7, 1911.

28. Milnor Roberts, "A Wonderland of Glaciers and Snow," *National Geographic* 20 (June 1909): 530, 534.

29. A. Woodruff McCully, "The Rainier Forest Reserve," *Overland Monthly* 55 (June 1910): 553–54.

30. "Glaciers and Gasoline: Motoring in Mt. Rainier National Park," *Sunset* 28 (January 1912): 41–47.

31. Carpenter Kendall, "Motoring on Mount Rainier," *Sunset* 31 (August 1913): 304–7. Kendall's observations were astute. In fairly short order, landscape architects would appear in national park management and set about reconciling autos and national parks further.

32. Enos A. Mills, "Touring in Our National Parks," *Country Life* 23 (January 1913): 33–36.

33. John H. Williams, *The Mountain That Was "God"* (New York: G. P. Putnam's Sons, 1911), 62–64.

34. Asahel Curtis and T. H. Martin to Walter L. Fisher, April 15, 1912, RG 79, Entry 6, box 135, file 12–7–2, "Roads, Trails, and Bridges," NA.

35. See, for example, Hal K. Rothman, *On Rims and Ridges: The Los Alamos Area since 1880* (Lincoln: University of Nebraska Press, 1992), on the relationship between the federal government and private interests in the management of public lands.

36. See, for example, "Mount Rainier National Park," in *Report of the Secretary of the Interior, 1903* (Washington, D.C.: Government Printing Office, 1903), 161–62; "Report of the Acting Superintendent of the Mount Rainier National Park, 1909," in *Report of the Secretary of the Interior, 1909* (Washington, D.C.: Government Printing Office, 1910), 459–60; "Report of the Superintendent of the

Mount Rainier National Park, 1911," in *Annual Reports of the Department of the Interior, 1911*, vol. 1 (Washington, D.C.: Government Printing Office, 1912), 623; "Report of the Superintendent of the Mount Rainier National Park, 1912," in *Annual Reports of the Department of the Interior, 1912*, vol. 1 (Washington, D.C.: Government Printing Office, 1913), 693–94; "Report of the Superintendent of the Mount Rainier National Park, 1913," in *Annual Reports of the Department of the Interior, 1913*, vol. 1 (Washington, D.C.: Government Printing Office, 1914), 767–69. This is not to say that park administrators stopped reporting mountain ascents altogether; the practice continued in later reports, but visitation by auto tourists figured prominently in the reports.

37. "Report of the Superintendent of the Mount Rainier National Park, 1913," in Department of the Interior, *Reports of the Department of the Interior, 1913* (Washington, D.C.: Government Printing Office, 1914), 776. In his testimony at the 1915 conference on national parks, T. H. Martin described "a great highway crossing from Puget Sound to the southern border of Mount Rainier National Park," and from there to the fruit valleys of Yakima. It would be an unforgettable drive, he noted. In the morning one could drive "through those heights, always with this magnificent dome in sight," and that evening dine in Yakima. Department of the Interior, *Proceedings of the National Park Conference Held at Berkeley, California, March 11, 12, and 13, 1915* (Washington, D.C.: Government Printing Office, 1915), 160.

38. C. G. Thompson, *The Rim Road—A Wonder Drive* (Portland: Scenic America Company, c. 1924), no pagination.

39. Francois E. Matthes to Clement S. Ucker, January 6, 1913, RG 79, entry 6, box 135, file 12-7-2, "Roads, Trails, and Bridges," NA.

40. Shankland, *Steve Mather of the National Parks*, 68, 78.

Chapter Twelve

Selling the Scenery: Advertising and the National Parks, 1916–1933

Peter Blodgett

When Stephen Tyng Mather assumed the post of assistant to the secretary of the interior for national parks in 1915, the cause of the parks received its ablest and most vocal spokesman within the councils of the federal government. The conservation movement, of course, had received increasingly favorable attention from Congress and the executive branch through the closing decades of the nineteenth century and had flourished for a season under the ebullient advocacy of Theodore Roosevelt. National parks, however, lacking the forceful direction and institutional security that Gifford Pinchot and the Forest Service provided for the national forests, never reaped a full share of the benefits that accrued to other conservation programs. The tiny band of scenic principalities, geologic curiosities, archaeological treasures, and historic sites that made up the national parks and monuments still suffered from considerable administrative and public neglect as they had, for the most part, since the founding of Yellowstone National Park in 1872. Scattered among three cabinet departments that displayed varying amounts of concern for their well-being, they fell prey all too often to the ministrations of poachers and vandals or to the exploitative schemes of commercial interests, abetted by corrupt or sympathetic politicians. Mather, disgusted at the impoverished and disorganized state of the parks he had visited, took on park preservation and improvement as his personal crusade and, for the most part, achieved considerable success. In particular, drawing upon his experience as a successful advertising executive in the borax industry, he tirelessly promoted travel to the parks and monuments, confident that public familiarity with them would generate the public support necessary to bolster their political standing.[1]

The efforts of Mather and his able successor, Horace M. Albright, to attract tourists into the parks between 1916 and 1933 involved forging alliances between the Park Service and a host of public and private organizations as one aspect of the burgeoning tourist industry in the Far West. Thus, the techniques adopted for this purpose by National Park Service leadership are part of a fascinating episode in the history of that region as well as the history of the national parks.

Mather's and Albright's work in promoting travel to the national parks, however, did not represent the first such efforts. Long before they came on the scene, a number of individuals and businesses had been urging the public to come to the parks. Not surprisingly, railroads serving the Far West were among the most fervent advocates of park travel. From the creation of Yellowstone National Park through the 1910s, those railroads gladly linked their economic self-interest to the development of parks in many sections of the trans-Mississippi West. Over the course of three decades, such lines as the Santa Fe, the Union Pacific, and the Great Northern invested considerable sums in advertising designed to induce travelers to visit the national parks in the domains served by their trains. Other commercial entities such as local "booster" clubs and chambers of commerce began to capitalize upon the proximity of national parks and monuments as especially attractive bait to lure tourists, often as a reminder to "See America First."[2] Finally, a handful of conservationists and preservationists had been calling upon Americans since the 1890s to visit these unexploited regions. Led by the preservation-minded John Muir, this loose but increasingly influential alliance of authors, editors, and scientists argued that exposure to the undisturbed reaches of the parks conferred psychological and physical benefits upon each visitor.[3]

The cause of the national parks thus had acquired a growing number of vigorous and eloquent allies late in the nineteenth century. Writers such as Muir and editors such as Robert Underwood Johnson of the *Century* magazine who espoused the cause especially exercised a powerful, if indirect, influence upon the fate of those reserves. Muir, Johnson, and their contemporaries, including J. Horace McFarland, head of the American Civic Association, and Enos Mills, the Colorado naturalist who fought for a national park in the Rockies, aroused the interest and sympathy of many Americans from both the socially and politically powerful upper classes and the newly ascendant professional classes. Their passionate arguments, broadcast by the leading magazines and publishing houses of the day, cultivated the expression of preservationist leanings and channeled those feelings into support for the preservation of scenic wonders. Park proponents early in this century drew upon the rising enthusiasm for untamed landscapes that Roderick Nash has termed the "wilderness cult" to claim that parks represented an absolutely essential element of modern urban life.[4]

Unfortunately for national parks, the good works accomplished by their friends often lacked a necessary unity of purpose. The railroads, the utilitarian conservationists, and the preservationists all had their own agendas for the parks' future. On occasion, their divergent interests hindered their ability to cooperate on behalf of the parks. Ensuring efficient administration, protection, and promotion of the parks meant placing an energetic and effective parks enthusiast inside the government. Such an individual would have to harness *all* the allies of the parks and draw upon their united strength to muster the political support required to acquire greater appropriations, more and better personnel, and an independent bureau to run the parks.

Stephen Mather filled the bill perfectly for all those purposes. Intelligent, vigorous, and exuberant, he had displayed great ability in several different careers after his graduation from the University of California in 1887. Most recently, as an executive in the borax industry, he had accumulated a sizable fortune, which freed him from any financial need for the rest of his life. Left at loose ends by his business successes, he found Interior Secretary Franklin Lane's challenge to him in 1914 to take charge of the national parks a perfect employment for his considerable administrative talents. The fate of the parks also absorbed his conservationist leanings and the boundless reserves of "generous enthusiasms" that led one observer to dub him "the Eternal Freshman."[5] Immediately upon taking office, he applied his skills as a manager and a promoter to organizing and implementing an advertising campaign on behalf of the parks that reduced every previous effort to insignificance by comparison.

Mather's elaborate program to improve the lot of the national parks involved many separate tasks but only two basic approaches: capitalizing upon Mather's enormous range of personal contacts in business, politics, and the conservation movement and erecting permanent machinery somewhere within the government to publicize the parks and attract the tourist. The foundation of a permanent advertising or publicity office had to await passage of legislation to establish a parks bureau, but Mather began twisting the arms of old friends and new acquaintances. By November of 1915, for example, he was already urging the major western railroads to send their chief passenger traffic officials to meet with him in Washington. Once assembled, Mather continued, they would all talk about the ways and means of expanding rail travel to the national parks and ways the promotional campaigns of the railroads could be bettered. In the same manner, Mather also recruited old friends from the newspaper world from his days as a reporter on the *New York Sun* to open their columns to stories about the parks and to print editorials supporting the creation of a national parks bureau within the interior department. He convinced editors of important periodicals, such as George Horace Lorimer of the *Saturday Evening Post,* to accept articles about the parks and enticed such prominent authors as Hal Evarts and Emerson Hough to write them. With his encouragement, publishers and editors with conservationist tendencies, such as Lorimer, commissioned stories and photographs on their own and threw their weight behind Mather's drive to improve the state of the parks. Finally, Mather and Albright took to the road themselves, as in a 1915 inspection tour of the parks. Like politicians on the stump circuit, they set out to win friends and influence people on behalf of the parks.[6]

Every opportunity for travel in the field meant, for Mather, another opportunity to spread his gospel of the parks. In some instances, such as his inspection trip of 1915, he preached his sermons about the crucial importance of the national parks to small-town newspapermen, local chambers of commerce, and the business clubs in towns and cities, such as Klamath Falls, Medford, Tacoma, Seattle, and Denver, that were neighbors to national parks. On other occasions, Mather arranged outings into the back country of the Sierra Nevada, such as one pack trip in 1915 composed of influential writers, editors, conservationists, and politicians. There, willing captives to Mather's enthusiasm for unspoiled landscapes, these opinion-makers would be bombarded with a steady stream of his arguments while professional packers, a first-rate trail cook, and air mattresses made "roughing it" easy.[7]

Mather's promotional labors on behalf of the parks bore fruit early on, with the passage in April 1916 of the National Park Service Act. Although the political momentum behind such a measure had been growing for nearly a decade, Mather's dynamic personal advocacy had focused the energy of this drive and won it important new friends in the press and within Congress. Mather, armed with that nearly arrogant confidence in his own abilities so often born of great success, assiduously courted an elite constituency whose influence on public affairs he had sought, successfully, to turn to his own advantage.

Mather did not make the mistake, however, of depending exclusively upon that constituency for his political support. Gifted with a strong sense of practical politics, he wooed the public at large with as much ardor as he expended upon the "taste-makers." Nothing could be as potent a tool for the parks as a steady rise in public visitation and a constant flow of compliments from satisfied "customers." Thus Mather laid the foundations for a formidable publicity machine that could produce favorable copy for the parks.

In one of his first acts, for example, Mather hired Robert Sterling Yard, a newspaper colleague of long-standing acquaintance, from the *New York Herald*, to run the publicity for the parks, even before a separate parks bureau had been created. Mather offered Yard five thousand dollars a year, to be paid out of Mather's own pocket, while Yard nominally graced the personnel lists of the United States Geological Survey at thirty dollars a month, on permanent loan to Mather's office. Working closely with Mather's allies in the press, Yard shepherded a monumental number of essays and press releases into print. After the establishment of the park bureau in 1916, Yard redoubled his efforts, writing, editing, or coordinating a vast array of news and feature stories. Mather's biographer, noting the effectiveness of this blitzkrieg, asserts that in a three-year period from 1917 to 1919, the almost unbelievable total of 1,050 articles appeared on national park topics in American magazines. Working almost single-handedly, Yard even superintended the production of the Park Service's two most important initial publications, *Glimpses of Our National Parks* and the *National Parks Portfolio*. In 1917 alone, service reports indicated that Yard's informal "news service" distributed nearly 250,000 pieces of literature (including 117,000 copies of *Glimpses of Our National Parks*), 83,000 road maps, and 348,000 feet of motion picture film, circulated without cost to outdoor clubs, charitable institutions, and schools all over the country, as well as blizzards of press releases, blanketing every newspaper that would take them.[8]

Among this assortment of publications, *Glimpses* and *Parks Portfolio* represented the most important element in the Park Service's effort to create an attractive image for the regions under its charge. Designed and written by Yard, the two volumes differed considerably in style and presentation. *Glimpses*, produced by the Park Service and designed for complimentary distribution, provided a general introduction to the parks for the public at large. The *Portfolio*, by contrast, produced for the Park Service by a commercial publisher, was aimed at a much more select audience, whose background, social connections, or professional interests suggested, in the words of one scholar, that they might prove "most likely to be moved by the *Portfolio* to visit the national parks, appreciate them, and spread enthusiasm." Composed of a series of well-written and attractively illustrated pamphlets bound in buckram, the *Portfolio* was mailed out to 275,000 people culled from the membership lists of men's and women's clubs, chambers of commerce, professional societies, the alumni rolls of the various universities, and social registers.[9]

The difference in presentation and approach of the two volumes belies the similarity of their appeal. Both sought to encourage the greater flow of tourists to the parks. Moreover, the whole process involved in producing the *Portfolio* aptly demonstrated the special links being forged between public and private agencies to achieve such ends. The *Portfolio*'s $48,000 price tag, for example, greatly exceeded any sums budgeted for publication in the Park Service's appropriations. With a $5,000 contribution from his own fortune, Mather cajoled the remaining funds from a combine of seventeen western railroads, who apparently saw the *Portfolio* as a valuable supplement to their own advertising.[10]

The Park Service's success in stimulating greater interest among a wider segment of the public in national parks with these initial measures led in quick order to the adoption of other promotional tactics. The new bureau depended upon the unrelenting support of the western railroads not only to provide money for special projects such as the *Portfolio* but also to issue a steady stream of attractive publication that would entice tourists to visit the western parks and monuments when they visited the Far West. The Denver and Rio Grande's advertising program in the winter of 1917–18 exemplified the unstinting response of many railroads. Using its network of ticket offices in such midwestern cities as Detroit, Cincinnati, and Cleveland, the railroad laid a foundation for the 1918 travel season by disseminating folders with double-page views of the national parks and monuments in Colorado, Utah, and New Mexico, as well as motion picture footage of the Mesa Verde National Park and the Royal Gorge. It also added its voice to the chorus urging Congress to support the parks more fully, supplying its brochures to every member of the House and Senate as one means to open their eyes to the wonders of the parks.[11]

Even after the individual lines were absorbed by the United States Railroad Administration (USRA) in 1918, promotion of travel to the parks by railroad interests continued. Before the war, the Chicago and Northwestern and the Union Pacific had jointly operated a tourist bureau reflecting their existing through passenger service from Chicago. Now, with the tacit approval and support of the NPS, the railroad executives who managed the USRA reorganized this agency into a Bureau of Service for the Western Lines, concentrating upon the national parks and monuments. That bureau, in their view, would carry on the private promotional campaigns of the railroads while coordinating those campaigns with the Park Service, the park concessionaires, and other interested parities.[12]

To justify the formation of this proposed Bureau of Service, railroads operating in the West pointed to their historical role in advertising and developing the parks, from the creation of Yellowstone National Park in 1872 through the establishment of the National Park Service. Howard Hays, former manager of the Union Pacific–Chicago and Northwestern tourist bureau, laid out this argument in a 1918 Bureau of Service memorandum that emphasized the railroads' sponsorship of park exhibits at the 1915 San Francisco Exposition and of the 1916 *National Parks Portfolio,* as well as the money spent by the railroads in promoting the parks. Hays concluded, not unreasonably, that the western national parks had "grown up, in part, through encouragement by the railroads, and, in whole, on a dependence on railroad service and publicity."[13]

The Park Service, however, despite its appreciation for such lavish assistance, never let itself become wholly dependent upon railroad service or publicity. The Park Service and the railroads shared the goal of increasing tourist travel to the parks, of course. For the Park Service, higher attendance figures would validate its management of the parks and justify requests for higher appropriations from Congress; for the railroads, growing numbers of park visitors would mean more business for the passenger trains they ran all over the West. Nonetheless, the bureau on occasion asserted its authority in the parks with vigor against the influence of some railroad magnates, such as Louis Hill. To help preserve its independence, it solicited the cooperation of many other private organizations besides the railroads in these early years.

Mather, perhaps because of his own experience as a journalist, had grasped immediately the press's importance to the work of his bureau and set about to instruct all his employees in that fact. During his many whirlwind expeditions around the national parks, he always made a point of conferring with representatives of the local newspapers, exercising all his charm and persuasiveness to win them over and make new allies. In the same vein, other members of the Park Service's Washington office learned to beware of such considerations and, in some cases, to mend political fences with publishers and editors.

Assistant Director Arno Cammerer, in outlining plans for a superintendents' conference in Denver, warned the superintendent of Rocky Mountain National Park that the 1919 meeting should be newsworthy enough to draw the interest of the local press and thus focus their attention on the parks for the conference's duration. At the 1919 conference, under the heading of "press notices," one superintendent described his elaborate routine of press work and, in doing so, demonstrated the lengths to which such publicity could be carried. In or out of the travel season, Superintendent Washington B. "Dusty" Lewis of Yosemite sought to put news of his park before the public's eyes by blanketing local newspapers with bulletins on weather and road conditions, statements of the general rules for park visitors, and every other conceivable kind of tourist information. Moreover, to broaden interest in his park, the superintendent cultivated not only the newspapers but chambers of commerce and other civic groups in the surrounding communities, just as Mather and Albright had cultivated political figures and opinion-makers on the national stage. First and foremost, Lewis sought public support for Park Service actions in managing Yosemite.[14] Such a program demonstrated what an innovative superintendent could achieve to publicize his park through local networks of private organizations, but also how all-consuming such publicity work could become.

In like manner, the Park Service responded to a host of inquiries and proposals from commercial organizations, civic groups, and enthusiastic individuals during the first years of its existence. Personally conducted package tours, pioneered in America during the 1870s by the firm of Raymond and Whitcomb on the model established by England's Thomas Cook, had begun to introduce the middle classes to travel in the national parks long before the Park Service had ever been contemplated. Now in the 1910s and early 1920s, the increasingly common practice of providing even wage-earners with paid vacations expanded the available pool of visitors greatly. The tremendous growth in the ownership of private automobiles and subsequent improvement in many public roads set loose a large new population of travelers who had previously lacked the free time or the means to visit the parks. Reflecting the increasing popularity of auto touring, they adopted the motto "See America First," originally publicized by the railroads, as their own battle cry. Now Americans were being urged to see the West through a windshield rather than a Pullman car window.[15]

As a result, much of the Service's promotional work not only encouraged people to visit the parks but also helped them to find their way. The Service routinely furnished maps and information to such national organizations at the American Automobile Association's Touring Bureau, the *Automobile Blue Book*, the American Express Company's Travel Department, and the Motorist Publishing Company, as well as dozens of local tourist agencies and civic groups. Between 1919 and 1921, for example, Park Service officials responded to requests for information from chambers of commerce, commercial clubs, automobile clubs, and state agencies in Wyoming, Montana, New Mexico, and Kansas, as well as numerous inquiries received directly from the general public. Many of these groups offered their enthusiastic support for the Park Service's efforts to spur travel to the parks, proclaiming in the words of A. L. Westgard that "it is up to this country to do all in its power to make our own attractions so well known and so get-to-able that we may be able to retain a large portion of that money which in former years was spent by Americans in Europe." Mather's answer to Westgard expressed the basic policy that would guide the Park Service's promotion of its system: "We will continue to hammer away with the 'See America First' idea, with every available means . . . to make the scenic resources of this country better known to our own people."[16]

To that end, the National Park Service collaborated with many private organizations on behalf of the increasingly motorized public. Beyond sharing useful tidbits of information about road conditions or new park regulations, the Service also urged travel promoters to sing the praises of the parks in their literature, gently corrected the factual errors promotional advertising made concerning the parks, and on occasion offered the imprimatur of the federal government for the final product. Mather in 1921 nudged the Salt Lake City Commercial Club toward amending the map in its brochure *Salt Lake City—The Center of Scenic America* after commending the club's president for the brochure's excellent presentation of "our great scenic country of the West." Similarly, Mather had solicitously assisted the publishers of the *Automobile Blue Book* in the preparation of successive editions because of its "very gratifying" presentation of national parks to "hordes of motorists who used the guidebooks" as reference tools. The Tourist and Publicity Bureau of the Denver Civic and Commercial Association and the chief cartographer of the National Highways Association, among many others, received supplies of photographs and essays for possible publication, exemplifying the Park Service's willingness to cooperate "with any other whole-hearted publicity scheme that would seem to have merit."[17]

Such cooperative relationships, of course, demanded that each partner contribute to achieving the common purpose. Just as the railroads had done since the 1880s, other organizations promoting tourist travel devoted money, energy, and publicity to advertise the parks in particular. Following the example of the western railways, groups such as the Denver Civic and Commercial Association subsidized Park Service productions or absorbed the subject of national parks into their own advertising matter. The one thousand dollars spent by the Civic and Commercial Association in 1917 for colored pictures clearly was seen as an investment whose return could be measured in the growing sums spent by tourists visiting the Colorado Rockies. The Denver Tourist and Publicity Bureau's offer in 1921 to distribute promotional literature on behalf of Mesa Verde National Park thus served the interests of park and promoter both. The Park Service had an opportunity to reach, without cost, potential travelers all over the Midwest with literature about the park, through the bureau's offices in Denver, Colorado Springs, St. Louis, Kansas City, Missouri, and Chicago.[18]

Besides the civic and commercial associations and the railroads that ballyhooed the charms of their respective cities or regions, great resort hotels, dude ranches, park concessioners, motorbus passenger carriers, and the highway and automobile associations all competed for the public's attention in order to inspire great new numbers of Americans to travel to the parks. Each group as well as thousands of small-town merchants and innkeepers hoped that a huge influx of travelers could be drawn into the West while visiting the parks. On the way to and from the parks, more tourists could be separated from more of their money.

As more and more tourists chose the automobile to carry them away on vacation, the automobile clubs and the private highway associations wielded particular influence with the National Park Service. From the beginning, Mather and his associates had worked closely and on generally cooperative terms with the American Automobile Association, the Rand McNally Company, and the Automobile Blue Book Publishing Company, among others, in preparing accurate maps and guidebooks for auto travelers. The Park Service shared a common interest with these friends of the motorist in fostering auto travel and in smoothing the way for the auto-borne tourist. Other promoters also appeared during the early years of the National Park Service, possessing a much more direct interest in western tourist travel and the national parks.

Before and after World War I, a great number of private highway associations sprang up, proclaiming their willingness to help put Americans onto good roads by pioneering new highways to be built with private funds, spanning the nation north to south and east to west. Watching the enormous growth in popular acceptance of the automobile, promoters of various associations began to see how increasing automobile travel could benefit their businesses and their communities. But to attract the patronage of the public and investors in their highways, these associations had to serve attractive destinations. In the Far West, many highway promoters made much of their proximity to the national parks.[19]

The western railroads and the great resort hotels (many of them owned by those same railroads) no longer dominated western tourist advertising as they had a generation earlier. As tourist travel to the West had grown into a mass movement, the number and variety of entrepreneurs seeking to profit from the tourists had grown accordingly. Western dude ranches, for example, took some pains to capitalize upon their common ground with the parks. Although many individual ranches antedated all the parks except Yellowstone, the dude ranch industry had greatly expanded in the 1910s and 1920s in response to the rising tide of tourism. Many of the newer ranches clustered in the vicinity of national parks such as Glacier, Rocky Mountain, and Yellowstone, sharing the same spectacular unspoiled landscapes that made those parks so popular. Some of the ranches promised pack trips into the parks as an inducement for potential customers; all of them benefited from the heightened public awareness of the Rocky Mountain West that the parks inspired.[20]

Hotels, motor courts, guest lodges, and all sorts of other hostelries for the tourist all over the Rocky Mountain West promoted themselves aggressively, either individually or through various cooperative arrangements with chambers of commerce, hotel associations, or travel clubs such as the state chapters of the AAA. *The Western Tourists' Auto Guide,* published in Salt Lake City during World War I, highlighted the fine roads that could carry motorists away to Yellowstone through Utah and Idaho, while it also emphasized the many fine establishments catering to tourists along the way. Hotels, lodges, and camps in the canyons of Utah's Wasatch Front and all across southern Idaho aimed directly at the park travelers, in hopes of waylaying them for at least a short time. Few were as blatant in their use of symbolism as Pocatello's "new" and "elegantly furnished" Hotel Yellowstone, but all certainly hoped to profit from the fact that the tourist "wonderland" they advertised lay so close at hand. Similarly, during the Depression, the Butte Chamber of Commerce, promoting travel to western Montana as the "land that enchants the traveler," drew upon Yellowstone and Glacier National Parks for further inspiration. Those two locations, "symbolic of [western Montana's] matchless scenic assets," only heightened the marvelous possibilities at hand "to revel in the day's play." Glacier National Park, the "Switzerland of America," offered scenic opportunities, especially along the soon-to-be completed Going-to-the-Sun Highway through Logan Pass, which outshone in beauty and "engineering supremacy" any European competitors.[21]

Scores of western cities and towns also took advantage of western national parks to pursue the tourists and their dollars. By themselves or gathered together into state or regional associations, western communities throughout the 1920s and early 1930s praised their special attractions and their unlimited opportunities for fun, especially in connection with the national parks. Salt Lake City's Chamber of Commerce described the city's location at "the Center of Scenic America." After exploring its "unique interesting and enchanting beauty," tourists could make the city of the Saints their "headquarters" for excursions to Yellowstone, the "scenic wonderland" of southern Utah, or even the Grand Canyon. Similar advertising prepared by Denver's tourist bureau in the same era proclaimed that its location astride a great network of western highways and railroads made it the "gateway" to all the national parks and monuments between the hundredth meridian and the Pacific Coast. Moreover, the city's closeness to Rocky Mountain National Park gave copywriters at Denver's Tourist and Publicity Bureau an opportunity to stress the "indescribable scenic magnificence" at hand.[22] Such advertising testified to the truth of an observation made by one student of the Park Service in 1922 that "private agencies . . . have discovered that advertising the parks in connection with their own business is . . . good advertising from the standpoint of . . . increased returns."[23]

The promotional work undertaken first by Mather and subsequently carried on by the Park Service thus had proven its worth early in the Park Service's history. The bureau's success with its own publishing campaigns and in its efforts to foster private business advertising of the parks encouraged the agency to refine and expand its publicity programs throughout the 1920s and early 1930s. It also continued to elicit cooperation in advertising from a host of private businesses who also favored increasing tourist travel to the Far West. Meanwhile, the Park Service's own publicity machinery continued to operate without interruption. Under the direction of an editor assigned to its Washington headquarters, the agency produced a steady stream of editorials, maps, and brochures, as well as issuing revised editions of the *National Parks Portfolio* and *Glimpses of the National Parks.* Missing no opportunity to charm the public with examples of the natural beauty in the parks, even circulars of rules and regulations were usually well decorated with scenic photographs.[24]

The Park Service also grasped the opportunities presented by the new media of communications already spreading fast in 1920s America. Recognizing the possibilities of radio, the Park Service put its message on the airwaves in 1932 with a series of evening lectures on WOC in Davenport, Iowa. Three lectures on Yellowstone National Park, "The Wonderland of America," Yosemite National Park, and the park system as a whole were announced with high hopes of reaching most of the station's estimated audience of one million people across the continent.[25]

Equally hopeful about the potential of motion pictures, the Park Service had gathered a large assortment of scenic movie footage shot in the parks to reproduce their natural beauty. These early productions, like the newsreels and travelogues of later years, tried to intrigue as well as inform and, by doing so, to excite an interest in travel to the parks. To that end, these films were screened before audiences all over the country until they were worn out. Meager bureau budgets did not allow the Park Service to film new reels as old footage deteriorated and so led it to ally itself with another type of commercial entrepreneur. The bureau depended upon the generosity of such private photographers as L. J. Burrud of Los Angeles to film park scenery and then offer copies to the government free of charge. In turn, photographers like Burrud (an aggressive hustler and bombastic self-promoter) sometimes found philanthropic gestures rewarding because of the free publicity and the frequent public viewings of their work that resulted. Capitalizing upon a slightly different use of the same technology, the Park Service also opened various parks to on-location shooting of the new motion picture "plays" such as

The Thundering Herd, filmed, with Horace Albright's approval, at Yellowstone National Park.[26]

However attractive these new media appeared, Mather and Albright still depended upon the written word as their primary tool in advertising the parks. An enormously varied literature *about* the parks developed in the 1920s, encouraged by a cooperative Park Service and supplementing the promotional literature sponsored by the tourist industry. Reflecting an undiminished public appetite for stories about the national parks, dozens of books and articles were published between 1918 and 1933. Many, in particular, celebrated the pleasures that awaited "sagebrushers" who came to the parks while touring the West by auto. Guidebooks to the parks proliferated, and many of those who motored west found the trip so memorable that they recorded their itineraries and their observations for posterity.

Ranging in quality from delightful and insightful to execrable and insufferable, these accounts often featured a visit to one or more national parks as one of the great moments of the expedition. Books with such evocative titles as *It Might Have Been Worse, Modern Gypsies, How's the Road?* and *Family Flivvers to Frisco,* as well as magazine articles describing "Roads That Rim the Rockies" and "The Wonderland of the Great Northwest" where tourists could be "Neighbors for a Night in Yellowstone" or use their cars to go "Motor-Lassoing the Gabled Rockies of Colorado," captured the excitement and the wonder of auto touring in the national parks. In doing so, they also generated an enormous amount of indirect, free advertising for the parks.[27]

No other advertiser, however, could compete with the western railroads in terms of the volume or the variety of advertising produced on behalf of the national parks. Despite the challenges posed by increasing automobile travel and by their own declining ridership, the western railroads continued to feature the parks prominently in their travel promotions. Railroad advertisements in the newspapers and periodicals during the 1920s and 1930s still glorified the "peaks of vacation pleasure" in Glacier National Park, the "startling loveliness" of Zion, or the "mystic wonderland" of Yellowstone. Colorful posters and timetables decorated with striking photographs of Zion's Great White Throne or Yellowstone's Old Faithful illuminated station walls, and handsomely illustrated brochures and booklets regaled the reader with visions of scenic magnificence and exhilarating recreation. The Union Pacific, for example, reached many of the great scenic parks in the Rocky Mountains, and through its Utah Parks Company subsidiary, it had invested heavily as a national parks concessioner in southern Utah. With a considerable stake in tourist travel to the parks, the railroad thus liberally advertised them in its promotional literature.[28]

One 1927 booklet, describing that season's program of escorted tours, opened with an invitation to "each and every American" from Park Service director Mather to visit the parks for relaxation, recreation, education, and inspiration. That publication outlined tours including Yellowstone and Rocky Mountain, Zion, Grand Canyon, and Yosemite. Filled with all the requisite details about lodgings, transportation, and expenses, the booklet also contained splendid photographs (color-tinted as well as black and white) and poetic descriptions of the national parks visited by each tour. Beneath a photograph of Big Thompson Canyon's towering walls in Rocky Mountain National Park, the text soared into rhetorical rhapsodies: "In nobility, in calm dignity, in glory of stalwart beauty, there is no mountain group to excel the company of snow-capped veterans of all ages which stands at everlasting parade behind its grim, helmeted captain, Longs Peak." There, in the Colorado Rockies, the tourists would find an unprecedented combination of "mountain outlines so bold with a quality of beauty so intimate and refined." Referring to the desert parks of southern Utah, it characterized them as comprising a realm of "grandeur" marked by "glorious, unbelievable color." Zion, the first of "Utah's Wonderlands" on the tour, presented an array of natural monuments blazing with "brilliant color" and "decorated with an endless array of fantastic sculpturing."[29]

A Union Pacific brochure of 1931, focusing upon the Utah "wonderlands" and the Grand Canyon, was even more unrestrained in its praise. Illustrated by new natural-color photographs in place of the previous technique of hand-coloring, the brochure depicted southern Utah and northern Arizona as "the Land of Sublime Canyons and Gorgeous Chasms" where "majestic peaks" and "glorious panoramas" would overwhelm the visitor. In those parks, tourists would discover scenery ranging from "friendly intimacy" to "awesome grandeur" in a "matchless geology of natural wonders."[30]

Thus, as it had since 1916, the National Park Service relied heavily upon the largesse of the railroads for assistance in attracting tourists. The cause of the parks benefited, as it had since the 1880s, from the enthusiastic support of private capital. Mather and Albright understood these facts and reciprocated with high praise for that support. One 1929 letter to the passenger traffic manager of the Baltimore and Ohio (B&O) Railroad demonstrated the care that the Park Service took in mending its political fences. Arno Cammerer, announcing a forthcoming conference of park superintendents, complimented the railroad fulsomely for its advertising campaigns that year on behalf of park travel. He commended the line for this "splendid representation" of the parks that "contributed materially to turning the attention of eastern people to the scenic attractions of our own country" and, at the same time, encouraging them to travel on the B&O. At the 1929 conference of park concessioners in Washington, D.C., Director Albright himself credited railroad advertising, along with that produced by the interior department, as responsible for the continued increase in visitations to the parks.[31]

The continued reliance upon the railroads and upon so many other sources of private capital for park advertising emphasized how the broad principle of public-private cooperation still conditioned Park Service thinking about national park advertising into the 1930s. Director Albright had personally assured the park concessioners during their 1929 meeting, "There is no disposition on the part of the Secretary or myself to develop a publicity bureau that will compete in any way with what you are doing." He still envisioned a productive partnership between private businesses or municipal boosters and the Park Service to promote park travel. Outside funds would supplement the Park Service's meager budget for advertising, while the Service would make the parks accessible and work with the concessioners to develop necessary services for visitors. The Park Service would not absorb the task of park advertising within itself nor establish its own advertising bureau. Through the end of the Mather-Albright era, the Park Service had adhered to the guidelines laid down for it in Secretary Lane's letter of May 13, 1918, to Mather. Lane's letter (drafted for his signature by the Park Service) described in some detail the Park Service's responsibilities as custodian of the national parks and the administrative tools at its disposal to carry out its tasks. Among the many subjects addressed by this letter, Secretary Lane urged Mather to "diligently extend and use the splendid cooperation developed during the last three years among chambers of commerce, tourist bureaus, and automobile associations, for the purpose of spreading information about our national parks and facilitating their use and enjoyment" by the traveling public. Over a fifteen-year span, the Service had followed that stricture with notable fidelity.[32]

The bureau's dependence upon a mixture of public and private initiatives to advertise the parks and thus increase visitation also typified increasingly common practice throughout much of the federal bureaucracy during the era of the "Republican ascendancy," from the election of Warren G. Harding in 1920 as president until that of Franklin D. Roosevelt in 1932. With the encouragement of government officials such as Secretary of Commerce Herbert Hoover, objectives set by public agencies, such as the Park Service's desire to promote travel to the national parks, were often pursued by a mixture of public and private means.[33] Such an approach, mixed with prevailing political sentiments that favored fairly strict limits on the exercise of federal authority in many fields, restricted the Park Service's ability to engage in any sort of activity, such as travel advertising, that might be seen as competition with private enterprise.

However limited the Park Service's power to further park travel directly, the advertising campaigns sponsored by private enterprise and abetted by government proved highly successful until the early years of the Great Depression. In achieving this success, advertisers benefited from the growing national enthusiasm for all kinds of outdoor recreation. What Roderick Nash has called "the wilderness cult," extolling rather than abhorring wild, unspoiled landscapes and the confrontation between human beings and "savage" nature, had become a powerful cultural force by the 1890s. The spread of its influence early in this century revealed how far removed from the struggle to "civilize" the continent most Americans felt as urban America grew without pause. Freed from the need to challenge and subdue wilderness in order to survive, many Americans now drew inspiration from it. Preconditioned by the popular wilderness literature and early photography that replicated wild lands in words and pictures, more and more middle-class tourists set out to partake of the special virtue of nature. They sought escape in "tem-

porary wilderness," especially in the Rocky Mountain West, far removed from most aspects of urbanization and long the last resort
in the popular imagination of untamed nature, including untamed
human nature. Although the reality of western savagery no longer
coincided with the stereotypes, the myths lured tourists and their
dollars.[34]

The national parks of the West seemed to exemplify the beauty,
isolation, and wildness idealized by many tourists who subscribed
to the wilderness cult. In their spectacular natural wonders such as
Half Dome and El Capitan, the Great White Throne and the Grand
Canyon of the Colorado, they also contained geologic monuments
that gave America a unique cultural identity to rival the antiquities
or the landscapes of European nations. Park advertising in many
instances accentuated a pervasive feeling of cultural nationalism and
tried to dispel the concomitant sense of cultural inferiority rooted
in our early national history. The parks thus appealed on many levels
to American tourists, especially the new waves of gasoline-powered
"vagabonds" or "sagebrushers." Cherishing the freedom offered by
their internal-combustion chariots, motor tourists flocked to the parks
in search of those qualities they had learned to associate with the
Wild West: "independence, open space, simplicity, a more leisurely
pace—all in direct contrast with the crowded, frenetic, compulsive
East." Thus many potential tourists had already been exposed to ideas
about the virtues of wild nature and natural beauty that made them
susceptible to advertising on behalf of the parks.[35]

The tremendous increase in the numbers of park visitors during the 1920s and early 1930s testifies to the impact such advertising had on many Americans. The cumulative number of visits to all
the national parks, for example, had risen in the four years preceding World War I from an estimated 229,000 to 356,000. Between 1916
and 1920, that number nearly tripled, rising to 920,000. During the
next travel season, park visits topped one million and continued to
climb without a pause for the next twelve years. The numbers of
visitors exceeded 1.5 million in 1925, 2 million in 1927, 2.5 million
in 1928, and 3 million in 1931. In 1933, despite the first decline in
total visitation since World War I, nearly 3.5 million visits were recorded. Furthermore, although some of this great expansion can be
explained by the growth in the number of parks managed by the
Park Service, the trend of figures held true for individual parks as

well. From 1919 through 1921, the estimated number of visitors reaching Yosemite National Park jumped from 58,362 to 68,906 to 91,513. Rocky Mountain saw an increase from 169,000 to 240,000 to 273,000 in the same years, with further growth in the 1920s and early 1930s, reaching the level of nearly 300,000 in 1933. And in Yellowstone, the crown jewel of the system, the sum total of visitors rose from 62,261 to 79,777 and then to 81,651. In 1923, the number of visitors broke well past the 100,000 mark, and it crossed the 150,000 level two years later. The 1927 travel season brought over 200,000 visitations, reaching an eventual maximum for the period of 260,697 in 1929.[36]

In their efforts to popularize travel to the national parks, Mather and Albright had created an enormous reserve of goodwill toward the parks among politicians, the press, and the public at large. The Park Service had been able to translate that goodwill into political support on many occasions to protect its budget, turn aside patronage appointments to senior positions, or reject plans for commercial developments within the parks.[37]

Mather's and Albright's alliances with business and civic interests for the purposes of advertising the parks served their bureau well on two counts. Private money expanded congressional appropriations for publicity work and supported each season's appeal to the prospective tourist. Moreover, the time and money invested by western railroads, chambers of commerce, and local civic booster clubs to make up the deficiencies in Park Service advertising drew all those groups deeply into park affairs. The Park Service could not rely upon them blindly for assistance since their interest in parks could evolve quite easily into a desire to dominate the parks to further their own purposes, such as unrestricted expansion of the tourist trade. Nonetheless, these many groups could be mobilized to support various measures, including larger bureau budgets, better facilities for the visitors, and opposition to destructive exploitation of natural resources in the parks. Because they would profit from a growing tourist trade, they had a stake in the fate of the parks that made them at least sometime-allies of the Park Service. The Service had built a base of support spread all over the Far West.

The Park Service's achievement in stimulating travel to the parks also bolstered the entire western tourist industry. Thousands of tourists who had never visited the Far West now were exposed to the region, and many were enticed to stay on or to return at another time. Tourist advertising throughout the Far West capitalized upon the presence of national parks and monuments. Dude ranches, resort hotels, chambers of commerce, and local booster clubs included national parks in their advertising whenever possible to capture the interest of the tourists. Reproductions of Old Faithful geyser at Yellowstone, Zion's Great White Throne, and the chasm of the Grand Canyon appeared in thousands of advertisements, leaflets, and brochures promoting tourist attractions all over the Far West throughout the 1920s.

Surging numbers of park visitors, however, also created new problems for the Park Service in managing the parks. As the crowds swelled without pause, the Park Service found itself hard-pressed to uphold its dual responsibility of preserving the parks intact for future generations and making them available for the enjoyment of the current generation. Commercial advertising produced to stimulate park travel often had blurred the lines of demarcation between national parks and private resorts by stressing only the recreational dimension of the parks. Many of the new visitors demanded new and more extensive services, forcing Mather, Albright, and their associates to reconsider their conceptions of the proper park experience. By the early 1930s, some conservationists were already bemoaning what they regarded as the vulgar and intrusive nature of many tourist facilities. A few years later, concerned rangers at Yosemite, such as Lemuel Garrison, began to worry about how to protect the park from the hordes who came every summer to camp in the valley. And, following the lean budgetary years of World War II, the tremendous increase in visitation after the war so strained the parks that Bernard DeVoto proposed in disgust that the parks should be closed entirely. The huge investment in facilities made in the 1950s under MISSION 66 and the repeated expansions of the park system in the 1960s and 1970s did less perhaps to reduce the sense of overcrowding than to make it possible for the system to accommodate even more millions in some semblance of order and comfort.[38]

Public enthusiasm for visiting the parks in our own times seems unquenchable, and its deleterious effects upon the parks seems clear. A host of events in this century, from the public's yearning to recapture the mythic frontier to the development of the passenger car and the interstate highway, have influenced this enthusiasm. The aggressive and systematic promotion of national parks travel by the Park Service and by an array of private groups between 1916 and 1933, however, set in motion a great migration for pleasure. To a degree, thus, the parks and the Park Service were victims as well as beneficiaries of the tourist industry and the travel advertising that fueled it. Although in some ways indispensable to the survival of the parks, the successful publicizing of the national parks also deeply influenced the directions in which the national park system developed. The enormous popular appeal of national parks emphasized their importance as "pleasure grounds" to which great crowds came for enjoyment rather than enlightenment. By the end of the twentieth century, in the face of skyrocketing attendance, the Park Service confronted one of its most intractable challenges in struggling to strike an acceptable balance between its mandates for preservation and use of the landscapes it managed.

Notes

1. To trace the evolving relationship between the conservation movement and the federal government from the late nineteenth century through the first three decades of the twentieth, see Samuel P. Hays, *Conservation and the Gospel of Efficiency: The Progressive Conservation Movement* (Cambridge, Mass.: Harvard University Press, 1959); Stephen R. Fox, *John Muir and His Legacy: The American Conservation Movement* (Boston: Houghton Mifflin, 1981); Roderick Nash, *Wilderness and the American Mind*, 2nd rev. ed. (New Haven: Yale University Press, 1982); Elmo R. Richardson, *The Politics of Conservation: Crusades and Controversies, 1897–1913* (Berkeley and Los Angeles: University of California Press, 1962); and Donald C. Swain, *Federal Conservation Policy, 1921–1933* (Berkeley and Los Angeles: University of California Press, 1963). For the early history of the national parks, see John Ise, *Our National Park Policy: A Critical History* (Baltimore: Johns Hopkins University Press, 1962); H. Duane Hampton, *How the U.S. Cavalry Saved Our National Parks* (Bloomington: Indiana University Press, 1971); and Alfred Runte, *National Parks: The American Experience*, 2nd rev. ed. (Lincoln: University of Nebraska Press, 1987), as well as the published biographies of Stephen Mather and Horace Albright, Robert Shankland, *Steve Mather of the National Parks*, 3rd ed. (New York: Alfred A. Knopf, 1970), and Donald C. Swain, *Wilderness Defender: Horace Albright and Conservation* (Chicago: University of Chicago Press, 1970), and Albright's memoirs as told to Robert Cahn, *The Birth of the National Park Service: The Founding Years, 1913–1931* (Salt Lake City: Howe Brothers, 1985).

2. For more on the "See America First" movement see Marguerite S. Shaffer's essays "Seeing America First: The Search for Identity in the Tourist Landscape" in this volume, "Negotiating National Identity: Western Tourism and 'See America First,'" in Hal K. Rothman, ed., *Reopening the American West* (Tucson: University of Arizona Press, 1998), 122–51, and "Seeing America

First: Re-Envisioning Nature and Region through Western Tourism," *Pacific Historical Review* 65 (November 1996): 559–82.

3. For a discussion of the railroads' interests in western tourism, see Alfred Runte, "Pragmatic Alliance: Western Railroads and the National Parks," *National Parks and Conservation Magazine: The Environmental Journal* 48 (April 1974): 14–21; Alfred Runte, *Trains of Discovery: Western Railroads and the National Parks* (Flagstaff, Ariz.: Northland Press, 1984); Carlos Schwantes, "Landscapes of Opportunity: Phases of Railroad Promotion of the Pacific Northwest," *Montana: The Magazine of Western History* 43, no. 2 (Spring 1993): 38–51; and Carlos Schwantes, *Railroad Signatures across the Pacific Northwest* (Seattle: University of Washington Press, 1993). For insight into the growth of a Western tourist industry in general, see Earl Pomeroy, *In Search of the Golden West: The Tourist in Western America* (New York: Alfred A. Knopf, 1957; reprint Lincoln: University of Nebraska Press, 1990), and Runte, *National Parks,* ch. 5. And for further details on the promotional labors of conservationists, see Nash, *Wilderness;* Fox, *Muir;* Carl Abbott, "The Active Force: Enos Mills and the National Park Movement," *Colorado Magazine* 56, nos. 1 and 2 (Winter/Spring 1979): 56–72; Peter Wild's chapter on Mills in *Pioneer Conservationists of Western America* (Missoula, Mont.: Mountain Press, 1979); and two fine examples of such writing: John Muir, *Our National Parks* (Boston: Houghton Mifflin, 1901), and Enos Mills, *Your National Parks* (Boston: Houghton Mifflin, 1917).

4. Nash, *Wilderness,* chs. 9 and 10; Fox, *Muir,* ch. 4; and Runte, *National Parks,* ch. 4.

5. Happily, Mather's life and career have been ably studied in Robert Shankland's first-rate biography. For other evaluations of this seminal figure in the history of the national parks, please see Wild, *Pioneer Conservationists,* 58–69; Swain, *Albright,* 35–46; and Albright, *Founding Years,* passim.

6. Stephen T. Mather to W. P. Kennly, Vice-President, Great Northern Railway, November 5, 1915, Central Files General "Cooperation—Railroads," pt. 1 in National Park Service, Record Group 79, National Archives (hereafter cited as NPS, RG 79, NA). Also Albright, *Founding Years,* 24; Ise, *Park Policy,* 196; Swain, *Albright,* 46–55; and Shankland, *Mather,* chs. 7 and 8.

7. Albright, *Founding Years,* 24–26; Shankland, *Mather,* 74–81; and Swain, *Albright,* 46–52.

8. Many of the figures cited in this paragraph are drawn from an internal accounting of publicity work entitled "Administrative Effort National Park Service" in Central Files General; Report (pt. 1), NPS, RG 79, NA. Please also consult Albright, *Founding Years,* 18–24 and 29; Ise, *National Park Policy,* 196; and Shankland, *Mather,* 83–99.

9. Albright, *Founding Years,* 38–39; Ise, *National Park Policy,* 196; and Shankland, *Mather,* 97–99.

10. Albright, *Founding Years,* 38–39; Ise, *National Park Policy,* 196; and Shankland, *Mather,* 97–99.

11. The letters cited, running from November 11, 1917, through March 29, 1918, are located in the Central Files; Mesa Verde National Park "Publicity Work," NPS, RG 79, NA. See Ise, *National Park Policy,* 196–97, and Shankland, *Mather,* 145–46 for the broader context of cooperation between the railroads and the Park Service at this time.

12. To follow the reorganization of tourist services under the United States Railroad Administration as it affected the Park Service, see Memorandum for

the Secretary from Stephen T. Mather, April 30, 1918, and Report of Howard Hays to P. S. Eustis, chairman, Passenger Traffic Committee Western Territory, May 29, 1918, in Central Files General; Western Lines Bureau of Service (pt. 1), NPS, RG 79, NA.

13. Hays observed, for example, that in 1917, twelve western railroads had spent $358,892.60 to spur park travel, with $59,252.82 spent on booklets and other printed matter and $217,639.43 invested in newspaper and maga- zine advertising. The Burlington alone had spent $115,666.66, while the Great Northern anted up $79,450 and the Santa Fe, $34,586. Report of Howard Hays to P. S. Eustis, May 29, 1918, Central Files General; Western Lines Bureau of Service (pt. 1), NPS, RG 79, NA. For detailed discussions of Bureau of Service operations, see USRA Western Passenger Traffic Committee, Circular No. 86, May 10, 1919, Hazen Hunkins, USRA WPTC Bureau of Service, National Parks and Monuments, to Horace Albright, June 5, 1919, and Hunkins to Albright, Aug. 14, 1919, in Central Files General; Western Lines Bureau of Service (pt. 3), as well as Bureau of Service Resume, Jan. 1 to Sept. 30, 1919, and Hunkins to Mather, Feb. 27, 1920, in Central Files General; Western Lines Bureau of Ser- vice (pt. 4), NPS, RG 79, NA.

14. Arno Cammerer to L. C. Way, Superintendent of Rocky Mountain National Park, Oct. 24, 1919, and National Park Conference Notes, Nov. 28, 1919, p. 5, in Central Files General; Convention of Superintendents (pt. 14 and pt. 15, respectively), NPS, RG 79, NA.

15. For more on the promotion of auto travel in the parks, see David Louter's essay "Glaciers and Gasoline: The Making of a Windshield Wilder- ness, 1900–1915," in this volume.

16. For specific examples of this cooperative exchange of information, see A. L. Westgard, AAA Touring Bureau to Mather, Jan. 30, 1919, Mather to Westgard, Feb. 4, 1919, Memorandum for Mr. Mather from A. E. Demaray, Feb. 19, 1920, and Editor, Motorist Publishing Company to National Park Service, Mar. 25, 1920, in Central Files General; "Maps" (pt. 1), NPS, RG 79, NA. Central Files General; "Maps" (pts. 1–3) documents the voluminous cor- respondence concerning travel maps that the Park Service carried on with organizations ranging from the Clovis (NMex.) Chamber of Commerce to the American Express Travel Department during 1919, 1920, and 1921, while the Park Service's efforts to influence the contents of the *Automobile Blue Book* can be traced in Central Files General; Publicity; Automobile Publishing Co. (pt. 1), NPS, RG 79, NA.

17. Mather to F. C. Schramm, President, Commercial Club of Salt Lake City, Dec. 21, 1921, in Central Files General; "Maps" (pt. 2), Mather to R. A. Woodall, editor, Automobile Blue Book Publishing Co., Nov. 19, 1917, in Cen- tral Files General; Publicity; Automobile Blue Book Publishing Co. (pt. 1), and Arno Cammerer to Harry Burhans, Secretary, Tourist and Publicity Bureau of the Denver Civic and Commercial Association, Dec. 8, 1919, in Central Files General, Publicity; Far Western Travelers' Association, NPS, RG 79, NA. For other examples of such cooperation during the Park Service's early years, see Mather to Woodall, Nov. 11, 1918, Central Files General; Publicity; Automo- bile Blue Book Publishing Co. (pt. 1), John C. Mulford, Chief Cartographer, National Highways Association, to Hubert Work, Secretary of the Interior, June 9, 1923, Central Files General; "Maps" (pt. 3), and E. C. Finney, First Assistant Secretary, Department of the Interior, to Mulford, June 23, 1923, Central Files General; "Maps" (pt. 3), NPS, RG 79, NA.

18. Harry Burhans, Tourist and Publicity Bureau of the Denver Civic and Commercial Association, to Mather, Mar. 29, 1919, Central Files General; Convention of National Park Superintendents (pt. 13), and circular letter from Harry Burhans, Executive Secretary, Denver Tourist and Publicity Bureau, May 15, 1921, Central Files, Mesa Verde National Park, "Publications and Circulars," in NPS, RG 79, NA.

19. Highway associations are discussed in James J. Flink's *The Car Culture* (Cambridge, Mass.: MIT Press, 1975). Their relationship, and that of the automobile tourist generally, to the national parks is discussed briefly in Horace Albright and Frank J. Taylor, *"Oh Ranger!" A Book about the National Parks* (Stanford, Calif.: Stanford University Press, 1928), 17–32; Richard A. Bartlett, *Yellowstone: A Wilderness Besieged* (Tucson: University of Arizona Press, 1985), 82–96; Runte, *National Parks*, 151–61; and Shankland, *Mather*, 149–50.

In regard to the highway associations, interested readers should consult Earl Pomeroy's *The Pacific Slope: A History of California, Oregon, Washington, Idaho, Utah and Nevada* (New York: Alfred A. Knopf, 1965), 359–60, for further discussion of their presence in the West. A brief but revealing firsthand discussion of the problems that arose in connection with private highway associations can be found in Virginia Rishel, *Wheels to Adventure: Bill Rishel's Western Routes* (Salt Lake City: Howe Brothers, 1983), 81–124. Joe McCarthy's article, "The Lincoln Highway," *American Heritage* 25, no. 4 (June 1974): 32–37 and 94, outlines the difficulties that confronted the most famous of these private highways.

20. The dude ranching industry has recently begun to attract the scholarly attention it deserves from western historians, culminating in Lawrence R. Borne's fine study, *Dude Ranching: A Complete History* (Albuquerque: 1983), which may be profitably consulted by those interested in dude ranching's place in the growth of the tourist industry and the development of the twentieth-century West. Earl Pomeroy's excellent volume *In Search of the Golden West* should also be examined in reference to the same topic, for his insights remain fresh and stimulating. On dude ranching and the national parks, see Borne, 150–59, as well as ch. 4, "The Outdoor Life," on the expansion of the industry, and Pomeroy, ch. 5, "Americans Move Outdoors."

21. For a general discussion of the expanding western tourist industry in this century, see Pomeroy, *In Search of the Golden West*, 112–38 and 150–55. The publications mentioned in the text are *The Western Tourists' Guide Utah-Idaho America's Wonderland* (Salt Lake City: no pub., c.1917) and *Western Montana, A Land That Enchants the Traveler, Enriches the Settler and Inspires Everyone* (Butte, Mont.: Chamber of Commerce, 1933); the quotations are drawn from page 54 and pages 8, 16, and 17 respectively. Other specific examples of the use private entrepreneurs made of national parks and monuments for advertising their resorts include the following publications: *The Olin Hotel* (Denver: no pub., c.1933); *Estes Park, Colorado* (Estes Park, Colo.: Chamber of Commerce, c.1930); *Steamboat Springs, Colorado* (Steamboat Springs, Colo.: Commercial Club, c.1930); *Welcome to Montrose* (Montrose, Colo.: Chamber of Commerce, 1925); *Western Colorado Scenic and Recreational Wonderland* (Grand Junction, Colo.: Chamber of Commerce, c.1932); *Center of Scenic America Official Guide* (Salt Lake City: Hotel Greeters of America, 1932); *Seeing Salt Lake City* (Salt Lake City: Grey Line, 1930); and *Jackson Lake Lodge* (Jackson, Wyo.: Grey Line, c.1929).

22. For Salt Lake City, some examples of this type of advertising include "A Stopover You'll Never Forget in the City of Seven Wonders," *Literary Digest* 85, no. 10 (June 6, 1925): 73; "Salt Lake City—Headquarters for Scenic America," *Saturday Evening Post* 198, no. 44 (May 1, 1926): 230; "See the Places You've Read About!" *Sunset Magazine* 56, no. 6 (June 1926): 88; and "Romantic Salt Lake City—The Storied, Gloried West," *Literary Digest* 93, no. 10 (June 4, 1927): 61. Also consult such publications as *Salt Lake City 7 Wonderful One-Day Trips in and Around Salt Lake City and Utah* (Salt Lake City: Chamber of Commerce, 1927 and 1931), and *Center of Scenic America Official Guide.*

For Denver, samples of this promotional work include "Denver the Gateway to 12 National Parks and 32 National Monuments," *Sunset Magazine* 38, no. 6 (June 1917): 92; "Rocky Mountain National Park in Colorado," *Sunset Magazine* 51, no. 1 (July 1923): 93; "Cool Colorado," *Sunset Magazine* 52, no. 6 (June 1924): 99; "Come Up to Colorado," *Sunset Magazine* 58, no. 6 (June 1927): 89; "Colorado," *Sunset Magazine* 60, no. 5 (June 1928): 86; and "Colorful Colorado Here You Can Learn to Live . . . and Play While Learning," *Saturday Evening Post* 204, no. 39 (Mar. 26, 1932): 69. Also see the following articles: Charles Rump, "Beauties of the Western Slope," *Colorado Highways* 2, no. 9 (Sep. 1923): 8–9, and C. L. Chatfield, "The Colorado Sun Circle," *Colorado Highways* 4, no. 2 (Feb. 1925): 4–5.

23. Jenks Cameron, *The National Park Service Its History, Activities and Organization* (New York: D. Appleton and Co., 1922), 12.

24. The quotation is from Cameron, *Park Service,* 58. For more information on the Park Service's publicity work, see Cameron, 62–63 and 78–79, and Shankland, *Steve Mather of the National Parks,* 145–46.

25. This episode in park promotion is drawn from Department of the Interior, Office of the Secretary: Memorandum to the Press, Apr. 7, 1923, Central Files General; Press Notices (pt. 1), NPS, RG 79, NA.

26. The Park Service's uneasy relationship with one commercial moviemaker is well documented in the correspondence between L. J. Burrud and the Park Service for the years 1921 and 1922 in Central Files General; Publicity; L. J. Burrud (pt. 1), NPS, RG 79, NA.

The Park Service's continuing interest in the utility of motion pictures is described in the Report of the Publicity and Public Relations Committee of the National Park Service Superintendents' Conference, Feb. 15–22, 1928, Central Classified Files General; 0-1.1 Conferences; Superintendents', 1928 (pt. 1), NPS, RG 79, NA.

The story of the production of *The Thundering Herd,* based on a novel by Zane Grey, and its unpleasant aftermath, is discussed in Bartlett, *Yellowstone,* 291–92, and Swain, *Albright,* 179 and 181.

27. The travel accounts cited in the text (only a handful out of many) are Beatrice Larned Massey, *It Might Have Been Worse: A Motor Tour from Coast to Coast* (San Francisco: Harr, Wagner Co., 1920); Mary Crehore Bedell, *Modern Gypsies* (New York: c.1924); Katherine C. Hulme, *How's the Road?* (San Francisco: privately published, 1928); and Frederick F. Van de Water, *Family Flivvers to Frisco* (New York: D. Appleton and Co., 1927). The four examples of periodical literature mentioned are Theodore G. Joslin, "Roads That Rim the Rockies," *World's Work* 60 (June 1931): [72]–75; Agnes C. Laut, "Wonderland of the Great Northwest," *Travel,* Jan.–May 1926; "Neighbors for a Night in Yellowstone National Park," *Literary Digest* 82 (Aug. 30, 1924): 44–46; and

Warren E. Boyer, "Motor-Lassoing the Gabled Rockies of Colorado," *Sunset Magazine* 56, no. 3 (Mar. 1926): 20–21, 62.

Two excellent bibliographic sources on the literature of western auto touring are Cary S. Bliss, *Autos across America: A Bibliography of Transcontinental Automobile Travel 1903–1940* (Los Angeles: Dawson's Book Shop, 1972; reprint Austin, Tex.: Jenkins and Reese, 1982), and Archibald Hanna, *From Train to Plane: Travelers in the American West 1866–1936: An Exhibition in the Beinecke Rare Book and Manuscript Library, Yale University* (New Haven: Yale University Library, 1979).

28. Every major popular magazine in the 1920s and 1930s carried travel advertising sponsored by the western railroads. A small selection of the many advertisements placed in the late 1920s and early 1930s, as quoted in the text, includes "For Graduation the gift of a lifetime. A tour of the Romantic Northwest Wonderland," sponsored by the Chicago, Milwaukee, St. Paul and Pacific in *Good Housekeeping* 99, no. 4 (April 1929): 104; "The World's Most Startling Loveliness Awaits You in Zion," sponsored by the Union Pacific in *Sunset Magazine* 64, no. 4 (April 1930): 67; and "Scale the peaks of vacation pleasure in Glacier Park," sponsored by the Great Northern in *Sunset Magazine* 66, no. 4 (April 1931): 48.

29. *Summer Tours under Escort* (Chicago: Department of Tours, Chicago and North Western Railway and the Union Pacific System, 1927), passim. The specific quotations are taken from pages 11, 21, and 22.

30. *Zion, Bryce Canyon, Grand Canyon: 3 National Parks* (Chicago: Union Pacific System, 1931), passim. The specific quotations are taken from pages 5, 9, and 35.

31. Cammerer to W. B. Callaway, Passenger Traffic Manager, Baltimore and Ohio Railroad, Aug. 2, 1929, Central Classified Files General; 0-1.1, Conferences; Superintendents (pt. 1); Proceedings of Conference of Public Utilities Operating in National Parks, Held December 6 and 7, 1929, p. 12, Central Classified Files General; 0–1.1, Conferences; Superintendents, 1934 (pt. 2), NPS, RG 79, NA.

32. Minutes of the Twelfth Conference of National Park Executives held at Hot Springs National Park, Arkansas, April 3 to 8, 1932, p. 17, in Central Classified Files General; 0-1.1, Conferences; Superintendents, 1932; Franklin K. Lane to Stephen T. Mather, May 13, 1918, Central Classified Files General; 0-201-15, Administration and Personnel Policy, NPS, RG 79, NA.

33. Pioneered especially by Secretary of Commerce Herbert Hoover, the concept of the "associative state" represented the evolution of "a new network of nongovernmental or quasi-governmental mechanisms" that would supplement and in some instances supplant preexisting federal regulatory agencies. The federal government's various departments and bureaus would not order the macroeconomic structure of the economy but would instead assist cooperative associations, commissions, and councils within major industries to create the "self-regulatory" organizations necessary to properly "manage" individual industries and the general economy. As Ellis Hawley notes, the 1920s thus could not be characterized as an era of retreat into laissez-faire theories and federal inactivity. For a general discussion of Secretary Hoover's efforts to foster cooperative arrangements between business and government, see two articles by Ellis Hawley: "Herbert Hoover, the Commerce Secretariat and the Vision of an 'Associative State,' 1921–1928," *Journal of American History* 61, no. 1

(June 1974), and "Three Facets of Hooverian Associationalism: Lumber, Avia-
tion and Movies 1921–1930" in Thomas McCraw, ed., *Regulation in Perspective:
Historical Essays* (Cambridge, Mass.: Harvard University Press, 1981). An interesting analysis of some applications of associationalism to the field of recreation during the Hoover era is Carl E. Krog, "'Organizing the Production of
Leisure': Herbert Hoover and the Conservation Movement in the 1920's," *Wisconsin Magazine of History* 67, no. 3 (Spring 1984).

34. Nash, *Wilderness,* 141–60; Peter Schmitt, *Back to Nature: The Arcadian
Myth in Urban America* (New York: Oxford University Press, 1969), 125–40, 146–
66, 168; and Pomeroy, *In Search of the Golden West,* 139–47.

35. Runte, *National Parks,* 11–47 and 82–105; Schmitt, *Back to Nature,* 167–
76; Pomeroy, *In Search of the Golden West,* 31–72 and 148–83; and Warren James
Belasco, *Americans on the Road: From Autocamp to Motel 1910–1945* (Cambridge,
Mass.; MIT Press, 1979), 8–16, 27.

36. The numbers of visitors for the park system were culled from annual
reports of the National Park Service, and especially from United States Department of the Interior, *Annual Report of the Director of the National Park Service . . .
1922* (Washington, D.C.: Government Printing Office, 1923), while figures for
the individual parks were gathered from the same sources and also from C. W.
Buchholtz, *Rocky Mountain National Park: A History* (Boulder, Colo.: Colorado
Associated University Press, 1983), 151 and 177, and Aubrey L. Haines, *The
Yellowstone Story,* vol. 2 (Yellowstone Park: Yellowstone Library and Museum
Association, 1977; reprint Yellowstone National Park: Yellowstone Association
for Natural Science, History, and Education; Niwot: University Press of Colo-
rado, 1996), 478–79.

37. The Park Service's efforts in the early years to forge alliances and to
secure its base of support are examined as a question of bureaucratic politics
in Ronald A. Foresta, *America's National Parks and Their Keepers* (Washington,
D.C.: Resources for the Future, 1984), 16–43.

38. For reference to "purist" opposition to Park Service policies, see
Foresta, *Parks,* 47; Ise, *National Park Policy,* 437–38; Runte, *National Parks,* 166–
79; and Swain, *Albright,* 247.

Lemuel A. Garrison's autobiography, *The Making of a Ranger: Forty Years
with the National Parks* (Salt Lake City: Howe Brothers, 1983), mentions some
of the first stirrings of concern about park use among the Yosemite ranger force;
see pp. 102–4 and 130–35.

Bernard DeVoto made his argument in "Let's Close the National Parks,"
Harper's Magazine 207, no. 1241 (Oct. 1953): 49–52.

Chapter Thirteen

A Dignified Exploitation: The Growth of Tourism in the National Parks

Dwight T. Pitcaithley

On New Year's Day 1997, warming temperatures melted an early and heavy snowpack, and steady rains contributed to one of the worst floods Yosemite National Park had experienced in its 130-year history as a park. The raging Merced River flushed the valley floor of campgrounds, employee housing, parking lots, roads, bridges, utility systems, and offices. The flood closed the park for months, caused the layoff of one thousand concession employees, disrupted the economy of the nearby gateway communities, emphasized the dynamic relationship between parks and tourism in the West, and sparked a broad reassessment of how overdeveloped Yosemite had become.[1] With 1996 visitation to the narrow valley at an all-time high of 4.1 million, it also brought back echoes of the *Field of Dreams* movie theme, "If you build it, they will come!"

The symbiotic connection between national parks and the tourist industry was evident even as Congress was considering the establishment of Yellowstone as the first national park. Indeed, the "development" of parks to accommodate tourists was seldom seriously questioned until the midpoint of this century, long after major hotel and cabin complexes, roads and trails, and utility systems had been constructed and become part of the "park experience."[2]

Long before President Woodrow Wilson signed a bill establishing the National Park Service (NPS) on August 25, 1916, however, a philosophy of use and enjoyment of parks and public grounds had been clearly articulated. When another president, Abraham Lincoln, authorized the transfer of the Yosemite Valley to the State of California in 1864, for "public use, resort and recreation," the national park idea took root. (George Catlin first articulated the idea of large western national parks in 1832, the same year Congress set aside the Hot Springs Reservation in central Arkansas, now known as Hot Springs National Park.) The chairman of the board of commissioners established to oversee the administration of the park, Frederick Law Olmsted, formulated a theory of use for this new type of land in an 1865 report that presented his views on how Yosemite should be developed.

Olmsted, the preeminent landscape architect of the nineteenth century, presented, however, more than a theory of use; he articulated a philosophy of leisure based on nature's regenerative powers for an urbanizing society. This builder of Central Park in New York City and countless other urban parks throughout the country believed that the essence of park land should be in establishing a contrast to the increasing pace of the modern world. Anchoring his thinking at the conclusion of the Civil War and amid the burgeoning Industrial Revolution, Olmsted envisioned a need for ordinary citizens to maintain perspective in their daily lives by being exposed to, and encouraged to contemplate, the natural rhythms of the natural world. Olmsted was not an advocate of wilderness; rather, he thought it most appropriate that parks have restaurants and hotels and carriage paths and trails, so that a leisurely appreciation of nature was possible. Their existence, however, should not interfere, visually or audibly, with the process of appreciation.[3]

Less than a decade later, with the establishment of the first national park, the public use of Yellowstone was assumed. Although the 1870 Washburn Expedition through Yellowstone stands in National Park Service lore as the beginning of the national park movement, it is now more completely understood as the origin of a happy partnership linking first the Northern Pacific and later other railroads with tourism and national parks.[4] Indeed, financier Jay Cooke and the Northern Pacific became active, although behind the scenes, as the principal promoters of the bill establishing Yellowstone as a national park in 1872. Once the act had been signed, the Northern

Pacific financed a number of hotels throughout the park, including the Old Faithful Inn in 1904.

A similar pattern of tourism in national parks is evident with the development of Glacier National Park by Louis W. Hill and the Great Northern Railway. Shortly after the creation of the park in 1910, the Great Northern adopted the slogan "See America First," and began both a promotional campaign to attract visitors and construction projects within the park to accommodate them. Between 1910 and 1915, Hill participated in the development of almost every amenity in the park. At the end of five years, Glacier (and the Great Northern) boasted of two rustic luxury hotels, nine chalet complexes, three tepee camps, and a series of roads and trails connecting them to the picturesque features of the park.[5] Other major western parks that also enjoyed considerable legislative and financial support from railroad companies included Grand Canyon, Yosemite, Mount Rainier, and Crater Lake.[6]

Thus, by the time Congress got around to creating the National Park Service in 1916, many western parks already had a full complement of tourist accommodations. What effect, then, would this new bureaucratic agency, with policies and regulations, and seemingly armed with a conservation mandate, have on the pattern of industrial tourism established by the railroads during the preceding forty-five years? In answering the question, we should look at the language of the enabling legislation and at its sponsors.

The legislation, known as the Organic Act, charged the new agency with conserving "the scenery and the natural and historic objects and the wild life therein and to provide for the enjoyment of the same in such manner and by such means as will leave them unimpaired for the enjoyment of future generations." The gentle tug between use and preservation created by Congress has been debated within and outside the Park Service for decades, with no clear resolution in sight. It is quite clear, however, that the word "unimpaired" was not intended in any literal sense, but more as a contrast to federal land that had been subject to extractive industries such as logging and mining. After all, the Yosemite Valley floor had been, by 1916, heavily "impaired" by tourist development, as had large portions of Yellowstone and Glacier. In fact, by 1900, four hundred miles of tour and administrative roads had been constructed throughout

Yellowstone. Certainly, the concept of preserving ecosystems in an unimpaired manner was still several decades in the future.

An assessment of the administration of the parks following the signing of the Organic Act results in the conclusion that "unimpaired" really meant unimpaired except for such development as was necessary to facilitate the enjoyment of parks by visitors. Or worded differently, the *primary* scenic features of the parks were to remain unimpaired for the enjoyment of future generations.[7] In this light, it can be argued that the word "unimpaired" was linked philosophically, as it is in the act, with the word "enjoyment." It was along those lines that Richard B. Watrous, secretary of the American Civic Association and one of the strong supporters of the Organic Act, remarked that tourism might be defined as the "dignified exploitation of our national parks."[8]

Indeed, a close reading of the Organic Act sheds considerable light on what Congress intended in 1916. While it is true that the act incorporated the words "conserve" and "unimpaired," it also included "enjoyment" and "use" and "accommodation" of visitors. The accommodation of visitors and perpetuation of park scenery (not to mention a pleasant park experience) could further be achieved, the act instructed, by granting permits or "privileges" for constructing visitor accommodations, removing diseased trees, and destroying animals that "may be detrimental to the use" of the parks.[9]

The *tasteful* development of parks for tourists was exactly what Frederick Law Olmsted Jr. and Stephen T. Mather had in mind as they championed the creation of the National Park Service. Olmsted, son of Frederick Law Olmsted Sr. and a renowned landscape architect in his own right, and Mather, a wealthy businessman, both supported the wholesale accessibility of parks to the American people. Mather, in particular, was a strong proponent of the automobile and its ability to transport ever increasing numbers of the public to national parks. He was present as the first automobiles rumbled into Yellowstone and personally financed the reopening of the Tioga Road in Yosemite.[10] And he enthusiastically supported a proposal by the nascent western tourist industry to construct a highway system that would connect all the western parks via one grand touring circuit.[11]

If there was any doubt about how the national parks should be managed with regard to tourists, Secretary of the Interior Franklin

Lane offered a corrective in 1918 when he wrote Mather that "every opportunity should be afforded to the public, wherever possible, to enjoy the national parks in the manner that best satisfies individual taste."[12] Although he needed no such encouragement (his assistant Horace Albright actually drafted the letter), Mather aggressively promoted the national parks to the tourist industry until his retirement in 1929.[13]

The Lane/Albright letter is interesting, for while it echoes much of the language of the Organic Act, it provides other clues to the thinking of the early administrators—and champions—of the parks. Lane seems to strengthen the act's emphasis on "unimpaired" by writing that "the national parks must be maintained in *absolutely* unimpaired form for the use of future generations" (emphasis mine). Lane informed Mather that he could thin the forests or clear vistas if by doing so he "improved the scenic features of the parks." (Obviously, the vistas were for the visitors and not for the wildlife.) Tourists could further be accommodated by permitting automobiles and motorcycles in all parks; in fact, wrote Lane, "the parks will be kept accessible by any means practicable." To protect the health of the visiting public, Lane continued, Mather should use existing federal scientific bureaus (at that time the service had no scientific capabilities of its own) to destroy insect pests in the forests, take care of wild animals, and propagate and distribute fish.[14]

Taking the Organic Act and the Lane letter together, one develops a clearer sense of the federal commitment to tourism as the new National Park Service began setting its course. The perpetuation of grand scenery was important; the preservation of natural systems was not. Insects that create ugly trees could be eliminated, wild animals that feed on other animals considered aesthetically pleasing could be exterminated, and fish could be added to lakes and streams. The use of terms such as "unimpaired" and "absolutely unimpaired" take on new meaning when assessed in this larger context.

Promoting the national parks was Mather's passion. He not only believed in the value of the parks to the American public but also thought that by increasing their popularity he would create a stronger political foundation for his fledgling agency. Increased visitation to the parks meant increased support for the park service. He proclaimed that "the greatest good to the greatest number is always the most important factor in determining the policy of the service."[15] Mather went to great lengths to encourage visitation and make the public feel comfortable. He and Albright led a vigorous campaign to have Yosemite National Park host the 1932 Winter Olympics, and encouraged the construction of a golf course and race track in the same park. He favored the development of a golf course in Yellowstone, and swimming pools and tennis courts in other parks. The first director also promoted "events" in the parks to attract visitors and ensure their enjoyment. He perpetuated the Yosemite "firefall," which employed concession employees to build a bonfire on the edge of Glacier Point at dusk and then push it over the three-thousand-foot-high promontory, creating a spectacle of falling fire and embers.[16] The Park Service, under the direction of Mather, also continued "bear shows," which capitalized on the popularity of bears by encouraging the public to watch them feed out of the trash dumps next to park hotels. In Yellowstone, bleachers were even provided to assure good views; tourists were protected from the bears by armed rangers.[17] Because of the popularity of large animals, to ensure that they contributed to the enjoyment of parks, both Yosemite and Yellowstone established zoos for the viewing pleasure of tourists.[18]

The Park Service's support of tourism during this period also included the categorization of the natural world into those elements that were good for tourism and those that were not. Predators—mountain lions, timber wolves, and coyotes—had no role in national parks and were hunted with enthusiasm. In several parks, populations of these animals were either eliminated or seriously reduced before the policy was amended during the mid-1920s.[19] Forest fires were also categorized as detrimental to tourism and were for years aggressively attacked, even though fire had been a part of the natural cycle of forest life for millennia. Mather termed fire the "Forest Fiend," and adopted for the National Park Service the same policy adhered to and promoted by the Forest Service.[20] Burned forests were ugly forests, and visitors did not go to national parks to see blackened landscapes.

Just as the Park Service believed some forms of wildlife hindered tourism, it considered others supportive. Perhaps the greatest manipulation of nature for tourists occurred in the area of sport fishing. While hunting game in the large western parks was illegal, fishing was enthusiastically encouraged. So that no hopeful angler would leave a park disappointed, the National Park Service, with the cooperation of the Bureau of Fisheries, established fish hatcheries in such parks as Yellowstone, Glacier, Mount Rainier, and Yosemite.[21] Lakes and streams were stocked with fish, and Crater Lake, which had originally been barren of fish, continued to be stocked—a practice begun by early army and civilian superintendents.[22]

As the National Park Service sought to develop a tourist constituency and enhance the popularity of the national parks, it also discovered there were limits on what tourist developments it could endorse. While swimming pools, golf courses, and tennis courts could be justified, a cable car across Grand Canyon could not. Proposed by a San Francisco engineer named George Davol in 1919, the cableway would link the south rim near the El Tovar Hotel to the north rim four miles distant. While Assistant Director Horace Albright favored the million-dollar scheme, Director Mather opposed it and, with the help of Secretary of the Interior John Barton Payne, killed it.[23] Other proposals to transport visitors within parks opposed by the Park Service included an elevator alongside the 308-foot Great Fall of the Yellowstone and a tramway from the Yosemite Valley to Glacier Point, three thousand feet above the valley floor. The latter had the complete support of President Herbert Hoover and then secretary of the interior Ray Lyman Wilber, but was successfully opposed by Director Albright.[24] Tramways seem to be ever popular. During the 1970s, one was proposed to carry visitors through the newly established Guadalupe Mountains National Park and ultimately to the top of Guadalupe Peak, the highest point in Texas. Like the others, this scheme fortunately died a quick death.

The seventeen years (1917–1933) that Stephen T. Mather and Horace Albright directed the National Park Service were formative years for the new agency and placed the service on firm political footing. They also, of course, made the National Park Service a popular federal agency, and the national parks accessible to tourists with increasing numbers of public facilities. Under Mather alone the National Park Service constructed 1,293 miles of roads, 3,903 miles of trails, 1,623 miles of telephone and telegraph lines, and numerous campgrounds, museums, offices, and, as we have seen, recreational facilities.[25]

During the 1930s, public works projects, such as those undertaken by the Civilian Conservation Corps (CCC), further enhanced tourist amenities within national parks. Between 1933 and 1943, the CCC built bathhouses in thirteen parks, cabins in fourteen, 1,850 miles of telephone lines, 5,310 acres of campgrounds, and 404 acres of picnic grounds.[26] Also during the Depression, the NPS conducted a survey of the Atlantic and Gulf coasts for their recreation potential. While the survey recommended that several large seashores be designated national park areas, only one, Cape Hatteras National Seashore, was established (in 1937).[27] (It was not until the 1960s that Congress established most of the other seashores in the study: Cape Cod in 1961, Padre Island in 1962, Assateague Island in 1965, and Cape Lookout in 1966.)

Developments in the national parks slowed and then ceased completely following the entry of the United States into World War II. In 1940, the budget for the NPS amounted to $33,500,000; by 1945 it had been reduced to a meager $4,700,000. To make matters worse, the headquarters office for the service was moved from Washington to the Merchandise Mart in Chicago. While the prospects for the service improved over the next several years, it wasn't until 1950 that the annual budget reached prewar levels.[28] By then park facilities were deteriorating faster than they could be repaired. And increasing visitation placed additional stress on roads, parking lots, and other park amenities.

To address these collective problems, the service developed a ten-year proposal for improving the parks, and designed it to culminate in 1966, on the fiftieth anniversary of the act creating the National Park Service. Mission 66, as it was called, funneled over a billion dollars into the parks for a wide-ranging assortment of projects. While considerable funds were devoted to administrative and utility buildings, employee residences, and the preservation of historic buildings, most of the money was spent on improving or constructing new visitor facilities. By 1966 the National Park Service had increased the number of parking lots fivefold; created 1,197 miles of new roads; added 575 new campgrounds and 742 new picnic areas; constructed 535 additional water systems, 521 new sewer systems, and 271 new power systems; developed 50 marinas; and constructed or rehabilitated 584 new comfort stations (the service's term for toilets).[29]

During the 1960s, however, the public perception of public lands began to change. In 1964, Congress passed the Wilderness Act, which placed ten million acres of land into wilderness status and created a process for the designation of millions more. At the same time came an increase in environmental awareness and concern for the ecological value of lands under the control of the federal government in general and the National Park Service in particular. Concern for the ecology of the parks led logically to the notion that parks were too crowded, too developed. Critics of the National Park Service argued that too large a percentage of the NPS's annual budget was devoted to accommodating visitors, and too little was going toward resource management.[30] A 1972 study illuminated the issue by comparing the research budgets of three agencies: the U.S. Forest Service, the Bureau of Sport Fisheries and Wildlife, and the National Park Service. The study came to striking conclusion that while the Forest Service and Fisheries and Wildlife devoted 11 and 19 percent of their annual budgets to research, the National Park Service allocated a mere 0.7 percent to scientific research.[31]

This came as no surprise to Edward Abbey, who had been a National Park Service employee and had watched western slickrock parks grow roads and parking lots and other "amenities" that encouraged large numbers of tourists to visit remote corners of canyons and plateaus and natural sandstone arches. His 1968 *Desert Solitaire: A Season in the Wilderness* was both a celebration of the desert, in this case Arches National Park, and an indictment of the NPS's development policies. In chapter five, titled "Industrial Tourism and the National Parks," Abbey proposed that the National Park Service build no new roads in national parks and allow no cars. Shuttle buses could move visitors into and within the parks just fine. "We have agreed," he wrote, "not to drive our automobiles into cathedrals, concert halls, art museums, legislative assemblies, private bedrooms, and the other sanctums of our culture; we should treat our national parks with the same deference, for they, too, are holy places."[32]

As Abbey knew instinctively, and the National Park Service has come to know by experience, the national park idea has succeeded beyond Olmsted's and Mather's and Albright's wildest imaginings. Over 280 million tourists visited national parks during 1998, stressing the facilities, the parking lots, the sewage systems, and the frayed nerves of their campground neighbors. (For most visitors, the contrast to their daily lives that Olmsted intended parks to provide was seldom present). The maintenance backlog for administrative and tourist-related structures stands at $2 billion.

Now let us return to where we began: Yosemite Valley. The cleansing flood of January 1997 has allowed the NPS to rethink its purpose and function and the ways it will accommodate tourists in the future. "We've known for 20 years many facilities were in the wrong place," observed Chip Jenkins of Yosemite's strategic planning office shortly after the flood. "They were poorly designed, poorly placed, bad for the habitat, and bad for the park experience."[33] Given a fresh chance to plan the valley, the NPS has engaged in a comprehensive planning effort that has combined several interim plans, allowing for a rethinking of all the important issues confronting park managers. Inspired by the devastation wrought by the flood, the National Park Service is focusing on reclaiming the valley's natural beauty, fostering the dominance of natural processes, and reducing traffic congestion and visitor overcrowding, with the logical consequence of promoting a heightened appreciation for and understanding of the Yosemite Valley on the part of park visitors. This new effort to confront the legacy of a century's worth of creeping park development will remove lodging, campgrounds, and park housing from the immediate confines of the Merced River, place any new facilities in less sensitive areas, remove most bridges, and remove day-visitor parking from the core of the valley. If executed as planned, this vision for the park will allow for the restoration of approximately 147 acres and promote access to the principal scenic features and interpretive or recreational sites in the valley via a shuttle bus service. The "Yosemite Valley Implementation Plan" further envisions the development of additional hiking and bicycling trails, with numerous picnic areas being accessible only by shuttle or bicycle or on foot. Bicycle rentals would be available at several locations in the park. What would Edward Abbey think?

Yosemite is indicative of many parks throughout the 378 park units that make up the National Park System. Through the Mather and Albright years, the Depression, Mission 66, not to mention the development that accompanied the celebration of the Bicentennial, the National Park Service has encouraged tourists to visit parks and has constructed facilities for their use and enjoyment. With the current population of the United States six times what it was when

Congress set aside Yellowstone in 1872, the National Park Service can no longer assume the suitability of Mather's policy of accommodating the greatest number of visitors. The National Park Service must reassess—and indeed is in the process of reassessing—its role in American society. During a period of introspection prompted by the observance of the NPS's seventy-fifth anniversary in 1991, a working group recognized the conflict between use and preservation and observed, "Visitors to park units use park resources: they take up space, they require transportation, food, (often) shelter, waste facilities, traffic control, viewing areas, and so on. Limitations on access and use are appropriate where they threaten impairment of a unit's special qualities, and where they significantly threaten the quality of overall visitor experience (through, for example, crowding or mutually disturbing recreational activities)."[34] Clearly the times have changed since Stephen Mather and Horace Albright conceptualized visitor amenities over six decades ago; it remains to be seen to what extent the National Park Service will change with them.

How Edward Abbey lived to see the flood and learn of the park's plans for reducing development on the valley floor, instituting a shuttle bus system, and providing extensive bicycle access, he would have smiled. In the middle of his polemic on industrial tourism and the national parks, he pauses and contemplates what could happen in one park should the National Park Service adopt a policy of less development. "Consider a concrete example," he mused in 1968, "and what could be done with it: Yosemite Valley in Yosemite National Park. At present a dusty milling confusion of motor vehicles and ponderous camping machinery, it could be returned to relative beauty and order by the simple expedient of requiring all visitors, at the park entrance, to lock up their automobiles and continue their tour on the seats of good workable bicycles supplied free of charge by the United States Government."[35]

How the National Park Service will ultimately respond to the opportunity created in the Yosemite Valley by the 1997 flood remains to be seen. The planning process at this time (November 1999) has not yet drawn to a close. Very real pressures, economic, social, and political, all come into play in the planning for our national parks, for Americans are of a decidedly mixed mind when it comes to these most public of places. They are seen as ecological reserves as well as playgrounds, places where history and nature can be studied, places to visit in motor homes, places to experience the wildness of wilderness. There are proponents of a minimalist approach to access and those who expect all the comforts of home. In the past, the National Park Service has attempted to accommodate large numbers of visitors while maintaining portions of parks in an undeveloped state. Guadalupe Mountains National Park, for example, can be appreciated only by hiking up the two-thousand-foot escarpment via a narrow switchback trail. For many, however, the south rim of the Grand Canyon is more the standard for park visits.

Managing the national parks into the next century will require greater attention to balancing visitor use with preservation of natural areas. In many parks, more roads, more visitor facilities, more parking lots are not even a temporary fix. By the time they are constructed, they are filled to capacity. Different ways will have to be found to accommodate an ever expanding population with proportionately fewer places to recreate. With no population corrective in sight, American society and the National Park Service will have to come to terms with park use. Parks cannot be expected to absorb, as they have in the past, all who seek entrance. At some point on the preservation and use and enjoyment graph, the enjoyment factor begins to decline as overuse of the resource increases.

These are not easy questions, and they do not engender easy answers. But serious questions must, indeed, be asked, for the large western (and not a few of the eastern) national parks are in danger of being loved to death. Americans must, along with the National Park Service, rethink how parks should be used in the future, what constitutes appropriate accommodations, what makes an enjoyable park visit. If national parks are to exist in perpetuity, then different models of park use must be found. There will always be, as there has been in the past, a supportive relationship between the tourist industry and the National Park Service. But both must work to redefine how parks and visitors connect during the twenty-first century. The National Park Service can no longer be expected to meet the growing demands of visitors. Limits must be placed, carrying capacities must be established, or parks will lose that which makes them attractive—the contrast they provide to our daily lives.

Notes

1. *Washington Post,* March 6, 1997 [A]1.

2. Richard W. Sellars, "Science or Scenery?" *Wilderness* 52 (Summer 1989): 29–32.

3. Olmsted's 1865 report was never used in defining the National Park Service or system, for it remained unpublished for almost a century. It was discovered by Olmsted's biographer Laura Wood Roper and published for the first time in the October 1952 issue of *Landscape Architecture.* See Joseph L. Sax, "America's National Parks: Their Principles, Purposes, and Prospects," *Natural History,* October 1976, pp. 59–87.

4. Alfred Runte, *Trains of Discovery: Western Railroads and the National Parks* (Niwot, Colo.: Roberts Rinehart, 1990), 13–16.

5. Marguerite S. Shaffer, "Swiss Chalets on the American Frontier: Seeing America First in Glacier National Park" (paper presented at the National Museum of American History Colloquium, June 15, 1993).

6. See Runte, *Trains of Discovery.*

7. I am grateful to Barry Mackintosh and Richard Sellars for helping me think through this interpretation of the 1916 Organic Act.

8. Quoted in Alfred Runte, *Trains of Discovery,* 39.

9. "An Act to Establish a National Park Service, and for Other Purposes," August 25, 1916, (39 Stat. 535), in Larry M. Dilsaver, ed., *America's National Park System: The Critical Documents* (Lanham, Md: Rowman and Littlefield, 1994), 46–47.

10. Robert Shankland, *Steve Mather of the National Parks,* (New York: Alfred A. Knopf, 1954), 147–48.

11. Ronald A. Foresta, *America's National Parks and Their Keepers* (Washington, D.C.: Resources for the Future, 1984), 27.

12. Franklin K. Lane to Stephen T. Mather, May 13, 1918, in Dilsaver, *America's National Park System,* 49–50.

13. For more on the Lane letter, see Horace Albright, *The Birth of the National Park Service: The Founding Years, 1913–33* (Salt Lake City: Howe Brothers, 1985), 68–73.

14. Franklin K. Lane to Stephen T. Mather, May 13, 1918, in Dilsaver, *America's National Park System,* 48–52.

15. Quoted in Richard W. Sellars, "Manipulating Nature's Paradise: National Park Management under Stephen T. Mather, 1916–1929," *Montana: The Magazine of Western History* 43 (Spring 1993): 5.

16. Alfred Runte, *Yosemite: The Embattled Wilderness* (Lincoln: University of Nebraska Press, 1990), 93–99, 140.

17. Sellars, "Manipulating Nature's Paradise," 9.

18. Ibid., 9; Shankland, *Steve Mather of the National Parks,* 269; Runte, *Yosemite: The Embattled Wilderness,* 133–34.

19. Sellars, "Manipulating Nature's Paradise," 8; Shankland, *Steve Mather and the National Parks,* 269–70.

20. Stephen Mather, "The Ideals and Policy of the National Park Service, Particularly in Relation to Yosemite National Park," in Ansel Hall, ed., *Handbook of Yosemite National Park: A Compendium of Articles on the Yosemite Region by Leading Scientific Authorities* (New York: G. P. Putnam's Sons, 1921), 79. See

also William C. Everhart, *The National Park Service* (Boulder, Colo.: Westview Press, 1983), 55.

21. Albright, *The Birth of the National Park Service,* 197–202.

22. Sellars, "Manipulating Nature's Paradise," 9–10.

23. Shankland, *Steve Mather and the National Parks,* 208.

24. Ibid.; Albright, *The Birth of the National Park Service,* 254.

25. Sellars, "Manipulating Nature's Paradise," 5.

26. Conrad L. Wirth, *Parks, Politics, and the People* (Norman: University of Oklahoma Press, 1980), 145.

27. Foresta, *The National Parks and Their Keepers,* 45.

28. Albright, *Parks, Politics, and the People,* 225–27.

29. Ibid., 262–67.

30. See Foresta, *The National Parks and their Keepers,* 93–98.

31. *National Parks for the Future: An Appraisal for the National Parks as They Begin Their Second Century* (Washington, D.C.: Conservation Foundation, 1972), 93.

32. Edward Abbey, *Desert Solitaire: A Season in the Wilderness* (New York: Balantine Books, 1968), 45–67; quote from page 60.

33. *Washington Post,* March 6, 1997 [A]17.

34. National Park Service, *National Parks for the 21st Century: The Vail Agenda: Report and Recommendations to the Director of the National Park Service from the Steering Committee for the 75th Anniversary Symposium* (working paper, 1991; published and distributed Post Mills, Vt.: Chelsea Green Pub. Co., 1993), 21.

35. Abbey, *Desert Solitaire,* 60.

Contributors

RUDOLFO ANAYA is professor emeritus of literature and language at the University of New Mexico and the author of numerous novels, dramas, stories, and essays. His books include *Bless Me, Ultima* (Tontatiuh International, 1972), *Tortuga* (University of New Mexico Press, 1979), *A Chicano in China* (University of New Mexico Press, 1986), *Albuquerque* (University of New Mexico Press, 1992), and *Rio Grande Fall* (Warner Books, 1996). His vast body of work has even been anthologized in *The Anaya Reader* (Warner Books, 1996). Anaya's numerous awards for excellence in letters include the PEN-West Fiction Award and the Before Columbus American Book Award.

PETER BLODGETT is curator of western American history at the Huntington Library, California. He is the author of various articles on tourism, recreation, and national parks published in *California History*, *Forest and Conservation History*, and *The Encyclopedia of the American West*, as well as *Land of Golden Dreams: California in the Gold Rush Decade* (Huntington Library Press, 1999). Currently he is completing a book titled *Vacations at Home: American Tourists in the Rocky Mountain West, 1920–1960*.

LEAH DILWORTH is associate professor of English at Long Island University's Brooklyn campus. She is the author *of Imagining Indians in the Southwest: Persistent Visions of a Primitive Past* (Smithsonian Institution Press, 1996). Dilworth is currently working on a book about collecting and domestic space.

PATRICIA NELSON LIMERICK is professor of history, cofounder, and chair of the board of directors of the Center of the American West, and associate director of the Minority Arts and Sciences Program at the University of Colorado, Boulder. She is also past president of the Western History Association and the American Studies Association. Limerick is the recipient of a MacArthur Fellowship and was named State Humanist of the Year in 1992 by the Colorado Endowment for the Humanities. She is the author of *The Legacy of Conquest: The Unbroken Past of the American West* (W. W. Norton, 1987) and *Something in the Soil: Legacies and Reckonings in the New West* (W. W. Norton, 2000) and coeditor of numerous volumes, including *Trails: Toward a New Western History* (University Press of Kansas, 1991).

PATRICK T. LONG is a professor in the College of Business at the University of Colorado, Boulder, where he directs a tourism impacts, planning, and policy research program funded by the US WEST Foundation. He is the immediate past president/CEO and a past chairman of the board of directors of the National Rural Tourism Foundation. He is also the founder and past director of the University of Colorado's Center for Recreation and Tourism Development and a founding member of the recently created Center for Sustainable Tourism. His articles have appeared in *Annals of Tourism Research, Journal of Travel Research,* and *Journal of Business Research* and *Tourism Management*. He is a coauthor of *Win, Lose, or Draw? Gambling with America's Small Towns* (Aspen Institute, 1994), a policy guide on community-based casino gambling.

DAVID LOUTER is a historian with the National Park Service in Seattle, Washington. He earned his Ph.D. in history from the University of Washington in 2000. Over the past ten years, he has written a number of studies documenting the histories of national parks in the Pacific Northwest. His most recent is *Contested Terrain: North Cascades National Park Service Complex, An Administrative History* (National Park Service, 1998). He is currently at work on a book about the way cars have shaped our ideas of parks as wilderness, based on his dissertation, "Windshield Wilderness: The Automobile and the Meaning of National Parks in Washington State."

DWIGHT T. PITCAITHLEY is the chief historian for the National Park Service. He has served the National Park Service as author, editor, educator, speaker, advisor, and historian during his professional career. In addition to numerous publications for the National Park Service, he has been published in several journals, including *Arkansas Historical Quarterly, New Mexico Historical Review,* and *The George Wright Forum.* He is the author of *Let the River Be: A History of the Ozark's Buffalo River.* In 1988, he received the James Madison Prize from the Society for History in the Federal Government for "Historic Sites: What Can Be Learned from Them?"

EARL POMEROY is professor emeritus at the University of Oregon and past president of the Western History Association and of the Pacific Coast Branch of the American Historical Association. He is the author of a number of seminal books in American western history, including: *In Search of the Golden West: The Tourist in Western America* (Knopf, 1957), *The Pacific Slope: A History of California, Oregon, Washington, Idaho, Utah, and Nevada* (Knopf, 1965), *The Territories and the United States, 1861–1890: Studies in Colonial Administration* (University of Pennsylvania Press, 1947), and of one of the most influential scholarly essays ever published on the West, "Toward a Reorientation of Western History: Continuity and Environment," *Mississippi Valley Historical Review* (1955).

HAL ROTHMAN is professor of history at the University of Nevada Las Vegas and editor of *Environmental History.* He is the author of numerous books, including *Devil's Bargains: Tourism in the Twentieth-Century American West* (University Press of Kansas, 1998); *The Greening of a Nation?: Environmentalism in the United States Since 1945* (Harcourt, Brace, 1998), *On Rims and Ridges: The Los Alamos Area Since 1880* (University of Nebraska Press, 1992); *Preserving Different Pasts: The American National Monuments* (University of Illinois Press, 1989); and *Saving the Planet: The American Response to the Environment in the Twentieth-Century* (Ivan R. Dee, 2000). He is also a syndicated columnist in *High Country News.* Rothman is currently completing a book on the transformation of Las Vegas entitled *Beyond Neon: How Las*

Vegas Shed Its Stigma and Became the First City of the Twenty-First Century (Routledge, 2001).

SYLVIA RODRIGUEZ is associate professor of anthropology at the University of New Mexico. She studies interethnic relations in the U.S.–Mexico borderlands, with emphasis on the Upper Rio Grande Valley of New Mexico. Her published works deal variously with the interaction among ethnicity, cultural politics, and tourism; ethnic relations and land and water issues; ethnic identity and expressive culture. Her book *The Matachines Dance: Ritual Symbolism and Interethnic Relations in the Upper Rio Grande Valley* (University of New Mexico Press, 1996) won the 1997 Chicago Folklore Prize. She is currently working on a book about the Taos Fiesta and a book on acequia (community irrigation ditch system) custom and practice.

CARLOS A. SCHWANTES is St. Louis Mercantile Library Endowed Professor of Transportation Studies at the University of Missouri–St. Louis. He is the author or editor of fifteen books, including *The Pacific Northwest: An Interpretive History* (University of Nebraska Press, 1989) and *Railroad Signatures across the Pacific Northwest* (University of Washington Press, 1993), *In Mountain Shadows: A History of Idaho* (University of Nebraska Press, 1991). He has traveled to every county west of the hundredth meridian to obtain material for a book on perceptions of the roadside West. Schwantes is an avid photographer, and the first published collection of his images appeared in 1996 as *So Incredibly Idaho! Seven Landscapes That Define the Gem State* (University of Idaho Press, 1996). His latest books are *Long Day's Journey: The Steamboat and Stagecoach Era in the Northern West* (University of Washington Press, 1999), and *Columbia River: Gateway to the West* (University of Idaho Press, 2000).

PAUL SCHULLERY, a naturalist-ranger and park historian, lives and writes in Yellowstone National Park. He is also an adjunct professor of American studies at the University of Wyoming and an affiliate professor of history at Montana State University. His numerous books include: *Mountain Time: A Yellowstone Memoir* (Roberts Rinehart, 1995), *Searching for Yellowstone: Ecology and Wonder in the Last Wilderness* (Houghton Mifflin, 1997), and *Royal Coachman: The Lore and Legends of Fly-Fishing* (Simon and Schuster, 1999). Schullery is the recipient of an honorary doctorate of letters from Montana State University (1997) and the 1999 recipient of the Center of the American West's Wallace Stegner Award. He is also the former director of the American Museum of Fly Fishing.

MARGUERITE S. SHAFFER, assistant professor of American studies and history at Miami University of Ohio, is the author of *See America First* (Smithsonian Institution Press, forthcoming, fall 2001). She has published articles on western tourism in the *Pacific Historical Review;* in Hal K. Rothman, ed., *Re-Opening the American West* (University of Arizona Press, 1998); and in Shelly Barnowski and Ellen Furlough, eds., *The Development of Mass Tourism* (University of Michigan Press, forthcoming, spring 2001).

DAVID M. WROBEL is associate professor of history at the University of Nevada Las Vegas. He is the author of *The End of American Exceptionalism: Frontier Anxiety from the Old West to the New Deal* (University Press of Kansas, 1993) and coeditor, with Michael C. Steiner, of *Many Wests: Place, Culture, and Regional Identity* (University Press of Kansas, 1997). He is currently working on a book titled *Promised Lands: Boosterism, Reminiscence, and the Creation of the American West.*

Index

319